Given to me in
March, 2006
by Chaplain's Office
with COTN in KC

[signature]

Spiritual Marketplace

✛

Spiritual Marketplace

BABY BOOMERS AND THE REMAKING
OF AMERICAN RELIGION

✣

WADE CLARK ROOF

PRINCETON UNIVERSITY PRESS

PRINCETON AND OXFORD

Copyright © 1999 by Princeton University Press
Published by Princeton University Press, 41 William Street,
Princeton, New Jersey 08540
In the United Kingdom: Princeton University Press,
3 Market Place, Woodstock, Oxfordshire OX20 1SY
All Rights Reserved

Third printing, and first paperback printing, 2001
Paperback ISBN 0-691-08996-5

The Library of Congress has cataloged the cloth edition of this book as follows

Roof, Wade Clark.
Spiritual marketplace : baby boomers and the remaking of
American religion / Wade Clark Roof.
p.   cm.
Includes bibliographical references and index.
ISBN 0-691-01659-3 (alk. paper)
1. United States—Religion—1960–   2. Baby boom
generation—Religious life.   I. Title.
BL2525.R654   1999
200′.973′09045—dc21   99-22825

British Library Cataloging-in-Publication Data is available

This book has been composed in Baskerville

Printed on acid-free paper. ∞

www.pup.princeton.edu

Printed in the United States of America

5   7   9   10   8   6   4

FOR LINDSAY, LAUREN,

MADDIE, RACHEL,

AND EMMA

THE "LITTLE WOMEN"

OF MY FAMILY

✢

✢ *Contents* ✢

❖ Acknowledgments ❖

I AM INDEBTED to foundations whose support made this book possible. A decade ago, the Lilly Endowment, Inc., provided funds for studying the Baby Boom generation. Funding from the Pew Charitable Trusts and the Randolph and Dora Haynes Foundation made possible supplementary research. The Henry Luce Foundation supported a "Consultation on Spirituality," which brought together a small group of scholars for discussion of themes in the book. There was actually no foundation support for the second round of interviews in 1995–96 on which this book rests, which means that I did a good deal of the interviewing myself. I am very grateful to those graduate and undergraduate students at the University of California at Santa Barbara who, with little compensation, gave so much of their time to help carry out various phases of the project: Marianna Pisano and Cybelle Shattuck for the interviewing, David Mahacek and Sandy Miller for coding and computer assistance. Martha Finch and Donna Moran early on read portions of the manuscript; John Bauman read it in its entirety and made very helpful comments. Shawn Landres discussed with me various topics I cover. Sara Duke, secretary at the Center for the Study of Religion, kept a watchful eye over our research operations and greatly assisted me with grant administration. And I am especially indebted to Nancy Ramsey, a research assistant relentless in her quest for information and obscure references, who also assisted in the final preparations of the manuscript.

This book took longer to write than I expected, in part because the interviews led to unexpected pursuits. My perspective on the subject also evolved as I listened to people and revised my thinking. Responses to my lectures in academic and religious audiences over the years were helpful, too, in formulating my views. Fortunately, I am surrounded by highly knowledgeable colleagues and students in the Department of Religious Studies at UCSB, a great sounding board. I have been much influenced by the growing attention within the social sciences and humanities to cultural approaches in the study of religion. Readers will detect those intellectual influences, and no doubt my freedom in drawing off them. A. Deborah Malmud, acquiring editor in religion at Princeton University Press, was enormously helpful and a pleasure to work with.

My indebtedness extends as well to personal realms. Jezebel, the cat who perched herself by my keyboard throughout much of the writing of my earlier book on Boomers, showed no interest in this project. But my new dog, Millie, an active yellow lab who was passing through a difficult adolescence as I was writing, was good enough on most days to allow me to work uninterruptedly up until about 4 in the afternoon, when almost invariably she demands a walk. At first this seemed to be an intrusion into my work schedule, but in time those walks came to be cherished as "wind-down" moments so necessary to keeping one's balance when so deeply immersed in a writing project. My wife, Terry, listened when I needed to talk something out and provided wonderful excursions of her own, reminding me of the things that really matter most. And for that I am especially grateful.

Spiritual Marketplace

✤

On Maps and Terrains

THIS BOOK IS ABOUT religious change in the United States as viewed through the experiences of the post–World War II "Baby Boomers." This large generation that grew up in the tumultuous decades of the 1960s and 1970s, was, and still is at the vanguard of cultural transformations in this country. Baby Boomers have long been the focus of debate about moral values and the tone they set for this country—controversial from the time they were in youthful rebellion right down to the more recent crisis of the Clinton presidency. An aging generation, its members are increasingly ensconced in midlife, at a juncture where we can better assess their impact religiously and morally. Hence, as we move into another century, it is appropriate to reflect upon where this "lead" demographic cohort may be taking us. My purpose is to examine how the religious terrain itself is being transformed, and how trends now in place among members of this generation may be altering our most basic conceptions of religion and spirituality, our interpretations of historic religious beliefs and symbols, and perhaps even our understanding of the sacred itself. So sweeping a range of religious and cultural shifts underscores the key role and long-lasting impact of this generation on the nation.

This much attention to change may come as a surprise considering how much continuity of religious faith and practice there is in the United States. The polls indicate that 94 percent of Americans believe in God, 90 percent report praying to God on a fairly regular basis, nine out of ten claim a religious affiliation, and the proportion reporting weekly attendance at religious services remains remarkably high compared with other Western countries. Moreover, many of the often-repeated statistics on American religiosity have not dramatically changed over the last several decades. Yet to focus on just these statistics as sociologists and commentators frequently do is too restrictive. There are other, highly significant changes occurring within religion—"soft" undercurrents, so to speak. Since midcentury especially, the images and symbols of religion have undergone a quiet transformation. Popular discourses about "religion" and "spirituality," about the "self" and "experience," about "God" and "faith" all point to subtle—but crucially important—shifts in the meaning of everyday religious life. While beyond our full grasp, these symbolic and subjective aspects of religion are most crucial since they influence our interpretations of our lives and experiences.

These "soft" undercurrents of change interest me and, I believe, occasion the need for a new mapping of the religious scene. New maps are called for when old ways of describing religion fail to capture what is happening in our everyday lives. "Events in the last decades of the twentieth century seem to demonstrate," say the authors of a recent textbook in the sociology of religion, "that there is no longer such a thing as 'religion as we know it.'"[1] Boundaries separating one faith tradition from another that once seemed fixed are now often blurred; religious identities are malleable and multifaceted, often overlapping several traditions. Trends and events stretch our imagination, even as we try to predict the direction of religious change. Some indicators point to institutional religious decline, others to a profound spiritual ferment, confusing the picture and making it difficult to describe what is really happening. A good example occurred a few years ago when a local newspaper in a Massachusetts town carried two headlines on religious trends, both on the same day and on the same page: "Spiritual Renewal Flourishes: People Seek Lessons of Universal Church" and "Religion Influence May Be Fading." The two scenerios portrayed quite differing religious futures, both drawing on information from reputable sources. Commenting on this double-entry a few months later, editors at *The New Republic* summed it up simply: "God is in the Details!"[2]

Of course, shifts in American religion are fairly common. Especially for religion as most people know it—in "the God-tangles of actually lived lives"[3]—there is always a volatile element, the sacred never quite contained in its familiar forms. American religion has long been known for its dynamism and fluidity, its responsiveness to grassroots opinions and sentiments, its creative capacity in relation to the cultural environment. It takes on colors drawn from its surroundings, its boundaries always shifting and porous. Religion in the United States is like a brilliantly colored kaleidoscope ever taking on new configurations of blended hues. Not just popular religious beliefs and practices, but religious institutions themselves undergo transformations in form and style, encouraged by a democratic, highly individualistic ethos and rapid social and cultural change. "Observers of American religion regularly need to map the terrain," writes historian Martin E. Marty. "Its bewildering pluralism, they soon learn resists a single or permanent outline."[4]

MAPS AND TERRAINS

A "map is not territory," so it is rightly said.[5] Maps set cognitive boundaries and shape our consciousness of what is taken to be "real" or "primary"; they direct us to certain features of the world around us, and not to others. To a considerable extent, we see what our culture and socialization—including the paradigms that consciously or unconsciously shape our thinking—predispose us to see. Thus our choice of maps for looking at religion becomes crucial: they construct our sense of religious reality and then undergird and perpetuate that with a degree of ontological certainty even greater perhaps than our better senses would want. Even if his is an overstatement, poet Wallace Stevens captures the situation when he writes, "We live in the description of a place and not in the place itself."

In his *Nation of Behavers*, published in 1976, Martin E. Marty wrote about three earlier maps in American religious history, plus a new one he proposed at the time.[6] First, there was the colonial territorial map of established churches in states organized on the basis of the ruling powers; second, there was the denominational map of separately organized institutions and distinct religious identities of individual believers in the nineteenth and early twentieth centuries; third, at midcentury there was a political mapping that focused on civil religion and democracy supplanting creed and institution, giving us a generalized "Protestant-Catholic-Jewish" United States. A fourth map, which Marty thought appropriate for the 1970s, focused attention on group identities and social belonging, sensitizing us to socially conscious constituencies in contention with one another.

Identity as a theme figures prominently in all these maps, despite its changing configurations and meanings over time. Marty's mapping, or some extension of it, was reflected in much of the discussion on religion during the late 1970s and 1980s. Identity and belonging found expression in group consciousness and polarized conflicts surfacing at the time: mainline versus Evangelical, tensions between blacks and Jews, secularists versus religionists. Abortion, school prayer, and homosexuality all became highly charged issues in the public arena, leading to more firmly drawn boundaries—morally, politically, religiously. Confrontation was often intense, culminating in a vision proposed by some commentators of a nation caught up in "culture wars" between liberals, progressives, and secularists, on the one hand, and conservatives, moralists,

5

and hard-core religious believers, on the other. Except for the colonial case, all such maps continue to influence to some extent the way Americans think about religion. Newer maps do not necessarily replace old ones nor necessarily should they. Maps persist because no one charting ever fully captures the scene, for reasons of nostalgia and ideology. Maps are influential, subtle forms of power, and hence often vigorously defended by religious scholars no less than by ecclesiastical and political authorities. Debates mount over the assumptions, or organizing principles, on which the maps themselves rest: the denominational map looks upon religious institutions as central; the civil-religious map points to affirmations of American values; the group map focuses on social boundaries and behavior; "culture wars" emphasize the polarization of values and constituencies. Defenders continue to debate about the privileging of one or another of these organizing principles, sometimes even after the terrains themselves have greatly changed.

For us today, the question is, which map best describes our religious situation? Denominational maps certainly continue to be of some importance: Baptists, Episcopalians, Methodists, Lutherans, Roman Catholics, Jehovah Witnesses, and the like are recognizable constituencies just about everywhere. Yet clearly, theological and cultural boundaries that once distinguished denominations and faith communities have faded over the decades. The "Protestant-Catholic-Jew" map is inadequate in an age when religious pluralism is expanding and civic-assimilationist themes are less pressing. Group boundaries of a religious kind are real enough, although many seem less important today than they did a decade ago. "Culture wars" continue to attract attention in the media because of controversial issues like abortion and homosexuality; but it too is a limited mapping of the world as we experience it today. The large cultural and religious middle in this country, whose attitudes and views are not so clearly crystallized on many moral and ideological issues, is easily misconstrued when so much focus is upon ideological extremes. All such maps have their limitations, of course, as do any new ones we might propose. Because the religious terrain is always in flux, no one map can serve well for long.

IN SEARCH OF A MAP

Observing the religious scene today, one is struck by a distinct change of mood since the time of Marty's mapping just two decades ago. Identity is still a powerful theme, but its mode of expression is now different: the energizing forces arise out of quests not so much for group identity and social location as for an authentic inner life and personhood. Activated more at the inner level, Americans are asking questions such as, "Does religion relate to my life?" "How can I find spiritual meaning and depth?" and "What might faith mean for me?" This inward search for greater spiritual depth was evident in a poll in 1994 which reported that 65 percent of Americans believed that religion was losing its influence in public life, yet almost equal numbers, 62 percent, claimed that the influence of religion was *increasing in their personal lives*.[7] If, as many social scientists argue, religion has to do with two major foci of concerns—*personal meaning* and *social belonging*—then most certainly it is around the first of these that religious energies revolve primarily today. Martin E. Marty himself has noted this recent turning inward on the part of Americans. Drawing off William James's notion of a "habitual centre of energy," he suggests religious energies now flow in channels very different from those he described in the mid 1970s:

> ... the personal, private, and autonomous at the expense of the communal, the public, and the derivative; the accent on meaning at the expense of inherited patterns of belonging; concentration on the local and particular more than the cosmopolitan or ecumenical; concern for practical and affective life accompanied by less devotion to the devotional and intellectual expressions; the feminist as opposed to the male dominated; and attention to separate causes more than to overarching civil commitments.[8]

A great variety of terms now in vogue signal such a shift in the center of religious energy: inwardness, subjectivity, the experiential, the expressive, the spiritual. Inherited forms of religion persist and still influence people but, as Marty says, "the individual seeker and chooser has come increasingly to be in control."[9] Nowhere is this greater emphasis upon the seeker more apparent than in the large chain bookstore: the old "religion" section is gone and in its place is a growing set of more specific rubrics catering to popular topics such as angels, Sufism, journey, recovery, meditation, magic, inspiration, Judaica, astrology, gurus, Bible, prophecy, Evangelicalism, Mary, Buddhism, Catholicism, esoterica, and the like. Words like *soul, sacred,* and *spiritual* resonate to a curious public. The discourse on spiritual "journeys" and "growth" is now a province not just of theologians and journalists, but of ordinary people in cafes, coffee bars, and bookstores across the country. Interest in the spiritual is voiced

7

both inside and outside the religious establishments: in growing Pente-costal, Charismatic, and Evangelical churches; in oldline congregations as they struggle to overcome the malaise that has settled upon them; in innovative religious forms such as "seeker churches" and "refreshings"; in spiritual seminars and popular lectures at retreat centers; in house churches, prayer cells, women's ritual groups, and support groups of all kinds; in courses on spiritual formation in seminaries; in an expanding psycho-spiritual culture of best-selling books and videos; on the World Wide Web and in the chat rooms of the Internet; in business and corpo-rate worlds; in medical schools examining the impact of prayer and med-itation on health.

Not surprisingly, all of this is happening at a time when the United States and other Western nations are undergoing massive social and cul-tural changes. The emergence of a global world, an influx of new immi-grants and cultures, widespread changes in values and beliefs, the im-mense role of the media and visual imagery in shaping contemporary life, an expanding consumer-oriented culture targeting the self as an arena for marketing, the erosion of many traditional forms of commu-nity—all point to major realignments in religion and culture. Mean-while, discoveries in quantum physics and astronomy lead scientists to back away from Newtonian notions of a deterministic universe and to speak of awe, holism, and even of "an observer-created universe."[10] Old certainties collapse as new mysteries arise. It seems not just coincidental that the metaphor of a spiritual quest takes on significance just when many of traditional religion's underpinnings of the culture have become more tenuous. One hears about the "crisis of modernity," and terms like post-traditional, post-dogmatic, and post-Christian are commonplace. Yet the search for spiritual meaning and direction takes on increasing momen-tum. A reclaiming of the interior life and renewed stress upon inner truths surface just when passionate voices on behalf of "personal knowl-edge" as opposed to the "unity of knowledge" attract mounting atten-tion. Talk of renewal and of the holistic flourishes at a time when tradi-tion as memory and its hold upon people's lives, or lack thereof, is widely discussed in intellectual circles, most notably in the debates over moder-nity and postmodernity.[11]

Some might say that there is nothing new in all of this: that Americans have always been spiritual seekers, ever ready to rebuild their lives and communities. And in one sense they would be right. The history of re-vivalism, utopian experiments, and positive-thinking movements in this country is well-known. Americans are always starting out on new spiritual ventures. But there does appear to be something distinctive about today's spiritual mood. "Ride down the back roads of Pennsylvania or Ohio or Oregon for two hours," writes historian R. Laurence Moore, "and you can bring back a list of signboard announcements that will baffle any panel of experts. Just who are the "Jews for Jesus" singers? Who runs the "Faith for Today" chapel at the entrance of a trailer park? What tradition are we to make out of signs welcoming 'questers' after religious and psychic counseling?"[12] Moore's vivid imagery captures so well this effusive quest culture and the proliferation of new spiritual suppliers now making their appeals. The mood of the times, the new discourses, the institutional innovations, all signal a changing religious environment.

Three aspects of the situation today particularly stand out. One is the sheer numbers of people involved: spiritual searching is hardly limited to a few bold spirits, to either marginalized or privileged classes. Surveys show that large sectors of the American population today are interested in deepening their spirituality. Many who seem to have lost a traditional religious grounding are striving for new and fresh moorings; many with a religious grounding are looking to enrich their lives further. Second, dominant amid all this ferment is an emphasis on self-understanding and self-reflexivity, a product of late modernity with its pluralism, relativism, and ontological uncertainties. Thus my use of the terms *quest*, *seeking*, and *searching* arise out of this particular historical and cultural context.[13] Third, and somewhat paradoxically, the spiritual yearnings are leading many Americans beyond the self-centered, therapeutic culture in which they grew up. Self-fulfillment as a cultural theme in the 1960s and 1970s set in motion a powerful quest, but now for a generation older and more mature that quest has moved beyond the solutions that were promised in consumption, materialism, and self-absorption. Popular spirituality may appear shallow, indeed flaky; yet its creative currents, under the right conditions, can activate our deepest energies and commitments. Even in its most self-absorbed forms, today's spiritual ferment reflects a deep hunger for a self-transformation that is both genuine and personally satisfying.

In my judgment, the current religious situation in the United States is characterized not so much by a loss of faith as a qualitative shift from unquestioned belief to a more open, questing mood. Underlying this, so I shall argue, a set of social and cultural transformations have created a quest culture, a search for certainty, but also the hope for a more authentic, intrinsically satisfying life. At times, as pollster Daniel Yankelovich reminds us, the "giant plates" of American culture[14]—like the geological plates beneath the earth's surface—shift positions, and those living closest to society's fault lines—most notably, the younger generations—are the first to alter their views. Hence the thesis of the book: *the boundaries of popular religious communities are now being redrawn, encouraged by the quests of the large, post–World War II generations, and facilitated by the rise of an expanded spiritual marketplace.* The notion of a "spiritual marketplace" is itself captivating, with the image of a quest culture shaped by forces of supply and demand, and of a remaking of religious and institutional loyalties. Much has been written about popular spirituality and especially its relation to such developments as feminism, the self-help movement, environmentalism, and so forth, but much less attention is given to why such spiritual concerns surface as they do today, how they find expression organizationally, and the larger issues of religion and modernity.[15] This book attempts to offer a more balanced perspective on these developments and pleads for more serious attention to the subtle undercurrents of change in contemporary religious life.

LIFE HISTORIES AND SURVEYS

The analysis here offered relies on survey data, in-depth interviews, and field observation. Fortunately a large-scale study I have conducted over the past decade provides such a rich source of information. Beginning in 1988 my research staff and I have interviewed hundreds of young Americans born after World War II, trying to understand their worlds and the changes in their life trajectories. We explored their religious and spiritual lives in some depth as well as their work and careers, their marriages and families. We created a huge biographical data bank with self-reported information on their life histories and about their parents and children. Findings from this early phase (1988–90) were in *A Generation of Seekers: The Spiritual Journeys of the Baby Boom Generation,* published in 1993.[16]

In this volume we rely on follow-up data obtained from an additional round of interviews. We have followed the same people over eight to nine years, beginning with a survey in 1988–89, follow-up telephone and face-to-face interviews in 1989–90, and now again a telephone survey in

1995–96 plus in some instances repeated interviews up through 1997. Properly speaking, this makes for a panel study. Panel studies are rare because they are costly and take so much time, but they have the great advantage of showing patterns for the same people over time: Have they become more religious? Have their spiritual views changed? Did those who dropped out of religious organizations return? Did those who returned actually stay once their own children were getting older? What are the major religious constituencies today, and what distinguishes them? Many of the people have talked with us for more than an hour, and almost a hundred were visited in their homes. In addition to the survey respondents, I have talked with dozens of religious and spiritual leaders, church consultants, directors of retreat centers, and sat through many spiritual seminars, religious services, and training sessions trying to learn more about the religious and spiritual mood of the country over the past four years. I have had access as well to bulletin boards on the Internet, including one on "Religion and Generations" designed to augment the general base of information. For further information on the data and statistical analysis upon which the book is based, see the Appendix on Methodology.

Throughout the pages that follow, my aim is to link people's life histories and stories with information gleaned from large-scale surveys. Personal narratives are rich in meaning and nuance, a means of exploring the many webs of cultural meaning that people spin. Surveys allow for generalizations, absolutely indispensable for describing social trends. Combining the two methods makes for a balanced approach for understanding what is happening to religion "on the ground," to its meaning and function in everyday life. The book attempts to describe popular religious culture, to look at sacred symbolism, meanings, and discourse—all extending beyond religious organizations and institutions, but also very much a part of them. It tries to capture the climate in which those institutions and organizations now function, and to which in one way or another they must adapt if they are to be competitive in the current religious climate. As a barometer of the religious and spiritual environment created by the influential Boomer generation, it falls into the tradition of books like Will Herberg's *Protestant-Catholic-Jew*[17] and Robert Bellah et al.'s *Habits of the Heart*,[18] which portrays the nation's cultural and religious milieu in earlier decades. Like those volumes, this one is a portrait in broad strokes, attempting in this instance to map the reshaping of moral and religious life at the turn of the century.

11

PLAN OF THE BOOK

In Chapter 1 the reader is introduced to five characters: John McRae, Karen Potter, Sam Wong, Sara Caughman, and Vicki Feinstein. Their life histories reveal a wide spectrum of spiritual searching, on the part of individuals acting alone and within communal contexts. Here we see the complex, multilayered character of contemporary spirituality and the importance of analyzing religion across pre-existing boundaries of traditions and institutions. "Lived religion," as described in this chapter, takes us into a world of diverse scripts and practices and of varying and evolving relationships of individuals to scripts, practices, and institutions. Agency, or the role of the individual actively engaging and creating an ongoing personal religious narrative in relation to the symbolic resources available, is set forth as crucial to our understanding of contemporary spiritual quests.

Chapter 2 examines social and cultural trends that have helped to create a spiritual quest culture in the late twentieth century. Major trends include Western rationalization and social differentiation, shifting conceptions of the religious, cultural emphasis on individuality, the impact of the media, and globalization. The impact of these rapid changes is intense on the part of the post–World War II American generations. Collectively the trends have brought about further structural dislocations for institutionalized religion and greater individual autonomy in the modern era, all encouraging a reflexive spiritual style, or a more intentional, self-directed approach to cultivating spiritual sensitivity and religious consciousness that is, in some very important respects, functionally different from what we have known in the past. The theme of a "reflexive spirituality" is central throughout the book.

Today's spiritual marketplace rests on this enhanced level of self-reflexivity. In Chapter 3, we look specifically at current spiritual themes and the dynamics of this changing marketplace. Particular attention is given to the interplay of demand and supply, and how a new cadre of suppliers is redefining religion in experiential ways and providing the popular categories now used in thinking about spiritual well-being. We look as well at innovations within religious institutions and the rise of new-style spiritual entrepreneurs and structures now influencing the religious culture. The making of meaning in this expanded, spiritually driven and consumer-oriented context emerges as a crucial enterprise on the part of suppliers, both old and new.

Chapter 4 describes the dominant religious trends for the large Boomer generation: how they identify themselves using religious and spiritual vocabularies, how they relate to institutions, and how their views toward religion and involvements within religious organizations are changing as they grow older. Members of this generation are shown to be somewhat more predictable in their commitments now than they were ten years ago, but still considerably fluid and open-ended. Paradoxically, they want to be both fluid and grounded, to look upon spirituality as a process yet not without anchors of some sort to fall back on. This protean-style religion is, I argue, an outgrowth of a more self-examining, searching stance toward religious symbols, meanings, and practices. Theoretical insights from Ernst Troeltsch and more contemporary scholars inform our perspective on what appears to be a distinctive religious ethos fitting to our time.

The fifth chapter looks at the construction of religious narrative in the contemporary setting. Drawing off the "cultural toolbox" metaphor, we explore the linkages between individuals and institutions, and the interplay between the "spiritual" and the "religious" as identities: when the spiritual is lost to frozen religious forms, when the religious and the spiritual are creatively fused in lived narrative, when religious rhetoric is rejected in favor of the spiritual, and when even both the religious and the spiritual fail to provide a meaningful language of self-construction. The chapter proposes a typology of narratively constructed identities fitting to a period when religious tradition is highly fragmented and individuals themselves exercise considerable autonomy in matters of faith and spiritual development.

In Chapter 6 we look at the emerging religious boundaries in the popular culture. Five major subcultures are proposed: dogmatists, mainstream believers, Born-again Christians, metaphysical believers and seekers, and secularists. Here we set forth social and demographic profiles as well as theological and metaphysical characteristics that distinguish among the constituencies. The interpretation stresses the role of believers and followers themselves in using symbols, doctrines, experiences, and concerns as "cultural tools" in defining who they are and for marking themselves as distinct and different from others. Particular attention is given to the vanguard movement, or the small but spiritually creative sector, within each of the religious subcultures who are leading the way, reconfiguring religious identities and relations among subcultures.

Chapter 7 looks at family patterns for the five religious subcultures. Historically family and religion were linked in mutually supporting ways,

13

and in the late twentieth century massive structural changes have radically altered links between the two institutions. We look at a broad spectrum of family types pioneered by the postwar generations, and how these changes affect religious socialization and family-based activities. Examined as well are how current patterns of intimacy, marriage, and family now serve as the carriers of distinct religious subcultures. In addition, we follow people through the course of their lives: from the time as children they were socialized in religious values, to when they became parents and the concerns they had for their own children, to more recent times when their children are growing up and leaving home. Particular attention is given to mixed-faith families, to both the challenges and the opportunities they present for religious socialization.

Chapter 8 explores moral visions and ethical values for the religious subcultures. If there is a spiritual resurgence, does it have any impact on moral commitments? Do these commitments vary from one constituency to another? Here we also examine the currently prominent "culture wars" thesis and offer a more balanced perspective on the moral and religious diversity in the nation today. We look at several major ethical concerns where strong ideologies have developed in recent times, particularly family life and values, work and material values, environmentalism, and the public role of religion. The usefulness of our mapping of religious subcultures becomes particularly evident here because we are able to show new formations of moral and spiritual values now emerging.

The Conclusion offers some final comments on where the country seems headed religiously as we move into the twenty-first century. More speculative, here we look at what the spiritual quests may foretell about individual and institutional well-being and changing religious patterns for the future. Risky as predicting may be, some assessment of the nation's "spiritual capital" as we move into a new century seems appropriate. An Appendix describing the database on which the book's argument rests, the research procedures utilized, and some extended statistical analysis offers additional detail for the interested reader.

Finally, a word about myself. It seems appropriate in a book remapping religion in a more reflexive mode that the author reveal something of his own identity. I grew up a Methodist in the South and became religiously and politically conscious during the 1960s. The civil rights and peace movements in those years challenged many of the comfortable alliances of religion and culture that I had grown up with and put me on a course asking tougher questions of religion—and of myself. I remain a Christian, though one open to the wisdom of other traditions

14

and never quite at ease in any taken-for-granted Zion. I remain ever conscious of what Peter Berger years ago called "the precarious vision,"[19] or the necessity modern life thrusts upon us to be self-conscious about even our deepest affirmations and commitments. I confess to being a seeker of sorts, to a restlessness with boundaries that overly contain, and certainly to my own struggles with faith and institutions even as I recognize their hold on me. No doubt these experiences have shaped my empathy for all those searching—who, as we shall see, differ greatly in what they seek.

Varieties of Spiritual Quest

[Religious experience] redeems and vivifies an interior world
which otherwise would be an empty waste.
(*William James*)

OF ALL HIS PENETRATING INSIGHTS into religious psychology, James's comment on the power of a religious experience to redeem and vivify—to fill an empty interior world—is especially fitting to our time.[1] There is an element of pathos in his comment, appropriate also to our time. The specter of life as an "empty waste" would prompt an anxious response in most any time, but particularly now given that those born after World War II have pursued so many dreams of material and psychological deliverance. Not that members of this generation have turned their back on affluence or hopes of deliverance though personal fulfillment, pleasure, and happiness, for certainly many have not; but the tone in which many of them talk about their hopes and aspirations is different now than it was even a decade ago. There is less certainty of a material or psychological deliverance, and a restlessness for something more—call it "values," "faith," "being centered," or finding "spiritual wisdom." A change of mood and of what seems worthwhile is evident. Admittedly all such words and phrases as now espoused can mean many things and may be shallow in meaning, but in their most feeble expression they mask a deep and profound hunger. Were William James alive today, he perhaps would not be surprised, seeing in the reactions to the prospect of an "empty waste" the logic of an emerging spiritual quest. Certainly, some aging Baby Boomers sense a need for that which transcends themselves and gives meaning and purpose to their lives and are able to articulate that need very clearly. Already deeply touched by a post-1960s psychological culture, now in midlife they seem to be searching further, in a more mature and focused manner.

Here in this opening chapter, we look at the life stories of five people I have interviewed—three times or more—over the past ten years: John McRae, Karen Potter, Sam Wong, Sara Caughman, and Vicki Feinstein.[2] I have tried to listen attentively to what they have said about their yearnings, hoping to discern their own growth and maturity. "Stay with" people long enough, listening carefully to what they have to say, the writer Robert Coles reminds us, and chances are you'll learn more than you ever expected.[3] What I discovered is that their spiritual quests are at the core of their personal narratives and that these quests bear directly upon not only their inner feelings but their religious identities, their family life, and moral and ethical issues. The spiritual currents they embody certainly flow in quite differing directions—which poses a challenge for any thorough analysis of popular spiritual discourse today but also promises to tell us a great deal about Americans and their sensibilities at the turn of the century.

JOHN MCRAE: REAWAKENINGS

"Do I think of myself as religious?" John asked, repeating slowly the question I had just put to him. It was a question I had looked forward to asking him ever since I arranged for a second interview. From an earlier interview I knew that his relationship with organized religion was ambiguous, that he was born into a Presbyterian family but had not been active in any church for many years. He was 41 years old, of Irish and Scottish descent, majored in engineering while in college, an architect with a large firm, married for five years, divorced, recently engaged for a second time, and now living in Ohio. I knew about him about as much as standard survey questions uncover—which, I discovered, isn't very much.

He now seemed unsure of what to say, which was strange for a man I had remembered as so articulate and for whom conversation seemed to flow naturally. Pausing a few moments, he replied: "I really don't know how to answer that."

"Do you go to church?" I queried.

"No. I used to—Presbyterian. I quit going when I left home twenty years ago."

"You told us when we talked to you on the phone that you were Presbyterian. Is that important to you?" I asked, thinking this might get him to respond in a frame of reference he would understand.

"A Presbyterian?" he said smiling, pondering as he spoke. "I don't know. It's not that I am opposed to church or anything like that, it's just that I got out of the habit of going and never got back."

17

"Do you believe pretty much as most other Presbyterians believe?" I asked, coming at him from yet another angle.

"I haven't the slightest idea," he said in a straightforward, honest manner. "What do Presbyterians believe?"

Set back by his responses, I wondered how best to proceed with the interview. According to my interview guide, I was supposed to classify him—based on his responses—as either "Presbyterian" or as "None," and then to ask the appropriate battery of follow-up questions. Then it occurred to me that maybe the questions themselves were the problem. What do Presbyterians believe? I wondered how I would answer that question myself. And why had I asked him at the beginning about going to church as if that was the most important aspect of his religious identity? Obviously we had reached a juncture in the interview where I had to make a decision. With a moment's pause, I switched altogether from what I knew from the telephone survey about him and set out upon a new line of questioning: "Are there things that excite you these days—causes, activities, anything that might make your heart sing?"

"Well, I'd have to think about that," he replied.

"Think about it," I said, hoping that we had found a basis for a more informed conversation.

"Well, Becky's been a big influence on me, I'd have to admit."

"How so?"

"Becky is my fiancée. She's Catholic. We're planning to get married. She knew this priest back at Ohio State. She was involved in a group at the student center where they talked a lot about their Catholic experiences. Very open-minded priest. He influenced her and helped her to deal with a lot of questions she had about religion."

Before I could comment, he continued. "Ever since, she's been a part of a group here in Cleveland like they had at the Newman Center—most of them Catholics, who read books and discuss them, sing with guitars, sort of like what they used to do back at the university. They are Catholics who meet as a small group. Probably some of them wouldn't feel comfortable at a church. I've been going with her to this group for several months."

"Does that make you religious?" I queried, wondering as quickly as I uttered the words if perhaps I should not have raised that question again.

"I don't know, but I like the group. I'm not going to become Catholic, but nobody really asks you to do that. I enjoy the discussions. We've read some good books. It's all very open, we mostly talk about our own lives and experiences. Becky does the Mass but I haven't done that yet. I don't even know what I believe anymore. But I've learned a lot about Thomas Merton, the Berrigans, and Mother Theresa—people I really admire. They all stood up for things that were important, they definitely impress me—so you tell me, am I religious?"

His question caught me off guard just as had mine with him minutes earlier. Quickly, I uttered something like "I don't know," and picked up on the names of the people he had mentioned. "What is it about these people that impresses you?"

"Their conviction and compassion, I suppose. Something about the courage and determination that forces you to do something with your life. For someone like me, caught up in the rat race of hustling the next client, drawing my next set of plans for building a mall, an architect for almost twenty years who hasn't thought much about what he was doing except making money and living the good life, it makes me think."

John doesn't know if he is religious but he is experiencing a spiritual reawakening of sorts in this informal Eucharistic community of dissident Catholics and their spouses. The group has touched him in surprising ways; he is inspired and finds his compassion rekindled by the lives and struggles of some contemporary Catholic figures. As with many of his generation for whom institutional religious ties and identities are fairly weak, it hardly helps to categorize him anymore as Presbyterian. At the same time, to think of him as a "None" (or a nonaffiliate) overlooks the fact that something profoundly moving is happening within him. Doubt and lack of a clear conviction about what to believe do not here translate into a secular outlook; rather they appear to signify just the opposite—a more open, questing posture born in no small way out of disenchantment with secular alternatives to faith. John's profession and scientific mode of thinking have for a long time filled the gap created by his drift out of the church of his childhood; however, at this moment in his life, influenced greatly by Becky's self-reflexive stance toward Catholicism, he questions the secular and material values that have dominated his adulthood. Through this reawakening of religious emotions that have long been dormant and a reconnecting of his life to a larger religious narrative privileging love and compassion, he finds himself searching in his own life for greater depth. Participation in this group has triggered experiences of joy, optimism, and hope—elementary religious responses, yet potent enough to raise possibilities of a transcendence forcing him even in his doubt and uncertainty to ponder the priorities of his own life. The "religious," at least in some sense of its meaning, is recaptured for him as its deeper spiritual meaning is opened up.

Such experiences are perhaps more common than we realize among people who, for one reason or another, opt out of the religious establishment. House churches, Catholic Eucharistic groups, Jewish *havurot*, Bible study, prayer groups, and other such groups are often invisible yet by all accounts are flourishing today.[4] Many of the people involved in these groups are rediscovering who they are in relation to a religious tradition despite feelings of alienation and some degree of doubt and uncertainty of faith. The openness of these groups and the sharing that goes on within them is spiritually revitalizing. Many who participate do so as couples and often discuss marriage, family, and work-related concerns. Often such groups are organized in the workplace and make possible opportunities for exploring religious and spiritual matters in a neutral context where honesty, doubt, and questions can be genuinely expressed—a situation not always found in the larger, more formal religious structures.

KAREN POTTER: FEMINIST JOURNEY

Raised Southern Baptist and long active within a local congregation, Karen Potter is now 40 years old and working on a graduate degree in counseling. A school psychologist, she is married with two school-age children and lives in one of North Carolina's largest cities. Deeply introspective, she wants to "feel" a spiritual dimension in her life and likes, as she says, "to talk from my own experiences." Touched deeply by the feminist movement, she is caught up in a struggle with herself. Unlike John, who in midlife is caught up in surprise as he reconnects with religious emotions that have grown dormant, she has made a more conscious break with her Southern Baptist heritage and deliberately sought a women's group in which to share her experiences.

Karen is unusual in that she credits her spiritual journey to a theologically moderate congregation where for the past five years she was a member. She is not so much hostile as she is searching for new avenues of meaning and belonging; in fact, she speaks of being enormously grateful for the opportunities the church has given her. "It's been a real catalyst," she said, but then in the same breath added, "but I have come to find out that it doesn't corner the market on spirituality. Still it's a tool for those that it works for. This church has helped me, but right now it doesn't have much to offer me."

Rarely have I met someone who had greater empathy for religious participation yet for whom it seemed like an unfulfilled experience. In Karen's view, churches and other religious organizations function best instrumentally—helping people to initiate their *own* spiritual journeys. People come and go as their lives unfold. "If they start growing, they will change," she insisted. "It all depends on where the journey leads." Pressed further on this, she suggested that congregations should be thought of as "enabling institutions," there to help people to deepen their spiritual lives.

"So this church has been a catalyst for you?"

"Yes, it has, but I had to give up the notion that the only place you could find spirit was here. It was like I thought spirit is at the church. Then I'd go and I wouldn't feel it. I love some of these people. And miss them. But I just don't feel like being a part of it now . . . and don't want to have somebody telling me that it is right for me right now." She acknowledges that for many people, maybe most people, church is appropriate in certain phases of their lives—in settled times—but this is not such a time for her; this is an unsettled time, a moment of searching and growth.

Karen has found new life in a group with four other women, all of whom, she says, have taken a "leave of absence" from their churches to pursue their own spiritual depths. These women decided to take some time out exploring their own needs, even to the point of disengaging from other activities in the community. For them it is a very intentional activity, undertaken with considerable seriousness and great expectations. It has also been a most unusual experience, realizing that this has been something unlike anything any of them has ever done before. Their husbands and children have tried to be supportive but haven't always understood why or just what they are doing. But overall, as Karen says, "it's been empowering" and has helped to put her in touch with her deepest feelings which she now recognizes were long stifled by a southern, Bible-belt culture obsessed with guilt and control that didn't allow her to trust her own feelings. Now, she says: "I feel my connectedness with other people. When I feel the feeling, it's very much feeling like I'm okay. And I am the source of the spirit. It's coming from within, not without, and that's what it feels like. And I feel that. I have that now with the women. We get together and we sit in a circle and we meditate and we share and spirit is there with me."

"Spirit is there with me" is a fitting description of Karen's moment of truth, a mystical insight that has come to her, something greater than just self-discovery or self-esteem. It is an inner awareness and rejuvenation arising out of a bonding experience with other women. Having recently read Jean Bolen's *Goddesses in Every Woman*, she finds herself on a path exploring with other seekers, unsure of where this path will take any of them, but nonetheless convinced that the path is essential for her. "It was time for me to find God inside myself. My timing. Not yours or theirs or anybody else's." What she most wants is a direct experience of the divine, more than what she has found within traditional religious women's groups and psychology books or manuals promising five easy steps to a deeper understanding of self.

When asked about religious figures important to her, she speaks of Artemis, the Greek goddess of the hunt, as a source of new life within her. Artemis is independent, a warrior, someone who doesn't "get run around" by men in the woods. She admits she has become more assertive and that it feels good, relating no doubt to experiences with her father and her first husband, both of whom were strong-willed, dominating men. She does worry about her children and admits that family needs might at some point outweigh her own personal agenda, but "all that will have to be resolved later." For now, she is committed to her own spiritual exploration and open to insights from wherever she can find them— lectures, workshops, local bookstores, wise women, other churches with special programs.

What do we make of Karen? She is not really all that different from many women over the years who have been drawn into what amounts to a "parallel church." Because religious organizations tend to be patriarchal in structure and ideology, women have long had their own separate spheres of female institutional development.[5] Within their own sphere women exercise a great deal of symbolic power and cultivate spiritual resources that shape identities and emotions. Women's stories of bonding and of claiming responsibility for their own lives underscore the depth of resources they have created in a gendered world. One study, for example, appropriately entitled *Defecting in Place*, documents a broad spectrum of alienated women nurturing their own spirituality on the peripheries or outside of the religious establishment and doing so on their own terms; those who stay within religious organizations express hopes of effecting change, others have given up on the institution altogether and created their own separate structures. In many places women seek to deepen feminine consciousness by supporting and affirming one another, and by celebrating their own rituals and liturgies—examples of a gender-based alienation as one theme in today's spiritual quest culture.[6]

The range of exploration in Karen's case, and for many other women, is quite wide: she reads all she can find on ancient wisdom, Eastern religions, goddess literature, and portions of the Bible ("those parts the Baptist preachers never told me about!"). Having for a long time repressed feelings about her body, she now enjoys trips to a local spa where "they have all those powders and sweet-smelling things." Lately, she has discovered *Star Seed Transformation* and *A Course in Miracles*. "I used to not say anything about what I believed," she says, "for fear people wouldn't have anything to do with me. Then I discovered there were others that believed as I did." Such discoveries are sustaining, reassuring her that she isn't as weird as perhaps some people think. In listening to other women's stories, she finds a depth of bonding that is exhilarating. "I didn't know how many other women there were like me—going to workshops, taking meditation classes, and going to the spa," she comments, reflecting upon her years in the Baptist church.

Karen experienced the gender revolution somewhat later than did many other women of her generation; but now that she's experiencing it, she is asking serious questions about her own feelings and delving deeply into the religious heritage in which she was reared. She may or may not return to her Southern Baptist church, but, she'll certainly never be the same again; her personal journey in the past six or eight years has led her to new insights into herself and about how she was "made to feel and do" what she once did. She says: "I try to find my own power and actually affirm the things that were sort of criticized for being feminine; I'm seeing the contrast and I'm seeing the sexism. So I think it has a lot to do with my life experience. I'm thinking in these radical ways and I'm in the South. I'm in the Bible Belt, so I have to come to terms with all that."

In southern cities as elsewhere today, middle-class Boomers are exposed to New Age bookstores, self-help gurus, feminist workshops, and spiritual teachings of many kinds. "The spa where I get my bath oils and powder, you know, is a franchise. It's down in Birmingham where my sister lives." A new, rapidly expanding network of commercial enterprises, and not just religious organizations, are sensitive to spiritual themes—including a strong emphasis on accepting oneself and one's own body. Whatever the repressive legacies of a religious past among white, Anglo-Saxon Protestants, there is now a reclaiming of the body and an overcoming of older suspicious views of bodily pleasure and pampering. There are substantial numbers of Boomer Americans who for one reason or another feel some ambivalence toward the faith tradition in which they were raised and are spiritually hungry—enough so for smart entrepreneurs to cater to their concerns. Spirituality as linked to resolution of repressed feelings flourishes at present, indeed, in no small part because suppliers have discovered new venues for creating this market.

Sam Wong: Evangelical Seeker

We have seen that spiritual awakenings can reconnect people with religious heritages or may lead them to pursue alternative spiritual identities altogether. A third pattern—the Evangelical seeker—is common as well. Consider Sam Wong, member of a large Evangelical church in San Jose, California, second-generation Chinese-American, 37 years old, lower middle class, married with a young child, employed as a software programmer. His parents were not very religious, nor was he at the time he was growing up. It was not until he went to California State University at Long Beach that he confronted and engaged Christianity for the first time. There he met his wife, and both were introduced to Evangelical Christianity. They were in and out of churches, never really all that active, until they moved to San Jose six years ago when he got a better job as a computer programmer.

In his home it is obvious that he likes computers and is a committed Evangelical Christian. In many places there are manuals about computers, and in talking with him it becomes clear very soon that he is engrossed in the technically based "digital revolution"—he speaks freely about "information flows" and computerized "inputs" and "outputs." His faith is evident not just in his speech but visibly as well: his coffee cups are inscribed, "Jesus is the Reason for the Season" and on a table in a workroom a stone adjacent to a computer has the engraving "WWJD." When asked about the stone, Sam replies, "It stands for 'What Would Jesus Do,'" and then quickly adds, "I ask myself that question every day when I have a decision to make, wherever I am. I figure you can't go wrong when you ask what he would do and then try to do it." Present on a table are books by James Dobson, the well-known family psychologist, books on prosperity theology and church growth, and magazines featuring stories on the radio counselor who speaks directly, and often abruptly, to moral issues raised by her listeners: Dr. Laura Schlesinger. The combination of computer technology, family psychology, moral advice, and material religious culture makes for a distinct religious gestalt.

Sam belongs to a Vineyard Fellowship congregation organized only a few years ago, one he describes as a "seeker church." Seeker churches make a deliberate overture to those, particularly of his age group, who are searching for answers to religious questions. In Sam's own words: "This church has a class where you can ask about Christianity. Most of the people there don't know what to believe. A lot of us don't know about all the teachings. But it's okay that you don't know, or maybe even don't always agree with some things as long as you believe in Jesus Christ, and learn and grow in your faith." Seeker churches organize activities and programs with the expectation that people have questions, maybe even doubts. They assume that people probably know very little about religious traditions—the meaning of symbols and teachings, why the faith is practiced as it is. The music, the preaching, the programs are oriented to contemporary life and relating faith to spiritual seeking. Such churches cater to a psychological culture and try to connect the language of self with a language of transcendence. The question, "What would Jesus do?" in this context is obviously such a link, and one that endows personal life and moral questions with divine guidance. In this way Evangelical churches build bridges to a changing culture and to people like Sam, whose ties to religion in the past were virtually nonexistent and for whom a narrative of growth in faith is important for understanding both himself and Christianity. He conceives of faith especially as a growth experience, a process of learning and exploring its meanings for moral and spiritual life.

Sam's Evangelicalism and interest in computers blend to create a distinctive style of spiritual seeking. This is not altogether surprising considering that Evangelicalism has long used up-to-date media and information technologies in its programming and recruitment efforts. But the profile of an "Evangelical seeker" is particularly evident in the way that Sam came to join his church, in his religious style, and the manner in which he witnesses to his faith. This all became more clearly focused when I asked him, "How did you get involved in this particular church?"

"David, my friend from college," he said, "told me about this bulletin board on the Internet where Christians talk to each other. We talk to one another about what it means to be a Christian and what Jesus would do in a particular situation. We share our experiences and pray for one another." Further in the conversation he mentioned that he and his friends were extending the network all across the country (the "Jesus Network," as he called it). It was clear that they saw the Internet as an opportunity to create chat rooms for people around the world who were searching for the Lord. "Our church has a computer club and we plan how to reach people and to answer their questions about our faith. That's why I like this church."

Sam belongs to the Jesus Network! He is obviously very perceptive and knowledgeable about adaptable Evangelical churches and how the computer can be used for extending the Christian message. For him, the computer is a window to a larger world of Evangelical challenges and opportunities, a nexus of interaction where faith and mission come alive for him. More than just for testimonials, the computer is a means to effective programming and marketing in a spiritually hungry world. Through sharing with his friends on the Internet, he sees himself as helping to create new ways of winning people over to Jesus and even organizing a worldwide Evangelical campaign. The Internet is a tool for witnessing to those who are asking questions about what to believe—an extension of the "seeker church" into cyberspace. Listening to him was like taking lessons about the escalating speed of religious technology, of the marriage of God and the Internet. It was also a lesson in sociometry: at first, one close friend, next, a computer club in a local church, and then, an interactive network of global strategies. His world is one where talent and religious imagination are being harnessed anew to the latest of Evangelical Christian recruitment methods—something quintessentially American, but now in a Boomer techno-culture style.

SARA CAUGHMAN: REDISCOVERY OF TRADITION

Spirituality in the 1990s finds diverse expressions within congregations. Sam Wong's is one such style, Sara Caughman's is quite another. She is 44, married, a graphic designer, and member of an Episcopal Church in southern California. Though raised as a Christian, she was not active in any church for many years. Like so many in her generation she dropped out in her twenties, disillusioned with organized religion. But to hear her tell it, there was a "great turnaround" in her life. She dates her religious rebirth in her early forties to the time her older brother died from cancer at 46—a sobering moment that led her to think through again what her own life was about. But it was the turnaround in her congregation she spoke about that first grabbed my attention in an early interview; hence my question, "What's happening at the church now that's so different?"

"We're no longer squabbling about what it means to be the church. There is a new mood. You know when you walk into the place it's now an inclusive church, open and ministering to people of all kinds and lifestyles. It's alive spiritually. It's been a great turnaround from the old place it used to be."

"You like it a lot better, I can tell."

"You bet. We're serving people, representing Christ to the needy and not just to the comfortable middle-class people. People are genuinely excited about what we are doing. The place had become dry and empty. It was death to the spirit. Rote religion."

In some respects, St. Michael's past is not all that different from that of many mainline Protestant churches. Many of them were, and still are, engaged in "rote religion"; and, not surprisingly, declining in membership. But what is striking about this downtown church is that it has sought for some time to find a style of ministry consistent with its largely white, middle-class constituency that nonetheless engages that culture and tries to overcome the Episcopal malaise of becoming overly comfortable in Zion. Moreover, the church is fortunate in having a cadre of young members like Sara who have pushed for more involvement in the local community, to do more for and with marginalized groups. Because of its weather, southern California attracts many homeless people. For a church, this makes, as Sara says, "for a test of the spirit, especially in a place that enjoys an economy of abundance." For her and other Boomers, who basically took over the church determined to rebuild it, "it is essential," she says, "that Christian communities help those left behind by modern technology, unable to compete economically, and who struggle simply to survive."

The turnaround in the congregation came several years ago when a young group of members, with the leadership of the new rector, organized a study group to explore new methods of ministry. "It was a small group when we started," she says, "but we had great enthusiasm and a sense that we would not stop until we felt marked by the Spirit and bound to our mission." Almost all in this group were Boomers and many of them—as with Sara—had read books on improving the self, dealing with stress and feeling good about themselves, and enhancing their lifestyles. Yet something seemed missing. Their first major accomplishment was to establish a soup line, which now provides lunch for about one hundred homeless and hungry people daily. Others were drawn to this activity and related opportunities for involvement in justice issues. So many young adults were drawn to one activity or another that a "Boomer workshop" was organized to inquire into how best to utilize the many talents available. Then came the creation of a base community of six to eight people, meeting weekly to read the Bible and study liberation and feminist theologies and varying styles of Christian spirituality. Especially important to these groups was the focus on practices, and learning that spirituality—if it is to have depth—requires cultivation by means of habit and shared activity. Participants also discovered that through practice it is possible to reach back in time and find roots in a tradition that are far richer often than what is generally known about them at any given time. Additional base communities were formed. Next came a workshop on Celtic spirituality exploring in some depth its earth-based insights and significance for a contemporary, religiously based environmental ethic.

The latest venture is a "Human Sexuality and Lifestyle" study group looking at gay and lesbian issues as well as single parents and cohabitation among heterosexuals. For over a year this group has been meeting, and just recently members delivered a report to the church encouraging it to bless same-sex unions openly. This is by far the most controversial undertaking to date, but one that has pushed many members to probe deeply into their own understandings of themselves as sexual beings. Openly discussed are the links between sexuality and spirituality. While some tensions have arisen around blessing same-sex unions, the church has weathered the storm precisely at the time when an Episcopal bishop was charged (but later the charges dropped) with heresy for ordaining an openly practicing gay man. There is a growing gay and lesbian community within the church, and frequently the meetings of Integrity, an Episcopal gay group, are announced in the morning worship service. The group's next project will probably be a report on responsible heterosexual relationships, which no doubt will prompt further discussion in the parish.

"Equality and tolerance toward all lifestyles are our things, you know," Sara emphasizes, leaving unclear whether "our" here refers to the Christian tradition or her generation. The two seem to mesh together in her mind, considering that she and others like her are now leaders at St. Michael's. A middle-class Boomer culture pervades the congregation with its sensitivities to women, child care, single parents, singles and divorced, gays and straight. The congregation's spiritual style is shaped by its celebration of openness and diversity; its members will tell you that here, unlike many other churches in their experience, they feel accepted. They come with their questions, doubts, abuses, and even resentments originating from previous church experiences. Some people leave because the openness and diversity is too great for them, but those numbers are few in comparison to the many who are drawn to the parish climate.

Sara describes her own turnaround as "a journey in faith toward greater understanding of the meaning of life." Important to observe is the language and symbols she uses to describe her own self-transformation. Though she uses popular spiritual terms in speaking of her religious life, clearly her story is infused with "we" language: words and phrases such as "community of faith," *church*, *God*, and *Christ* flow easily; her adopted Anglican liturgy and community is the setting for her own personal exploration, which she prefers to describe as a shared experience. Journey extends not only forward but into the past, toward rediscovery and reclaiming of Christian spirituality as understood within her tradition. Her spiritual style reflects an accommodation to the larger seeker themes in today's culture but without sacrificing historic religious language or religious self-understanding. Indeed, as for much of this congregation, this cultural accommodation is rather obvious. Recently the church has obtained a labyrinth, which is the most visible of the institutional innovations undertaken to accommodate the quest culture. This circular pathway—leading into a center, and then back outward—dating to medieval times, if not earlier, makes for a bodily based spiritual experience appealing to contemporary sensitivities. But as she points out, as in Chartres cathedral, a labyrinth should be located at the entrance of a church, a reminder that "in walking it one is awakened to a shared life in faith." Many people, she says, "start out walking it as if they are alone but discover fellow travelers along the way." At St. Michael's such people are welcomed in their spiritual pursuits.

VICKI FEINSTEIN: ECLECTIC SEEKER

Unlike John, Karen, Sam, and Sara, all self-proclaimed Baby Boomers, Vicki Feinstein is not sure of her generation: she was born in 1964, right on the cusp, "either at the end of the Boomer era," she says, "or at the beginning of the Busters." She admits she doesn't really identify with the Boomer generation but she's also unsure if she belongs to the younger generation. "Busters, Generation Xers, Slackers, Thirteeners . . . who are they or we? *Time* magazine says we may never know." Never married, she works as a physical therapist in a veterans hospital and lives in a Maryland suburb outside Washington, D.C. She is far more settled now than when we first met her ten years ago, although the tattoo on her upper left arm and small ring on her right ear clearly mark her as belonging to a younger generation.

When we first met her in 1989, she was living near Boston. After high school she had attended a secretarial college and held several part-time jobs but decided some years ago to train to become a physical therapist. Like others of her age, she has a clear sense of life's ironies and hardships. Finding work to support herself has not always come easily. Her parents were divorced when she was 6. She has two older sisters, both of them now divorced. She herself has had several failed romances (including "lesbian relationships," she volunteers). She expresses many of the cynical attitudes of Generation Xers: skepticism about the future, doubts about marriages succeeding, and uncertainty about any religious or metaphysical claims as "objectively true." As she sees it, the world is not only a place of many differing religious beliefs, it is hostile and unpredictable, somewhat like in a video game. "Sometimes you win, sometimes you lose," she says, "but you are always calling the shots and trying to figure out what's happening."

Her sense of aloneness and uncertainty became even more apparent in our second interview. When asked about connections to family and religion, her answers revealed little of the family warmth or sense of religious belonging that is common to many Americans. Asked about her parents' religious affiliation, she replies: "My father was Jewish but not religious. We never went to synagogue. Maybe a time or so when I was a kid. I don't know what my mother is. Nothing really. Catholic, I suppose." Growing up, she was exposed neither to church nor synagogue. She occasionally goes to synagogue but only for special events like an art show or a visiting lecturer. By her own admission, Judaism as such has no particular or deep religious meaning for her; its religious narrative offers little memory and basis for organizing her life. When asked about it, she dismisses the question saying, "I'm a secular Jew."

When asked further about religion, again she dismisses it, saying she isn't religious and admits that she doesn't know what it would really be like to be religious. She says she cannot imagine herself belonging to any religious organization. The closest thing to church or synagogue for her was the short time she spent in the Church of Scientology when she was much younger. As a teenager growing up in Massachusetts, she read about dianetics and was drawn to the philosophical teachings of Scientology. She liked the idea that human beings are basically good but in need of greater self-knowledge for expressing goodness and escaping from painful past experiences. She and some friends got involved in the religious movement. Suffering at the time from anorexia and low self-esteem, she was drawn toward, as she says, "motorcycles, drugs, and Scientology." The latter offered what she felt at the time she most needed, a practical means of improving her life. Scientology promised hope and survival. "I liked what Scientology taught about how my mind was shaped, and how I could know myself better." Its teachings were meaningful, but also it was something she and her friends had themselves freely chosen—a "venture all our own," as she says.

"What about any other religions? Did you check any others out?" I inquired.

"Oh yes," she said. "I read all the books I could on Buddhism."

"What about this religion did you like?"

"I like the fact that it encouraged me to focus upon myself. To look within my self and to find out what was right and true for me. I also like *Star Trek*—is that a religion? I don't know."

"Why *Star Trek*?" I asked curiously.

"I like the fact that people all work together, to explore and expand the world we live in. Doesn't matter who you are, what race, sex, religion, whatever planet you come from, all get along well and look to a future together. It's promising. If we lived that way we would have a better world," she says.

"Would you describe yourself as New Age?" I asked, searching for a label that might fit her.

"I don't know" she replied, adding that she doesn't agree with everything she has read about it. She has checked out various 1-800 telephone lines connected to New Age teachings and in the past subscribed to several newsletters. Most recently, she participated in a Reiki workshop and before that attended sessions on "body talk" and "relaxation responses" at a local health club. She regularly browses books at the Borders bookstore in her suburban mall on topics relating to mind, body, and spirit. In her small apartment, she is surrounded by books and magazines on consciousness expansion, techniques for finding joy and happiness, self-esteem, and physical therapy. Her work as a therapist and personal spiritual exploration appear to have fused somewhat, giving her some degree of unity of experience in work and life. If there is a center in her life right now, it would have to be her work and related activities.

One does not easily put a religious label upon her. Very much an independent thinker, she is on a spiritual quest characterized largely by pragmatism, self-reliance, and hope for a happier life than she knew as a child. There are themes of science fiction and utopianism, bound up with her search for deliverance from a world that seems chaotic, violent, and at times hopeless. She is simultaneously drawn to aspects of her Jewish heritage and a mythic vision of a future humanity—an imaginary script—promising a way that she, and others like her, can exist in a supportive, caring manner. Like many others in our survey who know little about a family-based religious tradition, she found questions about purpose of life and finding meaning very salient—indeed, she wants very much to live in an ordered world and to feel that her life fits into some larger narrative. Even if she cannot articulate very well that larger story, she senses that it exists, that there is a story for her. Asked if she believes in God, she says, "Yes, in my own way."

Of all the people we met, Vicki comes closest to being a "tourist" of religion.[7] One religion is as true as another from her vantage point, and shopping around is appropriate. Truthfulness lies in a religion's—any religion's—meaning for her. She approaches all of them somewhat skeptically; the fact that she was not brought up in a particular faith tradition means that she thinks of herself largely as an outsider to religion of any kind. For any religion to "work" for her, it has to grab her and deliver on its promise—in effect, it must break through her cynicism and convince her of its hold on mystery and meaning. She wants the latter and thinks it might actually lie within her reach. She is aware of various techniques designed for cultivating spirituality—personality inventories, meditation, visualization, bodily movement—and has explored many of them, to see what "they can do" for her; yet no one single technique seems to provide fully in an instrumental way what she is looking for. Perhaps most importantly, she speaks in multiple religious vocabularies: in Jewish, in Buddhist, in Star Trek and New Age terminologies. She moves across conventional religious boundaries with great ease, trying not so much to blend them as to understand in what ways religions are similar and different. She speaks of "inner strength," "the God within," "energy," "*chakras*," "archetypes," even "the God of the Hebrew people," aware that these imply quite differing ontological realities, yet she is hardly flippant or dismissive about them. All are important to her in a quest seemingly dominated by concerns for meaning and personal healing. While a tourist in the realm of religion, she is open to, but seemingly not all that desperately in search of, a spiritual unity within her life.

Even so, one is struck by the eclectic—at times seemingly contradictory—mix of symbols, teachings, beliefs, experiences, and practices she claims as her own. There is a makeshift quality in her lifestyle that suggests that spirituality plays a role in her life even as she navigates through, in, and around religious alternatives. What is lacking is any fixed, neatly ordered religious system we can identify as hers. One senses, within her overlapping boundaries and juxtapositions of identities, a Jewish father and a Catholic mother; shifting configurations of spiritual teachings and practices drawn from many traditions; a spiritual self-understanding defined in part by its opposition to a conventional religious identity. The formation and negotiation of her own sense of self take precedence over any single set of culturally inherited prescriptions about who she is. In sum Vicki's life and commitments force us to rethink our notions of a unitary religious self or of religion itself as a self-contained entity consisting of mutually exclusive components; she points us to what one commentator calls a "problem of boundaries" in the contemporary study of religion.[8]

FOCUS ON THE SPIRITUAL

These stories introduce us to a rich and textured religious terrain. Far from a random selection, these particular accounts are chosen because they highlight spiritual themes prominent in the United States today. Stories are insightful when, as is true here, they open up the intersection of personal and collective experience and expose the inner worlds of experience and meaning, and show (or demonstrate) how those worlds connect with families and communities, with moral life and responsibility, and contemporary values. Indeed, as many researchers have come to realize, storytelling is crucial to both religion and the human condition: it is a creative act, an exercise in making meaning, the constructing of personal identity. By focusing on people's own accounts of their lives, we begin to appreciate the complex, multifaceted face of religion, as symbol, belief, practice, experience, identity, community, institution, and how these various aspects fluctuate in importance in an individual's own religious world over time.

Clearly the attention in these stories is on the "spiritual." More than any other, it is the experiential face of religion that takes on current prominence: in story after story the quest is for something more than doctrine, creed, or institution, although of course these are usually

involved. What is sought after has to do more with feelings, with awareness of innermost realities, with intimations of the presence of the sacred—what amounts to the very pulse of lived religion. For if people do
not encounter the sacred in profound, life-transforming ways through
meditation, prayer, or other practices, the latter lose their force and risk
becoming empty exercises. All the stories reported here give expression
to some degree of searching for that deeper level of encounter with the
sacred, that deepest "ground of being"—yearnings that are among the
most deeply rooted of all human responses and the means by which
humanity becomes defined as human.[9] Historically, in many languages
and cultures, the spiritual was conceived as wind and breath, that which
moves, the force that mysteriously and invisibly animates: the Latin *spiri-
tus, anima,* and *animus,* the Greek *psyche,* the Sanskrit *atman,* the Hebrew
ruach. The spiritual comprehends but cannot be contained by intellect,
cognition, or institutional structure; it reaches out for unity and the ordering of experience; it abhors fixity in the interest of transformation.
Both the notion of ordering experience and that of transformation suggest something deeply existential, directed to connections with ultimate
meanings, values, and ethical commitment. Theologian Paul Tillich defined the spiritual as "the unity of power and meaning" arising out of the
depths of a person's being.[10] In Tillich's way of thinking, this union becomes possible by means of constitutive symbols that affirm the self, generate hope and joy, and motivate the wish to live, over against the adver-
sities of existence. That is, spirit is the fundamental life-force giving drive
and direction to human existence. Without it there would be no such
thing as the human.

Yet words like *spirit* and *spiritual* remain difficult to grasp. As Augus-
tine said about time, their meaning seems fairly obvious until we try to
define them. Classical definitions have come down through all the great
religious traditions, yet as we have encountered such terms in the five
stories described here, quite clearly they take on particular meaning in
the vernacular. As Americans speak of spirituality today, the term may,
and most often does, include religion in the sense of a tradition, yet for
many it is not bound by doctrinal, creedal, or ecclesiastical categories.
Some people claim to be spiritual but with little, if any, grounding in any
faith tradition; still others claim to be spiritual but are opposed to the
religious. And if that is not confusing enough, people readily refer to
differing types of spiritualities, such as feminist spirituality, eco-spirituality, Latino spirituality, Native American spirituality, and the like. Thus we
have multiple discourses about spirituality, and seldom is the term pre-

cisely defined in any of the discourses. Faced with such discursive ambiguities at the level of everyday usage, a recent panel of judges consisting of two dozen corporate executives, educators, clergy, and community leaders, when asked to define contemporary usage of the term among Americans, concluded as follows: "Spirituality is a very difficult word to define. An adequate definition would include reference to a relationship with something beyond myself (known as "Creator," "God," "transcendent power," etc.) that is intangible but also real. It would recognize that spirituality is the source of one's values and meaning, a way of understanding the world, an awareness of my "inner self," and a means of integrating the various aspects of myself into a whole."[11] Spirituality encompasses all four above-mentioned themes: a source of values and meaning beyond oneself, a way of understanding, inner awareness, and personal integration. All are "big" themes, indicating the depths of spiritual challenge felt by many people in our time. In a very fundamental sense, what is at stake is a viable conception of the "self." Viewed against a backdrop of fragmentation and commodification of the self in modern society, its cultivation and maintenance become problematic. Contemporary quests for spirituality are really yearnings for a reconstructed interior life, deliberate and formative efforts aimed at forging an integrated self and transcending the limits of the given. In keeping with spirit as that which moves—like wind and breath—but utilizing a quite different language, anthropologist Thomas J. Csordas proposes that we look upon the self as "an indeterminate capacity to engage or become oriented in the world, characterized by effort and reflexivity." Plasticity and creativity are attributes of the self, and, as Csordas says, self-making involves "orientational processes in which aspects of the world are thematized, with the result that the self can be objectified as a person with a cultural identity or set of identities."[12]

Contexts for Analysis

Put into simpler terms, religious identities in contemporary society are fluid, multilayered, and to a considerable extent personally achieved. The experiential, deeply spiritual aspects of religion most especially assume these features, something obvious from the stories reported in this chapter. Open-ended accounts of religious life are likely to reveal some degree of eclecticism, or constellation of elements and themes from differing faiths and traditions, put together by individuals exercising their creative agency. There may well be underlying, unresolved tensions among elements or themes. In modern pluralistic settings people become "heteroglossic"—they speak in many voices.[13] The pertinent question becomes, What are the relevant major contexts for understanding these voices?

Religious Belonging

Almost ninety percent of Americans claim an institutionally based religious identity, as Southern Baptist, Lutheran, Presbyterian, Roman Catholic, Reform Jew, Quaker, African Methodist Episcopal, Assemblies of God, and so on. Hundreds of religious denominations in the United States make for a vast array of "communities of memory."[14] They serve as an important basis of social belonging, especially in the United States because, as sociologists point out, the country is religiously pluralistic and lacks an established church; and given the legal distinction between membership in religion and membership in society which ensues, quasi-Gemeinschaft groups are not only possible but structurally encouraged as centers of belonging.[15] Protestant Christianity has spawned movement after movement, in what is described as the sect-to-denomination process: splinter groups break away but in time join the cultural mainstream, becoming yet another, respectable religious option. New splinter movement or old established group, Americans continue to identify with them. These movements are a recurring source, too, of an ascetic moralism deeply rooted in biblical tradition and Reformation theology emphasizing duty to family, church, and work. Reaffirmed are the twin ordering principles so embedded within this legacy, love of God and love of neighbor, that have long shaped religious and even secular notions of purpose in life, goodness, responsibility, and justice.

Religious communities overlap with racial, ethnic, regional, and social class constituencies. In the United States the religious mingles easily with ascriptive and achieved statuses—reinforcing group consciousness. Religious identities are deeply rooted in families, the latter providing a sense of self-definition and social location in a world of alternatives and creating for many people warm fuzzy feelings—as with John McRae, despite his having strayed from his childhood religious past. Nor should we overlook more conscious religious identities rooted in congregations, most of which are linked to a historic tradition and carry a biblically based morality. Religious communities in fact thrive in the United States as nowhere else. Even in settings where the religious content may appear to

be weak, denominationally based communities can be spiritually supportive for inner circles and still define boundaries of social interaction that
extend well beyond Sunday morning. They function as a basis for voluntary organizations and civic activities, less today than in the past, but
more so than secular commentators are inclined to think in a highly
mobile and seemingly rootless world.[16]

But there is a downside. Organized religion can be experienced as
distant and out-of-date; spiritually it can be dry. People may, and often
do, feel somewhat removed from whatever religious heritage they have
inherited. "I happen to be" religion is common in the United States (for
example, "I happen to be Catholic"), that is, a person may have a family-
based religious identity but not really claim it in any deep way as his or
her own. "Happen to be" religion is mostly a leftover: an ethnic or cultural past, preference for a particular food, family connections, inherited status, and belonging. Moreover, the fact that for many Americans
religious participation is sporadic, that is, they move in and out of active
participation within their religious communities, means that the sali-
ence, or significance, of that participation and belonging varies enormously over the individual's life-course. At any given moment a sizable
proportion of those identifying with any of the historic religious communities that form the bulk of the population—say Catholics, Protestants, and Jews—can more appropriately be described as "cultural" (as
opposed to "religious"), as "nominal," as "unchurched," as "nonobservant," as "nonpracticing," as "inactive," all depending on the heritage.
For those especially who feel cut off from a religious past, this is true. It
is not that denominational and faith-community identities are irrelevant,
indeed far from it, but such identities must be critically examined rather
than simply presumed in contemporary society: in what ways are they
important in people's lives, and more generally, what is their place in the
larger process of constructing religious identity?

Popular Religious and Spiritual Culture

If denominations represent an established, "official" form of religious
belonging, popular religious culture is more diffused, less contained by
formal religious structures: widespread belief in angels and reincarnation; the appeal of religious and quasi-religious shrines, retreat centers,
and theme parks; interest in metaphysical and theosophical teachings,
prosperity theology and "possibility thinking"; and large proportions of
Americans reporting mystical experiences.[17] At this level we observe an

eclectic mix of religious and spiritual ideas, beliefs, and practices. What such examples share is that they are less institutionalized and distinct as separate meaning systems; they persist largely as a result of loosely bound networks of practitioners, the publishing industry, and the media. Much of popular spiritual culture currently goes by other names, such as the paranormal, Neo-Paganism, astrology, nature religion, holistic thinking, healing, New Age, or New Spirituality. Historically, religious ideas stemming from the time of Emerson and the Transcendentalists, and then later the movements known as Theosophy and New Thought, constituted a metaphysical strand in American life that diffused fairly widely into the culture and set forth quite distinctive ideas about the connections between the individual and a divine mind and the flow of spiritual energies. This metaphysical tradition is identified with an expressive moralism that, counter to more ascetic moral styles, puts greater emphasis on personal happiness, growth and self-fulfillment, and harmony with nature and universal truth. Close links between the spiritual and the material mean that this tradition, or at least portions of it, take a positive stance toward economic prosperity and align it with moral and religious practice focused to a great degree on personal interests.

The mixing of official and more popular religious themes is very evident in our stories: especially in Vicki Feinstein's do-it-yourself eclecticism, but also in Sam Wong's popular Evangelicalism. Popular versions of Christianity allow Sam Wong to share similar spiritual styles with other Evangelicals, within his church and outside of it. Aside from the Christian video games, the church growth teachings, and the testimonials he and others exchange on the Internet, he relies on a widely used inspirational literature demonstrating prosperity through faith in God and describing religious techniques in almost-magical fashion (biblical passages to be read with investment brokers when setting up IRS accounts) to secure that prosperity. Capitalism, the entertainment industry, and modern technology interface with his congregation to create a multi-layered religious environment. Vicki Feinstein delves into metaphysical and New Age teachings and lives in a world vastly different from Sam Wong's, but hers is no less spiritually inviting. Her inquiries have taken her back to the metaphysical movements of the nineteenth century. From these teachings she has settled on a conviction about spiritual energies and how they can heal the body; on an understanding of the "higher mind" and subtle ways that intentionality influences personal energies; and on a view generally of the role of "positive thinking" in healing and facing life's dilemmas. Her spiritual quest makes clear that the nineteenth-century metaphysical teachings are not a thing of the past but indeed are a continuing source of spiritual vitality in the United States. That popular religious themes mesh so easily with the religious cultures found in established institutions, organizations, and social activities implies a horizontal dimension of spiritual influence, one that cuts across existing structures and, inevitably, pops up in surprising places.

As already implied, this fluid, less contained form of spirituality does have its limitations. If official religion can become encrusted and rigid, highly personal religion easily suffers from a lack of institutionalization. Mystical experiences, so much a part of religious life, are highly sporadic and volatile; they tend not to encourage lasting loyalty to social organizations, privileging instead the individual's own inner world. But without an institutional and communal context, it is difficult to regularize religious life around a set of practices and unifying experiences, to mobilize people around causes, or even to sustain personal religious identity. Individual religious identity is itself rooted to a considerable extent within community.

Therapeutic and Post-Therapeutic Cultures

A closely related phenomenon is the therapeutic culture and its explicit attention to the self. Members of the Baby Boom generation grew up in years when the "human potential" movement deeply influenced American life, and now in their midlives its successor movements, known variously as "twelve-step," "self-help," and "recovery," attract considerable followings. How many Baby Boomers are involved in these particular programs, including Evangelical Christian versions of them, is unknown, but the numbers are considerable. One national survey finds that one out of four Americans are involved in small groups of one sort or another, many of which are therapeutic in type and include a great proportion of members from this generation.[18] The "triumph of the therapeutic," to cite Phillip Rieff, created a broadly based cultural movement with characteristics similar to popular religious meaning systems: it privileges the felt needs of the ordinary person, offers direct access to God or "a Power greater than ourselves" (once the person has recognized he or she is powerless over an addiction), and encourages moral and spiritual transformation. Deciding to seek help—especially self-help—takes on features comparable to a religious conversion, even among Evangelicals who often are ambivalent about so explicit a focus on the therapeutic. One commentator describes the religious similarities as follows: "In language evocative of Christian confession, the steps require the addicted to admit their 'wrongs' to God, to themselves, and to others, by taking a 'fearless moral inventory' of themselves. They are then enjoined to make amends to all whom they have injured and to remain alert to further wrongdoing in the future. The final step advocates spreading this message to other addicts and continuing to live out this transformation in all areas of life."[19]

This movement reflects a profound effort within contemporary culture to address psychological health and personal well-being openly and candidly in a supportive context and amounts to, as R. Marie Griffith observes, "a kind of spiritual shift in American life, in which the boundaries between the public and the private have been repeatedly challenged and redrawn."[20] What had begun in the 1960s as a quest for the "ideal self," an excessively individualistic quest, had by the early 1990s become more contained, opening the way for people in the presence of other people to share aspects of their lives, even their very intimate lives, in ways that were potentially nurturing and transforming. It offers an anonymous setting where people can reclaim their feelings and inner resolve, deal with their addictions and abuses, and experience the spiritual in small groups. As judged by people's accounts within small groups, much is involved in the process of spiritual transformation: individual stories become enmeshed in group experience, people arrive at their own understandings of truth in a supportive and negotiated context, the sacred becomes more personal, and the interior self is deepened.

The current recovery movement is both a product of, and a backlash to, an earlier "self-ism" that was so highly focused on individual needs. Its spiritual force is rooted in the paradox of surrendering control over one's life, while simultaneously discovering the power to take charge of life. For people who want more than what consumption, materialism, faith in science and progress, and narcissistic searching for self-fulfillment can provide, the movement offers not just liberation from addictions but also depth, authenticity, and integration of life experiences. In a very real sense, self-fulfillment became a trap: with so much emphasis upon the self—with its inflated images of being special, unique, and only potentially realized—maintaining the self became a "burden," a psychological crisis brought on by encounter with one's own self-delusions.[21] Having confronted that "empty waste," to quote William James again, awareness of a need for a stronger interior world and spiritual resources is a powerful motif in contemporary American culture. For this reason, the spiritual ferment we observe today may be far deeper and of greater significance than many commentators, who point simply to its faddish qualities, would have us believe.

Scripts, Practices, and Human Agency

"Lived religion," that is, religion as experienced in everyday life, offers a model for integrating the official, the popular, and the therapeutic modes of religious identity.[22] Lived religion might be thought of as involving three crucial aspects: scripts, or sets of symbols that imaginatively explain what the world and life are about; practices, or the means whereby individuals relate to, and locate themselves within, a symbolic frame of reference; and human agency, or the ability of people to actively engage the religious worlds they help to create. Scripts as found in religious traditions would include symbolic formulations such as the command to love God and to love one's neighbor within Christianity, the prophetic call for social justice in the Hebrew scriptures, meditation on selflessness in the teachings of the Buddha, the sacredness of the earth in Native American traditions, or the harmony between the individual and the universe within the metaphysical traditions. The two great faiths in the West—Judaism and Christianity—have sought to nourish the *Imitatio Dei*, the imitation of God and the imitation of Christ, respectively, as a means of connecting the individual with God. Hence the significance of practices like prayer, devotion, meditation, worship, observance of sacred time, and service in helping to create and maintain the presence of the divine. Practices, as philosopher Alasdair MacIntyre reminds us, arise from a social context: religion as a symbol, myth, and narrative is maintained through shared activities and practices oriented to a given place and time. If indeed we were to single out one aspect of lived religion as central, that which makes for the encounter with the sacred, it would be practice, or "religious culture in action."[23]

But at this juncture in history, inherited religious traditions face severe challenges. Tradition as memory and authority, or as a means of organizing the past in relation to the present, is eroded in a secular world; religious scripts that once communicated deep meanings, symbolic frames of reference, and defined modes of action must now compete with other stories in a pluralistic and media-saturated society that encourages a mixing of religious themes. Religious truths that were once closely linked to place and context are undermined by high levels of geographic and social mobility, rapid social and technological change, and by a mass culture made up increasingly of images and symbols that often retain very little to locate and anchor them in a particular place and time. The result is a proliferation of religious scripts, greater selectivity of practices from a variety of sources, the possibility of multilayered religious worlds, and often a softening of personal commitment resulting from what has been described as a shift "from a world in which beliefs held believers to one in which believers hold beliefs."[24]

Thus in a very real sense, the self is elevated to a higher level of making spiritual choices and negotiating frameworks of meaning drawing off institutional and more popular-based religious discourses, all in a context where for many Americans, especially those born after World War II, relationships with organized religion are often rather tenuous. Many in these generations know very little about specific teachings, or how one faith community differs from another; many just nominally involved within churches, synagogues, and temples find it difficult to articulate what they believe. That is to say, many of them are not very well versed in religious scripts and moral codes, even when they continue—as is the American custom—to claim some affiliation with faith communities. Still others are more cut off from organized religion. In this respect Vicki Feinstein stands out sharply from all four of the other characters: she is less rooted religiously, to the symbols, beliefs, and practices of any tradition, than we would expect for most Americans. Religion for her remains largely something distant and to be "tried out," making her situation somewhat akin to that of a voyeur adrift in a sea of symbols, beliefs, and practices. Religious symbols, texts, and rituals are more a *resource* for her exploration than elements of a living faith. She exemplifies what some say occurs in a society where religion has become partially severed from its traditional anchors of family, community, and social institution, and hence, in its everyday practice becomes more eclectic and radically self-constructed. Her situation resembles that of a growing number of people for whom no singular inherited religious vocabulary exists to describe who they are and to express their deepest spiritual yearnings.[25]

But Vicki Feinstein is on the extreme end of the open searching spectrum, positioned differently from our other characters who seek either stronger spiritual support or some vital balance of that and spiritual openness.[26] It is helpful to think of a continuum—spiritual support, or grounding usually involving a core tradition, versus spiritual openness, or searching for insights with a much higher level of tolerance for uncertainty—on which our characters, and Americans more generally, might

42

be placed. Karen Potter is deeply involved in her own personal transformation, negotiating her way through her inherited religious tradition with the help of a feminist support group; Sam Wong's voice is influenced by a Christian Evangelical "seeker" language blending faith and journey combined with a moral defensiveness; John McRae speaks in an idiom of institutional disclaimers, yet also of subtle reawakenings of deeply felt religious sentiments; Sara Caughman wants a deeper grounding within a faith tradition and a moral sensibility balancing self and others. Each relates in his or her own way to whatever script is involved. Indeed, the situation is even more complex considering, as religious scholar Robert Orsi puts it, we must pay attention to "how particular people, in particular places and times, live in, with, through, and against the religious idioms, including (often enough) those not explicitly their own."[27]

BOUNDARIES, EXCHANGES, AND QUEST

To be sure, people in modern society live in, with, through, and against many religious idioms at any given time in their lives. People make choices, selectively engage scripts and practices, reflect upon themselves as meaning-making creatures. In this process biography and faith traditions interact to produce discursive strategies toward religion. As Rabbi Debra Orenstein writes, "Jews no longer necessarily discover Judaism through Jewish texts, rituals, and traditions. Often, Jews discover Judaism through their personal quests and journeys—finding, as a seemingly belated surprise, that Judaism has something to say about their lives and circumstances after all."[28] The same can be said of other religious communities, or of people who just "happen to be" linked with some tradition but are not self-conscious of who they are until in some existential moment they rediscover themselves. Without recognition of these "lived"—or spiritual—qualities of religion, we risk losing perspective on the diversity and texture of religious life and of its deep personal groundings within an individual's experience. Certainly any analysis that would do justice to the religious lives of the post–World War II generations must look broadly at the meanings assigned to terms like *religious* and *spiritual* and at social and psychological processes involved in the construction of religious identities. It is difficult to proceed without such polarities as religious and secular, or even religious and spiritual, yet on moment's reflection it is obvious that, as R. Laurence Moore observes,

"However much we conceptualize with binary minds, however much bureaucratization encourages us to differentiate functions, reality remains hybrid."[29] Thus, for a variety of reasons, all having to do with the hypermodernity of our time, the turn of the century marks a moment when the mapping of the religious scene calls for serious attention to boundaries, exchanges, and quest.

To call attention to boundaries and exchanges is to emphasize that in the contemporary United States, fluidity within religious groups and institutions is extraordinarily high. Boundaries are porous, allowing people, ideas, beliefs, practices, symbols, and spiritual currents to cross. And as a result, religious boundaries themselves become redefined, and personal and group identities reconfigured. Further, participation in religious congregations, in special purpose groups, and in loosely networked spiritual constituencies overlap: churchgoing United Methodists read "positive thinking" literature, join support groups, commit themselves to special causes, not infrequently believe in reincarnation and psychic powers, watch *Touched by an Angel* on television. To ask a United Methodist, "Are you religious?" is to evoke response frames of varying kinds and of varying intensities. At a still deeper level, even the definition of what it means to be a United Methodist, or any other collectively defined religious identity in the American environment, is itself shaped by a long history of encounters between whites and blacks, between southerners and northerners, between East Coast tradition and West Coast frontier, between Social Gospel and Evangelical theologies, and more recently, of encounters between men and women and between straights and gays. Rather than being isolated or static, religious traditions are "made over and over again in encounters with others."[30] Much the same might be said of popular religious culture, and of its changing moods and styles. In the current context, religious meanings and identities are contested and negotiated over considerations of generation, gender, morality, and lifestyle. The process itself is hardly new, only the dimensions that support those debates, and the scale and complexity of modern encounters in general.

To emphasize quest is to make the point that in an age when boundaries are especially permeable, when exchanges freely occur, spiritual searching should come as no surprise. Flexibility and movement encourage creative, soul-searching processes; the actual practice of religion in a context of overlapping religious cultures and blurred boundaries encourages a degree of self-scrutiny and reflection. Both faith as traditionally conceived within religious communities and spirituality conceived in its extreme as its alternative require deliberation and a sustained act of will, certainly under conditions where no single *type* of religious institution or spiritual activity monopolizes symbolization of the sacred. With so much religious diffusion, old ways of looking at religion simply in terms of established institutions or acceptance of a single tradition as normative, and others not, becomes less and less appropriate. And to speak of "syncretism" to describe this diffusion is to perpetuate old, misguided notions of religious purity spoiled by contamination. Thus it is that in scholarly discourse on religion psychologists increasingly, and more appropriately, speak of a "quest orientation,"[31] and sociologists call attention to a "new quest for community" and "religious quest" engendered by confrontation with pluralism, individualism, and modernity.[32] Labeled one way or another, spiritual ferment both for individuals and within institutions is apparent to any interested observer. In short, to talk of religion in a place like the United States currently is to raise a host of unresolved issues pertaining to symbolization, the power of tradition, and individual agency.

What exactly are the sources of this quest mentality? How is the impact of modernity upon religion to be understood? How are we to better understand the characters introduced in this chapter? To address these questions requires a close look at demographics, social and cultural dynamics, and religious developments in this latter half-century. The task is difficult because both modernity as context and the religious terrain itself are complex. But cartographers, or mapmakers, must themselves be seekers of sorts—that is, explorers ready to chart terrains anew. And that is what we here set out to do, beginning first with the broad social structural developments that are now reshaping American religious life and culture.

The Making of a Quest Culture

*Modernity . . . would not be defined in terms of this or that
attribute, but rather as an ingrained mistrust of anything stable
or inherited and the constant quest for the new.*
(*François Ricard*)

THE STORIES FROM the previous chapter bear the imprint of distinct religious sensibilities, and particularly an emphasis on personal experience and deep spiritual yearnings: a shift in consciousness hardly limited to the social margins of contemporary society, and for that reason not to be confused with seeking in some narrow, "cultlike" sense. This more open, spiritual searching style is apparent among feminists, liberationists, and self-declared "seekers"—for their inner life is now opened up and they claim some degree of control over it. This increased openness is evident also among Christian Evangelicals, Pentecostals, and Charismatics, and in addition, many mainline Protestants, Catholics, Jews, and others who might not think of themselves immediately in such terms, yet for whom the languages of "journey" and "walk" and "growth" are commonplace. Religion as quest, whether for spiritual support or in search of broadened horizons, or some vital mix of the two as is usually the case, engages emotions and impulses involving not just heads and hearts but bodies. Or perhaps better put, contemporary spiritual quests give expression to the search for unity of mind, body, and self. Generally, primacy is placed not on reason or inherited faith, but on experience, or anticipation of experience, engaging the whole person and activating, or reactivating, individual as well as collective energies. In subtle if not always very explicit ways, such yearnings easily combine sentiments of protest against the religious and cultural establishment. Talk about the "spiritual" can be, and often is, a boundary-defining mechanism while at the same time it signals transition into a world where many older religious boundaries have faded. For this and other reasons, popular spirituality has its surprising and somewhat paradoxical features.

A good example is doubt, or the fact that doubt is now more openly acknowledged and perhaps even assumes a more significant religious role. Doubt is as old as faith itself, of course, but in today's quest milieu

NAZARENE THEOLOGICAL SEMINARY

1700 EAST MEYER BLVD., KANSAS CITY, MO 64131
816-333-6254 ▪ FAX: 816-822-2468

the relation between these two is being redefined. Jack Miles, author of *God: A Biography*, the Pulitzer Prize–winning book describing God not as an object of reverence and theological reflection but as the literary protagonist of the Old Testament, makes an insightful observation along this line. What struck him most in conversations with people he met on book-promotion tours was, he says, "a note of defiance, the defiant rejection of the widespread assumption that doubt and religion are incompatible." By avoiding theological and doctrinal formulations neatly separating these two, people were more open and comfortable sharing their views about religion with him—revealing a far greater depth of honesty, skepticism, and inquiry about God than he had expected. Old conceptualizations of God as literalistic, exclusivistic, and distant from the realities of everyday life had ceased to be persuasive; struggle, self-engagement, and doubt were very much a part of the negotiated religious worlds in which they lived. Miles writes: " 'Take it (belief) or leave it (religion)'—this was the dilemma I heard brusquely rejected in favor of a third alternative: *If I may doubt the practice of medicine from the operating table, if I may doubt the political system from the voting booth, if I may doubt the institution of marriage from the conjugal bed, why may I not doubt religion from the pew?*"[1]

Miles further ponders whether the doubts relate mainly to God or society: is it religion that is really in question, or is it the secular loss of faith? That is a perplexing question. Miles speculates that Americans are in an open, questing mood not so much because they reject religious belief, but as a result of having perhaps lost faith in the secular alternatives—in progress, science, therapy, politics, consumption. The case for belief need not be established, he says, but rather only "the case for unbelief [should] be somewhat neutralized." This latter is insightful, and very much so for the people we interviewed. Hopes pinned to old salvations have dimmed, and there is uncertainty on the part of many as to exactly what to believe or where to find answers to pressing questions. That uncertainty, not just about religion, extends to most social institutions. For the boomer generation trust in institutions has been, and continues to be, a vexing and unresolved matter. Not unexpectedly, in the current milieu religious questions take on distinctive features. A hunger for certainty leads some people to embrace neotraditional formulations of faith and truth, but great numbers, it seems, simply *acknowledge* the possibility of belief but do not necessarily *affirm* belief—people sociologist Peter Berger recently referred to as "uncertainty wallahs."[2] Certainly, many people are not convinced by older beliefs and notions about religion that were once more widely accepted; they combine skepticism with varying degrees of faith, or openness to faith. Recognition of uncertainty in many realms of life is widespread and is hardly the province of a handful of postmodern theorists. Yet, it is equally clear, there is no wholesale rejection of the possibility of belief. History has not gone the way of the demythologized world that liberal and existentialist theologians only fifty years ago predicted as the future course: current popular belief in angels, near-death experiences, and UFOs lay that secular hope to rest. To the contrary, there is a staggering openness to *exploring* possibilities of belief and a willing suspension of hesitancy to confront the grounds of faith and morality. "Uncertainty wallahs" want to believe in something but are unsure what and find it difficult to settle upon a firm conviction.

Even more broadly in American culture, this openness to possibilities manifests itself anew at present. Ideas and imageries of recreating the self, of improved personal health and happiness, and of material well-being are widely diffused across religious and nonreligious sectors alike. At the hands of skillful merchandisers, these ideas and imageries pop up in the strangest of places: Explorer, Voyager, Pathfinder, Discovery, Odyssey, and even Quest are all model names on 1990s cars, vans, and trucks; Quest is the name of a magazine, a frequent word appearing on Internet pages for churches and spiritual-growth networks; there is a "Quester's Bible" cast in terms of questions and answers. But why now? What social and cultural changes have brought these concerns and imageries to the surface in the late twentieth century? Why is so much contemporary discourse, both inside and outside the religious establishments, couched in terms of self, experience, and spiritual need? What are the implications for the way that people frame their identities in relation to religious symbols, teachings, and traditions? All these questions beg for further attention.

Generations as Cultural Carriers

Much has been written about the religious developments in the United States since the 1950s: the decline of the Protestant establishment, post-Vatican Council II Catholicism, the Evangelical and Fundamentalist resurgence, the rise of new religious movements and increased diversity, the rise of televangelism, the growth of special-purpose groups, and the polarization of religious liberals and religious conservatives. All are singled out as important aspects of the "restructuring" of American religion.[3] Whatever one makes of so many major developments, *in toto* they amount to a wrenching experience for rank-and-file Americans who have lived through them and have been faced with making sense of their lives in the midst of so much turmoil and unrest. Here in this chapter, we focus on those most directly involved in this religious restructuring—those born after World War II—and on aspects of the underlying structural and cultural changes that have had important consequences for grassroots religious outlook and styles. It might be said that demography collided with religious and cultural changes to make this sector of the population the principal carrier of an emerging spiritual quest culture.

Canadian philosopher François Ricard advances the thesis that members of the large Baby Boom generation are "collaborators with modernity," his point being that it was in their formative stages as youth and young adults that Western modernity truly triumphed.[4] Older definitions of the world and how it operated gave way to new ones including, as Ricard says, a growing preoccupation with the "new," whether as the latest material gadget, the remaking of a person's self-image, or the most promising vision of salvation. The advent of nuclear warfare, the birth control pill, advances in communications technology, the expansion of multinational corporations, and changing global patterns of political and economic alliances coalesced to remake the world in their time. Mass culture especially took on an unprecedented influence in human affairs. To cite Daniel Bell, there emerged a "disjunction" between the techno-economic and cultural realms in a postindustrial society, resulting in an expanded role for expressive symbolism and opening the possibility where, increasingly, cultural innovations would reach much further into people's lives—shaping tastes, styles, fashions, and mind-sets.[5] Earlier in an industrial society, personal identities were linked to production; one's occupation or profession was a major source of a relatively stable identity. But beginning with the post–World War II United States, personal identities came to be linked more to lifestyle and consumption, and less to an economic ethic that had long been undergirded by religious values. This reversal in historic influences, giving greater autonomy to the cultural sphere, set in motion a proliferation of popular cultural forms, less and less bounded by the social locations in which they originated, and gave rise to a whole new set of industries—the "cultural industries"—whose business it would be to spin new and compelling narratives about virtually all aspects of life and experience. It was a reversal with far-reaching implications for an expanding production of culture, reaching deeply into religious and secular life.

These developments extend throughout much of the Western world. The latter half-century in many countries witnessed major breaks with older normative cultures, increased personal autonomy, greater reliance on mass media and the cultural industries, and a great deal of spiritual ferment and experimentation among the younger generations.[6] Old symbolic frameworks began to fade, and new ones catering to individual choice emerged. To pick up on the metaphor mentioned in the Introduction, the "giant plates" of culture greatly shifted in this period, rocking the foundations especially for those born after World War II. The younger generations are in this respect carriers of cultural innovation, but also of change that, while not originating with them, became more pronounced in the 1960s and 1970s. Among mainline Protestants in the United States, for example, an erosion of religious commitment is discernible dating from the early decades of this century. Declines in Sabbath observance, strict moral standards, and traditional norms regarding sexuality and family life were all well in place in the decades prior to the arrival of the post–World War II babies.[7] But the early Boom cohort did in fact accentuate the trends: because there were so many of them born between 1946 and 1955 (the so-called "Vietnam Generation") and because they grew up in a period of intense cultural turmoil, they quickened the pace of social and religious change. What the early Boom cohort did in a very real sense was not so much to initiate as bring to the surface tensions in religion and morality that had long been festering. They were a catalyst leading to the release of a good deal of pent-up frustration and ambivalence. Further, this early cohort—and the generation more generally—became the carrier of cultural and religious values that would permeate "upward" to older generations and "downward" to those born after them. Feminism, ecology, and tolerance of gay and lesbian lifestyles exemplify a new consciousness associated with this generation in its youth, but which is now broadly diffused in American society. Values, lifestyles, and moral sensitivities that were once more specific to particular generations are now widely spread throughout American society.

Yet we should not overlook the depths of this generation's experience. For those born from 1946 to 1964, there was a break with institutional religious authority that has had lasting consequences for both institutions and individuals. It is well documented that many in this generation dropped out of active involvement in churches and synagogues in their youthful years.[8] As children they were born into families that were by most indicators fairly religious, but this all changed rather quickly during the countercultural years of the 1960s and early 1970s—a period now remembered for anti-Vietnam War protests, civil rights struggles, gender revolution, environmental awareness, and experimentation in new lifestyles. Few historians would question, in fact, that the ten-year period from President Kennedy's assassination in 1963 to Watergate in 1973 was one of the most turbulent, chaotic periods of American history, which left its imprint on the entire society, and particularly on those at a formative stage of their lives at the time. A major consequence was the plummeting of confidence among the young in all the dominant social institutions—political, economic, cultural, and religious. Politically, that loss of confidence is well-known and associated with declines in voting and lack of party loyalty; religiously, it is less obvious but yet catastrophic in some ways. So widespread were the religious defections, in fact, that mainline Protestant churches began to experience a noticeable downturn in membership and influence, beginning in the mid 1960s and continuing to the present. Children born into any faith community are the primary means by which that community replenishes itself, and for the mainline religious communities these defections have created a serious problem of institutional replacement. Catholic and Jewish losses were felt, but not to the same extent as for oldline Protestant groups like the Presbyterians, the Episcopalians, the United Church of Christ, the United Methodists, and the Disciples, denominational bodies that had long been identified with the liberal Protestant cultural establishment. Forty years of downward trends, even if now abating somewhat, have left this tradition in a much weakened public position.

But there was more than just institutional defection. Sabbath observance and conventional forms of piety, suffering from erosion for decades, experienced even more precipitous declines during this time. My own survey shows that roughly two-thirds of those born in this century prior to World War II claimed a "strong" religious preference; for those born afterward, only about 40 percent did so. Whereas only 16 percent of Protestants (mainline and conservative) and 18 percent of Catholics born in the years 1926–1935 thought that church rules on morality were too strict, 30 percent of conservative Protestants, 34 percent of mainline Protestants, and 48 percent of Catholics born between 1955 and 1962 held such views. Judeo-Christian notions of morality existing at midcentury came seriously into question, especially for those most influenced by the rapidly expanding centers of higher education in the late

1960s. Middle-class college youth experimented with alternative ways of living, openly rejecting bourgeois family values; they insisted on finding more meaning for their own lives, greater self-expression, and living their lives to the brim. And within a relatively short period of time, their values spread to other alienated constituencies, for example, to women and blue-collar constituencies, altering views on sexuality, marriage, family, lifestyle, and personal fulfillment across a fairly broad social spectrum. So striking were the value changes spearheaded by younger Americans at the time that one survey researcher, who sought to get to the heart of what was happening in the culture, Daniel Yankelovich, simply entitled his book *New Rules*.

Those "new rules" continue to play out in one after another permutation, deeply absorbed within the cultural mainstream. Seventy-six million strong, the Boomers are the "lead cohort" of the society: they define societal values and set the moral and political tone. Their influence is particularly felt in the "soft" cultural realms of style, taste, belief, and consciousness. Religiously, their influence is far greater than we generally realize. National surveys point to cohort shifts in religious styles, and particularly in the direction of greater institutional abandonment and increased attention to the "experiential" and "spiritual" dimension of religion. Boomers and the Generation Xers, or Busters, following them are all less likely to value faith in God or to say they feel close to God than did older generations; they are less likely to say that events such as marriage or a death in the family have strengthened their faith; they are far less inclined to rate churches or religious groups very well as meeting their spiritual needs. Yet in some other respects, just the reverse is the case: both Boomers and Busters report having more déjà vu experiences and mystical visions. Mysticism in its broadest sense—as personal moments of encountering the sacred—appears to be on the rise. A close look at cohort patterns shows that religious lines are more sharply drawn between those born before World War II and those born afterward, than are those between Boomers and Busters or within the large Boom generation.[9] Older generations remain more loyal to institutions and doctrinal beliefs whereas younger generations register higher scores on experiential measures not directly related to "church religion." Quite clearly, the consensus language of Judeo-Christian faith that dominated at midcentury, now at the century's end seems empty to many in the younger generations and does not come as readily as does talk of experiences and encounters associated with the occult and the paranormal, which now penetrates the cultural mainstream.

Another barometer of long-term change is the Princeton Religion Index, calculated by the Gallup Organization now for over fifty years. This index is based on eight key indicators such as belief in God; confidence in religion, church, and clergy; religious membership; church/ synagogue attendance; and self-perceived importance of religion in one's life. Heavily based on 1950s-style, Judeo-Christian religious values, beliefs, and practices, this index reached its highest levels in the 1950s, a decade well remembered for its high levels of popular religiosity. But after the 1950s the index plunged decade after decade, reaching its lowest levels in the 1990s.[10] While many factors bear on this decline, it in fact occurred during the years when the Baby Boomers were growing up and taking their place in society as adults: as the "lead cohort" of the society, they redefined the nation's religious norms, beliefs, and practices.

Important to recognize is that the Princeton Religion Index continued to decline even during the years when members of this generation were in passage from the *young to middle adult years.* Boomers are an aging population, many of them now rapidly moving into their late forties and early to mid fifties. Generally it is expected that as members of a generation age, religious belief and religious involvement will rise. Even rebellious youth, once they married, had children, and settled down—so the old cultural script had it—would once again reaffirm their childhood faiths and reconnect with religious institutions.[11] But with Boomers this did *not* happen; indeed, just the opposite appears to have happened—as measured by the Gallup indicators. The general religious climate as measured by 1950s-style religious values declined even more rapidly than did church and synagogue membership. Such observation suggests that growing numbers of church members are themselves increasingly nontraditional in belief and commitment; that is, cultural changes from the outside continue to reshape norms, beliefs, and mind-sets even within religious communities. A culture of choice and spiritual exploration prevails—both inside and outside the religious establishments—and not without demographic consequences. Age-based religious patterns are now more visible than at any time since mid-century; then such differences were quite small and hardly noticeable, but in the sixties they began to widen and continued to increase during the 1970s and 1980s. Today patterns seem to have stabilized even as the younger cohorts have grown older. "One result of the religious transition of the sixties," writes sociologist David A. Roozen, "appears to be the creation of an enduring stratification of religious expression by age."[12]

Decline of Traditional Theism

One crucial change is the decline of traditional theism. By traditional theism is meant belief in God as the Supreme Being who governs all things in nature and human history. The God of Western piety is viewed—or has long been viewed—as an awesome and holy presence, actively engaged within the world. But ever since the Enlightenment, an all-encompassing belief in divine agency has been difficult to affirm. Modern science and rationality have pushed back the boundaries of faith, limiting the scope of divine presence increasingly to individual, personal matters. Scientific discoveries provide explanations for natural phenomena such as diseases and disasters that once evoked notions of divine causation. In all of this, theistic beliefs did not disappear but were redefined; modernity forces people into negotiating an accommodating worldview, allowing for some divine action in the world but recognizing other possible influences as well. For a long time, this mix of natural and supernatural influences governing life appeared workable as a world-view: people affirmed a belief in God either unaware of the incongruities of their faith while simultaneously explaining more of the world around them in natural terms, or if they were aware, they seemed not greatly bothered.

But this appears to be changing. It is not that the contradictions of belief are necessarily more apparent or that people ponder inconsistencies in their lives more now than before, but rather, as a whole they are more open about their doubts and uncertainties. Whereas at mid-century polls showed that Americans, young and old, professed belief in a traditional, anthropomorphic conception of God, during the sixties and seventies such belief declined. Increased numbers said they did not "feel close" to a God who seemed removed from the affairs of this world, and they openly questioned traditional doctrines (for example, "hell" and "Satan") favoring instead symbolic interpretations.[13] Moreover, there was erosion of firm belief in the existence of God. Young Jews found it difficult to reconcile faith in God and the sufferings of the Holocaust. Polls asking if Americans could affirm the statement, "I know God really exists and I have no doubt about it," reveal a distinct break in responses between cohorts born before World War II and those born afterward.[14] Older Americans are more likely to "believe" that God exists, younger Americans to have "beliefs about the possibility of believing." The latter is a means of keeping open the range of outcomes in the world of belief without having necessarily to commit, a strategy much in keeping with a popular quest mentality.

This break in the way beliefs are held is, unsurprisingly, more pronounced among the better-educated. The expansion of higher education and its emphasis on science and technology beginning in the 1950s, partly in response, ironically, to the fear that the atheistic Communists would get to the moon before a God-fearing United States, helped to bring about a major confrontation with an older pattern of religious views. Technology combined with the advent of the computer gave rise to the so-called knowledge class, that sector of the population oriented largely toward the production, interpretation, and dissemination of information and more inclined to look on cultural symbols, religious or otherwise, as humanly created. For Boomers, this would result in a cultural and religious cleavage of considerable proportions, pitting the more educated scientific and technologically oriented class with its more open, constructionist approach to religious symbols over against those more inclined to hold more literal or objectivist views. Educating college populations in the humanities and the social sciences, on critical biblical scholarship, the world religions, semiotics, and hermeneutics further contributed to a more relativistic understanding of religious truth.[15] Thus, education would emerge as an important catalyst of a new category of religious differences.

During this time other meaning systems gained acceptance as well, such as mystical, social scientific, and secular-individualistic perspectives. Often these latter, overlapping with theistic views, created diffused, more personalized interpretations of the forces governing life. Such individually, critically constructed religious meanings thrive on introspection and boundary-crossing explorations. And partly as a result of this proliferation of individual meaning systems, a greater variety of divine imageries now flourish at the grass-roots level—more intimate and feminine, less distant and patriarchal, deeply personal and inwardly focused. "The Goddess is entitled to her day," as Karen Potter likes to say, staking a claim for the legitimacy of her views. These new imageries are a source of spiritual meaning and empowerment for many who find an older, patriarchical conception of God unsatisfactory. No doubt such imageries owe something to the earlier Death-of-God movement fashionable when many Boomers were teenagers or entering college—a movement that faded quickly but encouraged people to think more for themselves about what they believed and not simply to accept conventional notions. The intellectual critiques of popular piety of the 1950s and early 1960s further helped to shape an environment that deeply questioned the religious establishment. A central theme in these critiques had to do with widely accepted cultural faith—belief in God, country, and the American Way of Life. The cozy relations of an Ameri-canized Deity with bourgeois culture and blind patriotism came in for serious appraisal.[16]

Of course, such critiques—or jeremiads, as they were once called—did not destroy popular faith in God, but they did help to create a mind-set less inclined to accept such faith on face value. Moreover, questions raised at the time the Boomers were young persist. Our survey showed that those who were most caught up in the countercultural values of the 1960s, when interviewed some fifteen to twenty years later, were still highly suspicious of the country's leaders. Despite the passage of time, confidence in the major social and political institutions has not returned to levels of the 1950s, and neither do traditional views about God register as they once did despite the aging of the Baby Boom generation. Nor is it likely that these older views could be revived. Put simply, the legacy of doubt, suspicion, and distrust of institutions and of religious authority permeates the mainstream culture even if the voices are now largely muted. As one writer says, that legacy "rekindled perennial questions about the identity of American culture, the integrity of religion as prac-ticed in the nation's churches and synagogues, and the moral responsi-bility of those with resources toward those without them. The jeremiads succeeded most, therefore, in moving these religious and cultural issues to a central place of concern in American society."[17]

Scripts and Codes

Another far-reaching change relates to religious scripts and codes. As described in Chapter 1, scripts are stories dramatized in rituals and prac-tices: biblical stories like that of Moses and the exodus out of Egypt, so central to Jewish history, and narratives of the death and resurrection of Jesus Christ, as told by Christians. For many people influenced by the Hollywood mystique, these stories are not so much lost as pushed into the background by popular myths and tales. Grand narratives as handed down through history with appeals to universal truth have lost force be-cause of greater skepticism, relativism, and the shaping of more personal metaphysical constructions. These scripts are also often not very well known, much less understood, by many younger Americans who are highly illiterate with respect to the Bible and other religious texts. Many have grown up with little connection to religious "communities of mem-ory"; their participation in congregational rituals is limited largely to baptisms, weddings, and funerals. As is often pointed out, the word reli-

gion is derived from the Latin *religare*, meaning "to tie, to fasten, to bind." Historically, ritual functioned to bind, or rebind, people to heritage and community, but, as one 31-year-old on an Internet bulletin board writes, "Traditional religious experience can't 're-*ligare*' relationships that were never bound in the first place."

Much the same holds for religious codes—the moral and behavioral prescriptions that members of a religious community share. Issues like abortion and gay rights take center stage, and faith communities—like people—are deeply divided in their responses. This generation is not of course the first to face difficult moral and ethical challenges, but moral passions over such perplexing issues have deeply gripped the nation. People have been, and continue to be, pulled into taking moral positions and are often led to a religious explanation. Even ordinary religious behavior itself can be baffling. For example, many people never exposed to a religious culture, or who dropped out of churches and synagogues when they were quite young, report that when they go to religious services they often feel awkward, not sure of what to say or how to act. Tensions often arise at baptisms and services of the Eucharist, because people are unsure of what the vows and symbols mean and whether or not it is hypocritical to participate if they are not fully committed to the faith. What does it mean for people who are not active members of a church to be godparents for a neighbor's child? Should one partake of the Eucharist if not a committed believer? A decade or more ago, these questions were raised by Boomers who felt at odds with the religious culture of the mainline churches; today, these same concerns are most likely raised by those younger, the Busters or Generation Xers. In either instance, it is less a protest of religion in the deepest sense of its meaning than a response to institutional and cultural styles that are unfamiliar or seemingly at odds with life experiences as these people know them.

Turning Inward

But disenchantment with organized religion is just one side of the coin; the other side is the turning inward in search of meaning and strength, which is happening with people both inside and outside the churches, synagogues, and temples. Uprooted in faiths and family traditions, many Americans are looking within themselves in hopes of finding a God not bound by older canons of literalism, moralism, and patriarchy, in hopes that their own biographies might yield personal insight about the sacred.

Encouraged first by the antiestablishment climate of the 1960s and then later by the therapeutic culture of the 1970s and 1980s, they continue to look inward—either trying to find the self in greater depth or to escape the burdens of maintaining its social presentation. Personal crises in the form of addictive behaviors contribute to this refocusing of the self and to greater attention to spiritual resources and personal transformation. Reliance on such resources further encourages the democratization of theology and the privileging of grassroots views about the sacred. More than just leading people to choose among established doctrines and theologies, as in earlier periods of American history, this democratization encourages a much deeper personal appropriation of belief and commitment, essentially making theologians of everyone.

Political scientist Ronald Inglehart uses the term *postmaterialist* to describe the generations born after World War II. By that he means they are more oriented toward self-expression, quality of life, environmentalism, peace, and inner well-being—values and concerns that take on greater meaning in advanced societies where material concerns either are largely met or have failed to make life sufficiently happy and satisfying. Such values took on greater importance after the Holocaust and explosion of the nuclear bomb, after the rise of television and expansion of a consumer culture, after technological advances that have enhanced living conditions for millions of people. They appear to be on the rise throughout the Western world, replacing an earlier emphasis on physical and economic security. This "cultural shift," Inglehart argues, is a lasting effect, emphasizing the significance of subjective definitions of truly life-sustaining values, despite the fact that as these generations have aged they have abandoned much of the radical rhetoric, leading to the suspicion whether the commitments they once professed were sincere.

Further, Inglehart's cross-cultural research suggests that the value-orientations *and* religion go together. Whereas materialist values are linked to institutionalized religious culture, postmaterialist values are associated with more personal, deeply felt spiritual concerns. "Postmaterialists are significantly less likely to believe in God, and less likely to describe themselves as religious, than those with Materialist or mixed values," says Inglehart. But such diminished religious commitment does not guarantee they have any less concern about finding meaning in life or seeing themselves in relation to some larger order. As Inglehart goes on to say, "Post-materialists may have *more* potential interest in religion than Materialists do. A religious message based on economic and physical security finds little resonance among Post-materialists—but one that conveyed a sense of meaning and purpose in contemporary society might fill a need that is becoming increasingly widespread."[18] As Inglehard distinguishes so well, the problem so many in this generation face is that of finding a sustainable discourse, deeply spiritual, which embraces the kinds of existential concerns they feel.

Important, too, in this cultural shift is the sheer force of demographics: every year now millions of Boomer Americans are turning 40, and increasingly, many of them 50. Numbers stack up reinforcing the value changes. People are redefining midlife as an extended period of a longer life expectancy. They are also asking lots of questions about the deeper meanings of their lives as they move into the years beyond midlife.[19] And the demographics assure that these questions will continue to be raised for some time to come. Between now and 2004, when the last Boomers turn 40 and large numbers of them will be past 50, the great majority of that generation will have accomplished the midlife passage—considered by psychologists as a time of heightened reflection about life and its meaning. Also increasingly, as they inherit financial resources from their parents, they will be called on to choose how to use such resources to support worthy causes and concerns. As they settle into the second half of their lives, their concerns about generativity, or the intangibles they will pass to their children and grandchildren, will continue to perpetuate a quest culture.

SOCIAL AND CULTURAL CONTEXT

To better grasp the making of a spiritual quest culture, we look in greater depth at various of the religio-cultural developments in the latter half of the twentieth century: (1) modernity and its discontents, (2) the cultural meaning of religion in the United States, (3) the rise of the expansive self, (4) the role of the media, and (5) global influences. Obviously these are overlapping influences, but it is best to disentangle them as much as possible and to sort out their direct effects.

Modernity and Its Discontents

Crucial in the late twentieth century is the quest for wholeness—a theme that runs through the life stories of people we interviewed. To place this in context, we have to look at the twin processes of rationalization and

59

differentiation and how these have shaped the very meaning of the term *religion* in Western culture. History has conditioned our sensibilities, giving the term a peculiar usage and connotation. Following textbook definitions, religion might be thought of as either of two types: as "ordinary," involving fundamental cultural symbols that provide a picture of the everyday world, including sentiments and values; and "extraordinary," involving an encounter with a world beyond this one, with special languages about God (or gods), and more encompassing, universal conceptions of an extended order.[20] The distinction captures two fundamental levels of sacred reality and provides a natural basis for understanding religious experience as either immanent or transcendent. In theological formulations the distinction takes on added, far richer significance and lays the basis for a broadly encompassing "sacred canopy" of order and meaning.

Unlike the situation in traditional societies, where the ordinary and extraordinary types of religion tend to be highly fused, in the modern world they are more separate. Today much of what might be called ordinary religion is widely diffused in the culture as expressed, say, in nature worship, holiday rituals, sacred myths, and healing practices. Extraordinary religion, in contrast, is more formal and institutionalized, as found in churches, temples, sectarian movements, and the like. Though not necessarily any more influential than ordinary religion, extraordinary religion is more visible and identifiable; it can easily become defined as "official religion" and experienced apart from everyday lived religion. Moreover, official religion is typically associated with supernatural theism—a God "out there" or "up there." As such, imageries of supernatural theism may seem distant to modern people, adding to their doubts and encouraging the search for a more personal, experiential encounter with the divine. This very split of religious worlds in modern life—between the ordinary, the felt, and the lived versus the extraordinary, the reified, the distant deity—is a continuing, unresolved source of spiritual malaise. People on the periphery of religious organizations, "in" but not really "of" them, and those who are curious but do not find it easy getting inside the religious world as institutionally defined, often experience an inner split. For without a felt experiential unity there can be no real spiritual depth, no personal integration, no genuine "wholeness."

Historically, forces have pulled the two types of religion apart. Protestantism, so influential in shaping religious consciousness in the modern West, generated an internal momentum toward a more institutionalized and doctrinally privileged style of religion cut off from, as Peter Berger points out, some of the most powerful aspects of the sacred—mystery, magic, and miracle.[21] The greatest forces pushing in this direction arose out of the confrontation with modernity itself. Enlightenment philosophers and the industrial revolution in the early modern phases pushed toward a more rational basis for truth and the understanding of social organization. The rise of a global economy in more recent times continues to fan an ongoing clash of religious and secular realities. But the causal influences are historically complex. Protestantism both "acted upon" modernity and has been "acted on" by it, and in this respect it serves as an example of what every religious tradition now faces in late twentieth century. Modernity, with its pluralizing and privatizing tendencies, challenges absolutes of all kinds and relativizes the beliefs, values, and practices linked to every religion. Similarly, it unleashes mighty forces of rationalization and institutional differentiation, which in their advanced stages undermine wholeness of life-experience and rob the world of its remaining mysteries.

Suffice it to say that rationalization, in its most basic sense, encourages an ordering and interpretation of life on the basis of logical principles. It is the extension of this process now, under conditions of late capitalism, that leads Jürgen Habermas to fear the "colonization of the life-world" and, in particular, the technicizing of the life-world.[22] Why such worries? Simply because rationalization substitutes mastery for mystery; it standardizes rules and procedures, thereby creating formal structures called bureaucracies; it encourages instrumental criteria and approaches to life; it favors rational and scientific-technical ways of knowing and ordering experience at the expense of the intuitive and nonempirical; it privileges mind over body, the cognitive over the imaginative and the emotional; its hold upon the individual is far-reaching and threatening to the human spirit. As a result, the meaning of the word *belief* itself has undergone a shift—away from its earlier connotations of an essential human activity to a more impersonal assent to an abstract proposition such as, for example, supernatural theism. Likewise, the notion of *faith* takes on a more static, objective status separated, as one scholar puts it, "from the personal, subjective, affective, visceral, and passional dimensions of being and knowing."[23] This amounts to a formalization of a person's relation to the sacred and a subject-object split that is increasingly problematic under conditions of modern rationality, a situation social philosopher Georg Simmel saw emerging as far back as a century ago when he distinguished between "religious forms" and the "spiritual quality" that precedes them. As Simmel observed, "A person not only *has* religion as a possession. . . . His very *being* is religious."[24]

Institutional differentiation is the social process by which specialized structures emerge creating, in effect, a separate institution like religion. Religious values, beliefs, and sentiments were in some earlier time integrally a part of other social realms, especially diffused in the family, the ethnic group, and society at large; but the process of differentiation encouraged greater compartmentalization or separation of the religious from other realms. The result is more than just a shift in the social location of religion, but can result in a loss in meaningful integration of life experiences, and especially under conditions of high levels of structural differentiation. People may continue to be involved in rituals and practices but not share in the underlying goals and sensibilities on which they rest, or they may hold such goals and sensibilities but feel that institutional forms fail to fully express them. In either instance there is a disconnection, the stifling of the experiential dimensions of faith. Sara Caughman's comment on what had happened in her congregation before the "great turnaround spiritually" is telling in this respect. She writes: "The place had become dry and empty. Rote religion. Death to the spirit." John Murray Cuddihy captures the same point writing more generally about the impact of differentiation on people's lives: "Differentiation is the cutting edge of the modernization process, sundering cruelly what tradition has joined. It . . . separates church from state . . . ethnicity from religion. . . . Differentiation slices through ancient primordial ties and identities, leaving crisis and "wholeness-hunger" in its wake."[25]

"Wholeness-hunger" is an apt description of what underlies much of today's spiritual malaise. It is something felt by many people, something that underlies comments about "centering your life" and "finding connections" that are so frequently voiced in the populace at large. Once identified as originating in New Age discourse, now such terms permeate the religious landscape in a more generic sense (Episcopalian Sara Caughman speaks of "centering prayer" and evangelical Christian Sam Wong talks about testimonies as a means of "connections"). Modernity severs connections to place and community, alienates people from their natural environments, separates work and life, dilutes ethical values, all of which makes the need for unifying experience so deeply felt. Interest in holistic health is one such example. As a species we may be reaching limits on the extent to which we can, or will, tolerate compartmentalization: once wholeness-hunger sets in, it manifests itself in processes of "de-differentiation"—that is, in constructive efforts at reintegrating life experiences, whether specifically in the form of holistic health, "total living" communities for senior citizens, or on-the-job spiritual workshops. These are all aimed at healing the wounds of minds, bodies, and souls—deliberate searching, it might be said, for experiential unities people feel they have been robbed of. Ultimately, what we see are perhaps acts of political defiance, rebellious attempts to reclaim the fullness of life arising out of a deeply felt alienation and meaninglessness brought on by a situation where people's lives are sliced into arbitrary parts.

Religion as Culturally Defined

The more immediate context for the rise of "wholeness-hunger," of course, is the latter half of this century when so many of modernity's discontents have found expression. For all five of our characters discussed in Chapter 1, their life histories and religious voyages really begin in the aftermath of World War II. For Americans the immediate postwar years were times of prosperity, suburbanization, an emerging mass culture, and optimistic hopes for the future.[26] The Communists were a threat, but God was expected to be on our side in a war against atheism. The development of the atomic bomb was seen at first as a sign of progress—not just for winning a war but a symbol of humankind's dreams of scientific advances for the future. Psychology flourished with its promise of locating the innate goodness within every individual and, by means of therapy, of correcting that which stood between the individual and her potential. Belief in God was at a high point at mid-century. Churchgoing flourished and was closely identified with a pro-American, pro-religious ideology. On the surface it looks to have been an ideal time to grow up and to follow the old ingrained scripts, culturally and religiously. Popular magazines at the time predicted just that—*Look* magazine in January 1960 carried an article stating that Americans "naturally expect to go on enjoying their peaceable, plentiful existence—right through the 1960s and maybe forever."[27]

What happened? Here is not the place for a full accounting for the 1960s or its aftermath. Rather, our focus is on what happened to religious language and, in particular, to the cultural meaning of the "religious" in those years. Subtle changes in religious language may have contributed in bringing about, interestingly, both a loss of faith in the institutionalized form of religion and its rejuvenation as a personal, spiritual quest. Sociologist Robert Wuthnow points out that in the post-war years, particularly during the late forties and early fifties, religious discourse shifted in its style toward greater emphasis on the spiritual growth of individuals. Throughout the nation's history, individualism had been deeply ingrained in the American experience, but religious conceptions and language underwent an even more marked change during these years—away from emphasis upon community and social obligation characteristic of the period between the World Wars and toward a more privatized view that looked on the religious institution increasingly as "a service agency for the fulfillment of its individual members."[28] That represented a transition of some magnitude. Fellowship, or community, was coming to be regarded as a by-product, a derivative of personal needs; individual faith and a conformist piety were primary, the most essential of qualities as Americans saw it at the time.

Victory in the war provided a chance to rebuild this country, and to do so by means of greater individual initiative. Because of the large generation of youth and emphasis at the time on the American Way of Life, much attention was given to the socialization of children through the teaching of values, faith, and morals. Individuals were examples who through their own lives and actions could shape a public religious consciousness. Values would influence behavior, and in turn, society would be made stronger. This very synthesis of moral, religious, and civic values obviously fell apart in the mid to late 1960s; however, these years of turmoil must be read in the context of the personal beliefs and values that had already emerged as the dominant mode of religious discourse. Thus, when the hard times came, particularly the years from 1963 to 1973—from the time of John F. Kennedy's assassination to the Watergate debacle—primarily it was the loss of confidence in beliefs and values, and how they could bring about a better society, that contributed to the larger crisis of institutions that so gripped the country during those turbulent years. Religious institutions, and most especially the more liberal, progressive ones, would be drastically affected by this loss of confidence.

But the cultural definition of "personal" religion—including concern for one's own inner world of truth and meaning—was very much in place. Optimism in the nation's future gave way to optimism about the individual's own potential. Popular interpretations of religious psychology in the tradition of William James's "varieties" of religious experience and Abraham Maslow's attention at the time to "peak experiences" reinforced the autonomy of the individual in religious matters. Linkages between religion and culture were shifting as well, reflecting greater individualization. Religious identities that had long been rooted in the historical "social sources of denominationalism"—social class, region, race, ethnicity—began to lose much of their anchorage in an age of greater social mobility and were replaced by a more tenuous, vaguely sounding "Judeo-Christian" synthesis. Liberal Protestantism was in hegemonic decline, even though it enjoyed a cultural triumph of sorts: values long identified with its heritage, such as individualism, freedom, pluralism, tolerance, democracy, and intellectual inquiry, came to be thought of as the dominant liberal values of the society.[29] Its institutions were in trouble, but the values it advanced found wide acceptance. The young who dropped out of the mainline Protestant churches, in effect, did not so much abandon the heritage as embrace deeply the values that had been taught to them—most notably, to rely upon their conscience and to think for themselves about moral and religious matters. For Catholics, Vatican Council II encouraged a more democratic and pluralistic church and, at the personal level, styles of faith that were driven more by conscience than by traditional religious authority. Generally, during this period a new cultural context for religion was emerging, one in which faith was increasingly psychologized and viewed as a matter of one's own choice and in keeping with one's own experience. For the religious mainstream in those years, Catholic, Protestant, and Jewish, it was a time of greater openness, dialogue, and a more individualized mode of religious discourse.

In this new religious context, words like *preference* and *opinion* came to be commonplace. Nor is it surprising that the traditional doctrine of God was becoming less a shared reality and more a matter about which individuals made their own judgments. Talk about God was becoming less "weighty," as David F. Wells says,[30] describing what happens when the locus of religious authority shifts from an external transcendence to an internal individual source. People still spoke of God but the talk no longer had the power to shape and to summon people's lives in ways it once did. Talk *about* religion was for some replacing the language *of* faith; speculating about God was easier, and in some ways more reinforced in the culture, than believing in God. Put simply, belief in the *objective* reality of the religious world was tottering but God-talk itself had not diminished; if anything, it had increased as individuals pondered to themselves and to others what God, or the sacred, must be like. What appeared to have emerged in practical religious experience on the part of the upwardly mobile classes was, as one commentator put it, "the church of the solitary individual."[31]

Expansive Selves

As religious discourse was changing, so too were notions of the self. More and more attention was coming to be focused around the "expansive self"—usually described in terms of feelings, sensitivities, expressiveness, or simply as "individuality." Individuality, as opposed to individualism, has largely to do with cultivating the inner life, with seeking meaning and purpose, and the elaboration of the self. More than simply an individuated sense of self as revealed in historic democratic rhetoric, this more expansive mode of individualism is distinctive in that it "focus[es] on the moral responsibility of the individual toward his or her own self."[32] That is, the individual deliberately assumes a posture of exploring the interior life, of marshaling effort and energy; the self is defined, shaped, and sustained through such effort and energy and looked upon as if in the process of creative transformation. In its most radical expression, it becomes what psychologist Robert Jay Lifton calls the "protean self," named after Proteus, the Greek god of many forms.[33] The protean self is adaptive, fluid, many-sided, chameleon-like, fitting colors to environments.

Terms like *expansiveness* and *proteanism* seem particularly fitting as descriptions of the contemporary religious psyche. These qualities are apparent in a wide range of religious phenomena: in human potential movements, in charismatic and neo-Pentecostal faiths, and in increased attention to spirituality as "journey" and "walk." The style of discourse that cuts across all such examples focuses on the inner world, its meanings and depths, and the need for cultivating a change of consciousness. Privileged in this discourse is a "subjectivist expansionism" and, above all, a quest for an *individualized*, authentic identity, one that, as philosopher Charles Taylor says, is "particular to me, and that I discover in myself."[34] The source we must connect with is not external—for example, God, or some notion of the Good—but deep within us. And if we are beings with inner depths, the ideal of authenticity encourages inner discovery and an instrumental approach to religion as a means to that discovery. It is an easy jump to seeing spirituality as linked with "techniques of the self," as when Vicki Feinstein tries to produce desired effects and to learn more about how she can "become" spiritual. Techniques for securing instrumental benefits are the handmaiden for generating creative experiences, of opening oneself to new possibilities of self-realization, of becoming; hence the proliferation of "how to" manuals, workbooks, and rationalized procedures and formulas, all designed to be of service to the expansive self. Quest has no identifiable essence other than its own inner revelations, bound not by cultural conformity but focused around one central ideal—being true to oneself.

Corresponding to an expansive self is the rise of a consumer culture catering to a proliferation of whims and desires. Baby Boomers especially, growing up in an age of affluence and high expectations, are highly conscious of themselves as consumers. They were the first generation of children defined by Madison Avenue by means of television as having distinct needs and wants. "From the cradle, the baby boomers had been surrounded by products created especially for them, from Silly Putty to Slinkies to skateboards," writes Landon Y. Jones. "New products, new toys, new commercials, new fads—the dictatorship of the new—was integral to the baby boom experience."[35] As they have grown older, the consumer culture has not withdrawn its promise of replenishing ever-hungry lives: the cosmetic lines, the exercise business, the body-appearance industry, the self-improvement mania. Advertising images continue to designate youthful, slender bodies and successful corporate executives as objects of sex, power, desire, and pleasure—replacing older models of virtue and what should be sought after. Not surprisingly, "How can I feel good about myself?" emerged as a far more pressing question to many Americans than "How can I be saved?" That shift of questions offers clues not just to a fundamental change in religious identities, but to the construction and stylization of spiritual concerns of an individual living within a self-focused, therapeutic culture.

The Impact of the Media

Of great importance in shaping this more expressive self through symbols and discourses is the mass media. Never before has human life been so caught up in mediated image and symbol. And never before have the people themselves been so aware that ours is such a world of image and symbol. The role of cultural industries and communication technologies continues to expand, and at the expense of traditional institutions of socialization—the family, the school, the church. Television, more than any other medium, sensitized us to visual media and electronic communication. More than just that, it would begin to have an enormous influence in shaping moral and religious perceptions. Perhaps because we stand so close in time to these major advances in communication technology, we cannot fully assess how rapidly meaning systems are changing, or appreciate the extent to which, as a result, the process of religious socialization itself is undergoing a transition.

Media influence religion in so many ways, one being simply as a source of information and authority. A good example would be a few years ago when the Religious News Service reported that "United Methodists are far more likely to rely on newspapers and television as resources for opinions than they are to look to religious institutions or the Bible."[36] In an age of mediated information, traditional religious authority even in matters of belief and moral choice suffers; views and opinions, as well as their legitimating rationale, come to be shaped elsewhere. The powerful role of the media redefining religious image and symbol was evident at the Re-Imagining Conference in Minneapolis in November 1993, attended by 2,200 women from mainline Protestant and Catholic churches. Once in the control of the media, the conference proceedings became something of a "public event" accentuating the deep split between radical feminists and religious conservatives.[37] Feminist images of divinity and sexuality (with prayers to Sophia) became an object of controversy in the larger cultural struggles over conceptions of Deity and religious narrative, generating debate across the country—illustrating how, in a media age, religious bodies can easily lose control of symbols and their meanings. Beyond that, those very symbols and meanings once in the domain of the media come back and shape discourse among members within the religious bodies themselves.

In television programming there is what might be called a "leveling effect"—a softening of religious rhetoric and of truth claims, making it acceptable to Christians, Jews, Muslims, Buddhists, and others. Old dichotomies like private/public and holy/unholy fade. Belief in Hell, the wrath of God, and sin are de-emphasized; even "religion" itself is often played down as a humanly created thing in favor of "spirituality," or a God-thing, as a frame of reference.[38] The discourses in which religious themes find a home tend to be highly psychological: terms like *experience, fulfillment, happiness,* and *inner peace* all reflect a preoccupation with the self as a dominant motif. Casting religion in subjective terms meshes well with a highly individualistic, inward-looking culture, and particularly its emphasis upon spiritual openness and expansion. Symbols are selectively retrieved and interpreted, or re-interpreted, in the creation of alternative universes of meaning. For example, when Vicki Feinstein talks about *Star Trek*, we see how a television series utilizes symbols to evoke strong sentiments of a religious or quasi-religious kind, tapping deeply rooted American feelings about progress and science along with intrigue about explorations of space and time.

Visual media reinforce a cultural conception of an expansive self, if not an empty self, in need of constant filling. An expansive self is sustained through one after another experience in what amounts to a seemingly unending search for moments of transcendence. In this respect the media create "spiritual omnivores,"[39] that is, people hungry for new experiences and insights with the hope that some encounter or a revelation lying just ahead will bring greater meaning to them. This heightened level of anticipation is apparent in much media production. It occurs on Evangelical soap operas on television when the audience identifies with a Christian confronted with personal dilemmas and must make decisions about how to respond (e.g., to abortion or infidelity). Or perhaps even more the case, it happens with rock concerts on MTV where viewers can shift from one symbolic code to another in the music (e.g., from Contemporary Christian to Heavy Metal or Satanic), sometimes even within a single performance. With the recycling of images and lyrics, the viewer is cast into a position of "negotiating" between one's own existence and these symbolic worlds, a process carried out increasingly by means of visual communication. That changes the sensory mechanisms and shifts the locus of all forms of communication— including religious communication. With visual media it is sight and vision, not hearing or reading the word as was traditionally the case, that emerge as the privileged modes of religious interpretation.[40] The full impact of this transition on religion is not yet known.

But in this changing religious-symbolic marketplace, we know that religion is subject to considerable recasting.[41] The recasting takes on features of *instrumentality*: the practical ways in which belief or practice can meet the perceived needs of individuals. Often it results in *commodification*: the turning of religion into a product, something to be sold. Frequently the recasts are *adhesive*: blendings of symbols, imageries, practices, and technologies into some form of coherence often linked to a personal-identity theme. Typically they emphasize *accessibility*: a direct relation between the consuming practioner and spiritual goods in a religiously deregulated and demonopolized world. In all these ways, the media remake religion into a more dynamic, self-reflexive activity on the part of the individual and reinforce the view that, whatever else it might be, religious consciousness involves an active process of meaning-making, of interpreting one's own situation in relation to media discourses as well as those in traditional religious institutions. Bombarded by media input, the individual is left having to do a lot of cognitive negotiating and bargaining.

Popular television programs like *ER* and *Chicago Hope* address questions of meaning, if often in an oblique manner. Examples include moments of decision about whether or not to pull the plug on an aging parent; the discovery of one's deeper self in the context of love and relationships; the rediscovery of faith and kindness in a world filled with hardships and horrors; the joys of friendships and finding support within a community. Doubt is commonly expressed, but less as rejection of faith than as a means of engaging its possibility. A program like *Touched by an Angel* infuses its mix of spiritual ideas drawn from evangelical Christianity and New Age into everyday life, cultivating mystery, expectancy, and a sense that one is being watched over even in the most ordinary of moments. *Oprah* offers a steady diet focused on self-improvement, where notions of inner peace and empowerment mix freely with ideas borrowed from the world's religious traditions and great philosophers. By focusing on life's struggles and critical moments, all such programs lift up the sacred in a prefiguring of potential possibilities. Reality is transformed through the immediacy and instancy of rapidly flowing images, signs, and significations. Visual scripts provoke powerful moments of reflection about characters and situations and make possible the extension of those reflections to people's own lives. Cinematic spirituality tends to be subtle, more a subtext relying on the audience to identify and to apply to their own lives themes such as love, journey, recovery, redemption, and moral and personal transformation; it is also rather generic, encouraging tolerance, forgiveness, redemption, and the like, cutting across the boundaries of particular faiths and institutions.[42] Yet another genre of television programs like *The X-Files* and movies like *Contact*, depicting aliens from other worlds, abductions, or supernatural phenomena, intensify conceptions of a world in which the "paranormal" shades into the "normal." Boundary-crossings are a stock in trade for the media and cultural industries, helping to reinforce a popular mind-set of shifting imageries and ontologies.

Television and film thus assume some of the functions traditionally assigned to religious myth and ritual. They are the cultural storytellers of modern society formulating narratives of good and evil, of hope and promise, at times reinforcing, at times redefining, the operative religious worlds in which people live. Visual media approach something of a Durkheimian community, creating "communities of interpretation" that shape and contest religious and ideological narratives. Electronic communication is opening possibilities for relational communities across spatial boundaries on a scale we have yet to fully fathom. The very fact that Neo-Paganism and Witchcraft can just as easily have web pages on the Internet as the Roman Catholic Church means that religions once considered esoteric, if not blasphemous, now gain legitimacy and acceptance, and thus increasingly take their place in this country's evolving religious pluralism. The Pope and leaders of a pagan community become equals in the cyberspace staging of religious possibilities. "Cyberchapels" draw seekers into on-line communities, and "chat rooms" encourage exploration and discussion of religious topics, doing what this medium does well, creating opportunities for conversation. Further, the medium encourages the democratization of religious opinion and, through interactive technology, allows an individual to engage those aspects of a belief system, or of the discourses surrounding it, which one chooses to enmesh oneself and to carve out personal claims to faith or spiritual values. What all this will do for faith and symbols as traditionally understood within religious communities remains unknown, though we might speculate further undermining of notions of eternal immutability and encouragement in the long run of conceptions of the divine as a more dynamic, evolving process.[43]

Lack of face-to-face interaction in electronic communities is obviously a limitation in sustaining spiritual support. Television provides only fleeting insights, glimpses really, into life, healing, and transcendence; the viewer is left to interpret such epiphanies as well as possible without much help from the medium. Images and narratives contain multiple encodings and decodings, thus allowing for negotiated cultural and religious meanings through appeals to the individual's own biography and self-reflexivity. Yet these very limitations have a positive side: they create a sense of liminality, of in-betweenness, and thereby open up opportunities for the sacred to come alive at the boundaries between life as experienced and visions of its greater possibilities. To the extent that people find spiritual support in personal testimonies, in shared experience, and identification with religious causes and concerns, a more universal mode of community is possible; indeed, Sam Wong's involvement in the Jesus Network would suggest this to be the case. Through the media, Evangelical Christians can see themselves as part of a larger constituency than a local church; they can redefine symbols, moral values, and political agendas in keeping with a translocal constituency which, in turn, can have implications for local congregations.[44] But in all such instances of mediated religion, the challenge is to ponder life's meanings in a world seemingly without foundations and where there is a large pool of symbols to choose from and to interpret, a challenge all the more formidable to the many people for whom these amount to "broken symbols," that is, symbols known to be humanly created and thus inherently finite and limited.[45] That they are broken need not necessarily imply people cannot engage the divine with them, but it does mean that people are more aware of the precarious enterprise in which they are involved.

A Global World

Finally, there are the globalizing trends of modernity. In a global world social life is increasingly ordered *across* time and place and thus in many ways swept away from its traditional, locally oriented moorings. Everywhere, it seems, rapid social change threatens to engulf even the most remote of places; and the scope of that change ever broadens as one after another realm of life is pulled into its orbit largely by means of expanding communication and information technologies—the latest being the fax, electronic mail, the Internet, satellite pagers—oblivious to boundaries that once separated villages, cities, and nation-states. Modern systems of transportation, communication, and, above all, information have "stretched" our social contacts beyond previously self-contained environments, opening up promising possibilities but also reorienting time and space and separating both from the preeminence of place. As a result, psychologically we live somewhat in a realm between somewhere and everywhere, or between "nowhere and now/here."[46]

Globalization has many consequences for religion. One is the similar styles of spirituality in response to an increasingly generic culture in large Western cities—the same T-shirts, the same movies, the same music, no matter which continent. One observes as well racks of mass-marketed books on spirituality in places like London, Paris, and Los Angeles; "Doubting Thomas" masses in Finland and "seeker services" in churches in various European countries not unlike those in Evangelical megachurches in the United States; widespread interest in the occult, in angels, and in Jesus as a spiritual teacher; rediscovery of saints and mystics; and growing numbers of the spiritually curious signing up in monasteries and retreat centers for secluded moments in quiet places. But more than just reaching out for new spiritual experiences, there is much interest in search of spiritual support by means of Bible study, prayer cells, and small groups of many kinds offering opportunities for sharing faith.

Another consequence is the changing mix of peoples and cultures now emerging in American cities. The so-called "new immigrants" have pushed forward the nation's boundaries of cultural and religious plural- ism. But more than just that, Sam Wong's parents and millions like them hold to faiths more deeply embedded in traditional practices than for most acculturated Euro-Americans; they bring with them a spiritual vital- ity that is reinvigorating and resourceful. Increasingly, the religions of the world are present, especially Buddhists, Hindus, Muslims, and Latino Catholics, as real people practicing their own faiths. Since the mid-1960s new religious leaders and spiritual teachings, practices, and techniques have all flowed into the country in a steady, unabated stream, creating a more diversified, dynamic spiritual life. Americans virtually everywhere, in cities and in small towns, are becoming aware, if not al- ways happy about, the changing religious demographics. Pluralism as a religious reality is extended, adding to perceptions of a growing lack of religious unity.

The implications are quite enormous. Once perceived as worlds apart, the distance between Jerusalem and Benares has greatly shrunk: people move more freely between religious worlds via travel, reading, televi- sion, and other media. Religious symbols, teachings, and practices are easily "disembedded," that is, lifted out of one cultural setting, and "re- embedded" into another.[47] Meditation techniques imported from India are repackaged in the United States; Native American teachings ex- tracted from their indigenous context pop up in other settings. A global world offers an expanded religious menu: images, rituals, symbols, med- itation techniques, healing practices, all of which may be borrowed eclectically, from a variety of sources such as Eastern spirituality, Theoso- phy and New Age, Witchcraft, Paganism, the ecology movement, nature religions, the occult traditions, psychotherapy, feminism, the human po- tential movement, science, and, of course, all the great world religious traditions. Yet depth to any tradition is often lost, the result being thin layers of cultural and religious meaning. What often follows is pastiche, collage, religious pluralism *within* the individual, bricolage, mixing of codes, religion à la carte, to cite some of the terms now in vogue describ- ing how the individual is thrust into a position of having to pull reli- gious themes together from a variety of sources. Given the extraction of symbols, teachings, and practices from their cultural origins and their instrumental use elsewhere, it is not surprising that questions are often raised about the authenticity and appropriateness of these new religious blendings, on the part particularly of indigeneous peoples who sometimes feel "spiritually raped" in the process.

Globalization can have quite deleterious effects: it de-traditionalizes in the sense of fragmenting unities of experience, truth, and wisdom that took thousands of years to evolve. The binding power of religious traditions in providing meaning and identity is easily eroded: individuals feel less bound to a collective past or a shared present. Trust in others, so essential a foundation for personal identity, faith, and social relationships, becomes problematic. Definitions of the "other" shift as older notions of insiders and outsiders break down; the "other" now may be living next door or even within one's own family. And not least of all, hypermodernity opens up new risks on a scale hitherto unknown to humankind—possibilities of nuclear attacks, environmental catastrophes, and global warming. Perhaps better put, we should say that globalization leads to mixed, often paradoxical, consequences. It creates a condition of living on the edge in a way that humanity has never lived before, yet at the same time creates possibilities for greater global solidarity. It threatens inherited religious beliefs and customs, yet can produce universal theodicies and religious symbolism. It threatens the survival of the small village, yet creates a world that looks more and more like a village. It uproots tradition, yet in the process provokes powerful yearnings for wisdom from the past. It might be said that globalization creates for people everywhere something of a perpetual liminal state—of being caught in between old ways of living and believing and the possibility of a new world in the making.

REFLEXIVE SPIRITUALITY

For all these reasons, Americans are in transition in their responses to the sacred in the late twentieth century. We stand much too close in time to grasp fully this transition, but we can discern shifts in the ways individuals are relating to religious communities and, in a broader sense, to traditional religious symbols and narratives in an increasingly mediated world. Under conditions of advanced modernity, connections with the past and to overarching systems of belief and practice are fractured; spirituality once oriented to place and context gives way to process-oriented conceptions; and perhaps most important of all, fundamental trust and a sense of ontological security, so crucial to maintaining social and religious order, are radically transposed in a world where, as Anthony Giddens says, we rely increasingly on experts and knowledge bases far removed from our own immediate worlds of experience.[48] In such contexts religious idioms become highly textured and multilayered; whatever else religion may be, in a mediated and consumption-oriented society it becomes a *cultural resource* broadly available to the masses. Responsibility falls more upon the individual—like that of the *bricoleur*—to cobble together a religious world from available images, symbols, moral codes, and doctrines, thereby exercising considerable agency in defining and shaping what is considered to be religiously meaningful. It is much too simple to describe these changes as secularization as is all too commonly done; far from being a linear, cumulative historical process in the diminution of the religious, the modern religious situation is much more complex and adaptable. What we have is what I am calling "reflexive spirituality," that is, a situation encouraging a more deliberate, engaging effort on people's part for their own spiritual formation, both inside and outside religious communities.

Reflexive spirituality involves, in William E. Paden's words,[49] a "contemplative act of stepping back from one's own perspective and recognizing that it, too, is situated" in a plurality of possibilities. This capacity of understanding one's own view as just that—*a view*—forces attention to biography, history, and experience and creates consciousness about the positioned nature of all our perspectives. Such awareness is basis for understanding not just oneself in a deeply personal sense, but encourages a profound sociological imagination, or recognition of one's own views, values, and identity in relation to others. Generally it encourages a more open stance toward religious teachings and spiritual resources; more experiential and holistic views; and active incorporation of religious input into constellations of belief and practice, or greater agency on the part of an individual in defining and monitoring one's own spiritual life. The effect is to create greater self-engagement with religious tradition, indeed, a deeper awareness of who we are and how we became who we are or, as is sometimes said, "fundamental moments of the self."[50] This does not mean that the "religious"—including the traditionally religious as found in a faith community—is about to be replaced by the emergence of a vague, unbounded spirituality; rather, it suggests that spiritual seeking is elevated as a prominent religious theme and can itself be a creative, revitalizing experience, even a venue to transforming the meaning of the religious itself.

Of course, belief and quest do not exist independently of each other. Healthy belief now as in the past involves some degree of quest, and quest pushes as it always has toward resolution of belief. Despite some inherent tensions the two blend in popular faith and spiritual discourse, not unlike the ways in which the paradoxes of doubt and belief work themselves out. Probably most Americans today fall on a spectrum somewhere in the middle as believers who also seek, or as seekers who are believers of one sort or another. The biblical admonition, "Seek and you shall find" embodies an element of religious truth as valid now as ever before. Quest may edge in on belief but need not replace it; indeed, some people exploring their spiritual lives are discovering, or rediscovering, faith in ways they never knew existed. But quest often does result in a reassessment of belief, and often its reconfiguration resulting in a deeper meaning; and for this reason, the late twentieth century may well be in some respects a formative religious period in history. Certainly, the quest culture of our time poses a challenge to anyone trying to make sense of the religious scene. Hence we must look more directly at its dynamics and at the interplay of supply and demand operating in today's spiritual marketplace. As we can anticipate, that interplay is complex indeed.

Spiritual Marketplace

The making of meaning is a serious business.
(*Marsha G. Witten*)

I<small>N HER BOOK</small> *Cities on a Hill,* Frances Fitzgerald observes how Americans have long followed a pattern of "starting over"—creating new religions, or perhaps better put, new versions of old religions. In times of great population shifts, occupational and geographic mobility, and rapid cultural changes, religion reinvents itself in response to its social circumstances. That we can, and do, start over—as evident in the rise of so many utopian communities, moral and religious reforms, schismatic sectarian faiths, new religious movements—is, as she says, one of the great legends of American life. Moreover, argues Fitzgerald, the period stemming from the 1960s down to the present is one of those fertile times, and particularly significant because cultural transformations are originating from the center, as opposed to the periphery, of the society. This places the developments of our time in even more focused perspective. She writes:

> There were very few periods in American history in which the dominant sector—the white middle class—transformed itself as thoroughly as it did in the sixties and seventies: transformed itself quite deliberately, and from the inside out, changing its costumes, its sexual mores, its family arrangements, and its religious patterns. In fact since the Revolution there was probably only one other such period, and that was the period when the American evangelical tradition was born: the Age of Jackson and the Second Great Awakening.[1]

As her comment suggests, the post-1960s is a time both of significant continuities and discontinuities. There is continuity in the prevalence of visionaries and innovative leaders holding up the possibility of a more promising, fulfilling future and organizing mass followings—a repeat of old religious and cultural movements. But there is discontinuity in the extent to which the white middle class seems to have been so thoroughly transformed by the religious and cultural changes she identifies. One might go even further than does Fitzgerald to argue that, based upon the reasoning in Chapter 2 above, the greater evidence of self-reflexivity in modern life further accentuates the discontinuities. We get clues of this not just in the diversity of religious discourses, but in subtle ways these vocabularies among rank-and-file Americans, including Evangelical Christians, now presume an awareness of religious choice and of reliance upon self-cultivation and self-monitoring. Doubt is more openly accepted, even endowed with potential theological significance. Instrumental approaches to religion are highly vocalized: what was once accepted simply as latent benefits of religion, for example, personal happiness and spiritual well-being, we now look upon more as manifest and, therefore, to be sought after and judged on the basis of what they do for us. Many individuals consider their own personal religious narratives as evolving, as open-ended and revisable. "Twentieth-century identities no longer presuppose continuous cultures or traditions," one commentator argues,[2] and even if this is an overstatement intended to provoke postmodern debate, we can hardly deny the level of inventiveness of contemporary culture, religious or otherwise.

Reflexivity is not just an individual trait; institutions themselves engage in interpretive and monitoring processes. Religious functionaries within institutions have at their disposal a rich symbolic heritage from which to draw, allowing them to reshape and alter religious and spiritual styles to meet social and psychological needs. As the social demographics of religious constituencies change over time, religious and spiritual leaders are in positions to envision beliefs and practices appropriate to changing circumstances. In recent times especially, religious messages and practices have come to be frequently restylized, made to fit a targeted social clientele, often on the basis of market analysis, and carefully monitored to determine if programmatic emphases should be adjusted to meet particular needs. An open, competitive religious economy makes possible an expanded spiritual marketplace which, like any marketplace, must be understood in terms both of "demand" and "supply." In a time of cultural and religious dislocations, new suppliers offer a range of goods and services designed to meet the spiritual concerns; and, in so doing, respond to and help to clarify those very concerns. Religion in any age exists in a dynamic and interactive relationship with its cultural environment; and, in our time we witness an expansion and elaboration of spiritual themes that amounts to a major restructuring of religious market dynamics. That ours is, as Fitzgerald says, truly a time of "starting over" prompts us to delve further into ways in which religious production and its consumption are now remaking spiritual styles and religious identities.

PRODUCING RELIGIOUS CULTURE

Religion is socially produced, or more accurately, we might say it is constantly being reproduced. Far from being handed down from the heavens, religious symbols, beliefs, and practices are created and then maintained, revised, and modified by the often self-conscious actions of human beings. It is easy to overlook this fact, to take religion for granted, when actually its changing forms and styles are themselves a product of a complex set of factors—changing interpretations of religious heritage, social location and influences, new leadership, groups contending for power and control within a religious tradition, and so forth. Even our notions of the sacred and of life's deepest meanings are in a process of continual social conditioning. On this latter point, sociologist Robert Wuthnow observes: "First, individuals, communities, and organizations are indeed in some ways responsible for the continuing existence of the sacred in our society; and second, it is not just religion about which we must ask, especially if religion is regarded as a bland, gray-suited creature already, but also the sacred, that is, the symbolic frameworks that are set apart from everyday life, giving a sense of transcendent, holistic meaning to life."[3]

Several points implied in his comment are worth noting. One is that revision of religion or the symbolic frameworks by which people live rests greatly upon the initiative, creativity, and energy not just of individuals, but of communities, organizations, and social networks. Since the production of religion is preeminently a social activity, not only is face-to-face interaction of paramount importance, but, increasingly, as a result of advances in electronic communication, so are faceless exchanges. Successful religious groups adapt to their environments—whether geographical neighborhoods, social clienteles, or spatially dispersed networks of people bound together by common causes and concerns. Expressed in market terms, they are the ones that compete well, providing a compelling "religious product" in exchange for resources—most notably, time, money, and commitment. To considerable extent, religious organizations are all similar in that they respond to fundamental human needs for meaning and belonging. Their answers to people's needs tend to resemble one another, making them isomorphic—otherwise we would not regard them as religious organizations. Yet in another sense, each one is quite special in that it carves out a particular niche for itself, responding to and performing a service for, some distinct constituency. Churches do this when they recruit people of certain social classes or of a similar ethnic origin. New religious movements do this when they reach out to people who feel alienated from the established faiths and offer them a more satisfactory alternative. And much the same is happening today with a variety of religious and quasi-religious groups and agencies, some visibly, some less so, catering to a deep hunger for spiritual meaning. By defining and articulating these quests in relation to human needs and intangibles, they claim a place for themselves in the larger universe of symbolic frameworks.

Important, too, in modern, pluralistic society, the sacred is far greater than any single institutional embodiment of it. The sacred is contained in the historic, time-bound systems of religious beliefs and practices but is hardly equated with them. And especially today, the spiritual marketplace overlaps with, but extends well beyond, the established religious structures. If we think of this larger spiritual marketplace as a "social field" where all the agents, conventionally religious or not, try to generate and/or preserve religious capital, i.e., legitimacy, acceptance, and influence, then we can begin to grasp the breadth and depth of a huge, highly competitive spiritual marketplace.[4] In this expanded and diverse field, the older established faiths try to hold on to or improve their position; new players on the spiritual scene look to ways of gaining leverage within the field. Spiritual themes cut across religious institutions—some faith traditions resist them while others more readily absorb them. Individuals may, or may not, embrace spiritual beliefs and practices, regardless of what religious establishments do. Under conditions of religious pluralism, some tension always exists among the many players, but reflexive spirituality as we see it emerging today opens up a set of personal and collective dynamics far more complex than those associated with an older denominational religious order. The number of players is greater, and the overlap of themes across organizational and institutional boundaries is considerable.

Today's spiritual quest culture can be analyzed in terms of four interrelated components: *the social world, producers, the audience,* and *cultural objects.*[5] Already in Chapter 2, we looked at factors shaping the first of these—the social world. Globalization, fragmentation of historic traditions, mediated symbols and meaning systems, and an expansive self are all features giving rise to or characterizing this social world, and especially for a Boomer audience. The discussion thus far has attempted to bring these two into juxtaposition—the social world and the audience. But we must go further and look at the religious producers operating in this environment and the cultural objects, i.e., symbols and spiritual themes of particular prominence in relation to this social world and audience. Carefully sorting out how these four components relate to one another is essential to our understanding of the spiritual marketplace and of how it is now reshaping the religious economy. And as we shall see in this and subsequent chapters, this expanded marketplace is fluid and evolving, and subject to a degree of unpredictability insofar as its dominant spiritual themes are concerned.

INTEREST IN SPIRITUALITY

From the time our research began with a survey in 1988–89, we were struck not just by the extent of expressed interest in spirituality but by particular themes that suggested a distinctive religious climate was in the making. Building off the experiences of the 1960s and 1970s, the quest culture by the late eighties was well articulated, especially by those passing through their formative years during those decades. Here we describe those themes shaping that culture as we first encountered it, and save for later chapters discussion of how trends and thematic emphases have changed over the past decade. To start with, for a considerable number of people at that time, "religion" appeared to be in disfavor, and "spirituality" was in vogue. It was not always clear just what was meant by the latter term, but its usage to refer to something distinct from religion and deeply subjective was obvious. Others did not draw the distinction, but it was clear from what they said that organized religion, its belief, practice, and ritual seemed cut and dried, encrusted and culturally bound; in contrast, the experiential aspects of religion were much more inviting. Even if they did not use the word, the term *spiritual* better described them than did the term *religious*. Their comments underscored William James's distinction between "secondhand" and "firsthand" religion: institutional forms of religion, or that which comes to one by way of tradition, as compared to experiential religion, or that which is direct and immediate, and truly the individual's own. Of course, the distinction is not altogether unproblematic, since it is virtually impossible, especially

81

in a place like the United States where religious scripts are so deeply embedded in the culture, to know where the boundary lies between what is inherited in some deeply impressionable sense and what is truly the individual's own;[6] but the point is that the distinction had emerged into a full-blown rhetoric and was meaningful in its own terms. Most members of the Baby Boom generation at the time were in their thirties, some in their early forties, and the prevailing climate was considerably suspicious of institutions of all kinds. Exploring the inner life seemed far more promising as a means to self-authenticity, if not downright exciting.

Another way of describing what we observed was an emphasis placed upon personal *power*—a fascination with finding a key to unlocking one's life, discovering the force or energy that can invigorate and give direction to life. Time and time again people with no strong ties to religious organizations talked about a need for finding a spiritual centering and for the strength that might come with it. So, too, did many Born-again Christians, Catholics, mainline Protestants, and almost all of the Orthodox Jews, Muslims, and Buddhists that we interviewed, whose religious or spiritual views were much more clearly articulated. As would be expected, the religious discourses took many forms in relation to personal empowerment, some people speaking as if they were "outsiders" looking in upon religion and curious about what it might offer them, others speaking as "insiders" claiming a faith tradition as their own and finding within it the symbols, beliefs, and practices to express their deepest yearnings. But for both outsiders and insiders, what was clear was the extent to which they relied upon a language of personal transformation—sometimes describing what was already an inward reality for them, but more usually something they wished could be real for them. For religion to be alive and real, it had to arise out of their own experiences and encounters; anything less failed to grab their attention.

Talk about spirituality was often rambling and far-ranging, although several themes stood out that underscored its reflexive style. One was the rhetoric of a self-authored search, of looking inward, of wanting to grow, of "journey." Journey had an obvious meaning of life unfolding and of insights obtained in the process, but for some people we talked to it was understood in more visual terms. Journey involved extended mental trips, voyages into other traditions, imaginary movement across time and space in search of spiritual resources available to the self. In its strongest form the reflexive self entails, as sociologist Anthony Giddens points out, "a more or less continuous interrogation of past, present, and future."[7]

People seemed amazingly open to spiritual exploration: more than a few were attracted to the paranormal and to divine intervention, as evident in conversations about space-age narratives, near-death experiences, shamans, angels, and past-life regressions. Striking among these more self-reflexive types was the degree to which such spiritual phenomena mixed rather freely with Judeo-Christian symbols and themes such as God, Jesus, faith, and salvation. Fully a fourth of our respondents said they believed in reincarnation, many of whom also professed to be committed Christians. We posed the following question: "Is it good to explore many differing religious teachings and learn from them, or should one stick to a particular faith?" The intent of the question was to discriminate between a seeker mentality that is open and inquiring as opposed to a more particularistic faith commitment. Sixty percent of our respondents said they preferred to explore, 29 percent said stick to a faith, and 11 percent could not choose or said do both. Whether as 60 percent, or the larger 71 percent opting for a position other than "sticking to a faith," clearly there was considerable openness toward exploring religion. Even half of the Born-again Christians chose to explore—indisputable evidence that the questing mode of spirituality was not limited to a handful of eclectic experimenters but found expression even in traditional faith communities demanding a strong personal commitment.

Another theme was the instrumentality of faith and spirituality. People spoke openly and frequently about the benefits of believing and/or cultivating an interior life. Self-reflexivity encourages such a vocabulary and conscious clarification of that which is sought—be it peace, joy, happiness, health, personal power in its many forms. Indeed, in its strongest form it entails a careful monitoring and evaluation of rewards in relation to that which is sought or deemed desirable. Self-declared spiritual seekers were the most inclined to evaluate their personal growth or inner development in terms of how well they were able to achieve the desired benefits; phrases like "it helps you," "you discover things about yourself you never knew," and "it works" were not uncommon. Others in virtually every religious tradition, including Catholic charismatics and evangelical Christians, often described the rewards of faith but seldom spoke so directly about them in a conscious framework of self-monitoring and self-evaluation. Among these latter, there was far more confidence and assurance that their path was deeply spiritual and would likely lead to an even richer, more meaningful life. When we did hear of the benefits of faith or spirituality discussed in a more reflexive manner in Evangelical circles, usually people were referring to or quoting from religious texts or inspirational literature that offered rather simple, rationalized formulas of why one should commit oneself to a particular faith or religious group. Such formulas (rules, guidelines, questions and answers), of course, arise out of a high level of reflexive engagement on the part of those who designed and distributed them; and in turn, they prompt serious-minded believers to offer their own interpretation as to how adequate or rewarding they found them to be.

Another theme evident was a religious relativism. While not always stated in such bold terms, large numbers looked upon all religions as having an equal footing with one another. Relativistic (or universalistic) views toward religious truth were even more widespread than we expected. For example, 48 percent in the survey agreed that "all the religions of the world are equally true and good." An equal proportion disagreed, and the remainder were unable to decide. This was significant because of the deep split it revealed in how they looked upon religious truth, with many of this generation regarding all religious traditions as symbolic resources, but with no single tradition necessarily regarded as having a monopoly on truth-claims. As might be expected, fewer Born-again Christians opted for the relativistic approach: slightly more than one-fourth as compared to 63 percent of all others. But the very fact that more than a fourth of Evangelicals held to a radical universalistic view toward all religions is worthy of note. It points to just how far notions of religious relativism had spread and awareness that truth can be expressed in symbolic forms from widely differing traditions—even those outside of Christianity—thereby suggesting the difficulty any particular faith faces in trying to confine truth to itself today. A posttraditional world of increased pluralism, relativism, and tolerance virtually assures a shift of perspective on truth and ontological certainty.

In a world where symbol, belief, and practice are easily disembedded from their original context, the autonomy of the individual believer or practitioner is greatly privileged. Individuals begin to assume that they are the masters of their own spiritual fate. We inquired into this by asking about individual versus group religious activity in the following way: "For you, which is most important: to be alone and to meditate, or to worship with others?" The question was aimed at tapping the extreme form of an individualistic, self-focused approach to the sacred, recognizing of course that the two are not mutually exclusive. Half of the respondents answered that they preferred to be alone, and another 18 percent said both were important (or they were unable to choose between them), which means that two-thirds leaned toward a spiritual style with an emphasis on meditation and aloneness. Forty percent of Born-again Christians opted for the importance of meditation and aloneness as well. This does not mean that they regard worship with others as unimportant, only that of the two, the more personal mode of relating to the sacred is deemed preferable. Even in instances where there was a strong preference for group worship, the reasons given in the in-depth interviews were often couched in a language of individual rewards, a reflection of just how much individualism permeates religious thinking in the American context.

What about attitudes toward religious institutions and reasons people give for their involvement within them? Knowing the great significance people attach to religious belonging, we wanted to find out if they looked upon religious institutions as helpful, or not very helpful, to their own spiritual development. According to the survey, 54 percent agreed "that churches and synagogues have lost the real spiritual part of religion." Not so surprisingly, over half of the Evangelical Christians agreed with the statement as compared to slightly under a half of all others. This perception of a lack of spirituality within the churches is consistent with the strong emphasis placed on the interior life, as well as a generalized suspicion toward institutions, religious or otherwise, on the part of many in this generation. A third of the respondents also agreed that "people have God within them, so churches aren't really necessary." Given the pro-religious views of most Americans, we were surprised that this many actually indicated their agreement with the statement. Even 13 percent of Born-again Christians agreed! It is unclear whether agreement is mainly with the notion that "God is within us" or that "churches aren't necessary," but the two notions together amount to a strong statement for Americans of any generation to endorse. Whatever lies behind this endorsement, the fact that one-third of the Boomer population said yes revealed a considerable level of dissatisfaction at the time with organized religion and serious doubt that it could provide a sufficient reserve of spiritual power and nurturance for them.

Finally, there is the question of why people chose to be involved in religious organizations. From a traditional point of view, the reason should be obvious: if people are committed to faith and have convictions, they usually feel some sense of duty and obligation connected with their religious belonging. The traditional religious script prescribes loyalty to a religious community. But how well does this hold in a consumer culture that emphasizes the personal rewards that should go with religious attachment? Given so much attention to choice and personal growth, it seemed reasonable to expect a shift in religious motivation. Actually, three-fourths agreed with the statement that "going to church/ synagogue is a duty and an obligation" as opposed to "something you do if you feel it meets your needs." Two-thirds of Born-again Christians concurred—powerful evidence of just how far the psychoculture has penetrated the churchgoing United States. The crucial consideration was not loyalty to an institution or to family tradition but whether religious involvement was deemed effective in meeting personal spiritual needs. For this generation, it was clear, the right to ask the question, "Is this a place that can nourish me?" was largely taken for granted. In effect, what has long been understood to be a latent, undisclosed consequence of churchgoing—psychological benefits—had become the manifest reason for religious participation.

Thus by the late 1980s, large sectors of the population—including mainline Protestants, Catholics, Jews, Born-again Evangelicals, and New Agers—were deeply focused on spiritual matters. As judged by a variety of survey indicators, the Boomers were drawn to a more intentional, self-conscious spiritual style concerned with not just greater awareness of themselves and of what they sought, but with also a sense of how well they were doing, or not doing, in achieving their goals. It was equally clear that such spirituality was not just something bubbling up from the margins of the society; rather, it claimed the attention of mainstream constituencies, across social classes, ethnic and cultural enclaves. It was expressed in a multiplicity of discourses—as exploring religious teachings, searching for spiritual growth, the cultivation of faith, concern about one's own needs, empowerment, enriched family life, and reaching out to others with renewed strength and conviction. While the better-educated were more articulate, traditionally religious people voiced deep spiritual concerns as well. Young adult Americans at the time, it was clear, were looking for a more direct experience of the sacred, for greater immediacy, spontaneity, and spiritual depth—in short, they were very much into a quest mode.

THE NEW SUPPLIERS

In this 1980s environment, the situation was ripe for "new suppliers" catering to spiritual quest themes. But how were these suppliers any different from other, more conventionally religious suppliers? What symbols, themes, and cultural objects did they seize upon? And what would be the impact of this new cadre of entrepreneurs on the spiritual marketplace generally? In one reading of the situation, these new entrepreneurs are not all that different in how they function from those in other periods of American history. From the time of the great antebellum revivals right down to the present, there have been major, and largely successful, efforts at mobilizing religious constituencies by means of effective leadership and organizational skills. Innovative means of proselytizing new members, often along kinship and friendship lines, and of subsequently cultivating them spiritually as a means of holding on to them, are important mechanisms for organizational success. And outside of formal religious organizations there have long been other spiritual suppliers—wise women, herbalists, occult leaders, folk healers, and the like—who were able to organize informal networks and develop constituencies. The fact that religion operates in this country as a voluntary commitment obviously works to its great benefit, since it is free and able to harness popular democratic tendencies by recognizing pluralism and the freedom to choose, and encouraging competition among, for the most part, equally acceptable religious alternatives. Religion flourishes in an open, deregulated market where it can respond in innovative ways to changing social realities and to people's own recognized, but changing, needs and preferences. Hence certain isomorphic tendencies are found in all religious and spiritual movements, whether old or new, and the leaders of all such movements have much in common.

Crucial, too, is the supplier's skill in defining and articulating a message for an audience. Suppliers must know their audience and be familiar with and able to reconfigure their religious stories, beliefs, and symbols in ways that capture attention and speak to felt needs. Whether in the message of spiritual rewards that can be experienced now or in the life to come, in carefully calculated "costs" of sacrifice in keeping with what a believing public will accept, or in strategies for winning adherents through circuit-riding on the frontier or, more recently, by means of televangelism in a mass society, the history of U.S. religion is replete with innovators who found a way to carry a new spiritual message to the people. Preaching skills and leadership styles are especially important given that popular faiths in this country have been, and still are, largely revivalist, emphasizing grace, hope, and a deeply personal relationship between the believer and God. A play upon these symbols is almost a guaranteed success on the American religious stage, and the plays have been, and continue to be, amazingly innovative in their narration and pitch to human needs, hopes and aspirations. Evangelical know-how and the American propensity to believe in the divine come together, making for abundant and seemingly unending possibilities. Time and time again Americans experience, as literary critic Harold Bloom says, "the perpetual shock of the individual discovering yet again what she or he always has known, which is that God loves her and him on an absolutely personal and indeed intimate basis."[8]

Is this shock of discovery any different today? Obviously there is much continuity with similar discoveries in the past. Any phenomenon recurring so often over the course of American history can hardly be considered new. What is recurrent is that, in times of spiritual awakenings, Americans fall back on their own conscience and solitude, on inner resources. They turn to popular faiths and practices, to popular dramas and cultural narratives giving expression to the individualism extolled in the American imagination, pursuing, as Robert S. Ellwood says, "some single, simple, sure key to peace and power (faith, prayer, the image of Christ), transmitted by accessible stories and images." Simplicity and accessibility are critical. Ellwood goes further to suggest how popular religion works in such times: "It first directly addresses the raw inner yearnings of the individual, juxtaposes religion and those needs in an easily understandable way, and provides a striking image or technique that ameliorates them by making religion the answer—the point of popular religion being not coherent wisdom or meaning so much as power. In all of this it [is] unlike elite religion, which [tends] to view one's raw inner yearnings as sinful—selfish or materialistic."[9]

Considering that belief in God *and* the power of faith are ubiquitous in America, the post-1960s period stands out in its resistance to elite religion, with its emphasis on theological consistency and universal judgments, and in its striking openness to the force of "raw inner yearnings." So much attention to these popular yearnings, combined with an abundant imagination of spiritual possibilities, made for a significant shift in religious narrative style—out of the hands of theologians and established religious leaders and into those of ordinary people. With such a shift in theological language and in the authority underlying it, we can most certainly speak of the period as a time of "starting over," in Fitzgerald's sense, a period when Americans were thrown back upon their own inner resources and, particularly, on the foundational assumption that God knows and loves them in a deeply personal and redeeming way, and that something inside them is—or wants to be—in contact with this divine reality. It makes for a powerful affirmation of human potentiality, reinforced by the most basic of religious claims as the people themselves understand them. But the pressing question becomes: how, or in what ways, did this shift in narrative power occur? Answers to this question can help us to gain perspective on just how the new entrepreneurs operate.

LEGITIMATING NEW VOCABULARIES

To begin with, the recent rise of the "spiritual" as a category of popular religious idiom cannot be understood apart from considerations of religious and cultural power. In periods when religious establishments enjoy social prestige and cultural capital, and thus exercise strong monopolies, the term appears to languish. Actually not all that long ago—even in the early 1960s—the word *spiritual* was conspicuously absent in the public arena; religious language and social ethics captured the day, prompting theologian Paul Tillich to speak of "the almost forbidden word 'spirit'" and of the spiritual dimension of life as "lost beyond hope."[10] But that public discourse was short-lived, indeed, muted in great part by the social and cultural transformations described in Chapter 2, and even so by the late 1960s and early 1970s.

Major legislation in 1965 rescinding immigration exclusion also opened the doors to migrants with cultures and religions from around the world. The resulting shift in migration streams into the United States from China, Vietnam, Korea, India, the Dominican Republic, and Mexico, to name the major points of origin, would be momentous, opening the doors to spiritual traditions (including Christian traditions) that are strikingly different from those of European heritage. In addition, a change in policy by the Federal Communications Commission about this same time democratized the airwaves. This new policy was pathbreaking considering that prior to this time religious broadcasting was provided mainly as a free service to the public, but henceforth it would be available to groups who could purchase airtime. Televangelists who could raise the funds now had much easier access to television programming and could use the medium for reaching an extended audience. Both of these developments were crucial in opening the way for new religious leaders and ideas, from the East especially, in the case of the first, and in the use of more recent communication technology by Evangelical and Charismatic Christians to reach new and growing constituencies, in the case of the second. Combined, the two developments represented a major step forward toward a more deregulated religious market,

89

broadening the base of religious competition within the country, opening up possibilities of new spiritual styles geared to the media, and turning the airwaves into an arena for proselytizing. The American religious terrain would never be quite the same again.

Cultural changes during this period were equally significant: with the decline of an older Protestant consensus and of even the broader Protestant-Catholic-Jewish canopy of religious identities prevailing at midcentury, there were subtle losses in power and control over religious discourse. Aside from declines in religious membership and participation, there was the more significant loss of "religious capital," or the cultural power to define and maintain a hold upon spiritual styles.[11] Organized religion's monopoly on symbolic frameworks was never complete, of course, but we can speak of periods when its control was much greater than in other times. Throughout much of the nineteenth century and well into the twentieth, religion exercised considerable control over spiritual styles through an expanded range of institutional structures such as youth camps, retreat centers, community centers, colleges, Bible schools, publishing houses, and hospitals. By means of these extended structures, organized religion exercised control and influence over a broad sector of life experiences. But this broad religious canopy had greatly diminished by the 1960s. Public facilities had replaced many of the older religious structures across many sectors, particularly in health, education, and leisure. By the early 1970s, an increasingly heterogeneous religious population combined with several decisive Supreme Court decisions meant that an older religious culture could no longer sustain its hold on the public school, much less the public realm more generally. So-called "alternative spiritualities" flourished as a result of this loss of religious control. New Thought and the metaphysical traditions, long marginalized by other religious voices, now enjoyed a revival. Eastern and metaphysical ideas, beliefs, and practices found an increasing acceptance, particularly among the educated middle classes rapidly expanding during this period.

Social conditions thus encouraged the emergence of a "spirituality industry" in response to people's deep concerns and questions. Books and videos on many differing types of spirituality, praise music, self-help groups, retreat centers, holistic health, spiritual seminars, workshops on corporate spirituality, and now cyberspace as a medium for spiritual teachings, all emerged as new or expanded "outlets" for those seeking spiritual resources. In Pierre Bourdieu's terms, the number of players not only increased but became a more varied set of agencies, catering to lifestyle niches and quandaries, and posturing to affirm legitimacy and a claim to distinct spiritual resources.[12] This meant enhanced competition, but more importantly, a restructuring of spiritual styles and practices catering to a wide range of people's causes, interests, and curiosities (for example, people interested in "eco-spirituality," "Motorcyclists for Jesus," "channeling sessions"). With this increased elaboration of spiritual styles, individuals were challenged to examine and to think through which options might best serve them in their own personal growth. All in all, what emerged was a more expanded, redefined religious market at the very time when many young people were becoming, or were pressured to become, more thoughtful about their own biographies and self-identities. Boomer demographics offered incentives to suppliers for creative attention to the psychological needs of an increasingly diverse, highly segmented marketplace.

Today, the new spiritual suppliers—inside and outside the religious establishments—cater to this more open religious climate. These suppliers take religious pluralism for granted and play to themes of choice, individuality, and the desirability of a cultivated and spiritually sensitive self. Knowing that pluralism is experienced as expanding psychological boundaries, they consciously define themselves in relation to a broadening and intensifying menu of spiritual possibilities. They recognize the fluidity of the self and the popularity of current psychological motifs like "personal growth," "womenspirit," and "holistic spirituality," and by means of definitions and labels claim on this more subjective space, thereby legitimating it and enhancing their market shares. They appeal to primitive desires for ecstasy, for bonding, for health, for hope and happiness, for the resacralization of everyday life. Often they go to great length to point out that personal awakenings and growth can best be achieved beyond the arbitrary limits set by formal institutions. Frequently, they redefine older religious language in ways to make it more acceptable or create alternative concepts altogether to such older notions as sin, grace, and discipleship. In all these ways, spirituality "invades" pre-existing religious forms, reconfiguring and revitalizing life-experiences.

A good example is the spiritually based dieting movement. Whereas in the not-so-distant past being overweight was seen as a result of gluttony or greed (to use "deadly sin" language), now, increasingly, it is viewed as an addiction. "One confesses no longer to being a penitent sinner," as an observer puts it, "but rather to being an acute 'foodaholic,' one whose compulsive eating is triggered by forces that were previously beyond one's knowledge or control (whether chemical, demonic or a combination of the two)."[13] As with other addictive behaviors, it is the *act* of overeating that is defined as the problem and that points to an underlying spiritual problem that must be addressed. One does not rely on traditional religious language or authority, but on self-help, workshops, or some form of guided deliverance from unwholesome food, with a goal of greater happiness, health, and self-esteem in mind. Dieticians claiming expertise in medical science working together with specialists knowledgeable about food and the tensions surrounding it have led the way toward recasting it as part of a larger cultural narrative about addiction and the necessity for self-discipline and self-monitoring. In this new narrative "the cure begins not with denying the flesh," a concept at the center of an older religious interpretation and ethic, "but with revealing the deeper, spiritual needs that trigger anxious eating."[14] Recast in this way the window is opened to a greater subjectivity in addressing concerns of the body.

Because the body generally is a basis of increased self-reflexivity, it becomes a basis for the restructuring of traditional religious practices. Consider prayer, for instance. Prayer, as perceived by many people, as a rather pious solitary or congregational act, is often reconstituted as bodily activity. In synagogues, for example, classes combine traditional Jewish prayers and Hebrew chants with modern-dance movements that add physical emphasis to the words. Similar body-based activities are to be found in Catholic retreat centers and in aerobics classes within Evangelical and Charismatic Protestant churches. Even in some resort centers and vacation spots, "spiritual awareness coordinators" and "stress care specialists" are now employed to provide demonstrations of mind-body meditation, to show the benefits of relaxation, and to encourage "innercise," a mode of dealing with stress by focusing on positive images and banishing destructive thoughts from the conscious mind. Legitimacy of such activities is sought in scientific studies demonstrating their practical results, and also through tracing the combination of body motion with prayer to ancient religious traditions. "New spiritual techniques" are thus not altogether new, only a repackaging and reinterpretation of older religious practices, as culled from both Western and Eastern religions. People who consider traditional prayer as a remote and alien practice, might attach new meaning and efficacy to it in this re-defined context.

WITHIN THE RELIGIOUS ESTABLISHMENT

In many mainline churches and synagogues, the quest theme finds explicit expression on various fronts. There are the appeals to learning more about religious traditions as they relate to personal life. Round-table discussions, forums, and crash courses on the Bible and the Torah, the basics of religious traditions, and spiritual wisdom and practices are flourishing. Typically, in such activities, and in crash courses on religion especially, the aim is to repackage the message and present it in a way that is culturally relevant and addresses existential concerns such as suffering, sexuality, and moral and ethical dilemmas.[15] A mild version of this is found in contemporary worship services, in Shabbat services, in support groups, and in other specialized ministries, all aimed at helping people relate to a religious tradition by means of their questions, interests, and doubts. There are as well the direct overtures to human potentiality and self-actualization. Living life to its fullest, overcoming stress and burdens, and making the most of the circumstances that come a person's way are held up as spiritual ideals.[16] An emphasis upon the positive, practical benefits of faith and spiritual anchors is not uncommon. But there is also appeal to social conscience and human bondings. This is apparent in Sara Caughman's congregation, where the latent idealism and activism of the Boomer generation have now been rekindled, offering ways for integrating historic faiths and contemporary issues like environmentalism, feminism, peace, social justice, and inclusive community. Skillful religious leaders engage religious symbols showing how they connect to causes and concerns, fashioning new interpretations of religion and of its relation to the world.

Special-purpose organizations and parachurch publications pitch their causes and concerns to particular constituencies. Literally scores of such organizations and publications vie with one another trying to capture a following, most focused on personal faith and spirituality, but also many addressing social causes and a "prophetic spirituality" that encourages relating biblical faith to specific programs working for social transformation.[17] What these organizations and publications accomplish is an expansion of opportunities for "tailoring" one's spiritual style around a particular issue, for example, prison ministry, the environment, the homeless, family life, abortion. Organizations and activities like these, usually operating independently of denominations and faith communities, have greatly increased in number over the past half-century and help to create a much more structurally diverse religious environment, for the country as a whole but also for local congregations and other religious gatherings.

This more differentiated religious context is important in another, but less obvious way: it encourages individuals and groups toward selective exploration of religious heritage as a means of gaining interpretive autonomy over it. Parties discover that they can use tradition as a mechanism for opposing unfavorable practices that have come to be institutionalized within that same tradition. Catholics who disagree with Rome, for example, may draw selectively on doctrine in the church's tradition to argue against positions held by the church. Vatican Council II created an environment more open to the deliberate reappropriation of religious teachings and symbols, resulting in internal skirmishes and sub-constituencies, or what has come to be called "contested knowledge."[18] Dissident Catholics may remain Catholic knowing and celebrating the fact that the tradition is bigger than any one interpretation—including the official ecclesiastical interpretation. The case of Catholicism is particularly interesting because it points to a situation where interpretive differences may not lead to affiliation with a different faith or formation of a splinter group, as so often occurs within Protestantism. The impulse to switch to another religion or to break away in schism is bridled by the force of long continuous tradition and collective memory, and also because, according to sociologist Michelle Dillon, "Catholics' doctrinal reflexivity . . . maintains the 'universality' of the Catholic community."[19] In this instance a rich heritage interacts with a quest culture resulting in reinterpretations of Catholic teachings and identity.

The quest culture permeates much of Evangelical Christianity, most visibly in its many special-purpose groups and megachurches. Tapping the deep activist and reform impulses of Americans, Evangelical groups currently link faith to a search for answers in the face of vexing moral dilemmas such as abortion, but also in rallies for chastity among teenagers, in antismoking campaigns, and in efforts at converting homosexuals to a "straight" lifestyle. Other types of special-purpose groups, including some for-profit agencies collecting "fees" and combining 1960s-style therapeutic goals with spiritual messages, hold inspirational rallies in sports arenas playing soft Christian rock music—calculated to appeal to those seeking help working out their feelings about themselves and others.[20] Prominent as well are the growing number of megachurches, also known as "full-service churches, seven-day-a-week churches, pastoral churches, apostolic churches, 'new tribe' churches, new paradigm churches, seeker-sensitive churches, shopping-mall churches."[21] Rapidly emerging in the late 1990s, these churches attract the "unchurched," the "superficially churched," and simply those who for whatever reason dislike more traditional churches. In contrast with the "believer's church," the "seeker church" has as its top priority programming to reach those people who are curious about religion, asking questions and open to the possibility of faith. A long-term goal is to make believers of them, but to start with, programming and preaching center around the doubts and questions people bring with them. Framing of religious styles and of spiritual steps involved from "seeking" to "believing" are carefully planned and programmatically managed.[22] Strategies for building "seeker churches" are advanced through a fairly sizable network of leadership consultants, church growth experts, and clergy who hold their own workshops and institutes. Nondenominational and community churches are popular since they bring with them little of the baggage often associated with the historic denominations. In a variety of ways, the public face of religion is altered, giving it more of a "user friendly" appearance.

These churches are skillful with small groups, creating "a church of options" and offering a range of programs and ministries largely in response to a Boomer culture of choice and the wish to participate in hands-on activities. Groups and fellowship opportunities are organized largely on the basis of experience, life-situations, and interests. Efforts at playing down conformity and offering options for people to "create" their own religious styles within some boundaries are intentional. Visiting one such church, a commentator observed the following programmatic options:

> . . . a seminar on effective single parenting; twelve-step recovery meetings by category (alcohol, drugs, abuse) and freeway coordinates; a parents-of-adolescents meeting; a class for premarital couples; another for "homebuilders"; something called Bunko Night (Tired of shopping? Low on funds?); a "woman in the workplace" brunch; a "fellowshippers" (seniors) meeting; a men's retreat ("Anchoring Deep"); women's Bible studies; a baseball league; a passel of Generation X activities; "grief support ministries"; worship music, drama, and dance; "discovering divorce dynamics"; a "belong class" for new members; and "life development" ("You will learn to know yourself and begin to see where God has a place of service for you. This is a can't miss class").[23]

"Seeker churches" work at developing forms of worship, and most especially utilizing music, that convey a sense of authenticity and reality about contemporary life. Above all, they try not to be boring. Sunday morning is defined as prime time for "unchurched" seekers—little is expected of those attending, they may participate if they like, and financial contributions are definitely not expected. Praise music and extensive sound systems create an inspirational context. Overhead projectors and large screens making possible visual connection with lyrics, cartoons, and Bible verses add to the overall experience. Drama and clips from film and television—mininarratives describing the joys and dilemmas of life—communicate effectively and relate to common, everyday experiences. Meeting in auditoriums, if not in warehouses, where there are few religious symbols and no stained glass plays down the "churchy" atmosphere and sends the message that persons are accepted for who they are, welcome even if they have doubts, know little about religion, and are just curious. The absence of a chancel gives the appearance that the sacred resides in the experience of the people. In sermons they hear about God, but it is a God usually less dogmatic and more tolerant of contemporary lifestyles than is the case for Fundamentalists and other Evangelicals not identified with the seeker movement.

WITHIN THE BROADER CULTURE

Outside of the churches and synagogues, seeker themes find eclectic expression in a variety of workshops, seminars, conferences, and retreat centers. Newsletters, meditation cassettes and videos, and 1-800 psychic lines create information networks and audiences. The self-help group and the professional counseling session, or group workshop, are the most common quasi-communities. Often information is provided to clients for a fee.[24] In all such instances, the quest culture finds its strongest version in explicit appeals to "seekers" using highly rationalized procedures and techniques aimed at self-transformation. An omnipresent theme in such activities is the promise of greater discovery, experience, and connection: participants are encouraged in their pursuits to discover the sacred, archetypal dimensions of life; to experience the divine energy that is within all of us; to discover the inner child; to reunite with their inner guidance; to discover the joy of personal healing; to experience or at least get close to experiencing one's own underlying perfection; to connect with universal life forces; to experience their own bodies and sensual selves; to discover the infinite love that is within; and to experience more fully the powers of beauty, creativity, life, and joy within each person. The spiritual comes alive in the celebration of powers arising from within each and every individual; participants seek to find ways to unleash those powers and to awaken new insights, in a context usually charged with energy and excitement about an unlimited potential of new insights possible.

Spiritual networks and workshops amount to followings hoping to learn more about themselves and to discover inner truths about life, but not stable long-term memberships based on faith. Rather than demand shared belief or a creedal affirmation, they insist only on spiritual authority as residing within the self. Meaning and truth are derived from feelings, intuitions, and personal disclosures, as opposed to religious claims of an external authority, i.e., belief in God. The contrast with religion has to do with the locus of authority. For example, when Vicki Feinstein says, "I didn't know where to look for God ... so I looked within myself which was the best place, I suppose," she expresses a current tendency toward trying to find a spiritual center within one's own self. Much of her seeking consists of simply turning inward looking for something she can rely on, a quest for authority. After exploring a variety of spiritual technologies, she settled on a local Tibetan Buddhist center with its East-West spiritual dialogues as a place that nurtures her sense of well-being. The additional appeal of this particular center is its program directed at people like Vicki who, for whatever reason, find conventional Judeo-Christian language unsatisfactory and want to cultivate their own inner awareness as a valid source of spiritual meaning. Sometimes that which is found within the inner self is called God even though its meaning may be very different from the more orthodox usage of that term; at other times the term *God* is replaced by any number of possible substitutes, such as Goddess and Sophia in feminist circles, or simply Higher Power or Universal Force. Symbols, imageries, icons, and discourses of virtually all kinds have burst upon the scene in recent decades, creating a prolific display of spiritual energies and commodities or, as one writer says, a "divine supermarket."[25]

The "Spirit Movement," as it is sometimes called, not only creates networks and quasicommunities but utilizes and builds on existing structures—for example, businesses and corporations. A cadre of management and organizational consultants invading the scene in the last decade are dedicated to renewing corporate and business cultures in which team spirit, community, creative intelligence, and authentic leadership cooperate. That this is happening within this arena points to a fundamental affinity between the spiritual and work-based experiences and identities. It is not uncommon to hear about the "soul" of corporations and the merging of the individual's life and work around a Higher Purpose. There appears to be a renaissance of values within the workplace as corporations and business commit themselves to becoming more socially responsible, more supportive of employees, and more humanistic and holistic in their approach to the marketplace. Obviously the bottom line is still very much in place—businesses must make a profit—but increasingly in many circles one hears talk of the work environment as a place of "support, renewal, and insight"—signifying an elevation of consciousness within this sector at the turn of the century.[26]

Increasingly, the book publishing, magazine, and music industries play a significant role in the production of spiritual themes. The printing and sale of books on spirituality and the sacred during the nineties is nothing less than phenomenal.[27] As one rather obvious indicator of this growth industry, the American Booksellers Association in 1995 opened at its convention and trade show a new and expanded section on "religious/spiritual/inspirational" books. But more than just sales or innovative marketing techniques, the book publishing industry is creating the categories commonplace in popular conversations about spirituality: wisdom, self-help, human potential, healing, meditation, channeling, inner child, body, mind, and soul. All are terms whose content is shaped at least as much by the quest culture as by historic traditions. What is most remarkable about the changing styles of God-talk in our time, observes religious commentator Phyllis A. Tickle, is "not that it is going on, but that it is going on with almost no sectarian or even tradition-oriented guidance."[28]

Popular books are effective carriers of teachings and symbols, in no small part because the publishers have done their homework figuring out what sells. Analysis of book sales (and by extension, music sales) in recent years suggests that there are distinct "belief constructs," or subcategories of experiences, interests, and concerns known to tap deep, often subterranean levels of consciousness.[29] The books address subjective spaces defined by the normative religious culture, but yet for many people often lack clarity and conviction. Addressing these spiritual vacuums, books help to reshape and fill them and often in ways that are highly formulaic and homogenized. This shift in the production of religious themes reflects a shrinking market for denominationally based publishers and the rise of large commercial conglomerates, some of which have bought up independent religious publishers, and all of which are captive to a commercial mentality. Much the same can be said about magazines and the music industry, both in their increased volume and way in which spiritual themes have overtaken a considerable portion of mass marketing. Magazines routinely carry articles on spirituality, either explicitly or implicitly in the context of a person's health, body image, pleasure, or self-esteem—the best example being the magazine that goes by the name *Self*.[30] Evangelical publications like *Aspire, Excellence,* and *Sports Spectrum* play upon themes of sexuality, achievement, and personal challenge. Simple songs of worship—"praise music"—currently flourish in what amounts to a burgeoning Christian industry. Boundaries between secular and Christian record companies are often blurred. Christian record companies increasingly produce music in virtually every category known to the popular music industry: heavy metal, light pop, jazz, folk, grunge, reggae, country, funk, gospel, and hip-hop. Whatever the category, the Christian sound is not all that different from its secular counterpart, despite differences in lyrics.[31]

Based on book sales, four categories of religious books top the sales charts. Most popular are books on near-death experiences, angels, and the invasion of aliens, all catering to an audience caught, as one commentator says, "somewhere between belief in and curiosity about such possibilities."[32] Americans want to believe that someone really cares about them, that there are realms of meaning and acceptance beyond their sight. Next are books on ancient wisdom, books that generally assume that something terribly important to human life has been lost but must, and hopefully can, be regained. Buddhism, Native American spiritual experiences, feminist spirituality, and assorted New Age teachings all fall under this rubric, and in one way or another all promise greater fullness to life. Third are self-help books pitched to the well-being of the practitioner and the use of spiritual disciplines for gaining power and control over whatever ills beset us. Here technique is privileged over sectarian doctrine; pragmatic instrumentalism, not commitment to any particular faith, is held up as the solution to life's dilemmas. Finally, there is religious fiction, a rapidly expanding genre with labels for ceaseless permutations of religions and cultural themes. "Call it religious fiction or inspirational fiction or by any of its sectarian names of Jewish, Catholic, Christian, or Evangelical," to quote Tickle again, "Or call it by some combination of them, like religious mysteries, Jewish historical novels, Evangelical Christian westerns, inspirational romances, and so on."[33] Generally, what the book sales tell us is that ours is a fluid religious context characterized more by its restiveness than a sense of security, more by keeping the quest alive through one after another iteration of the narrative formula than any genuine resolution of the truth-claims that are put forward. Perhaps the best examples of a narrative formula are the "Chicken Soup" books that recount inspirational stories of personal tribulation and triumph—one after another designed to fit special markets or "niche areas."[34] Even "niche Bibles" are available, aimed at one after another audience in an expanding, highly segmented economy. In this revived and highly rationalized market, the old "religion" section is replaced by a more differentiated bookshelf of specialized topics and narrative styles pitched to carefully defined audiences.

SYMBOLIC CONSTRUCTIONS

In addition to the producers, the audience, and the social world, we must look to the "cultural objects," or symbolic themes, that figure prominently in the current quest culture: God, or the sacred; personal growth; struggles; the body; and identity. All involve cultural constructions, or reconstructions, well suited to the salient concerns and sensibilities of a post-1960s world.

God or the Sacred

The supernatural theism that is declining, as was argued in an earlier chapter, is that which emerged in relation to the Enlightenment and the modern worldview: a God "out there" but increasingly distant and removed from the world. It is an outcome of a "domesticated" transcendence of God, of a closed system of natural laws of cause and effect in which God has really no place other than "beyond" the universe. But in the contemporary spiritual marketplace, pressures mount in the direction of reconstructing the sacred: reconnecting the transcendent and the immanent, reclaiming God in everyday life and experiences, natural and otherwise, and asserting the dialectical presence of the divine, both "right here" and "beyond." Biography and relationships are reinfused with sacred meaning; individual experience as well as group sharing offer opportunities to learn about the place and meaning of the sacred in life; there is "more" to reality claimed than just what is visible, material, or natural; there are enhanced moments of consciousness, often presumed to have a noetic quality, that is, as involving not just a feeling but a knowing of other, deeper levels of reality. In this cultural climate

100

old patriarchal notions of deity are giving way to newer, softer imageries of a more accessible God.

Some commentators see these trends as worrisome, as reducing the sacred to feelings, individualism, or in the case of group sharing to the group itself; still others foresee the rise of a promising panentheistic conception of God, replacing an outdated conception with the discovery of "the God we never knew."[35] Popular discourses reveal a blending of religious notions of the "divine" and broader cultural conceptions of the "sacred" reflecting ideas and themes originating from a variety of places: from Eastern religions, from metaphysical traditions, from humanistic psychology, and from a democratized Judeo-Christian theology. Much God-talk bespeaks a fundamental conception of a self informed by reliance on one's own inner resources and thought by many to contain a spark of the divine. Even if not expressed in metaphysical language of this kind, the belief runs deep that God—or the re-imaged God—is one who is best known deep within the self, that here is where life at its deepest is encountered. Religious communities continue to sustain traditional discourses about God, but in contemporary society there are other places for religious talk as well—small groups and sharing sessions, the Internet, even bookstores, cafes, and coffee shops. Borders, Barnes and Noble, and Starbucks, to cite some well-known commercial establishments, themselves function as places where people come together and carry on conversation in an open, nonsectarian atmosphere. Through book discussions, lectures, films, story-hours, music, and poetry readings, bookstores engage a variety of themes relating to health, personal well-being, and spiritual growth and in so doing sustain networks of shared discourse around ideas and symbols appealing to a deep, largely unresolved hunger for community. In a very real sense, the popularity of such informal places signals the shift in spiritual mood that this book attempts to describe—the searching and striving on the part of ordinary people that has broken out of, and extends beyond, formal religious structures.

Personal Growth

No terms are more common in the seeker culture than "journey" and "growth"—metaphors the people themselves use to describe a process-oriented conception of spirituality. Inside and outside the religious establishments, it is how people speak of faith and spirituality; even those people who are quite traditional in religious orientations are greatly influenced by such constructions placed upon the religious life. An evangelical Christian woman told us of her decision to join a Bible study group because, as she said, "I knew it would help me to grow, make my faith stronger." "Growth" and "faith" are interfused. Others spoke simply of cultivating a deeper spirituality. As one fifty-year-old man who has spent the last twenty years seriously pursuing his spiritual growth said, "I have grown a lot in my thinking, but most of all I now have a better sense of who I am and where, I think, I am headed." "Growth" and "identity" are interfused. Whether for Evangelical Christians who speak of "walking the walk" or people with more expansive spiritual horizons, or even the considerable numbers of Jews, Catholics and mainline Protestants who themselves not infrequently talk of "journeys" or "paths," there is a remarkable degree of clarity about themselves as engaged in a process-oriented spirituality and what that engagement may involve for them. Reflexive spirituality is not haphazard, or left to chance; it seeks self-understanding and self-management, governed by some sense of how one ought to be progressing in life, which all resonates well in a culture where so many things—from making money and improving love lives to overcoming personal disorders—are typically cast in popular form as a series of procedural steps toward reaching such a goal.

Journey language meshes well with humanistic and developmental psychology, the basic ideas of which are widely diffused in middle-class culture. A few of our respondents were conversant with the language of "peak experiences," "archetypes," "flow," and the like, derived from theorists such as Maslow and Jung, and actually used such terms to describe themselves at an enhanced level of self-reflexivity. But far more common is a language of spiritual growth infused with biblical teachings and therapeutic values. People attracted to specific causes and programs, such as overcoming drug addiction, feminine spirituality, and marriage encounter, rely on spiritually infused language, sometimes very self-consciousness about the mix of religious and psychological themes, but often simply taking such language on face value. Religious literature, even that published by denominational presses, is saturated with themes of the self, much of it either implicitly or explicitly focused on personal growth and fulfillment, and far more so than was true in earlier decades of this century. The autonomy of the self, the importance of taking charge over religious and spiritual matters, and the necessity for some degree of managing one's own interior life and its cultivation are all motifs, while not always boldly asserted, clearly present in this literature.[36]

Technology makes possible new, unprecedented possibilities for the servicing and monitoring of the self. For example, an organization like Focus on the Family, the conservative Christian parachurch and counseling agency led by Dr. James Dobson, makes ample use of personal growth language. Focus incorporates "spiritual growth boosters" into its magazines, which are carefully prescribed in content for varying age and life-situation constituencies, and in its radio narrative for children entitled *Adventures in Odyssey*. But most striking is its use of computer technology for counseling. Focus stores its thousands of phone calls, letters, and E-mail every day in a huge data-bank, so that when a "client" calls in counselors can bring up the person's record on the screen and pick up on conversations where they left off, interjecting here and there computer-prodded responses giving moral and religious advice, asking further questions about how the person is dealing with spiritual problems, citing biblical verses that are appropriate.[37] By means of prototype responses and standardized procedures, emotions are structured and to some degree personal stories are amplified as they get incorporated into collective scripts appropriate to people with certain "problems," "concerns," "questions," or "life-situations." Or to take another example, consider the spiritual service offered by the channel Lazaris, which is aimed at a much different audience. Lazaris makes available on the Internet mail-order tapes with instructions on hundreds of topics such as "Avoiding Failure," "Overcoming Fear," "Expressing your Feelings," "Embracing Feminine Energy," "Granting Forgiveness," "Controlling Frustration," and "Awakening the Future Self," just some of those listed under the letter F. Not only can a person choose the tapes and the order in which they are dealt with, in effect plotting his or her own spiritual development, but the tapes offer a sufficient variety of metaphysical formulae, techniques, and psychic insights such that each person is likely to interpret its applicability to his or her life quite differently. In this way journey language is elevated to an even higher level of individual reflexivity and self-monitoring. Since there is little sense of communal belonging and services are rendered in exchange for fees, the product is separated from the producer more than for other types of religious providers, and even more than for the highly computerized "constituent services" of organizations like Focus on the Family.[38] But both are examples of how with the aid of technology spiritual needs are becoming more rationalized, monitored, and more directly accessible, thereby fundamentally altering relations between religious producers and religious consumers.

Struggles

Time and time again, struggle as a theme surfaced in our interviews. It emerged in discussions of people's religious biographies, in their experiences with religious institutions, in family and lifestyle experiences. It emerged when we asked, as we did from 1988 to the present, about what books had most influenced them. Mentioned most frequently, and especially in the later interviews, was M. Scott Peck's *The Road Less Traveled.* When asked why this particular book had such an impact, many cited its opening line, "Life is difficult." That line resonates with many Americans born after World War II who have grown up with high expectations, but who for one reason or another have had to scale down their hopes and aspirations. Being laid off work, going through a divorce, never quite accomplishing what they hoped to achieve, along with being "sandwiched" between their children and aging or dying parents were all struggles cited—sometimes as a source of rich spiritual experience. Recall that the book of Genesis contains the story of Jacob's wrestling with an angel, a metaphor widely meaningful to people we talked to. Wrestling may refer to the struggle of conscience in making a difficult moral decision; it may signal cultural confusion and bewilderment; it may occur in situations where people are cut off or estranged from their spiritual roots and past; it can involve deep ambivalence and wrenching love-hate relationships; it can happen when life's realities fail to match youthful anticipations. All are instances Boomer Americans know well.

Today the metaphor expresses a depth of meaning and feeling, even among those who have difficulty articulating it. It is invoked particularly by those who feel oppressed or for whatever reason marginalized by the dominant social institutions—including religious institutions. Thus it is not surprising that many Americans, especially feminists, people of color, gays and lesbians, are engaged in a serious struggle with religious heritages and interpretations flowing from them; for many of them to talk about religion is to confront ironies, paradoxes, ambiguities, and inconsistencies that reach deeply into their lives. Engaging the tradition, its symbols and values is revealing, and opens up vistas hitherto unforeseen. Feminist writer Judith Plaskow, speaking out of her Jewish tradition, expresses the sentiment: "If the Torah is our text, it can and must answer our questions and share our values; if we wrestle with it, it will yield meaning."[39]

Wrestling is an apt symbol today because it symbolizes both confrontation with an external opponent and confrontation with oneself; it also combines in a single image the hostile energy of resisting an enemy with the affirming energy of embracing the other. Who is the other today? How do we embrace the other? Who are we in relation to the other? No American can boast of being without fears of the other in an age when acts of terrorism at home and abroad are unpredictable; when AIDS links us to sexual others we never knew; when it is easy, especially since the collapse of the Berlin Wall, to blame the new immigrants or the federal government for all our national problems; when jobs disappear and in a global economy we do not know who to blame; when the other is as likely to be living next door, possibly within our own family, as in some faraway place. Yet people continue to find spiritual resources to match their fears. In Western religious thought, spirituality embraces a dialectic expressed in at least five distinct types of polarities:

(1) internal (subjectivity) *and* external (God and neighbor);

(2) intentionality *and* power from beyond the self;

(3) conscious awareness *and* unconscious bodily processes;

(4) rest, fulfillment, and surrender *and* process, suffering, and struggle;

(5) positive (love, joy) *and* either the negative (hatred, suffering) or that which is beyond good and evil.[40]

Someone may be engaged primarily in one of these dimensions, or in more than one simultaneously. In a time of great cultural dislocations, energies unleashed in any one of them may be redirected toward re-union of the self, at overcoming its alienation and separation. Life on the margins—at the boundaries—keeps the horizons open and sustains an on-edge spiritual sensibility. In this respect wrestling as a metaphor is as apt today as it was in the past.

Importance of the Body

The body figures prominently in contemporary spiritual quests. Since we are unable to know ourselves apart from our bodies, it comes as no surprise that many of today's quests (and struggles) of the spirit are truly quests (and struggles) of embodied selves. Karen Potter's life is an example: after years of devaluing herself, she now talks about having "reclaimed" her body and is concerned to find out what this means for her. Feeling better about her body, she feels better about herself generally; spirituality and embodiment are integrally linked. We heard similar claims from others, especially from women trying to break from

105

pre-existing gender roles, underscoring just how crucial the body is to self-reflexivity. Feelings are grounded in the body just as is awareness of one's presence in the world. Bodies experience intimacy, emotions, relationships, spontaneity, and control—all fundamental to a sense of self *and*, many would argue, a sense of the sacred.[41] And of course, bodies are a visible sign of who a person is, of sexual identity and of cultural identities more broadly.

Again, dieting is a good example. As we have seen, it is widely understood as a spiritual practice in the United States; it is also very much a reflexively infused practice.[42] Dieting is based on knowledge of foods and nutrition and application of that knowledge to obtain the desired goal of weight control and health, and hence closely akin to reflexive spirituality. Thus it is not surprising that we observe the rationalization of this practice: the use of devotional fitness manuals, calorie worksheets combined with spiritual teachings, weight graphs plastered with biblical passages, appeals to scientific and motivational experts, and increasing numbers of workshops, support groups, and organizations, often meeting in malls or churches, and all trying in one way or another to get people to "substitute God for food."[43] "Christian dieting" as well as other types of spiritually based dieting flourish as people assume responsibility for the development and appearance of their bodies. What a person eats is a life-style choice, something one must "work on" relying on the best of nutritional advice and, most important of all, spiritual motivation. Being overweight is not so much the problem as is the lack of spiritual power to control it. As a mainline Protestant told us, "I know I'm fat, but I don't think God judges me because of that. But he does want me to be responsible for what I eat because he knows, and I know, I have this spiritual problem." Food has long been viewed as a source of temptation, indeed, in post-Augustinian Christianity, as a distorted desire. The fact of so many overweight Americans as well as the prevalence of eating disorders both signal serious spiritual struggles with food and account for why, within Evangelical Christianity especially, so many special-purpose groups now address these concerns.

Similarly, the body is central to healing experiences. We heard many more accounts of ritual healing in the later survey than we did in the earlier one: stories about how bodies, personal relationships, and inner feelings were healed. Whatever the type of healing, all such experiences are grounded in an embodied self that is in a continuous process of development and idealization. As one commentator who has studied a wide spectrum of healing groups in the United States observes,

106

" 'Health' is an idealization of a kind of self, and 'healing' is part of the process by which growth toward that ideal is achieved."[44] Whether the self is cultivated in relation to a transcendent deity, as in the case of Charismatic Christians, or is construed as more open and flexible, as in alternative healing, it is embodied in experiences and emotions that take on spiritual meaning through rituals and invoking a language of transcendence.

To speak of the body is to engage questions about power: who defines it, who regiments its rhythms? With regard to economically deprived and oppressed populations, the links between power and bodies are fairly obvious. Less obvious are the more general cultural constructions that shape the meanings and uses of the body, or the so-called socially informed body.[45] Behaviors ranging from dieting to working out, gender and work roles, sex appeal, health, and body appearance all bear the coercive imprint of existing social arrangements and often the legitimations of religious symbols and teachings. In an age when these constraints and legitimations are being challenged, the body becomes a major symbol both of dissent and affirmation. Women and homosexuals, both male and female, contest existing definitions and stereotypes and affirm who they are. People are insisting on taking charge of their bodies, and Boomers, especially as their bodies begin to fail them, are looking for, and finding, new ways of taking control—for example, in the use of Viagra, the virility pill, and other "lifestyle drugs" that enhance choices. Because feelings and passions are situated in the body, these are all engaged by means of the body in religious ritual: in healing rituals bodies are transformed; in pilgrimage rituals bodies experience movement through time and space; in trances body posture is the means by which consciousness is altered; and in dieting support groups, bodies are at the center of focus as people find ways to substitute God for food. In all such cases, bodily involved rituals structure spiritual awareness and transform individual identity.

Identity Themes

More broadly, the new suppliers cater to quests for identity in a rapidly changing culture. Identities themselves have become more fluid and adaptable than they were under conditions of greater social stability. In this respect Frances Fitzgerald's metaphor of American society as a centrifuge is suggestive.[46] A centrifuge is an apparatus in a science laboratory that rotates at high speeds and sorts out substances at differing densities. Centrifugal forces move outward away from a center, creating new clusters. Applied to society, it points to the breakdown of ascriptive unities and re-sorting of elemental qualities underlying new identities. Social class, color, region, ethnicity, and language are the historical bases upon which Americans have organized their religious lives, but there are now new sortings along gender, sexual orientation, lifestyle, and generational lines. These latter sortings tap emotions and latent identities that reach deeply in people's lives; they now emerge as a powerful source of religious interpretation and identity construction. Even though they do not define a person's identity, they filter religions experience.

A parallel exists with politics. In the recent decades, politics has come to be emancipated from tradition, leading to what has been described as "life politics," dealing with such issues as nuclear war, the environment, and the rights of a woman over her body.[47] "Life politics" as a term signifies the shift in the direction toward greater worries about quality of life and the individual's own life as an end in itself. The mobilizing principle in such politics is the increased personal autonomy of our time: the individual becomes free from social constraints of class, ethnicity, and nationality, but also empowered to act responsibly and to make informed political choices in keeping with the greater attention to personal concerns. Politics becomes more closely linked to existential concerns of a moral and spiritual kind. In either instance, in political action and religious identity, there is great appeal to authenticity and to thinking through how issues bear on one's deepest sensitivities and identities.

As the rich metaphor of a centrifugal process implies, American religion is dynamic and evolving, ever capable of relating to shifting life-spaces and of giving rise to new organizational and communal forms. Its openness and adaptability are its strength, for in the changing configuration of identities there may actually be more, not necessarily less, potential for spiritual vitality. As the cultural layers are stripped away freeing the individual, personal and experiential aspects of identity rise to the surface. In various settings today, one observes the centrality of experience, such as in the casual Evangelical setting of jeans, cotton sweaters, drums, and guitars, where members brag about not being "churchy," or in a goddess festival where women try to integrate feminine power, sexual ecstasy, and spiritual awakening, or in the emotional and heartfelt participation found at the Metropolitan Community Church, a gay religious community whose members are finally free to acknowledge who they really are and to celebrate their identity. Wherever it is happening, this centrifugal process results in a resorting of people and a reconfiguring of symbols and themes, offering positive definition of who people are and empowering them in fresh ways.

SERIOUS BUSINESS

In thinking about these symbolic reconstructions, it is clear the new suppliers are, paradoxically, simultaneously broadening and narrowing definitions of spirituality. There is broadening in the sense that spirituality is refocused around a multitude of causes, concerns, and life-situations; it is defined and made applicable to social and psychological spaces of modern life never before explored so fully. It might be said that spirituality enjoys a high level of narrative enmeshment: it is pulled into people's everyday lives in all their diversity and perplexity. But there is a narrowing, too, for when spirituality is recast in strictly psychological terms, it is often loosened from its traditional moorings—from historic creeds and doctrines, from broad symbolic universes, from religious community. There is narrative enmeshment, but in its specificity and inward focus the communal dimension so important historically to cultivating spirituality is weakened. The autonomous, often instrumentally minded individual can be left alone. Of course, autonomy and instrumentality are always both a matter of degree, and in some sense inevitable given how the religious sphere is defined in the modern world. Both are topics we must explore further in the chapters that follow.

The suppliers in this new spiritual marketplace are themselves diverse: some are specialists in turning old, dying churches into places that are coming alive again; others are capable of devising seeker churches with video screens, skits, and folk music appealing to people who otherwise would never get close to a church; others are skilled at organizing spiritual seminars on the environment, Native American spirituality, goddess worship, channeling, spirituality in business, and many other topics; and still others know how to cultivate readerships through newsletters, Webpages, and fax machines or a listening audience through cassettes on scores of topics, sometimes only vaguely aware how it is they are engaging the human spirit. To speak of them as suppliers, or entrepreneurs, is not to reduce what they do to economics, and certainly not to imply that their motivation is mercenary; many church growth and megachurch consultants, avant-guard theologians, and spiritual leaders—perhaps most—are doing what they do with good intentions. The nation's religious climate indeed encourages well-meaning entrepreneurs to enter the marketplace. Religious and spiritual groups of all kinds today operate in a context which William McKinney and I characterized in 1987 as the "New Voluntarism"; that is, a situation in which people are bound less than ever before to inherited faiths, are deeply subjective in their religious choices, and are looking to a range of experts and resources for help in cultivating their spiritual lives.[48] Some commentators decry this trend, but it seems clear that on the whole such voluntarism encourages creativity and has given rise to a healthy spurt of entrepreneurial activity within religion.

But as mentioned at the beginning of the chapter, the making of meaning is a serious business.[49] It always was for prophets and priests in the past, but arguably it becomes much more serious in the contemporary world. The number of voices addressing questions of meaning has increased many times over. Moreover, people now take a more active role in shaping the meaning systems by which they live and must themselves determine how to respond to this widening range of suppliers, all contending with one another in creating symbolic worlds. Storytelling and meaning-making inevitably become intertwined with marketing, technology, and consumption in a market economy. Inevitably, too, some scrutiny of meaning systems is essential to human well-being and survival. Because ours is an age when it is possible to appropriate religious symbols from many times and places, we are forced to become more self-conscious about all such choices. Not only do we depend on a vast array of producers, we recognize that the meaning systems that are created and by which we live are just that—systems that are created and by which we have chosen to live. Even if we regard the sacred as irreducible, as most religious people would insist, still the language we opt for in describing the sacred bears a cultural imprint. Knowing all this, that symbolic frameworks of interpretation express the search for meaning as filtered through the experiences of a particular time and place, is powerful and sobering, forcing on us a sense of responsibility for our decisions and binding us in a common undertaking.

On Being Fluid and Grounded

The protean self seeks to be both fluid and grounded,
however tenuous that combination.
(*Robert Jay Lifton*)

In 1993 *Time* magazine carried a story about the Walceks—a large Catholic family in Placentia, California. Back in the 1950s and early 1960s, the Walceks, like so many other American families, said grace together before meals and held family prayers before going to bed. All nine children were sent to parochial schools. On Sunday mornings they regularly attended Mass at St. Joseph's Church. Much of their social life revolved around the parish. As judged by religious indicators at the time, they were traditional Catholics whose belief and practice mirrored that of millions of other "good" Catholics who generally took their faith for granted. Like their grandparents and parents before them, Emil and Kathleen Walcek thought of themselves as faithful Catholics who would pass on the family's religious tradition to their children, who, in turn, would pass it to their children. Religion and family had long been bound together, and there was little reason to expect this not to continue into the future.

But as time passed, the children grew up and began making their own religious decisions. *Time*'s religion editor, Richard N. Ostling, describes what happened to each of them:

> Emil Jr., 45, and Edward, 32, dropped out of church, and stayed out. John, 43, was married on a cliff overlooking Laguna Beach, divorced—and returned to the Catholic Church, saying, "Maybe the traditional way of doing things isn't so bad." Joe, 41, also returned to the fold after marrying a Ukrainian Catholic. Mary, 40, married a lapsed Methodist and worships "God's creation" in her own unstructured fashion. Rosie, 38, drifted into the Hindu-influenced Self-Realization Fellowship. Chris, 34, picked Unitarianism, which offered some of Christianity's morality without its dogma. Theresa, 36, spent five years exploring the "Higher Power" in 12-step self-help programs. Ann, 30, called off her wedding when her non-

practicing Jewish fiancé embraced Orthodoxy, a crisis that "sparked a whole new journey for me."[1]

Few families could match the Walceks—or perhaps would want to! Obviously its members were deeply touched by the countercultural trends of the late 1960s and early 1970s, as evident in their having absorbed so wide a range of religious and spiritual styles. For Catholics, Vatican Council II had at the time unleashed a new freedom of expression and populism that meshed well with the broader cultural developments. And that freedom spread rapidly among young Catholics. But important to note, the story on the Walceks was not about rejecting Catholicism even though some of its members had done so at the time of the reporter's account; it was about a deeply psychological, self-focused, and selective style of religion that has remained in place in a milder version ever since, privileging themes of individuality, adaptability, fluidity and, at its most popular level, a do-it-yourself mode of spirituality.

Important, too, the story was written from the perspective not of the late 1960s and early 1970s, but of the early 1990s. The intent was to show how events and influences of an earlier time had transformed its members' lives in lasting ways. A quick glance at the adult ages of the children suggests just how lasting apparently these influences were; indeed, as was the point of *Time*'s cover story about Baby Boomers and religion, the climate of spiritual seeking that influenced members of this generation during their youthful years left a deep impression on them. Ever since, they have looked at religion differently, appropriating a level of individual choice and responsibility for decisions sometimes in concern with religious communities, often in defiance of them. Even the Walceks who remained Catholics, or who later reaffirmed their inherited faith, were—after the 1960s—very different Catholics.

OPPOSING VIEWS

But what was that mark? And was it really lasting? These questions have sparked a good deal of debate and controversy over the past few decades. By virtue of its sheer numbers, whatever this generation does captures public attention and almost always bears implications for society and its institutions. Throughout their lives, it seems, the Boomers were an object of religious curiosity: as children they crowded into kindergartens and church schools; as teenagers they dropped out of active religious involvement in record numbers; many of the college-educated explored alternative religions, although very few actually joined up. At every step along the way, people have wondered if they would follow in the footsteps of previous generations, or if they would create new patterns for themselves. Now many of them are 50 years of age or more, hardly the youth they are still remembered as being and certainly old enough to have established a religious record of their own, but the question remains unanswered: how are we to profile this generation religiously? The fact that this question is still unanswered is itself fascinating and a commentary on just how multifasceted, and perhaps blurred, this generation's religious culture has become.

Opinions are still very much divided. Many commentators regard the decade of the 1960s as a watershed period in the United States but disagree about its impact and how best to interpret the decade. Almost everyone would agree that the "spiritual marketplace" as we know it today has roots in those early years, but what to make of Boomer religiosity in terms of its depth and style is open to a good deal of debate. Some analysts see the period as a serious break in institutional loyalties, as nothing less than a profound rupture in the nation's moral and religious fabric. They look on the post–World War II youth as the generation that "forgot God," broke away from their religious roots, and turned to Eastern religions and meditation techniques. They recall how the youth drifted from the mainline churches, how they rebelled against a civic faith linking God and country, and how the proportion of young people professing no affiliation with organized religion skyrocketed during this time. As this scenario would have it, a self-absorbed, narcissistic generation abandoned theology in favor of psychology and self-help philosophies focused largely on their own individual wants and needs. They were born to be pleased, not to be saved. It is said that as children and youth of the late 1940s and 1950s, they were the product of a period, though highly religious, that was also shallow and superficial—born into a "culture religion" that was conventionally American, status-oriented, and focused more around the conformity of belonging than believing. It was not a religious ethos that encouraged a strong commitment of faith in God or a nourishing spiritual life; indeed, as a result of their rebellion many young people grew up biblically illiterate, agnostic, and with remarkably little understanding of, or loyalty to, a denominational or faith tradition. Some interpreters actually go so far as to portray the generation as "destructive," seeing in the left-leaning politics of rebellion during the 1960s and early 1970s a rejection not just of the conformity culture at the time but of core religious and cultural values that have long been a basis of continuity in American life.[2] In their view the generation is far more secular than was their parents' generation.

Other commentators paint a more optimistic scenario: they argue that despite a youthful rebellion, the generation is now "returning to God" in the midlife years. Having left behind their earlier experimentation with Eastern meditation and curiosities about new religions, they are now reclaiming the traditional faiths in which they grew up. Proponents of this perspective play down the moral, religious, and political disruptions of the 1960s, viewing them as youthful dabblings; and stress instead that in time rebels settle down and come to their senses. They point to the stunning growth of Evangelical and Charismatic churches and the more conservative moral and religious mood today as compared to the earlier period in which they grew up. Just as they postponed marriages, they have postponed returning to religion, but now all this is changing: more mature, married and raising children, they are becoming more involved in the communities they left behind. Previous generations, it is said, followed a similar pattern of rebellion and later reclaimed faith as they aged, so why not expect the same to hold for Boomers? "The older people get, the more religion becomes important to them, and the more they tend to go to church," writes George H. Gallup Jr.; hence, as he says, "there is no reason to believe that the Baby Boomers will be any different."[3] In other words, there have been no really significant changes altering their religious lives, only youthful experimentation and postponements; and they can now be expected to reconnect with institutions and re-establish religious and cultural continuities.

A third scenario strikes a middle position. There was a spiritual awakening stemming from the 1960s but it was, and still is, largely nonconformist—more a "people's revolution" in which the symbols of religion were seized on in a search for meaning and the cultivation of an inner life. This scenario focuses on the spiritual, but it is not presumed there will necessarily be a massive return to conventional religious life of the sort that flourished when they were children. It is emphasized that the age of strong religious hegemonies in the modern world is over; that cognitive, moral, and religious pluralism is now a reality in the everyday lives of Americans. Yet religious symbols, myths, and narratives in the popular culture play a crucial role enhancing spiritual growth and identity on the part of those hungry for a richer experience of the divine. Skeptical of established institutions and highly subjective in their approaches to religion, the post-World War II generations choose for themselves what to believe and what to practice; they are far less concerned about orthodoxies and inherited faith traditions than were their parents. As this perspective would have it, the notion of objective truth loses much of its persuasiveness, and consistency of belief and practice becomes less important than coherence—that is, a mix of beliefs, symbols, and practices may be personally meaningful even if they appear from the outside as unrelated or even internally contradictory. Mysticism, nature religion, the feminine, the primitive, the unity of experience, and ancient wisdom are all themes that, to one degree or another, gain prominence in what amounts to a process-oriented style of spirituality that abhors fixity and stagnation and privileges instead the religious imagination and exploration of the mind and spirit to achieve new heights of consciousness. Religion has not been abandoned but is expressed in a mood, style and discourse strikingly different from that of a half-century ago. In Robert S. Ellwood's words:

> The new religious imagination conceived of a church or temple that was egalitarian, concerned with subjectivity, driven by feeling rather than highly consistent doctrine: and it imagined a God who himself enjoyed rich subjectivity and was not very legalistic. This God was apparently also easy with pluralism, well aware that Americans are not likely ever to be very much alike in religion. That sixties God is pretty much the God that has been worshiped ever since in this corner of the world, whether by liberals or conservatives, Catholics, Protestants, or Jews.[4]

As Ellwood's comment suggests, this more subjective mode of religiosity permeates the contemporary scene—not only in the established churches and temples, but also in its diffused and popular idiom. It reflects a grassroots sensibility extending across a wide spectrum of American life, in both liberal and conservative quarters, in faith communities as well as in loosely connected metaphysical networks. In whatever context, this scenario has it that spiritual concerns, even if not always defined in traditional religious language, find widespread expression and are leading to major realignments of people and institutions.

A Return to Religion?

Which of these scenarios best captures the current religious situation? What directions are this generation's spiritual concerns taking them in as they settle into midlife? Seemingly these questions would be easy to answer, but hardly so on second thought considering that religious culture, as we saw in Chapter 1, is multilayered and polysemic, and thus open to so many interpretations. It is known that Boomers are generally less committed to religious institutions than pre-Boomers, but this fails to tell us anything about religious changes for the generation as it has matured. Nor can we equate religion and institutions in a simple way. Religious life is structured by a complex of organizations including but hardly limited to congregational participation. Further, studies looking at religious developments as the generation has aged lead to somewhat contradictory findings, depending on the research measures used. For these reasons we rely here on the results of a panel study, that is, on information gained from repeated interviews with the same people over the course of their lives. This promises to yield a more conclusive, clearer understanding of trends now emerging.

To begin with, we ask the foremost institutional question: is there a return to church, synagogue, and temple? This should be easy to determine, yet even here answers are not as easy to come by as we might expect. Beginning in the mid-to-late 1980s, speculation mounted that a "return to religion" was in the making. The February, 1987 cover of the *Washingtonian* magazine announced approvingly: "God is Back." Reference to "God" here had a clearly traditional ring about it, suggesting that young people were returning after a long absence to church, synagogue, and temple. Not only in Washington but elsewhere across the country congregations were experiencing an influx of young adults looking for a place they could call their own. Many of them were turning 40, and those especially who were married and had school-age children were "shopping"—looking for good music and worship, fellowship opportunities, and moral and religious education for the children. Both personal and family concerns dominated the news about the returnees. In retrospect we see that this so-called return to religion was something of a media event—hundreds of newspapers and magazines carried headlines about Boomers finding God and going back to religious services and activities after years of conspicuous absence. Writers found here an interesting "hot" subject to explore and comment on, including one writer who wrote about himself in a widely read book—entitled simply *Returning: A Spiritual Journey.*[5]

And clearly there was a return. Our 1988–89 survey showed that among the many who had dropped out of active religious involvement during their teens or early adult years, one-fourth had returned—often to a congregation or denomination different from the one they had left, but nonetheless they were driven by spiritual and religious concerns.

People were primarily focused on moral and religious training for their children, but concerns for themselves ran a close second. The return to religious participation was greater for conservative Protestants but significant enough to register across denominational and Protestant, Catholic, and Jewish boundaries; returnees were presumably deeply committed to their faiths (especially as measured by belief in God and the importance of religion) during their youth before they dropped out, and now they returned, renewing those commitments. Other studies documented increased levels of regular church attendance among older Boomers at the time.[6]

But what kind of a return was it? Were the returnees renewed in their faith and commitment to the churches and synagogues? Here the stakes get bigger and more difficult to sort out. From the beginning there was reason to suspect that levels of commitment were low; studies showed that Boomers in great numbers questioned religious authority when they were growing up and had remained somewhat distrustful of institutions even as they had aged. Based on our own earlier survey in 1988–89, it was evident from a range of institutional indicators that returnees were less committed than the loyalists, that is, those who had not dropped out of religious groups for any extended period at the time we interviewed them. Whether in matters of belief, congregational participation, subjective importance of religion, or religious self-identity, returnees scored lower than the loyalists, even after being back in the fold for as long as five years. This was true across all major faith traditions and across age and gender lines, a finding that led us to conclude at the time:

> Highly voluntaristic norms of religious belonging are deeply ingrained in this generation, among younger as well as older members, and this will likely be the predominate shaping influence on styles of congregational involvement in the future. Reginald Bibby's "à la carte" style of religious belief seems to be the wave of the future for this generation, which probably means that we can expect a great deal of continued shopping around for religious themes, and even within a religious community considerable picking and choosing of what to believe and how to practice what one believes.[7]

After a second round of interviews in 1995–96, we now have a better basis for an informed judgment on the matter. And the results are mixed. Among those who were identified as returnees in 1988–89, a majority of whom claimed at the time to have had a born-again experience, only 43 percent say they now attend services even as often as once a

117

month or more. More than a third of the returnees now report they hardly ever, or never, attend a religious service. This represents a considerable shift away from institutional involvement. Interestingly, too, we observe a parallel shift in beliefs. Whereas 86 percent of the returnees once indicated they believed in God, now they sort out in roughly three equal groups: a third saying they are "strong believers," a third having "occasional doubts," and a third saying they are "seekers not always sure what to believe." To speak of them—and perhaps of their generation generally—as "believers" is to overextend a category, to presume a firmness of conviction that does not exist. In actuality, their beliefs are quite fluid in the sense that at one time they may be firm, but at other times much less so. As the journalist Jack Miles had surmised, doubt and faith mix together in ways that are not easily separated, and often result in a creative conjoining of the two—of faith open to question and of doubt pushing toward affirmation. Subjective religious, not just institutional, fluidity is commonplace. What emerges, then, is a picture of large numbers of returnees having spent sometime in a congregation, or checked out several congregations, but then dropping out or becoming so inactive as to have effectively dropped out. Despite the attention of the media to the "return of the Boomers" to organized religion in the late 1980s and early 1990s, it is clear now that this was not a return to traditional faith and loyalty, certainly not of the sort that many clergy and laypeople pinned their hopes on for bridging what a decade or more ago had come to be called a "generation gap" in the churches.

In our interviews we asked returnees who now had dropped out if they had become discouraged with churches and synagogues. Some certainly had and gave all the typical reasons—boring worship services, inadequate programs for children, busy schedules, indifference, dislike for the clergy, not feeling welcome. But there was also the more positive aspect of spiritual searching: people who had once sought out a congregation often said that they were now looking for another congregation; some spoke of becoming more deeply involved in a small group, sometimes in a congregation, sometimes elsewhere. Still others spoke of turning away from the churches in which they had grown up and looking beyond religious institutions altogether for spiritual guidance—to reading books and inspirational literature, attending lectures, exploring the Internet, going to retreat centers. A church, synagogue, or temple was one place, and for many a good place, but not the only place to find spiritual guidance. The fact that people so often speak of spirituality as something to "find" suggests that in popular understanding it is seen as requiring some degree of scouting around, and very much depends on how a person goes about trying to find it and how much the person succeeds. Some people who previously were active in traditional congregations but no longer now, told us that their views of God had changed: once they had thought of God in conventional terms as a Heavenly Father, but now spoke of a "higher power," the "total realization of all human potential," "cosmic consciousness," "female energy," and the like. Some people said they questioned whether the reality of God could be defined, though they usually held to some kind of positive assumptions about the divine or metaphysical reality. Even among Evangelical Christians, presumably strong believers in a traditional God, we found more mixed imageries of Deity and an increasingly diverse and inclusive spirituality for those no longer as involved as they once were in organized religion. Other researchers have observed this same trend for Evangelicals, which suggests that mystical New Age–derived teachings may have penetrated the culture much farther than customarily assumed, and that barriers presumed to isolate the Evangelical faith communities from this invasion may not be all that strong.[8]

Yet the trends do not fit some easy notion of secular drift. This became evident when we switched attention from the returnees to the dropouts, those people who in 1988–89 had drifted away from active religious involvement for a period of two years or more. One-third of these dropouts now attend religious services weekly or more; one-half attend two or three times a month or more. Almost a half now say they are "strong believers," with the remainder divided about equally between "doubters" and "seekers." Some who once espoused New Age views now talk about God in a more 1950s-style Judeo-Christian manner, as a Father, a Comforter, a caring Shepherd. Surprisingly, our earlier dropouts are almost as active now in a congregation or some religious group as the religious loyalists, the people who were the most committed of all at the time of the earlier survey. By any institutional measure we select, only about a third of those once the most alienated from organized religion—across all faith traditions—can be still classified as dropouts; today the majority of them look pretty much like other religious people. Considerable numbers of them have reclaimed religion, or at least are involved in some kind of organized religious activity, thus making generalizations about trends a risky undertaking. And if we add to that number those who may not be so involved institutionally but profess a greater personal faith than they once held, clearly any simple secularization thesis does not hold.

Thus, regarding the picture as a whole, what is striking is *the dynamic, fluid character* of Boomer religiosity, which is almost like a game of musical chairs: loyalists and returnees drop out in sizable numbers while dropouts, some of them inactive for twenty or thirty years, find their way back to the churches, synagogues, and temples. Often in the polls religious indicators give us more of an appearance of stability than is really the case, for the more we observe the people themselves over time— treating them not simply as population aggregates but as individuals whose religious sensibilities and activities ebb and flow—the more we see a far more open, revolving pattern. This may be more so for Boomers, but it probably holds far more for Americans as a whole than we tend to realize; certainly any serious religious profiling must consider this movement "in" and "out" of institutions and groups in relation to people's changing social circumstances and life-course patterns.[9] Such movement bears directly on the debate over Baby Boomer religiosity. Some commentators see in this movement signs of religious defection and rejection of traditional religious authority; others interpret it as evidence of considerable, but largely unbounded, spiritual ferment. In such a situation, the analyst trying to get to the bottom of what is happening must examine the religious terrain carefully and attend to the deeper meanings people attach to their religious lives rather than relying too much upon surface observations. Flannery O'Connor is said to have once commented that "glibness is the great danger in answering people's questions about religion." It is a warning sociologists, journalists, and others would do well to heed; it is also important to be cautious in interpreting what people say, or at least query them deeply; as pointed out in the Introduction, with religion the truth lies "in the details."

Religious Attendance

In search of more details, we look first at religious attendance, the most cited religious indicator from polls and surveys in the United States next to belief in God. It is also among the most visible of religious behaviors, and thus a public symbolic act of some significance, indicative not just of religious involvement but of levels of confidence in religious authority. Certainly there has been no massive upturn within the country in religious attendance, either for this generation or for the country as a whole. But neither has there been any great turning away over the past twenty years. Possibly there is a gap—perhaps an increasing gap[10]—between what people "say" about religious attendance and what they actually "do," but we have no firm basis on which to draw any conclusions. What we do observe from the panel study is movement in *opposing* directions, that is, a slightly more polarized religious population today than we observed in 1988–89. Somewhat more people now say they are involved in weekly religious worship (39 versus 36 percent), but also more report being not at all involved (15 versus 12 percent). People with average levels of involvement may have become more, or less, involved, but in the aggregate scores look pretty much the same. But as is often the case, aggregate scores can be misleading. There appears to be both an increase of serious churchgoers *and* a falling away of casual attenders. And if so, then the cleavage between the so-called churched and unchurched sectors has widened for this generation. Such interpretation is consistent with other research pointing to an increasing gap in the perceptions of religious institutions among younger American cohorts: for those born since World War II, those most religiously involved are much more respectful of institutional authority than those with low levels of participation, or no involvement.[11] Should this gap of participation and respect for authority continue to broaden for succeeding cohorts, then most assuredly the result will be a more visible reconfiguration of institutional religious loyalties.

But here too, there is much fluidity. If we look at those who were weekly attenders at the time of the first survey, today we find that only slightly more than one-fourth remain active at this level, 37 percent are less active, though they still sometimes attend, and 35 percent say they now hardly ever or never attend. And the converse holds as well: among those who reported hardly ever or never attending in 1988–89, a third are now weekly attenders, 31 percent attend sometime, and 35 percent remain uninvolved. Knowing whether a person was an active attender or not in early adult life, thus, does not predict level of involvement at a subsequent time very well. Instability—not stability—as a conceptual model best characterizes the situation. Breakdowns by gender, social class, race, ethnicity, and region make little difference. The only social correlate that sheds much light is age: those more active now than in the past are the younger members of the Baby Boom cohort, who, when we interviewed them the first time, were less likely to be married or to have children; and similarly, many who are now older are less active in congregations than they once were. Such patterns suggest the importance of life-cycle effects, of family formation and raising children, a topic we return to and examine in some depth in Chapter 7.

To be sure, there are loyalists who stick with congregations over time, and a comparable sector who remain uninvolved, but in between these two is a sizable constituency for whom there is a great deal of fluidity. Our interviews suggest, in addition to life-cycle effects, that an enormous range of considerations affects levels of participation, such as work patterns, friendships, mobility, institutional programming, likes and dislikes about congregations and the clergy, and fluctuating spiritual interests. Even if boundaries between the "churched" and "unchurched" cultures are being redrawn, it is important to recognize that these are permeable boundaries, and probably more so in this country than in some others where religious and secular cleavages are more firmly drawn. Important, too, are trends for conservative Protestants, liberal Protestants, and Catholics—the three large American faith constituencies. Based on the self-reports of the people we interviewed, we are able to follow their church-going habits from the time they were children 8–10 years old up to the most recent survey when the oldest among them were beginning to turn 50. All three constituencies report high levels of attendance as children, followed by much lower levels in the early adult years. At the time of the 1988–89 survey, attendance levels had increased for all three but proportionately more so for Catholics. By 1995–96 Catholic attendance had leveled off while Protestant attendance continued on a slightly upward trajectory. For mainline Protestants, attendance remained substantially lower than for conservative Protestants, yet proportionately speaking, levels of attendance during this latter period actually increased at a greater rate. Because mainline Protestant involvement was so drastically affected in the years when Boomers were in their teen and early adult years, the modest increases more recently for this constituency are noteworthy. Sara Caughman, our spiritually minded Episcopalian, is not alone in becoming more seriously involved and reclaiming her Protestant heritage. Others like her—not all that many, but enough to register statistically—are rediscovering the richness of a religious heritage and opting for a more active involvement in a congregation after years of indifference and/or checking out other spiritual possibilities. In the reshuffling of religious affiliations that has been underway for some time, strikingly new patterns of religious commitment appear to be emerging within the old-line Protestant sector, even if on a modest scale—a topic we take up in Chapter 6.

RELIGIOUS IDENTIFICATION

Another significant indicator for Americans is religious identification, usually measured in polls and surveys as a "preference" for a particular denomination or faith tradition. Ever since Will Herberg's well-known *Protestant-Catholic-Jew*, written in the mid-1950s, Americans have been singled out for their high levels of religious identification, even if they are religiously indifferent in other respects. People might have a shallow level of faith and weak institutional commitments, yet maintain loyalty to a religious community as a means of affirming both a religious identity and the American Way of Life. With Herberg, as for later sociologists, religion provides a sense of "belonging," a means of socially locating oneself in a large, pluralistic society; to identify with a religious community is to declare one's cultural heritage and identity, and thus to set onself apart from other traditions and groups. Historic patterns of denominationalism and ethnic pluralism, separation of church and state, social mobility, and the pressures of assimilation are all thought to contribute to the strong sense of social belonging religions promote in this country. Today 90 percent of Americans still claim to belong to one or another religious community.

But what about shifts in religious preferences? In a dynamic society, the scope and direction of such preferences are an important index of what is happening religiously and culturally at any given time. To speak of a "religious preference" is of course a very American way of thinking; it reflects not only the individualizing trends within religious culture and the social reality of pluralism, but also the shifting bases of religious identity-construction. For members of the Boomer generation, the range of possible religious options expanded to levels hitherto unknown and, given a highly psychological culture, the significance and meanings attached to religious symbols became more richly varied and polysemous. At a time when Protestant, Catholic, Jewish and even more narrow denominational identities have lost much of their power to bestow social meaning, how *conservative/traditional* or how *liberal/progressive* one is religiously and morally has come to take on an even greater significance for many people. No matter what one's faith tradition may be, an ideologically infused religious identity is of great importance. Moral values and passions cluster around these ideological identities, although, as we shall see in Chapter 8, such clustering is far more complex and not as polarized as is often assumed. But for religious identity formation, as well as for structuring perceptions of the groups that comprise the contemporary religious landscape, ideology clearly serves important boundary-defining functions. For this generation particularly, ideological labels have become crucially important markers of personal identity.

Those of a liberal Protestant theological heritage continue to abandon their identities—a pattern quite pronounced since the mid-1960s. Both the magnitude and continuation of this downward trend signal the extent of this tradition's loss over the culture. The theological underpinnings of a normative culture derived in large part from old-line Christian traditions of the eighteenth and nineteenth centuries have by now largely vanished. More than just an institutional and normative decline, a spiritual crisis currently afflicts many theologically liberal-to-moderate churches.[12] In contrast, conservative Protestantism continues to attract a large number of Boomers as well as Generation Xers. Many dropouts from the old-line Protestant churches have found a home within this remarkably diverse set of Evangelical, Fundamentalist, and Charismatic traditions, but all emphasizing strong personal faith and commitment. Their populist teachings and championing of "traditional values" appeal to those who feel the country has lost its moral moorings. Roman Catholic preferences increased over the past ten years after an earlier period of some decline. Religious involvement for Roman Catholics dropped in the 1960s and 1970s but turned around, largely as a result, so it is argued, of the greater accommodation to choice and interpretation over church teachings.[13] Boomers have been, and continue to be, the spearhead of what has come to be called Selective Catholicism.[14] Both the widespread Protestant Evangelical appeal and the changing normative Catholic styles within the United States reflect institutional adaptations to popular religious moods and experiential faith.

Two other trends deserve attention. Ever since large numbers of this generation turned away from the churches, synagogues, and temples in their young years, questions have been asked about what happened to them. It is clear that some turned to "other religions," as the pollsters call them; over time there has been a steady, albeit proportionately small, growth in this diverse category. Other religions would include hundreds of possibilities, the major ones being Muslim, Buddhist, Hindu, Native American, Scientologist, Unitarian-Universalist, Jehovah's Witness, Baha'i, Sikh, Wiccan, Eckankar, and New Agers of varying stripes.[15] Many of these are traditions that reach into the ancient past, others are "invented traditions" of the modern era.[16] Of greater significance than their numerical size is the wide range of religious alternatives which they now make available to Americans. Of course, the "None" category has grown as well. Early on, members of this generation were overwhelmingly identified as religious (97 percent), but beginning in their youth the numbers rejecting a religious identification increased rather precipitously to 10 percent. So marked was this increase, one might have thought the secularizing forces of the society had brought about a major reversal in the American propensity to claim a religious identity. But this seems not to be the case. Our more recent data suggest that the "None" identification has leveled off at 9 or 10 percent. Trends appear to have stabilized and, quite possibly, the configuration of major religious identities we now observe will persist relatively unchanged into the foreseeable future. At the same time, a stable "culture of nonaffiliation" seems to have clearly emerged, implying that defection and/or the rejection of a religious identity is, as has been claimed, "an increasingly acceptable alternative in American society."[17]

GAUGING THE SPIRITUAL MOOD

Institutional indicators, of course, reveal only so much. The spiritual mood of the country, and for a generation so large and whose members are moving into midlife, is far more difficult to gauge. Demographic projections would suggest a generation that should now be settling down to stable religious affiliations and practices, and to some degree that is what we find. In talks with the same people over a period of almost ten years, it is clear they are better able now to articulate their spiritual values and do so with a good deal more conviction and confidence. There is less of a frantic obsession to find spiritual insight and more concern about its depth and meaning. More of them now prefer to "stick to a faith" rather than to engage in endless "exploration of spiritual teachings." Many are concerned about their children and what spiritual values they are imparting to them. As members of this generation grow older, they recognize that spirituality must be cultivated through practice, and that there is no "quick fix" when it comes to spiritual depth. They also recognize that preoccupation with self has its limits: genuine personal fulfillment arises not from continued self-absorption but out of a vital balance of commitments, both to self and to others. People who fifteen or even ten years ago were very vocal about their own self-searching now talk more about giving to others, about family life, about well-being and the quality of relationships; for most, spirituality is no longer viewed, if ever actually it was, simply as self-expansion. An "ethic of commitment," which pollster Daniel Yankelovich foresaw emerging in the early 1980s, clearly reached a level of fruition in the 1990s—an ethic emphasizing greater reaching out to others and alignment with good causes along with, and perhaps in direct relation to, the nurturing of one's own interior life. Members of this generation, far more so now than before, show signs of having reached spiritual maturity.

And yet it is easy to overstate their grounding. It would be more accurate to describe them as spiritually in flux, even as they appear to be more grounded. Nowhere is this more evident than in their involvement in the small-group movement. Boomers, like Americans of all ages,[18] spend a considerable amount of time in small groups of many kinds—Bible study, Torah study, prayer fellowships, twelve-step therapy groups, women's groups, men's groups, singles groups, support groups, special-interest groups, and the like. One-third of the people we interviewed in 1988–89 belonged to a small group, and by 1995–96 that figure had increased to 43 percent. A significant number of them belong to more than one such group. Many are seriously committed to their group actvities. Both religious and nonreligious in character, small groups attract because they offer extended opportunity for sharing, intimacy, and social support. A distinct impression one gets from people in these groups, however, is that of much sifting and sorting: well over half (61 percent) of the people who were involved at the time of our first survey were not involved when we got back to them in the second survey. When asked about why they were or were not still involved, the idiom in which their answers were cast had largely to do with "finding" a spiritual basis for life, with "personal growth," with "emotional support," with "becoming centered," and with "reaching out to others." The stories were largely about "starting over," about reorientation through participation in small informal groups, in house churches and *havurot*. So deeply an American theme, "starting over" captures for Boomers a sense of a self-in-movement, as opportunity for the expression and recrystallizing of feelings, attitudes, beliefs, and outlook not just once, but repeatedly, and as life circumstances change. A psychological culture encourages definition of the self as open-ended and revisable, and hence a self capable of transcending organizational boundaries and inherited identities. In this respect, even if the psychology within many small groups is overly expansive and potentially misleading in its extreme, such groups still serve an important function for their participants, assisting them in reorganizing their lives and assuring them that they can start over. It is a pattern as old as the United States itself, and one Americans still cherish.

At the same time, often the rhetoric gave hint of tension surrounding their involvement in these groups. There is the dilemma of wanting social support and community, yet resisting too much infringement on personal space. Finding a balance between spiritual support and spiritual openness is not easy, and certainly not for most people with whom we talked. This dilemma arises partly out of a disillusionment with an earlier culture of self-transformation with its excessive emphasis on openness; increasingly, serious-minded people know there must be some limits to the revision of the self. Recognized is an individual's own sense of purpose and direction, and the necessity of social attachments as an anchor stabilizing one's identity. But more subtle social realities come into play as well. The psychological language of the small-group movement betrays an underlying anxiety arising out of a deep-seated disjunction of modern culture, of being caught between a highly pragmatic, materialistic culture that celebrates possessions, status, and social achievement, on the one hand, and the deeper human needs for acceptance, happiness, and justification of shortcomings when measured against such high social standards, on the other. Many in the Boomer generation feel caught in between these two worlds of self-reference and often falter in finding words to express their feelings. More than a third of the people we talked to report scaled-down expectations; failures, disappointments, unrealized dreams, job layoffs, marriage and family breakups, and feelings of personal inadequacy in one or another aspect of their lives are real though often difficult to talk about. Failure is not a reality Americans are taught to deal with very well. Moreover, many say they find little help from religious people and institutions in dealing with it. Typically they resort to psychological explanations for what amounts to a culturally induced dilemma facing many Americans.

But this situation is hardly new. Since the time of Tocqueville, observers have noted that Americans espouse a this-worldly, secular-style religiosity adaptable to the practicalities of everyday life—to pluralism, to democracy, to making a living, and to getting ahead. So accommodating is the religious culture that faith itself for ordinary Americans is unlikely to interfere very dramatically with their views regarding work, social status, earning money, or desire for happiness. "A person of faith should still work hard," sociologist Robert Wuthnow says, "but enjoying life becomes even more important. Dogmatism should be resisted. Faith should result in joy, inner peace, tolerance, getting along with one another, and indeed just getting along."[19] Such easygoing religiosity is known for its affinity with the American Way of Life, with democracy and competition, with hard work and material acquisition. And in this respect, Boomers are no different really from other affluent, middle-class Americans, or even from those who are less privileged but aspire to success and upward mobility. Given the influence of the mass media and the cultural industries, the narrative scripts posed for Americans of all social classes except perhaps for the truly disadvantaged, who are seldom held up as models of achievement anyway, embrace a cultural faith combining notions of God, upward striving and prosperity, and desire for happiness. Those scripts are so deeply embedded in the culture that all Americans, whether they choose it or not, are touched by them. Religion as a great majority of people understand it is itself very much bound up with these larger cultural narratives.

Yet at the same time, significant numbers of those who "have it all"—money, status, comfortable lives—say they want more from life than material success alone. Money and worldly success conjure up a degree of ambivalence: they want it but know that it only goes so far satisfying their wants. Family and friends are deeply cherished; yet commitments even to them are moderated by their own individualism. The ease with which people today talk about spiritual values reflects an underlying discontent with lives trapped in empty routines, devoid of larger meaning and purpose. Many hunger for a spirituality that breaks out of such routines; and sizable numbers consider themselves resourceful and consciously try to cultivate an awareness of who they are in relation to God or whatever they regard as sacred. They seek to reorient their ways of looking at the material world, at the environment, at other human beings, at all forms of life. Tensions arise within families, and within individuals themselves, as they face compromises arising out of their everyday experiences and the need for a sustainable life. Even among those lacking a good vocabulary for expressing their inner selves, or for whom spirituality is vaguely defined and without much real power to challenge their secular values and assumptions, there is a yearning for something that transcends a consumption ethic and material definitions of success. If asked, many would deny such yearning, but a close reading of their comments and behavioral cues suggest otherwise. Deep down, many of them are looking for a language to express their real feelings and, more importantly, to find a way to feel happy with themselves and their circumstances.

But where is this spirituality to be found? Already we have seen the many forms that this searching takes—reaching inward and reviving old traditions, exploring new traditions trying to find out more about God or the sacred. By any reckoning, the "Born-again" movement figures prominently in this quest. The Evangelical, Charismatic, and Fundamentalist movements of the late 1970s and 1980s generated hope of a renewed synthesis of the spiritual and the material, of the inner and outer aspects of life, through a reaffirmation of traditional faith in God. And judged by the statistics, there is still considerable optimism and hope (44 percent of our respondents claimed to be "born again" in 1988–89 as did 40 percent in 1995–96). No other spiritual movement, or family of movements, has attracted so many younger Americans in the post–World War II period. Often interpreted as an antimodernist response, the Born-again movement should be cautiously interpreted as a dogmatic or Fundamentalist response to modernity. Since the 1940s and the rise of the "neo-Evangelical" movement, a break with an older style of Fundamentalism has been in the making, offering a more culturally accommodating and subjectively oriented religious style.[20] Popular evangelical styles continue to be driven by pressures of accommodation, and especially so within the Boomer culture. Despite resistance to the erosion of an older religious world, the drift over time, and still today, is in the direction of enhanced choices for individuals and toward a deeply personal, subjective understanding of faith and well-being.

Evidence that the appeal of popular Evangelicalism lies primarily in its attention to personal needs, and not dogma or even strict morality, is supported by careful analysis of national surveys.[21] Psychological categories like "self," "fulfillment," "individuality," "journey," "walk" and "growth" are all very prominent within Evangelical Christianity.[22] Moreover, close scrutiny of our own data reveal subtle shifts on the part of Evangelical Boomers in recent years. Despite much talk of a "return to stricter moral standards," almost half our Evangelical respondents indicated that they are uncomfortable with rigid moral rules and insist—above all else—on following the dictates of their own conscience. Freedom for the individual believer to make his or her own moral decisions, not rigidity of outlook, is the defining feature of mainstream religious life. This same insistence on freedom carries over to traditional doctrine: contrary to much public perception, Evangelicals, increasingly like other Americans, honor the individual's own decisions in matters of faith. In this respect the "weightlessness" of contemporary belief in God is a reality not just for religious liberals and many Evangelicals, for Protestants,

Catholics, Jews, Muslims, and many others, but is, as David F. Wells underscores, "the common form in which modernity rearranges all belief in God."[23]

Boundaries between religious liberals and religious conservatives from time to time are redrawn, and they continue to evolve, but largely because the psychologically oriented culture in which we now live is far more influential than either theology or ecclesial tradition. The rift between these two theological camps and the so-called cultural wars attracts much attention in the media, but the real story of American religious life in this half-century is the *rise of a new sovereign self* that defines and sets limits on the very meaning of the divine. An individualistic ethos, the rise of the therapeutic mentality, and a growing consumerism have all conspired to create a new cultural definition of the self in the United States, one which Philip Cushman describes as follows: "The new cultural terrain was now oriented to purchasing and consuming rather than to moral striving; to individual transcendence rather than to community salvation; to isolated relationships rather than to community activism; to an individualistic mysticism rather than to political change."[24]

What appears to have emerged is the "self-contained individual," in Cushman's words, "a self that experiences a significant absence of community, tradition, and shared meaning."[25] Even if his is a sweeping generalization we must later unpack, it can hardly be denied that an older moral asceticism that had long held sway over people's lives limiting their wants and defining social duties and obligations has run its course in a highly consumer-oriented culture. Installment buying in the 1940s and 1950s and then the credit card in the 1960s ushered in a world of consumption virtually assuring its demise. Nor can we overlook the considerable store of religious data, some of which we discussed above, pointing to a significant erosion of authority in religious communities and shift in religious identities, which occurred in large part in the very years when Boomers were passing through the early phases of adulthood.[26] The self-contained individual, buoyed by an appetite for consumption, directly contributed also to a reassessment of institutional values. Or, to invoke again Pierre Bourdieu's terms, we witnessed during these years a decline in "social capital" associated with attachments to organized religion. If by social capital we mean a variety of valued resources such as social status, cultural acceptance, friendship networks, and the like associated with religious membership and participation, then the evidence seems fairly clear: these resources are less valued by this generation. When asked about their religious identification, fewer in the Boomer generation say they are "strong" Methodists, Presbyterians, Catholics, or whatever than is true for older Americans. When asked if "being a church member is an important way to become established in a community," fewer in this generation answer positively compared to earlier cohorts of Americans. When asked if religious communities are a good place for making friendships, fewer Boomers agree than do their parents. Religion in its deepest, most personal sense may be no less important to them, but as an index of social location, privilege, and identification, institutional labels have lost significance.

PSYCHOLOGICAL RELIGION

From the standpoint of Cushman's perspective—less "community, tradition, and shared meaning"—we gain perspective on the protean character of contemporary religious life. This becomes apparent in our research in comparing responses to the same question, asked in 1988–89 and 1995–96: "Is it good to explore many differing religious teachings and learn from them, or should one stick to a particular faith?" As already mentioned, more people now opt for sticking to a faith: 52 percent as compared to 29 percent in 1988–89. But the more interesting finding is that gained from the panel study. What we find, once again, is considerable fluidity (or keeping the metaphor of musical chairs, let us say "musical selves"). Only half of those who once emphasized religious consistency do so now; and almost a half of those who encouraged exploring at the time of the first survey now say it is best to stay with one faith. Given an opportunity to identify oneself as "strong believer," "doubter," or "seeker," seven out of ten of those we interviewed in our last survey who had once said they preferred to explore teachings rather than to stay with one faith now claim to be "strong believers"—an indication again of the pull toward a more traditional faith. Yet two-thirds of those who once said it is better to stay with one faith now refer to themselves as either "doubters" or "seekers." A surprising number of people we interviewed, upward of one half, move easily from a discourse of seeking to one of believing, or vice versa, from believing to seeking. This would appear to be an important characterization of the present religious scene, and clearly strong evidence of how permeable the boundaries between believing and seeking have become. To what extent this is peculiar to this generation, or applies to Americans more broadly, we cannot say. But those born since World War II probably constitute a strong vanguard.

In a highly subjective religious culture, people move back and forth psychologically across what many regard as porous, somewhat artificial, boundaries, wanting at times a stable anchor, and open at other times to more expansive possibilities. Or put differently, people must hold to some fundamental basis of truth but may still fear being consumed by it, reminding us of Robert Jay Lifton's comment about the protean self wanting to be *both fluid and grounded at the same time, however tenuous that possibility.*[27] In questioning people about this, the most frequent explanation given was pragmatic, that following one and then another strategy "works" for them. Research on the life-course generally reveals that transitions are to be expected not just in the sense of marriage, divorce, or becoming parents, but psychologically and emotionally as people deal with adversity, stress, and the pain and confusion in life.[28] A psychological culture encourages awareness of emotional hurdles that must be confronted and dealt with. Spiritual hurdles are no less real and call forth a variety of responses: sometimes all that is required is simple faith, other times new insights are needed, as well as discussion about moral and spiritual problems, or even a change of faith or spiritual teachers. It comes as little surprise, then, that the popular religious idioms today by which people define and describe themselves are so colored by life's transitions, or that the terms that convey the deepest meanings are so deeply subjective and experiential in character.

Of course, subjective labels often surface in the revised institutional identities people claim as their own: when people define themselves as "good" Catholics or non-observant Jews. Pollsters often fail to pick up on this "added meaning" people attach to their identities given the way they ask questions about religious identity, but when given a chance people will often say much more, amplifying religious identities to fit their lives at the time. We were impressed with how often people invoked terminologies in our second or third conversations that were either more elaborated or reflected revisions from that of the first: a man who was a "loyal Presbyterian" is now a "religious survivor"; our one and only "Quakerpalian" is now a "Born-again Christian"; and an inactive "Reform Jew" says he is now "fulfilled" in a Four-Square Messianic congregation. More so than for Catholics, Muslims, Buddhists, or Jews, Protestant denominational identities are downplayed; but when Protestants do name the specific denomination to which they belong, often they add descriptors (for example, "Born-again," "Charismatic," "vegetarian,"

"ecologically minded," "Bible-believing," and the like) creating hyphenated religious identities. Popular expression of faith in the United States
is known for its adhesional quality, allowing belief to mix freely with
ideologies, experiential language, and cultural and identity themes.[29]
Purists may think of this as adulterating religion, but it is how lived religion functions in any cultural context and is, to some extent, a source of
its ongoing vitality and meaningfulness.

A related dynamic is what we might call "improvisation." Anthropologist Mary Catherine Bateson calls attention to "the arts of improvisation,"
or the recombination of partly familiar cultural materials in new and
adaptive ways. For her, jazz music exemplifies improvisation: "individual
and communal, performance that is both repetitive and innovative, each
participant sometimes providing background support and sometimes
flying free."[30] Lived religion is very similar. Improvisation amounts to a
creative refocusing of religious resources, often in response to a mishap
or a new set of challenges. "I had many doubts about God after I was
divorced," one man told us, "but the more I doubted the more I learned
about myself and the more I realized I had to put my life together
again—which I did, and now I know I was just coasting along back then.
Now I know what I believe. How I think about God is very different now."
Interesting is this man's use of the phrase "coasting along." For him it
means that his Catholic faith was simply taken for granted until he was
faced with a life-circumstance forcing him to question who he was and
what he believed. His story differs from the usual religious narrative
about hardship leading to a stronger faith, since for him the experience
led to a more *conscious* faith. Becoming conscious means taking charge
of the situation, and recognizing that one can redefine relations with
God or the sacred, and even evaluate how best to conceptualize that
relationship. Improvisation often involves a recombination of symbols
and practices, as in the case of a woman suffering from an undiagnosed
medical problem who told us about how in an informal healing ritual
she came to realize that visualization techniques are part of "God's ar-
senal in defense of health, every bit as powerful, maybe even more, than
medical doctors." This fresh insight about God and health is more than
an "add on" to her Methodist faith, it is a recasting of a religious worldview and a set of practices. In both stories we have examples of innovation within a context of continuity, of the personal in relation to the
communal, and of the unleashing of spiritual energies, all having considerable potential for revitalizing religious life. Religion—like jazz—
involves an ongoing reconfiguring of possibilities.

Yet another way of conceptualizing this is fixity versus movement, the one most akin to Lifton's perspective on the protean self. Ritual is often the setting in which this dialectic is observed. Symbolic anthropologists, especially those influenced by Victor Turner, speak of society as involving both fixed structure and process and see in ritual its potential of liminality, of a dialectic between affirming a static social entity and its recreation. In an age of shifting psychological and experiential frames, it seems reasonable to expect some degree of reformulated religious identities, or at least the potential for reformulation if conditions are right. In more extreme forms the dialectic encourages people not just to doubt but even to laugh at, to find irony in, even to mock religion, simultaneously affirming yet distancing themselves from it—what Lifton calls "lubrication,"[31] giving the self space and creating a dialogical relation with belief and symbol. Further, the dialectic is reinforced by the fact that people's identities and coping styles tend now not to be as highly bound by traditional roles and religious subcultures; and hence, adaptations are highly personalized and subject to continuing modification, and feelings and mental states take priority over fixed cognitive and behavioral patterns. Religiously, this amounts to a heightened self-awareness and sensitivity to "how that commitment is interpreted, and then, lived out."[32]

In a dialogical context, religion becomes less a matter of supernatural theism, of belief in a God "out there," and more of a direct relationship with, and experience of, God or the sacred as an encompassing reality, spirit, or presence "right here." Faith may postulate belief in an external religious authority, but in the reflexive moment, the self rushes to the center of the meaning-making process. In such instance, often it is the self in search of meaning, or a self inwardly focused upon itself. But it need not necessarily follow that the two—the transcendent and the immanent or, if one prefers, the beyond and the immediate—are necessarily distant or removed from one another. For even as polar opposites, these two realities of God or of the sacred become easily fused in lived religious experience. As sociologist Robert Bellah and his associates make clear, both "poles" in organizing religion value to some degree personal experience as a basis of belief and moral action and "shifts from one pole to the other are not as rare as one might think."[33] Indeed, such shifts are themselves revitalizing: in reconnections of the inward and the outward, spiritual energies are generated with sufficient power to reorient people's lives.

FLUIDITY AND RELIGIOUS IDENTITY

Religious fluidity is certainly greater for the large middle sectors of the American population, and for those who are neither religious dogmatists nor ideological secularists. A subjective, highly diffused religion finds its greatest expression among those in contemporary society most exposed to conditions where, as one sociologist says, "the symbolization of man's relation to the ultimate conditions of his existence, is no longer the monopoly of any groups explicitly-labeled religious."[34] Those most exposed to such conditions would include the so-called "knowledge-based" techno-literate classes but also many others for whom there is spiritual interest, including those who, for whatever reason, find many of the customary beliefs and practices associated with organized religion more an obstacle than a venue to involvement. It is in these sectors of contemporary society, in fact, where many of the older religious boundaries that once distinguished denominations and faith traditions from one another have greatly vanished. Hence religious anchors here are often weak. People are thrown back more on their own experiences and self-examination in search of the sacred, finding themselves often caught between a religious exclusivism, on the one hand, and a full-blown secularism, on the other. These latter two serve as outer limits to the greater fluidity within the religious mainstream, and function to limit switching from one faith tradition to another and, to some extent, movement between the internal and external dimensions of religion and shifts in imageries of deity, emotions, and cognitive states.

But there are boundaries, of course. One is the communal context of religion, which despite individualizing trends continues to exert some hold. Americans, even when highly exposed to a quest culture, hold on to communal-based identities as Catholics, Methodists, Lutherans, Jews, Quakers, and the like, even as they amplify those identities in keeping with their experiences and lifestyles. Typically formed in childhood and grounded in family and close friendships, and not just in theology or institutional affiliation, these collective, quasi-*Gemeinschaft* identities persist as badges of belonging. By and large, they no longer function as a vital link between individuals and society, or mediating structure, in the way Will Herberg proposed in the 1950s; for many people, being a Catholic, a Methodist, or whatever is more a religious frame of reference, a psychological anchor of sorts, than a strong basis of group belonging. Yet it offers a connection with the past, a cultural "memory" which for the least religiously involved is likely to surface at times when extended families come together, on holidays and during rites of passage.[35] Our character John McRae is a perfect example of this early childhood socialization. His Presbyterian origins are not of much conscious religious significance to him anymore, yet his emotions and latent commitments are aroused when he remembers his childhood and family celebrations. He has not forgotten going to church with his parents or the warmth and happiness of those Christmas experiences when he was a child. In a very real sense, those early family experiences continue to define for him what is most important in life and still shape his religious sensibilities and expectations. More than 80 percent of the people in our survey, actively religious or not, say they would call on a church, synagogue, or temple for a family wedding or funeral, and almost that many say the same about baptisms, which says something about roots, memory, and the need for religious ritual at critical turns in people's lives.

At present in the United States, there appears to be a functional relationship between communal religious identities and psychological fluidity: religious communities set some outer limits on fluidity for many people, and fluidity, as we have seen, is rejuvenating for religious identity. As an example, a young Jewish woman told us about a particular moment within her synagogue when she became really aware for the first time of the spiritual dimension and was led to explore her own tradition, especially the Kabbalah. "I believe in the Jewish tradition *and* I believe in the importance of cherishing the earthy, the feminine, and the mystical. I used my own experiences to 'fill in' the holes left by the scaffolding." Asked about what she meant by "holes" and "scaffolding," her responses reveal a great deal about how Americans approach religion. "Holes" for her refers to things she wished her religion had provided but had not, such as a closer connection with the divine, an experience of mystery, and spiritual empowerment. Her description of what she felt she lacked was shaped by her Jewish experience but the story might just as easily been told by someone from another religious tradition. But that was only one side of her story. There was the "scaffolding" to which she referred, too: her Jewish tradition had provided a structure on which she could build. She knows that she does not need to create an entire religious system. Judaism offers a rich set of symbols, beliefs, practices and, most of all, a story of a people that is the centerpiece of her own personal story. This might well have been the voice of a lapsed Presbyterian or Catholic—a voice in a different idiom but with much the same message.

It is the general situation of a person recognizing how deeply embedded he or she may be within a tradition, yet confronting the fact that the inner life may not be fully formed or contained by tradition as received, and that by pulling together from other sources, often resources neglected from within one's own tradition, new and enriched meanings are possible. The believer is thrust into the situation, of the *bricoleur*, who in cobbling together from a variety of imageries, doctrines, symbols, texts, moral codes, and spiritual disciplines finds new religious meaning and in so doing often discovers a nuance, an insight, an angle of vision that is revitalizing in its creativity.

Important is another boundary, one that is very much self-constructed: defining oneself primarily as "spiritual" or as "religious." Having examined this distinction in earlier chapters, here we need only to observe that this is an emerging boundary-definition of social and psychological consequence. More often than we expected, we encountered people who spoke with conviction about their discoveries of the spiritual and how it had changed their lives—including rescue "from religion" that was too limiting. A comment from a 44-year-old woman in Massachusetts, raised a Fundamentalist, Bible-believing Christian but who recently found a "more friendly Christian church," is worth quoting, since it captures so well this self-discovery. Asked about the difference between religion and spirituality, she had this to say:

> Well, religion, I feel, is doctrine and tradition, genuflecting, and you have to do things this way. Spirituality is an inner feeling, an allowance of however you perceive it in your world, in your mind, and however it feels is okay. This might be a little far out as an example, but the traditional picture of Jesus, the bearded man. Well if you picture him in a different way, that's okay. There's not these parameters on it. That you have to believe in it this way and only in this way. Spirituality, I think, is what enters you and lifts you up and moves you to be a better person, a more open person. I don't think religion does that. Religion tells you what to do and when to do it, when to kneel, when to stand up, all of that stuff. Lots of rules.

Several issues she touches upon we unravel in Chapter 5—the role of tradition and practice, and the complex relation of religion and spirituality as these terms have come to be understood in popular discourse. Here we simply underscore the force of the spiritual in all its fluidity and creativity, which she describes in two ways: one, the reflexive voice that frees her imagination to think of Jesus in new ways, and two, how she is moved in such experiences to be a better person. Freeing of the imagination allows for a more "playful" religious world where an individual can engage faith, imagine other religious realities, be creative.[36] For many people we spoke with, there was a distinct "marker" in their lives, a moment of double awareness when they remembered the shift to a more experiential faith, when spirituality took on a new depth of meaning, or contrariwise, when religion as a cultural form lost its force for them. Stories were told about how the spiritual had aroused their moral consciences. Hearing these stories, we were reminded of the place in religious research of the concepts and dichotomies proposed by religious scholars for grasping how the imaginal and inspirational often erupt within, and then break out of, institutional routines: Otto's category of "the numinous," Eliade's "hierophanies" and "theophanies," Victor Turner's "liminality" in contrast to "structure," Martin Buber's "I-Thou" replacing the "I-It," and William James's "first-hand" religious experience as distinct from institutionally mediated "second-hand" religion.

How are we to understand this fluidity, this dialectic of movement and fixity, in its broader social and cultural context? The question prompts reflection beyond the purely psychological on several fronts. One is that modern life erodes many boundaries that once better contained people and encourages adhesional impulses, leading even the most faithful to sort out what they really believe and what else they are curious about or searching to understand. In this case, faith and quest often turn out to mirror one another: faith turning into quest, and quest leading to faith. Communal identities often have staying power when faith is weak. Faith for many Americans, not just Boomers, involves little more than streamlined belief in a rather generic God, a doctrine widely held that can nonetheless be rather weightless and not very engaging. Overarching meaning systems, logically ordered and consistent, may be described in textbooks describing the world's religions, but the operative symbolic universes for people are often not so well-defined, certainly not in the modern world; instead, many people are drawn to "religious fragments" of the sort that Reginald Bibby speaks of when he describes how modernity pushes people in the direction of consuming religious symbols, beliefs, and practices selectively.[37] People adopt a particular belief or ritual practice precisely because it offers something to hold on to, without the need to fashion an integrated, or fully coherent view of oneself or of religion. Fragmentation might be thought of in one sense as the breakdown of a faith tradition, yet as Bibby points out, fragments have positive features: they work in a complex and pluralist society to reduce role tensions and, more to the present point, they make possible easy movement from one social role or psychological frame to another in what amounts to a "multiple-option" society. In this respect fluidity makes for psychological adjustment and adaptability to a highly differentiated society. In Martin E. Marty's words:

> Religion serves both to pocket people in enclaves, as in the case of the Amish, the Unification Church, Orthodox Judaism, the Nation of Islam, fundamentalisms, or high-churched Anglicanism, *and* to help people engage in criss-crossing between these subcultures. Thus at one moment being an *African American* Baptist defines a person, and a moment later, in a different context, being an African American *Baptist* is the vital identifier. Being a Catholic *feminist* counts for one set of questions, and being a *Catholic* feminist helps account in the case of another.[38]

Second, this fluidity is reinforced not just by multiple roles and social contexts but by a mass-produced religious culture. Religious themes reflect popular ideologies and cultural motifs of the time, such as in the 1950s when the Cold War encouraged strong American religious identities, or as happened in the 1960s, when many new religions and mystical faiths came to be more accepted. And in our own day, given how quest and spiritually infused themes and imageries permeate secular life (when advertisements for selling cars emphasize "Driving is Believing" and Viagra, the sex pill, is marketed as offering middle-aged men "new horizons of experience") the exploratory and creative dimensions of the sacred gain broad social support at the expense of traditional religious discourse). Vicki Feinstein expresses a similar cultural outlook: "One day I woke up and wondered: maybe today I should be a Christian, or would I rather be a Buddhist, or am I just a Star Trek freak?" Not that she has been any of these in any serious way, but she can *imagine* what it would be like being them; she possesses a mental mobility that allows her considerable freedom to put herself into one or another of these frames, even if it is more a "virtual reality" than what we take to be reality. American life encourages a popular religious imagination that breaks through existing boundaries. Even within traditions as different historically as Evangelical Christianity and the metaphysical teachings known as New Thought, trends in the late twentieth century encourage a convergence of themes. Practically, these traditions have been drawn closer together, partly as a result of the upward mobility of Evangelicals into the middle class, but also because of the spread of popular teachings on positive thinking, economic prosperity, and mental well-being by religious leaders like Norman Vincent Peale ("Think big, pray big, believe big, act big," he exhorted in one of his sermons). Today Evangelicals face the same psychological adjustments to modern life as do all other middle-class Americans, such as finding happiness, dealing with insecurities and anxieties, overcoming abuses and addictions, and coping with life. Pressures on religion to address its instrumental functions, that is, what it can provide, such as peace of mind, happiness, and comfort push toward greater functional similarity, no matter what the tradition or its historic theological or cultural distinctiveness. Commenting on this convergence some years ago, religious scholar Richard Quebedeaux wrote: "If revivalistic Christianity offered an experiential soul cure to the poor and would-be rich, New Thought offered peace of mind and emotional tranquility to those already on the way up. Salvation was mentalized."[39]

Further, the religious suppliers catering to contemporary spirituality help to create conditions for religious fluidity by using similar vocabularies and drawing on common imageries. Bible-study guides, New Age newsletters, promotions on self-help books, web pages on the Internet portraying the teachings of Jesus, the Buddha, and other spiritual masters, mailings describing churches and synagogues and what they have to offer—all can be remarkably alike in how they pitch their appeal. Social pressures and technology push in the direction of standardizing religious and spiritual themes. Both commercial and scholarly efforts go into creating "spiritual inventories" with items focused on activities, behaviors, and thought processes commonly associated with spirituality, which has the effect of enhancing levels of self-consciousness, of course, but also of eliminating those beliefs and practices that might in any way offend a particular religious constituency.[40] Not to be overlooked either is the "mainstreaming" of spiritual themes in recent years. Consider spirituality and health: when *Civilization*, the magazine of the Library of Congress, and the *Harvard Health Letter* carry stories on "alternative therapies" and "making a place for spirituality," respectively, clearly this is indication of the widespread appeal of such ideas and of a regularizing of themes related to prayer, meditation, and holistic healing in relation to more scientific medical approaches.[41] The fact that an Office for Alternative Medicine is now housed and funded in the National Institute of Health further legitimates and systematizes a rapidly changing paradigm of health, religion, and spirituality.

Within religious communities, there is considerable blending of popular spiritual and healing discourses. There is a mixing of Evangelical

Christian as well as New Thought and metaphysical codes, imageries, and practices.[42] Such codes, imageries, and practices depict differing answers to religious questions yet frame questions and answers in ways that are often quite consistent. Generally presumed is a culturally defined conception of a freely choosing, expressive individual, one who can marshal resources from various places and takes as almost axiomatic that an individual has an obligation—to oneself and to her own well-being first and foremost. Sam Wong admits as much when he says that his experience in Campus Crusade for Christ as a student continues to influence his thinking about his "journey to find Christ and all He can mean to me." His pastor at the time, trained in counseling psychology and taught by his sponsoring organization to relate faith to student questions, was well equipped to form Christian identities in a quest environment. The sheer demographic fact of so much movement in and out of congregations is an important factor as well. Clergy try to relate to spiritual nomads with sermons sensitive to their experiences in a world of rapid and fast movement. Even if a church knows that few of these mobile-minded people are likely to join and stick around, appeals to such identity themes make sense. A pastor of a middle-class church on the West Side of Los Angeles told us: "Our people are transient. We self-consciously style our ministry to meet the needs of people for the few years they are here. They come, they go." His comment reflects recognition of the realities of geographic, social, and mental mobility, and the need for modeling the Christian faith to the adaptable lifestyles of people on the move.

Broadening the Interpretation

Thomas J. Csordas, the anthropologist of contemporary culture, speaks of the "religions of the self," pointing out that the emphasis on subjective transformation, or internal psychological movement, intersects with three conditions of the world in which we now live: one, the dissociation of symbols from their referents allowing for the free play of signifiers; two, the decentering of authority in meaning, discourse, and social form; and three, the globalization of culture along with consumerization and the information glut. "Not only the self, but a particular form of self," he writes, "takes precedence" under such conditions.[43] In his research on Catholic Charismatics, Csordas argues that the primary goal of this religious movement is the subjective transformation of its followers in response to changing social conditions. He sees in its ritual language and performance an enormous outpouring of spiritual creativity, literally a transformation of self and habitus made possible through practice. This is not quite the same as the "shifting centers of energy" envisioned by William James and resulting in a unitary conception of psychological stability and wholeness; instead, with Csordas we have a more radical conception of transformation involving a multiplicity of meanings and a reordering of the self on the basis of selective image, rhetoric, and symbol. His is a postmodern vision of an oversupply of signs and the breakdown of boundaries between symbolic forms whose referents are no longer stable, and of a resulting medley of heterglossic voices. It is an extreme vision of the breakdown of contemporary religious culture, and fitting only to its extremes. Csordas's perspective sheds more light on Vicki Feinstein and her eclectic spiritual searching than on the other characters profiled in Chapter 1, all of whom are more grounded than she. If we think of his vision as analogous to an ideal-type, that is, as a sensitizing construct which stands in varying degrees of approximation to the empirical world, then we can better appreciate what it might tell us, and perhaps even recognize themes in the other characters that are elucidated by it. Fluidity always stands in some relation to groundedness, or creativity as over against constraint; and, as a variable feature it offers enormous insight into the current religious climate in the United States.

Almost a hundred years ago, Ernst Troeltsch anticipated the rise of a mystical religious style characterized, more than anything else, by fluidity and an ambiguous relationship with institutions—resulting from the larger transformations of both self and religion in the Western world. Mystical religion was known for its "direct, inward and present religious experience."[44] Distinct from either sectarian or churchly varieties of religion, this "third type" of religious consciousness would become, he predicted, increasingly common because of the confrontations of religion with modernity. He envisioned a decline in institutional authority, growing religious and cultural pluralism, increased individualism, and an affinity between mysticism and individualism.[45] Mysticism favors a monistic conception of reality, much the same as James saw happening with the alignment of spiritual emotions and the resulting psychological integration. A unified worldview arising out of mystical experience is not burdened with the dualisms, for example, mind versus body, that are so much a part of modern, fragmented culture. Mysticism encourages a universal religious consciousness, or a more relative stance toward religious truth, and accepts the possibility that truth can be found in many places and experiences. It focuses on what is subjectively real and the force of myth, symbol, fantasy, and metaphor in religious interpretation.

For Troeltsch, mysticism could be thought of in two basic senses. Psychologist Ralph W. Hood comments on them as follows: "In one sense, mysticism is simply a profound, primary religious awareness of the transcendent reality that serves as a human experiential basis for religious institutions and dogmas. Such a mysticism is compatible with almost any dogma or structure and is simply the existential foundation that religion molds into its various social forms. As such it has no unique sociological importance." He continues: "In another sense, mysticism as a separate form emerges historically as a deliberate cultivated act of transcendence, often rising in opposition to established religious institutions, if not independently of them. As such, it is an independent religious form, distinct from both church and sect."[46]

Mysticism in the first sense, then, functions within a tradition to keep it alive, to recharge its batteries, whereas in the second sense, mysticism is less bounded and more free-floating. Crucial is whether mystical awareness and enthusiasm are "religiously interpreted," and thus formative of tradition itself, or whether such awareness and enthusiasm result from a "deliberately cultivating" of the reality of God, or of the sacred, and largely independent of traditional dogma and sacraments. This latter notion overlaps with James's concept of the "transport" that triggers religious emotions and experiences through ritual practices and may, though not necessarily, involve deliberate effort on the part of an individual trying to make them happen. And clearly, the "new entrepreneurs" we have described are of both types, some working to regenerate individuals from within religious establishments drawing largely off internal symbolic resources, others outside of these establishments in parachurch groups, alternative organizations, or loosely knit spiritual networks drawing off a much broader repertoire of symbolic resources. But in either instance, deliberate efforts at revitalizing spiritual life involve what we have defined as a key feature of the contemporary religious situation—its greater reflexivity.

Looking at American religious life through Troeltschean lenses, our attention is drawn to several of its currently important tensions between personal religious experience and its institutional expression; between "religiously based spirituality" as found within the religious establishment and the less-structured styles of "free-floating spirituality" outside of it; and between individual subjectivity and history, tradition, and community that begs the issue of whether a disembodied spirituality effectively cut off from symbol, myth, and community can last for long. These are all problematic issues for religion at the turn of the century, and matters that figure prominently in any thorough analysis of current trends. Thus, whether as inferred from Troeltsch's perspective or from Csordas's more radical postmodern vision, the spiritual dynamics of the self are extraordinarily complex. It is even more complex still. For despite all that we have said about spirituality as an individual matter, it involves meanings, symbols, practices, and processes born out of, and shaped by, communal life and the confrontations of modernity and religious tradition; and for this reason, spirituality cannot be thought of simply as a matter of individual choice. This latter problematic lies at the very heart of the religious situation today and must be analyzed carefully if we are to grasp the major types of spiritual quests now emerging. It is to this problematic that we now turn, one that by any reckoning in modern, pluralistic society, is challenging to grasp.

CHAPTER 5

A Quest for What?

The unity of a human life is the unity of a narrative quest.
Quests sometimes fail, are frustrated, abandoned or dissipated
into distractions . . . the only criteria for success or failure in a
human life as a whole are the criteria of success or failure in
a narrated or to-be-narrated quest. A quest for what?
(*Alasdair MacIntyre*)

Pollster George Gallup, Jr., made headline news in 1978 when he reported that eight out of ten Americans agreed with the statement that "an individual should arrive at his or her own religious beliefs independent of any churches or synagogues."[1] On a related item, he found that almost the same number agreed that "a person can be a good Christian or Jew if he or she doesn't attend church or synagogue." With national figures hovering around 80 percent on both items, virtually any major subgroup of Americans—men or women, southerners or nonsoutherners, old or young—would necessarily possess high levels of what at the time was labeled "religious individualism." From our vantage point today, such individualism is not all that surprising, accustomed as we are to widespread choice and diversity in religious life; but two decades ago the Gallup report had an ominous ring about it. Individualism, so it seemed, had reached hitherto unknown levels among rank-and-file Americans. Or it might be said, the public was confronted with its individualism in a way that was deeply revealing. The tension of trying to be fluid while simultaneously being grounded appeared to have reached a breaking point—fluidity had triumphed, even in the realm of the sacred. Not surprisingly, the Gallup poll findings provoked a great deal of public discussion: What was the future of organized religion if people were themselves deciding about matters of belief and practice rather than respecting the authority of religious institutions? Was religious community falling apart? People still believed in God, even prayed and said grace before meals in substantial numbers, but were we becoming a country of "believers but not belongers"?

The questions had a pressing urgency at the time. A young generation of Americans born after World War II who reached maturity in the 1960s and early 1970s, especially those college-educated, had rebelled against institutional authority. As we have seen, the culturally established bourgeois faiths especially felt the brunt of that rebellion. Questions were being raised not just about moral and lifestyle issues, but about what to believe, what is sacred, and the nature of religious authority. The rallying cry was to turn inward, to look to one's own experience for guidance and truth. Spirituality was a word increasingly being voiced, but it was not at all clear where, if anywhere, interest in the interior life might lead. Eastern religions represented a visible alternative, but, despite lots of media attention, they never really were a big draw as judged by self-reported followings of new religious movements; even the Jesus Movement with its flower-child innocence and visionary fervor, which brought Evangelical and Charismatic Christianity to growing numbers of young people, was thought by many mainline Protestants, Catholics, and Jews at the time to be a poor substitute.[2] Both seemed strange, unpredictable, and hopefully a temporary phenomenon as viewed through the eyes of mainliners. But more worrisome than either the "new religions" or the hippie Christianity of the period for many, was the growing spirit of independence on the part of believers in virtually every tradition. Turning inward meant people were making their own religious decisions, questioning authority, and holding themselves up as the final arbiters of what to believe or practice. As one interviewee said, speaking for many of his generation, "I no longer looked to any church for what to believe. I could think for myself, believe for myself. Why not?" Behind so simple and straightforward a question lies a much more perplexing question, What is the relation of the individual to religious narrative, to community and tradition?

SHEILAISM

The question drew a good deal of attention in the 1980s among sociologists of religion. *Habits of the Heart,* the book written by Berkeley sociologist Robert Bellah and his associates, published in 1985, zeroed in on this very question, provoking considerable discussion among scholars, religious leaders, and civic officials. From the very first pages of the book, the authors expressed alarm that individualism was becoming increasingly "cancerous to American society."[3] They worried not just about organized religion but about the family, political participation, community involvement, and public life. Individualism had reached such alienating proportions, they feared, that the bonds of civic community might be threatened; particularly insidious they thought, was the rampant "expressive individualism," which combined with the historic "utilitarian individualism" of American culture, could well pose serious concern about the future of the nation's social institutions. They looked at the language of individualism, arguing that it was at odds with, and was helping to undermine, the language of community and shared memory. Its heavy price was a loss of commitment—to marriage and family, to religious and political institutions, to civic participation. At the very center of this discussion were worries especially about a younger generation of Americans who were rapidly making entry into the adult world at the time— the self-preoccupied, ambitious "Me Generation," as its members came to be called during those years. Other commentators writing before *Habits* was published had likewise expressed alarm about an increasing subjectivity expressed variously as "narcissism," "the fall of public man," and "civic privatism," often drawing character examples from the post– World War II generation.[4] In scholarly as well as religious quarters, there was heightened concern that cultural changes were mounting which, should they continue to spread, might threaten the moral fabric and institutional structures that had formed the country.

Much evidence in the mid 1980s did in fact suggest that the nation's social institutions were facing severe challenges: divorce rates had reached extraordinarily high levels, loyalties to religious denominations and faith communities were declining, attachments to local community were weakened by high rates of geographic and social mobility, and participation in voluntary associations was down. The civic culture was deeply fractured in the aftermath of racial struggles and the Vietnam War. Against a backdrop of the more stable period at midcentury, the social and cultural upheavals of the 1960s and early 1970s all loomed large, prompting concerns about an uncertain future. Many young Americans, including record numbers of young women, were entering the labor force. Their energies went into work and careers. Women particularly, with more opportunities to work outside the home, had less time for family, volunteer work, and religious activities than had young women of earlier times. A gender revolution, modern contraception, and the expansion of higher education all contributed to a greater freedom of choice in lifestyles and family planning. People were postponing marriage, and if married, postponing having children, both of which served to delay involvement in community and religious activities. Flourishing was a young adult culture that was turned inward on itself, focused around lifestyle, career, and pursuit of the individual's own personal freedom, epitomized best in the stereotypes of upscale, material-minded Yuppies and DINKS, the double-income couples with no kids. Though they represented an exceedingly small proportion of the total young population, they provided flashy imagery for television programs and popular magazines; while widely celebrated in their own circles, they were critiqued in other segments of the society. A culture known for youth-orientation, materialism, and self-focus for fully two decades now awakened to an adult profile, albeit stereotypical, that it had created.

This culture of choice seemed particularly troubling in the religious realm. In *Habits of the Heart*, readers were introduced to a young nurse, Sheila Larson, whose description of her own deeply personal style of religiosity—which she designated as "Sheilaism"—was held up as an example of this new-style religious individualism. Sheilaism would quickly become a household word among religious leaders, journalists, and sociologists, who saw in her a worrisome image of the future. Sheila understood religion to be an inward reflection about knowing herself, essentially independent of any involvement within a church, synagogue, or any other religious organization. At the most charitable level, she represented the deeply ingrained view of great numbers of Americans who look upon what to believe as the primary choice an individual must make, the secondary one being the decision whether to join a particular religious group. Affiliation follows a decision about faith. Even people deeply rooted in a faith tradition from the time they were children are likely to think of themselves as personally responsible for their religious affiliations. But Sheilaism was something more, a view explicitly and unashamedly focused around the self; Sheila herself spoke of her own "little voice" and of the realizations about life that come from listening to that voice. Privileged in her conception of religion was the inward, deeply personal dimension. Commenting on this highly subjective understanding of religion, the authors concluded that it involved "a kind of radical individualism that tends to elevate the self to a cosmic principle."[5] As such, her self-designated religion and its inwardly focused style raised serious questions about religious authority, about self and God, about the individual and community. As might be expected, Sheilaism was a lightning rod for those who saw in her and related kin a threat to, if not the demise of, organized religion.

148

Whereas the book brought attention to a significant aspect of American religious culture, much of the public discussion of Sheilaism was disappointing. Its focus was greatly one-sided, far more concerned about the health of institutions than of individuals. Sheila Larson became something of a caricature, an example of how religious individualism was undermining institutional commitment in our time. She was held up as the personification of Gallup's trends toward greater personal autonomy, of where religious freedom in the absence of community was taking the nation. Even though in *Habits* the authors went to some length to show that Sheila was a "perfectly natural expression" of American religious life, she fared much more poorly at the hands of less sympathetic critics. Largely overlooked were Sheila's experiences as a woman trying to come to terms with herself in an age of changing gender roles and feminist ideology. That she was unmarried was seldom pointed out, even though it is well-known that religious affiliation is closely intertwined with marriage and family structure. Even the possibility that she might be in a transitional phase of her life seemed not to matter. Dismissed were her religious views arising out of her experiences as a nurse, someone who faced human suffering every day and talked openly about mystical religious moments she experienced on the job. That she might be struggling to arrive at a relationship with a benevolent God in the midst of suffering, caught up in her own Job-like drama, went largely unnoticed. More generally, remarkably little attention was given to the fact that a Sheila-like expressive culture now generates, paradoxically, both highly individualistic spiritual quests outside of church, synagogue, and temple *and* deep experiential expressions of faith within religious communities, most notably within Pentecostalism, Evangelicalism, and the Charismatic movements. Commentators neglected the possibility that Sheilaism might be part of a larger religious and cultural pattern increasingly visible both inside and outside the religious establishments. Most telling perhaps, the possibility that Sheila's turning inward after an oppressively conformist earlier life might actually be *spiritually rejuvenating* was lost on religious leaders and most scholars as well. So little attention to this latter is surprising considering that breaking away from external religious authorities is seen by many feminist scholars as the first step on the part of women toward taking moral and spiritual responsibility for oneself; individualism might conceivably be a means of positive self-assertion and inner discovery, the cultivation of self—indeed, an instance of what we are calling "reflexive spirituality."[6]

The Crux of the Matter

Historically, individualism has been a noticeable feature of religious life in the United States. Alexis de Tocqueville, in his visit here in the 1830s, was very struck with the voluntary character of American religion and how easily people moved from one faith to another. "Voluntarism," as this quality of religious life came to be called, was seen as crucial to understanding religion's role and significance. For there was a paradox in that, on the one hand, people were highly individualistic, which might reasonably lead to religious abandonment, yet on the other hand, they were remarkably religious in so many ways. Tocqueville, as well as other visitors to this country, puzzled over this situation. How could this be? Would not individualism undermine shared faith and practice? Would not democracy undermine religious authority? But Tocqueville was hopeful since in this country, he observed, religion and democracy march together rather than at odds with one another. Democracy opens up opportunities for religion and, in turn, religion that is free and voluntary can use those opportunities, find ways of responding creatively to them. "Thus it is," wrote Tocqueville, "that by respecting all democratic tendencies not absolutely contrary to herself, and by making use of several of them for her own purposes, religion sustains a successful struggle with that spirit of individual independence which is her most dangerous opponent."[7] At the time of his writing, he could conclude that religion sustained a successful struggle with individualism by means of institutional adaptation and innovative ways of reaching people. The key to success was in redefining the religious message to fit the times, new organizational structures, and energetic proselytizing. But that was the 1830s. What of the year 2000? Is religion still powerful and creative enough to wage a successful struggle with individualism as we know it today?

These are difficult questions, more so now than in Tocqueville's day. More is involved than innovative methods for carrying the religious message to people or the adaptation of religious institutions to democratic conditions. Religion's relation to the wider culture must itself be considered. In Tocqueville's time, religion was largely "socially inherited," that is, it was passed down through families, and thus rather firmly linked to social class, regional cultures, ethnicity, and local community. Religion's social location meant that it was positioned to exercise considerable influence in reinforcing self-control and defining moral standards. That

would remain pretty much intact up until the 1920s, but after the so-
called "second disestablishment" that occurred about that time and
its greater religious pluralism, and certainly after the "third disestablishment" of the 1960s and its greater subjectivism, or internalized pluralism, religion had become more and more a matter of individual
preference.[8] Religion's powers to sustain a self, anchored within community, and to counter the corrosive influences of an increasingly mass-
produced cultural individualism were unquestionably weakened. With
declining solidarities of family, class, ethnicity, and community, religion's social-integrative potential was greatly diminished. But how diminished? And with what consequences for individuals and society?

Scholarly responses to these questions vary. Sociologist Phillip E.
Hammond argues that there was a decisive cultural turn, a "shift in the
meaning of the church from that of a collective-expressive agency to that
of an individual-expressive agency."[9] He sees the increased personal autonomy as bringing about a major alteration in the relationship between
organized religion and culture and an inevitable loss of religious cus-
todianship over core values. Bellah and his associates fall short of so
sweeping a claim, preferring instead to treat Sheilaism as a contemporary religious and cultural text and to use her religious style as basis for
a conversation about individualism and its impact on institutions. They
see themselves as fostering a public debate, hopefully resulting in the
renewal of core institutional attachments, but clearly they worry that if
trends toward fragmentation and privatism continue, religiously based
voluntary associations will lose what remains of their socially integrative
power. In the tradition of Tocqueville, these scholars are concerned with
the broader societal implications of changing styles of religiosity and,
particularly, whether institutional religion today has sufficient standing
to counter the massive influences of the media, of privatizing religious
trends, and powerful economic realities. They have less to say about the
individuals themselves, about what the trends might mean for personal
belief and well-being. Other scholars focus more on the moral and religious texture of people's lives in this current situation. In particular,
Robert Wuthnow explores narrative accounts of people's life-experiences and looks at ways in which individualism creates a variety of responses bearing on religious communities, acts of charity, use of money,
volunteering in service organizations, and moral and ethical values generally. His conclusions from a number of quite different studies point to
a thick religio-moral context, an embedded individualism that takes on
rich and multiple meanings in relation to personal and social commit-

ments. He leaves open possibilities for social institutions, religious and otherwise, and for the role of faith communities in society, though his is far from a dispassionate analysis and not without a tone of alarm at times about disturbing trends now on the horizons.[10]

My own position is akin to Wuthnow's insofar as it seems advisable to problematize the relation of religion and culture and to leave open institutional adaptations and responses. Rather than focus on a core religious culture and deviations from it, the approach here is to identify new religious subcultures now emerging and to look for "cutting-edge" developments within these subcultures. This makes for a more varied picture of the American religious terrain and recognizes not just religion's adaptability in a psychologically oriented culture but also its creative potential. Individualism is more than a one-way influence shaping styles of institutional commitment; it also opens up new possibilities for religious institutions and changing modes of personal commitment. Self-reflexivity is itself a potent aspect of modern individualism. Attention to its dynamics in contemporary life cautions against hasty generalizations or glossing over religion's rich terrain, especially in a setting where historically belief, practice, and religious identities have proved to be so variable and where religious and cultural moods often ebb and flow. It has been said that religion in America is "bumptious,"[11] that it has a quality of reasserting itself in unexpected ways, of taking new forms, of resisting containment within old boundaries. Now as in the past, religion presents itself in paradoxical ways—as socially inherited but as individually creative, as institutional but as anti-institutional, as highly privatized but in other ways deprivatized. Assuming this to be the case, the pressing task would seem to be, first, to sort out these paradoxical themes and then, second, after carefully surveying the contemporary religious terrain, to debate about the broader connections of religion and society.

SORTING OUT THE THEMES

The massive social transformations straining individual ties with tradition comprise the dominant force shaping the quest culture, but the historic context in which this occurs should not be overlooked. In many respects such culture today is an elaboration, or a working out, of a peculiarly American religious theme. Long before the human potential or self-help movements of recent times galvanized spiritual quests, there were the Theosophical, New Thought, and Transcendentalist movements, all of which placed great emphasis on the inner life and possibilities for its transformation, on mystical and harmonial experiences, and on the psychic frontiers of the mind. These latter movements, remarkably optimistic about the individual's own power to shape his or her own fate, emphasized the connection between the self and the universe and the divine spark within every individual, themes that all meshed well with the American spirit of freedom and self-reliance. Such themes were, and still are, reinforced by a dynamic, mobile American population—geographically, socially, and more narrowly psychological. So much movement across physical space and social class lines, and into the interior life all helped to form a normative spiritual style that is fluid and malleable, and capable of moving easily from one frame of reference to another. And likewise, Evangelical Christianity historically held up the promise of a richer life for those who would take Jesus into their hearts, a promise expressed directly to individuals who recognized their own need for salvation. Evangelical religion in the nineteenth century, as Nathan Hatch reminds us, both "democratized" the United States and "was democratized" as the religion of the people,[12] which in operative religious terms meant that every American Christian must have, above all else, his or her own encounter with Jesus, nothing less than a personal experience of "being saved" or "born again." No matter what the denomination or even if there was a denomination, whether churchgoer or not, the subjective world of the American was—and remains—a space open and spiritually revisable. To be American was to allow for cognitive and experiential shifts, to make and remake religious worlds.

This process of remaking religion need not be viewed as an erosion, as secularization, although this may appear to be the case. What may look like defection is often a temporary disengagement or dissent, hardly a full-fledged break with a personal faith or with institutionalized religious ideals. There is considerable "upward" religious movement in the status hierarchy of religious groups, which on the surface may appear to be a secular accommodation. Carefully analyzed, however, the evidence on religious switching, or the movement from one denomination or faith community to another, is disproportionately positive—that is, religious switchers tend to be serious about their decisions. As judged by various survey indicators, those who choose a religion typically are more committed than those who were born into the same religion.[13] Looking at movement into and out of religious groups, we find that most people who drop out at one time or another and then return to the group they left behind, or join a new group, do so at a higher level of commitment.

Even committed people who move to a new place of residence and affiliate with a congregation within the same religious denomination or tradition often report being challenged by a new setting. "We moved to Concord and finally found a parish that we liked," a Catholic man in Massachusetts told us. "I'm more involved now than ever before in my life." Asked further about his comment, he added, "Something about us and this place clicked." Landscapes, or settings, are intrinsically important to lived religion; the chemistry between people and community, between believers and a particular set of stimuli, remains a powerful source of energy.

Much energy is expended in creative realignments of belief and practice by individuals on the move, and there is also a corresponding energy on the part of religious and spiritual leaders attempting to reach people in their new settings. "People have to be won over and over again as they move geographically and as they change their class orientations and find different aspirations for themselves,"[14] one analyst observes, emphasizing that religious groups in a dynamic society must, if they are to survive, posture themselves primarily to dynamic people. More than just psychological readjustment, religious groups must assist people addressing notions of self and God in a new environment. Overall geographical movement and social mobility may have receded somewhat in the 1990s, but psychological energy born out of changing personal circumstances, aspirations, and soul-searching continues, maybe even more so, as a creative force reshaping people's religious narratives. It is a major factor generating a dynamic spiritual marketplace: encouraging people to adapt their spiritual views in ways that are fulfilling and empowering; to reclaim aspects of their lives that are underdeveloped or neglected; and, perhaps most important of all, to insist that they themselves must take charge of their own personal well-being. Because of so widespread a cultural mood at present, Christian Evangelical and New Age movements within the United States, despite obvious differences, share many themes: an emphasis on direct experience, physical and emotional healing, personal and social transformation, the democracy of believers and of followers, expectation of future change, a deeply based quest for wholeness.[15]

Viewed from this vantage point, we can see in William James's classic *Varieties of Religious Experience* a definition of religion that reflects so well an embedded American religious sensibility: *the feelings, acts, and experiences of individual men in their solitude, so far as they apprehend themselves to stand in relation to whatever they may consider the divine.* He further added that the relation may be "moral, physical, or ritual," giving religion a broad primordial grounding, and that out of this relation with the divine, "theologies, philosophies, and ecclesiastical organizations may secondarily grow." By looking at religion not in terms of an object (God or the universe) but as it appears in the subject, and in its shifting centers of energy and breadth of psychological movements—believing, doubting, practicing, experiencing, struggling—James established an affinity with the ordinary mysticism that pervades American life. So many of his themes are quintessentially American, and very much so, Boomer American: *pragmatism,* or the recognition that the religious experiences that make a difference are the ones that are self-authenticating; *pluralism,* or the reality of cosmological and theological diversity; *supply,* or appreciation for the vast spiritual resources affirming life, health, energy, power, and harmony; *religious experience,* or stress on how personal energy is mobilized and subject to its many centers; *moral transformation,* or the expectation of spiritual energy flowing and producing effects; *personal struggle,* or the conflict inherent between a morality of mastery and control and a spirituality of letting go; and *personal growth,* or the possibility of a healthy-mindedness that comes with overcoming divisions within the self and achieving a harmonious relation with the universe. James captured national mood and sentiment, and by articulating them, in turn helped to shape an American ethos with a vocabulary of religious speech that pervades, yet supercedes life inside organized religion.

Contemporary literary critic Harold Bloom echoes much the same when he speaks of an "American Religion" that teaches a purely inner freedom as its defining Gnostic-like characteristic.[16] By this he means that Americans typically find God in themselves and that in one reading of the situation, salvation is understood less as an experience within a communal context than as a reality of the individual's own innermost world. Many religious leaders and theologians take issue with Bloom's claim, but anyone who has ever attended a Southern Baptist revival or observed carefully how the invitation to accept Jesus at a Billy Graham Crusade is pitched to the televised audience (often to the lonely person sitting in a bar) knows that "accepting Jesus in your heart," wherever you are and whatever you are doing, is the message. Certainly we can say that revivalistic themes historically, along with Theosophical and New Thought teachings, blended to create a popular style of religious individualism that has touched almost every faith tradition, sometimes explicitly and identifiably, but more often than not only vaguely. For the great mass of American Christians other than Evangelicals, including

Roman Catholics, religious authority lies to a considerable extent in the individual believer—rather than in the church or the Bible. No matter the religious background, Americans are socialized into this heritage of privileging the individual and her encounters with the divine; it is the shape of faith born out of a mix of democracy, pluralism, and the operative principles of conscience stemming from the constitutional separation of church and state. Historian Catherine L. Albanese sums up this cultural complex in a simple phrase: "In the beginning was God—and the individual."[17]

Sociologists, far more inclined to look to shared faiths, institutions, and communities, are less likely to appreciate this aspect of American religious life. James, Bloom, and others of their persuasion are criticized for overlooking the collective and institutional dimensions of religion. Yet if we look at operative religious styles, and if indeed our aim is to get at the underlying American ethos and how it filters religious experience, we cannot dismiss the influence of individualism on the way people relate to religious groups. After the largest private survey on religious identification ever conducted in the United States had interviewed 113,000 Americans in 1990, sociologists Barry A. Kosmin and Seymour P. Lachman conclude: "For most, religion means a personal affirmation of faith in God and an identification with a religious denomination, but it does not necessarily mean joining or being an active member of that particular group. It is more of a private commitment than a shared experience."[18]

Religion as private commitment is even less bounded than institutional affiliation makes it appear: it involves multiple motives, disengagements and re-engagements, mixes and matches of spiritual themes. This recognition of the profoundly private character of American faith need not be interpreted as negative; to the contrary, it is a testimony of the depths of commitment and potential awareness of the divine as revealed in the overwhelming numbers of Americans who, whether regular participants in religious institutions or not, believe in God, report praying regularly, and say they believe that God loves them. This belief among so many Americans that God loves them is powerful: if one believes that he or she is loved by God, then the task becomes coming to terms with that love, either accepting that love as coming from a God external to the self, or seeking to know that love deep within one's own inwardness. Whether it is in the redemptive theology and idiom of walking alone with Jesus as found in conservative Protestantism, or in the language of American Catholics who prefer to go their own way in defiance of what

Rome dictates, or in the way mainline Protestants talk about their religious convictions in terms of doing good and not harming others, or in the words of Emersonian self-reliance and of the voice of the god within the self, the message is clear: for rank-and-file Americans, religion is deeply personal, not just in the obvious psychological sense but theologically and metaphysically. This bears in several ways on our understanding of the self in relation to religious community, to which we now give attention.

Self-Authentication

Throughout Western history, an upgrading of the individual's role meant the emancipation of faith from ascriptive loyalties—to family, to ethnic group, even to religious background—meaning that what a person *chooses*, rather than what one is born into, becomes decisive. With the Reformation particularly, the individual was singled out as needing salvation and having direct accountability to God. Individual choice and responsibility were held intact, however, since for centuries religious decisions were mediated in communal contexts. But today, this older framework of the responsible "person-in-relation-to-God" has lost some of its long-standing hold, while the notion that the individual is freed from the tutelage of religious institutions and therefore fully enfranchised for making religious decisions is widely accepted. The two in combination enhance self-responsibility, but also in the present cultural climate another theme is introduced: self-authentication. For Americans, this means that one can—indeed, one ought to—choose how to engage the religious question, that is, how to think about believing and practicing, on the basis of one's own deepest spiritual sensibilities. Thus, for contemporaries, "lived religion"—as opposed to official doctrines and rituals—increasingly encompasses a continuous, self-conscious process of narrative construction, born out of a sense of life's open-endedness and unexpected possibilities. The popularization of traditional Judeo-Christian symbols and teachings combined with the expressive individualism of recent times tend to intensify the subjective, expansionary character of religious life.

Given these trends, people increasingly look upon their spiritual life as an arena they control. The quest for self-fulfillment emanating out of the 1960s unleashed a powerful aspiration to "free" oneself from whatever constraints were limiting and to open up greater possibilities for the democratization of emotions and deeply based commitments. These aspirations have found expression in one after another liberationist or justice-oriented movement, most notably the women's and gay rights movements. But beyond this, there is a hankering for something more than the gods of narcissism, materialism, self-fulfillment, and even liberation ultimately can provide. Such search involves, as Peter Clecak persuasively argues, "the hope, to recall a phrase from the Gospel of John, of a more 'abundant life' characterized by an individual's opportunity to define and enact possibilities of feeling and mind as freely and as fully as possible."[19] Abundance as popularly conceived has connotations of a "spiritual supply" that resonates with Americans who like to think that plenty, not poverty, is their inheritance as spiritual children of God.[20] Not only do they want, they feel entitled to experiences that lead to fuller interior lives and to tapping their potential of "feeling and mind." Secular culture encourages this expectation, and the antinomian tendencies in particular, with their appeal to the authority of conscience, find affinity with this enlivened sense of freedom. But more so than anything else, as Clecak argues, it is the Judeo-Christian metaphor of salvation that still delineates the hopes and desires of millions of Americans, whether as found most vividly in the Evangelical and Charismatic faiths or more indirectly in the therapeutic expectations of wholeness and authenticity, offered through new spiritual movements but historically rooted in theological perspectives.

Yet we must not lose sight of a balance between personal freedom and institution. Fears that expressive individualism is destroying institutional loyalties are easily exaggerated and distract from its positive values for genuine religious conviction. Individualism also makes possible an affirmation of religious faith, identity, and belonging—as self-chosen. And as a result, people often possess a greater clarity of their own beliefs and metaphysical views as well as a sense of personal accountability; contrary to the view that individualism only erodes commitment, it can actually "tighten," and not just "loosen" ties to groups and institutions.[21] Internalized as one's own choice, religious decisions and practices are raised to a higher level of intentionality. Sara Caughman gives voice to this possibility when she acknowledges, "I never knew what I really believed when I was young except that in my family we all were Methodist, and we just went to church because it was the thing to do." Now having become engaged in her own, deeply personal exploration of the Anglican tradition and knowing better what is, and is not, very nurturing spiritually, she better understands herself, her faith, and what it is about this tradition that she really likes. Embracing it as her own, she finds it means more to her. "Now I feel like I have found myself," she adds, commenting on her active involvement in her Episcopal parish. For people who have been shaken out of their old cultural faiths and forced to arrive at their own convictions, such experiences can be deeply self-authenticating. And, in turn, this often revitalizes institutional commitments.

At a time when there is much emphasis on personal transformation, it may be the case too that people who think through their commitments are more likely to embrace them with feeling and enthusiasm than are many conventional believers who have never engaged faith or metaphysics seriously. This is not unimportant considering that more and more Americans are making religious decisions on the basis of their feelings. Polls and surveys show that motivations for religious involvement are undergoing a shift: subjective factors such as whether one feels warmly accepted within a congregation or some other religious group, likes what the group stands for, or enjoys being within it now assume greater significance in the calculation of religious options, while family background, social custom, and even belief itself seem to have all receded in importance as predictors of institutional participation.[22] People who switch from one faith community to another often do so because they feel more accepted and, consequently, are likely to speak more warmly and appreciatively of their new affiliations. Feelings and inner satisfactions thus become an added force in the sifting and sorting of religious choices. "It is decreasingly satisfying to respond to a query that one has one's religion 'because that's how I was brought up,' " sociologist R. Stephen Warner says. "One is supposed to be more self-actualized than that."[23]

Subtle Consequences

But does self-actualization lead to a break with institutional religious ties? That is the conventional wisdom, but the situation is not so straightforward as it might appear. Rather than thinking of individualism as having a one-way, corrosive influence on organizational involvement, it is better viewed as having an opposing set of religious consequences. In our survey we found that high levels of religious individualism are associated with declining religiosity but are *positively* related to interest in personal spirituality.[24] If it undermines one, it intensifies the other. Often the patterns are subtle and hidden. Highly autonomous people may be less involved in conventional religious activities but they may express concern about "finding connections" and pursuing "meaning in life"— concerns that often lead to involvement in new types of structures, in loosely knit networks and informal gatherings. These are the people who drop out of organized religion because the weekly routines, for whatever reasons, fail to impact their lives, but who might show up at a church or synagogue for special workshops on Celtic spirituality, on eco-spirituality, on centering prayer, or on the Jewish renewal movement. Or they turn to special-purpose groups of one kind or another, which draw them into particular causes or concerns. Seeker churches especially target people who are open to new ways of thinking and find old ways of "doing church" boring or ineffective—and then try to pull them into fresh routines. All of this suggests that spiritual concerns can, and often do, flourish under conditions of high personal autonomy, and especially when opportunities for expression are unrestrained by custom and people feel they can participate in more open, person-to-person conversations. Religious individualism thus has a double face: *while it might erode religious involvement as conventionally defined, it can also encourage self-reflection that can lead to greater clarity of conviction, greater ethical sensitivities, and new modes of participation.*

Karen Potter is a fitting example. Were we to score her on an institutionally based religious index, clearly she would not rank very high at present. But in search of someone deeply engaged spiritually, we could hardly find anyone who illustrates better how a break in institutional ties has been both liberating and soul-sustaining. Many women, along with African Americans, Latinos, gays, lesbians, the disabled, and other so-called "lifestyle enclaves," are emotionally bonded and share identities often at odds with the sense of community perpetuated by the dominant religious traditions. Having been excluded from power throughout history, they find theological and ecclesiastical norms alien, pushed upon them. Hence, more than just to "find themselves," they feel they must create new forms of community, either within or outside of existing institutions. Their energies turn to imaging Deity in supportive ways, to new forms of social solidarity, to claiming their own power, and to creating "parallel church" structures. Commenting on the experiences of women in the 1980s and 1990s, one observer writes: "They see the institutional church as arbiter of religion, which is often not meaningful or relevant to them. Their spirituality, far more inclusive, encompasses every aspect of their lives. . . . They are deciding for themselves how best to

160

name and worship God."[25] A powerful release of energies, this new free-dom challenges existing structures to make room for new, constructive expression.

Those who decide such things for themselves break with social con-ventions, to be sure, but in another sense, they do not so much break with as embrace and celebrate core American values. By their actions they affirm the individual over the group, personal experience over in-herited creed, and self-reliance over social conformity. And to that ex-tent, they align themselves with deeply embedded ideals celebrating the individual as a responsible and caring agent. Their values and actions resonate with religious and patriotic role-models long held dear by Americans. To believe for oneself and to follow one's conscience, even if it means breaking from tradition or withstanding strong group pres-sures, are closely aligned with popular religious teachings about the di-rect relationship between people and God. To assert one's own views in matters of faith and morality as opposed to blind loyalty to institutions was, and still is, a cherished ideal on the part of most Americans. More-over, they do not just leave behind old structures, they *create* new struc-tures thought to better embody their own spiritual ideals. Emotions and subjective experience often become the basis for organizing new groups. Therefore, it is misleading to assume that a greater personal autonomy necessarily results in a decline of collective-expressive identity; the two aspects of human agency are much too intertwined, and individual agency much too unbounded to rule out the possibility for the forma-tion of new communities.

Search for Community

The link between individualism and community deserves attention from yet another angle. In a very real sense, the quest for community is a defining feature of our time, yet we do not always fully grasp the nature of the relation between the individual and community. John McRae is our favorite example in this regard. It might reasonably be argued that *because of his individualism* he found a small Eucharistic community spiri-tually meaningful: an open, voluntary stance on his part ("I was willing to try it") led him to join his fiancée in attending the group and then later influenced his decision to become more involved. Choice opened the way for a new strategy of exploring options and discovery of a com-munity that was unlike anything he had known before. Here he finds a community that functions like a religion, yet it does not immediately come to him to think of it as religious. So different is the spiritual experience of sharing with others in this setting, that he was taken by surprise during the interview when he pondered the depths of his own question—"Am I really religious?" If individualism accounts for his departure from a Presbyterian background, an argument that might readily be made, it also brought him into this new informal group and to a rediscovery of religious community. Paradoxically, cultural trends that may erode an individual's ties with one group can create conditions for attachment to another.

So many other variations of community arise out of human quests. Karen Potter finds a sharing community in her women's group; Sara Caughman has her base community within her Episcopal parish; Sam Wong is in a Bible study group and on the Internet. Through sharing with others, they create narrative accounts of who they are, and of how their lives are anchored within a larger setting: "my" story evolves into "our" story, in which case profound changes in communal loyalties and identities occur. Religious stories arise at the intersection of individual and group experiences or, as Wuthnow says, "through storytelling individuals turn their own experiences into a collective event."[26] What seems like a very personal story centering around distinctive experiences—the "burdened self" is common—becomes more deeply enmeshed as a collective story of spiritual struggle, buttressed by an affirming and emotionally supportive fellowship. Many people feel that the structures of modern society force them into narrow roles or encourage stereotypic, one-sided views of who they are, and they, too, frequently find within small groups and temporary assemblies a more elaborated sense of self. Stated differently, the appeal of such groups is that they provide a space for the whole person. So-called new identity groups representing the whole person rather than just a segmented aspect of the individual appear to be rapidly growing.[27] Generally, we are coming to realize that modernity does not necessarily erode close bonds among individuals as was once feared by social scientists; rather, as sociologist Daniel V. A. Olson says, "modernization's major impact is to increase people's *choice* of associates and affiliations. People use this choice to develop relationships with others who share important aspects of their identity."[28] The point is that sociability has not so much declined as conditions have freed human agency to develop a much broader range of social attachments and shared identities, and thereby created greater cross-pressures upon people's involvements and commitments.

But why so much quest for community today? The most persuasive reason is that the small-group movement of recent years emerged out of the breakdown of traditional support structures.[29] A weakening of families, of ethnic and religious ties, of community, and other dislocations of a highly mobile society are all factors. Networks now replace neighborhoods as a primary sphere of social interaction. Electronic communication is a medium through which a growing amount of human exchange occurs. Consequently, people find that many of their emotional and support needs go increasingly unmet; or in order to meet them, they must turn to new types of bondings and communities focused around, most notably, self-expression and nurturance, group sharing, and helping others. It may even be that the very notion of community itself is undergoing a fundamental change. For whatever reason, people seem to be more intentional and deliberate about the communities they create— they choose to "make" community, so to speak. They do so when they consciously select a congregation to join, commit themselves to spend a week with Habitat for Humanity, go on-line to share Evangelical faith with others a continent away, or participate in a goddess spirituality workshop. And these are the shared experiences that mean the most to them—as much, sometimes even more, than family experiences. Bonding becomes more a matter of choice, deeply intersubjective; and inevitably, responsibility shifts to the individual to try to shape those bonds in a meaningful, self-sustaining way for all involved. In a context where institutional orthodoxies have lost much of their hold on people, shared experiences and mutual testimony emerge as an epistemological basis for "truth" itself.[30]

One thing seems fairly certain: high levels of religious individualism do not necessarily undermine spiritual vitality. Individualism often does erode certain forms of institutionalized religious participation—usually the older, more acculturated styles that have lost touch with everyday life—but it also opens up "free space" for forming new activities and solidarities as individual proclivities evolve in a seemingly endless, kaleidoscopic fashion. Claiming and filling this fluid space is a challenging opportunity for religious leaders and the new suppliers generally that we have described. That people today are bonding more around their emotions, experiences, and yearnings need not spell the demise of traditional religious structures, but it does mean that such structures as well as any new types of spiritual movements now taking form, must accommodate, indeed, actively embrace, personal concerns in its formation of community.

"Lived Religious" Narrative

Up to this point, we have looked at distinctive themes of American-style religious individualism. Experience, self-authentication, and community formation are all integral aspects of achieved, as opposed to ascribed, religious identities. In other words, identity becomes more constructed than given, something "worked out," a narrated selfhood—which means, as Alasdair MacIntyre observes, that increasingly "the unity of a human life is the unity of a narrative quest." But what does he mean with his eloquent words? In the most elementary sense, he means that it is through life stories that people bring order and direction to their existence. For Americans, this is no trite observation. Given so much pluralism, so much psychological interpretation, so much shifting of popular identity themes—so much movement—much responsibility rests on the individual to *bring* order and direction to life. This being the case, there is a second and related question MacIntyre poses: "a quest for what?"[31] He forces the hardest question of all, moral in its broadest sense, and having to do with some final *telos* to which life is directed. Quest is not about itself, but about the narration of human intentionality and purpose, ultimately about some object of value and fidelity. His is *the* question modernity forces on all individuals in a "post-traditional" context where the binding force of tradition is greatly diminished and agreed-upon, culturally embedded answers cannot be presumed from one generation to the next, and where individual choice in such matters becomes increasingly obligatory.

To say "post-traditional" is in one sense to say nothing really new about the American context. From the time of its founding, this country was post-traditional, meaning that it threw off the shackles of European tradition and instituted instead democratic values of individualism, achievement, and equality. Two centuries of immigration and an expanding multiculturalism reinforce these core values even as debate over their meaning and application is very much before us today. But to invoke the descriptor "post-traditional" also means, as Tocqueville and so many other commentators have made clear, either explicitly or implicitly, that religious narrative is bound up with individualism in a creative and compelling manner. Social structural and economic transformations of modernity have further created a situation where individuals find themselves pulled into an ongoing dialogue with tradition. Boomer

Americans, no less than others, feel a pull toward greater engagement with tradition. Despite all the rhetoric of individual preference, they know there is something profoundly important about connections with family, with community, with country, with religious heritage. The distinguishing feature of a self, and that which makes it reflexive, is that it is an object to itself, and possible only through responsiveness to others. Because the self is constituted socially, there is no self in the absence of history or of the stories of those communities from which one comes or chooses to claim as one's own. Or, as MacIntyre says describing narrative quests, "without those moral particularities to begin from there would never be anywhere to begin."[32] Despite the fact that Americans like to "improvise" with their religious stories, there must be something to improvise on. Tradition precedes choice. Community makes its coercive influence felt, like it or not. And in this respect, maturing Boomers are not so much antitraditional as they recognize they must negotiate meanings out of a matrix of histories, both personal and communal, and must do so in as conscious and responsible a manner as possible. To an extent more, perhaps, than they are inclined themselves to acknowledge, they recognize the limits of their individual freedom and choice, even as they are quick to draw a line on how far they are willing to allow tradition its hold upon them. The portrayal by Robert Bellah et al. of the two major languages for Americans—that of the self-reliant individual and of communities of memory arising out of lived traditions—is right on target as a statement about the tension many Americans live with.[33]

Thus tradition does not so much disappear as it is continuously revised and reformulated. One can speak of a "loss" of tradition, of its binding power, of its power to organize the past in relation to the present; yet in another sense, to speak this way is somewhat of a misnomer since tradition is always in a state of flux. There is no alternative, especially not in the context of modern life. Religious tradition persists, and will continue to do so, but in one of two fundamental ways: either as "lived tradition," and thereby in a continual state of reenactment, or hardened into rigid dogmas and moralisms. The latter is a dismal prospect, but the former signals the promise of renewal and reformation. Lived tradition is open to human agency and, therefore, to continuing narration of symbol, belief, practice, and image. Religious narration, like any "speech-act,"[34] is performative and opens up possibilities for the reconstitution of symbolic constructions and sacred meaning systems. As such, language is more than a tool for communication, but a vital source of creativity and human transformation. Tradition remains alive—vibrant and meaningful—only as its members engage it in a given time and circumstance.

Indeed, in an age of rapid social and cultural change, engagement with tradition becomes all the more crucial. Because of the changed relation of the individual to tradition, a person must assume responsibility not simply as a choice but more because it is an "imperative," Peter Berger would say.[35] It becomes necessary to carry on a creative dialogue with tradition. And in so doing, individuals configure new spaces for making meaning and engage in a process of interiorizing and authenticating their own affirmations. For many, this will mean consciously trying to learn more about a religious tradition, exploring its teachings, getting involved in religious communities, engaging its practices. Shared practices are particularly important since it is through them that one not just learns about, but actually participates in the religious world; they are essential to gaining, as William James would say, "a foothold on reality," to cultivating a depth of understanding about God and the sacred and of a life in response to such realities. It might be said that the modern individual must carry on a conversation with tradition, claiming its perspective as one's own, yet also arguing with it, seeing it not only from "within" but also having eyes to see it from "outside." In this way, the thoughtful individual discovers that tradition itself in a very real sense *is* a conversation. Far from being something closed, all worked out and formulated, living tradition is, as MacIntyre says, a "not-yet-completed narrative," or as he says elsewhere, a "historically extended, socially embodied argument, and an argument precisely in part about the goods which constitute that tradition."[36] To think of tradition as an extended argument underscores the point that spiritual practices and faith expressions are constituted—or preferably, reconstituted—always in a social environment responsive to changing circumstances and challenges. Elaborating on this point, historian Dorothy Bass observes that "the openness of a tradition's future is evident in the unresolvable argument that constitutes it (what exactly *is* redemption? is it what is happening in this case or not?) and in the quest it engenders in its bearers to learn both about themselves and about the fullness of the tradition, including what more and else it may yet become. The question of what any tradition means is part of that tradition itself, and as long as the tradition lives the question remains in dispute."[37]

Her comment underscores a process of reflexivity at two levels—for individual believers and for traditions. It is at this very juncture, where individual and collective stories intersect, that the contemporary spiritual quest comes into its creative focus. "Lived religion" engages the moment while simultaneously transcending it, the force that keeps any religious tradition alive; and conversely traditions provide, as Bass says, "the critical and inventive resources" that enable individuals and communities to transcend old configurations of meaning and to institutionalize new ones. If religion becomes too rationalized, too cut off from feelings and experience, it loses this internal dynamic. If religion becomes too closed to the human search for meaning, it loses touch with the human spirit. This happens when, as another writer says, religion becomes an "institution of acculturation," that is, a "self-contained system that leaves the spirit little to ask for . . . (and) is less a manifestation of the individual quest than an alternative to it: it says not 'Seek!' but 'Seek no further!' "[38] Lack of sensitivity to people's deeper needs and failure to cultivate a capacity for experiencing the sacred symbolically and engaging the present all serve to place limits on the spiritual, and thus risk turning religion—belief system as well as institution—into frozen forms.

But the role of narrative construction in transforming selves and institutions is itself a force with the potential for offsetting this possibility. Three such processes of narration, each with its own quite differing mechanism for resolving the serious tension inherent in the confrontation of tradition with modernity, deserve brief comment: reconnecting, reframing, and retraditionalizing.

Reconnecting

Reconnecting occurs in everyday encounters and experiences that create "liminal" moments, or a sense of "in-betweenness," that lead to personal reflection. If modernity creates lapses of memory brought on by a weakening of traditional ties, it is also the context in which people have experiences that "reconnect" them to a past and to a larger narrative of meaning and purpose. Traditional religious images and symbols retain a considerable amount of potency, particularly so in the face of the perennial circumstances of human life—death, suffering, personal crises, and aging. For many Americans, religion functions as a latent narrative lodged in memory, and one not very salient to them much of the time. But under the right circumstances, religious imaginations are reactivated, and emotional and cognitive responses follow. In a small sharing group, for example, a woman who calls herself a "lapsed Catholic" is overtaken by emotions when memories of her deceased mother's piety

167

surfaces. More than an outburst of feelings, the experience leads her to tell of her own deep Catholic sentiments about the sanctity of life—feelings largely suppressed by her pro-choice inclinations in adulthood, yet still very much a part of her childhood past. This all came about in a context of sharing stories about mother-daughter relationships, provoking emotions that she readily admits surprised her. Her reaction suggests just how deeply symbolic meanings may be buried in people's pasts and how, on occasion, they can erupt and arouse sentiments that have long been dormant.

A surprising number of people we talked with related experiences similar to this woman's, moments when they said they discovered all over again how grounded in a religious tradition they really were. They were "rugged individualists," "nonobservant," "unchurched" "disinterested," yet in the flicker of a moment recognized their relationship to a religious narrative, however distant it once may have seemed to them. Such reconnections are probably more common than we think. Reconnecting often also occurs in the least expected places and circumstances. Priest-sociologist Andrew M. Greeley offers a vivid description of such an occurrence, again, in the Catholic tradition:

> Discouraged and depressed with the futility of life, I wait for an endlessly delayed flight in December at Chicago's O'Hare Airport. I see a young mother holding her baby with passionate and protective adoration. In the beauty of that instant recognition of grounds for hope, my confidence in the purpose of life is revitalized and renewed. The friends who meet me at the end of the plane flight are astonished at my good spirits. Today, I tell them by way of explanation, I met a madonna.
>
> The madonna image, lurking in my memory on the threshold of consciousness, especially in December, disposes me to experience renewal in the presence of a mother with a child, shapes that actual experience, provides a "pigeonhole" into which I can insert my new experience, and becomes a shared symbol with which I can explain my unusual (after plane flights) cheerfulness to my friends. If someone should preach a Christmas homily about the madonna, I remember both images—Bethlehem and O'Hare—and "correlate" them; each gives emotional vitality and resonance to the other. Catechisms, creeds, doctrines, philosophy, and theology—essential reflection on and criticism of the moments of raw religious experience—all come later. The origin and raw power of experience re-

sides in life-explaining experiences. Religion is a meaning-bestowing story before it becomes anything else.[39]

Because religion is a meaning-bestowing story, it has great staying power, which resides in the capacity of symbols to link life-events with larger narratives—between O'Hare and Bethlehem—and to bring, as Greeley says, emotional vitality and resonance to them. Perhaps more than anything else, this feature of religious story explains how in the midst of so much fluidity of religious opinion and emotion, Americans continue to find in their religious affiliations not just social location and belonging, but some sense of ontological grounding. It is a grounding many, seemingly nonreligious people keep coming back to in between what might be thought of as intermittent memory losses.

Reframing

A more deliberate enterprise is involved in reframing religious language. Reframing occurs when religious speech or symbols are used not to convey some transcendent truth or reality as traditionally understood, but as a means of *creating* truth or *provoking* confrontation with it. Rather than looking upon symbols as fixed realities in some objectivist manner, they become negotiated and situational, used to construct a set of meanings in the face of serious human dilemmas and existential concerns. This amounts to a highly reflexive act, an undertaking designed to force interpretation either by dislodging old meanings and/or provoking new ones. Implicit is the assumption that it falls on the individual, or small groups of individuals, to weave a coherent narrative of meaning and life, and that religious symbols and practices are at their perusal and disposal. Since this usually occurs in a communal context, it is an opportunity for shared meanings to evolve that are different in narrative style, or for confronting existential realities anew. Even in the act of rejecting traditional religious definitions, there is the creative energy expended in arriving at alternative interpretations.

Reframing as a shift in speech styles can sometimes be observed in sermons within churches. Looking not only at religious themes but at the juxtaposition of symbols and meanings, sermons on occasion reveal a mix of languages and a deliberate openness to allowing the audience itself to define the meaning. Religious encounter becomes somewhat akin to that of a dramatic arts production where the audience is brought into the process of interpretation and emotional response. Unlike

169

traditional religious contexts where interpretation and response are highly structured, here the goal is to keep them open and polysemous. This more flexible, multivocal understanding of religious language underscores its constitutive power in an age when the meanings of words, images, and symbols can no longer be simply taken for granted; it also presumes, as sociologist Marsha G. Witten says, a "middle ground" between subjective and objective grounds of truth. Witten offers an example: "For some contemporary Christians, the symbol of the cross may no longer plausibly refer to the accounts of the crucifixion and resurrection of Jesus as they appear in the gospels. Yet the cross may take on significance in another way as speakers use it to condense and dramatize notions of suffering and its transcendence, or overwhelming love, or the possibilities of human transfiguration."[40] What she suggests is that the role of religion for some people may not be so much to signify objective truths as to offer a repertoire of symbols to draw upon in narrating and interpreting experiences that might seem at odds with conventional interpretation. Rather than approach a symbol as doctrinally formulated, allow the possibility that people may freely associate with it, drawing from their own experiences. The metaphor of a "symbolic toolbox" now often applied to religion suggests that people may draw selectively from its resources and exercise considerable agency in its interpretation.[41] It implies as well that a religious tradition has a broad set of "tools," and that in any one setting its members draw from a limited combination of texts, teachings, liturgies, symbols, and practices. By juxtaposing symbolic elements, selectively posing and presenting themes, even subverting taken-for-granted sacred realities, religious reframing is a means of breaking through encrusted tradition and opening up new possibilities for an encounter with religious and metaphysical truths.

Reframing has potential in a media age, where words and symbols are manipulated in ways that often disassociate them from a historic and grounded tradition. If we posit that highly reflexive persons are likely oriented toward linguistic relativism and recognize the socially constructed character of meaning, then it may well be that they are quite comfortable with negotiated interpretations of religious images and symbols, and interpretations that are understood to vary from one context to another and in relation to linguistic codes. For many Baby Boomers, suspicious of religious truth-claims but yet drawn to metaphysical questions, this approach to reformulating meaning and narrative has some appeal. It generates a sense of ownership, that the interpretations arrived at are theirs and therefore meaningful on those terms. Evangelical seeker churches, for example, often self-consciously play down conventional symbols and meanings in an effort to create a religious sensibility—to dramatize a Christ-and-culture relationship—both markedly different from that people normally expect, and one that Boomer audiences can claim as their own.[42] Efforts at redefining religion as spirituality by the new entrepreneurs, described in Chapter 3, involves, to one degree or another, reframing. Many writings on spirituality go to some length to show how new terms have replaced old religious concepts, and to demonstrate points of connection with sacred realities by whatever name or discourse they are described. Relating religion to psychology and to art and drama, common in liberal religious tradition throughout much of this century, is a similar, though not necessarily a full-blown, case of reframing religion.

Retraditionalizing

A third enterprise, a countertrend really, might be termed *retraditionalizing*, or creating new cultural formations that provide alternative visions of spiritual and ethical life. Here the emphasis is not on reinterpreting words or symbols embedded in a religious narrative but on the fact that new traditions arise and should be recognized as serious alternatives. It points to the rise of more universal and humanistic meaning systems that now compete with the historic religions. These newer discourses are sensitive to concerns about human dignity and equality, to suffering of all kinds, to fears of disasters and destruction, to human potential. Arguments such as these represent a major break with those who argue, to the contrary, that we live in an age of detraditionalization. As opposed to trends toward moral relativism, narcissism, and emotivism, retraditionalizing calls attention to newly emerging, culturally pervasive ethical formations.[43] Those advancing these newer ethical ideals infer powerful spiritual potential as found, say, in what Emile Durkheim called "the religion of humanity," with its recognition of human rights, the power of human bondings, and implicit enhancement of human personality.

Something like a "religion of humanity" seems to have found renewed favor in recent decades. The period is seen as a time of paradigm shifts, a rebirthing of a tradition of human kindness—as reflected in the civil rights movement, Vietnam War protests, concerns about the use of nuclear energy, environmentalism, the rise of multiculturalism, the politics of civility. Hardly restricted to the American situation, there is ample evidence of global awareness and recognition of similar concerns. Such developments share a deep respect for the human as expressed in inclusive, egalitarian values and a corresponding disapproval of discrepant hierarchies and ideological divisions within society as well as between societies. At the very heart of this ethic, as with Durkheim's original thesis, is a conviction about the sacred character of the human personality, which, if violated, amounts to a moral wrong against humanity. Among Boomers, in fact, such sentiment runs strong. Even among those who might not go so far as to associate sacredness with humanity, say, conservative Christians, there is considerable affinity with values placed upon the rights, freedom, and dignity of the individual. For great numbers of Evangelicals and Charismatics, those values increasingly extend to civil liberties and gender equality.

There would appear, then, to be growing acceptance of beliefs, values, and practices, whether acknowledged as such or not, associated with an "ethic of humanity." So strong is the base of approval, in fact, that it is arguably now the dominant tradition of the modern democratic state. The expansion of human rights—civil, political, economic, and cultural—would point to the growing hold of the tradition, appealing not just for its broad unifying influence, but for its effective identification of the self with universal and humanistic values that extend beyond any single society.[44] In this respect, the tradition may be viewed as a corrective both to exclusivistic tendencies that threaten to disrupt society and international relations and to the self-preoccupation so often associated with the Boomer generation. The ethic plays a critical role in "curtailing tendencies," so British sociologist Paul Heelas contends, "which lead beyond 'being human': either to the 'I' which is fundamentally differentiated from others because it *belongs* to a tradition, or the 'I' which simply dwells on *itself*."[45] Thus in his view, retraditionalizing is put forth as an alternative to reactionary Fundamentalisms, on the one side, and to psychological reductionism, on the other. Its proponents see it as a solution to the religious and secular ideological extremes that have evolved in modern society.

TOWARD A TYPOLOGY

If, as presumed here, the onslaught of modernity has led to significant religious dislocations, can we arrive at a typology that sensitizes us to this changing nexus of individuals and religious narrative? What analytic scheme would yield insight into the major religious subcultures now emerging? Any such scheme, and religious mapping derived from it, must of necessity take seriously the historic role of religious narrative and practice. As we have seen, modernity has given rise to an altered relation between individuals and traditions and thus problematizes the process of religious narration itself—of the way in which individual stories relate to the larger, so-called grand narratives. Further, implicit is a disruption between internal, or experiential ("spiritual") and external, or institutionalized ("religious") components. Under conditions of late modernity, it might be said that relations between these two have become "stretched," and people increasingly conscious of it. Unable to presume the two to be necessarily in sync with one another, it is helpful to look on them broadly as constituting a matrix of possibilities, of the two components varying independently of each other, or as being in a dialogical relationship. Indeed, it is this very problematic that prompts MacIntyre's concern about the unity of a narrative quest and his question, "a quest for what?" That he—and we—must ask so direct a question says something about the threat of disunity that modernity poses to inherited religious narrative. It also attests to the fact that narrative construction is a deeply reflexive process, opening the way to new self-understanding and self-presentation, and hence to new communal attachments and solidarities. To grasp the logic behind these—both the threat and the promise—is the challenge before us.

But also empirically, there are grounds for examining this internal-external distinction. As is obvious by now, the terms *religious* and *spiritual* point to quite differing phenomenological realities for the Boomer population. Both our survey and interview data underscore how emotion, cognition, group attachments, and cultures all crystallize around this distinction. Yet it is far from a simple distinction either conceptually or empirically. Even though 74 percent of our people say they are "religious" and 73 percent say they are "spiritual," there is no one-to-one relationship between the two self-reported identities: 79 percent of those who are religious also claim to be spiritual, but 54 percent of those who are not religious say they are spiritual as well. There is substantial overlap of the two, yet significant discrepancies at both extremes—people who claim to be spiritual but not religious, or religious but not spiritual. Certainly, the range of independent variation for the two components of religious identity is sufficient that, increasingly, we cannot assume that one implies the other. That ordinary people recognize this possible discrepancy is itself a significant shift in popular discourse, for in times past such a distinction would have been understood primarily by theologians and intellectual elites. It tells us something about the magnitude of cultural and religious transformation of our time and about why a spiritual quest culture takes on the importance it does today. It seems reasonable to infer as well that the emerging distinction signals a more reflexively infused discourse. "I've thought a lot about this," a school teacher in California told us. "I can feel my spirituality; it seems different to me than saying I'm religious, which I no longer am." Not all people we interviewed were so quick to draw the distinction, but clearly for substantial numbers of people, it is a matter either they have thought about or can respond to with ease when the distinction is posed; in either instance, the evidence suggests that the distinction is increasingly culturally defined. Other research as well points to clarity of the distinction and underscores the dialogical relation between the two identity-components.[46]

In a lived tradition, the religious should, to a considerable degree, contain the spiritual: people hold to a faith in a transcendent God, or a conception of the sacred, regarded by them as subjectively real and meaningfully present in their lives. By thinking of religion as a cultural-linguistic system, that is, as a set of rich symbolic forms or narrative script, we gain perspective on how religious language generates and sustains a sense of the sacred.[47] A comprehensive belief system, embodied in myth, symbol, ritual, and narrative, structures human experience, emotions, and conceptions of the self in relation to a larger world; both its vocabulary of symbols and its syntax provide a system for ordering and giving meaning to experiences. Faith communities historically have functioned in this way precisely because their symbols, imageries, practices, and stories have a powerful capacity to evoke religious sentiments and to maintain a plausible religious world. Sermons, testimonies, repetitive responses, music, icons, lights, candles, incense, and other such phenomena trigger experiences of awe, mystery, and ecstasy, thereby creating the presence of God or awareness of the sacred. That is to say, experience for believers is largely derivative; it follows from practice, or the rehearsing of myth and narrative. Encoded signs and symbols provide the means by which experiences are generated and described, even recognized, as religious. More than just trigger experiences, a religious system undergirds conceptions of a *transcendent reality* and supplies the *symbolic vehicles* for living in its thought world and responding affectively and intentionally. In this way continuity of religious experience and worldview is maintained; by means of a process of "traditioning," experience and worldview are recreated and passed on in a communal context. This requires not just persuasive symbolic formulations, but that they be "socially embodied." Again, to quote historian Dorothy Bass: "Living traditions . . . are embodied in the social world in two related ways: through *practices* and *institutions* where practices are sustained. Individuals can learn and participate in traditions only in the company of others; they do so by entering into the practices and institutions through which particular social groups, versed in specific activities and gathered into specific organizations, bear traditions over time."[48] Practices, both personal and collective, are embedded in a tradition's history and serve to "keep alive" that history and are the means by which a person learns, shares, and participates in its symbolic world. In fact a symbolic world "rests" on a well-defined and embodied set of practices.

For an individual embedded in such a tradition with its constitutive symbols, doctrines, and practices, ways of relating to the sacred are very different than for someone who is not so grounded. "Strategies of action" are fairly well prescribed: a believer reproduces tradition by habitually entering into its thought world, feelings, and practices. Meaning and action fuse in the sense that one "dwells" in a particular *habitus.*[49] In a plural religious context as found in the United States, dwelling for the faithful arises out of participation in a community of shared faith and practice; within this environment new experiences are interpreted in light of tradition, and tradition is also reformulated in light of experience. The Latin *religio* embraces the human capacity to perceive meaning and design in life—or as Wilfred Cantwell Smith says, "to see, to feel, to act in terms of, a transcendent"[50]—and in a shared religious context it prescribes a unity of faith, practice, and action. Despite rampant individualism and subjectivity, this unity is held together to some degree by means of rich symbolic and metaphoric language, through shared practices and communal belonging. Always in some degree of dialogical tension, form and spirit are drawn toward an equilibrium.

Yet some people may be pulled toward revering tradition for its own sake, in which case ritual turns into ritualism, dogma into dogmatism— spirit loses out to form. Seeing, feeling, and acting in terms of a transcendent are all robbed of experiential wholeness. Such a spiritual drought occurs for reasons both personal and institutional. The loss of tradition, decline of authority, and fears generated out of the psycho-historical dislocations of modernity, may all provoke defensive responses. Some people are drawn to traditions, or more precisely, interpretations of traditions, that promise to resist change in the name of preserving eternal values; such interpretations have as their appeal an offer of stability in an otherwise chaotic world. Religious institutions themselves, so oriented to their own self-perpetuation, can be their own worst enemies when they try to "box in" the numinous and resist accommodation to changing circumstances. It becomes quite possible, then, for people to adopt the outward forms of doctrine, morality, and institution without having, or feeling, any engaged relationship with the tradition. In this case people try to hold on to the religious but lack its spiritual dimension—a frequent event among dogmatists, Fundamentalists, and traditionalists claiming to have the definitive religious truth or among institutionalists of one stripe or another for whom a particular religious form easily becomes encrusted and lifeless.

In a post-traditional world, appeals to various types of religious narratives and experiences are inevitable. Even within a historical tradition, there is a range of idioms, normative styles, and interpretations such as liberal versus conservative theological discourses, as found, say, within Christianity in the twentieth century. A Born-again Evangelical Christian and an ecologically minded liberal, mainstream Episcopalian may both be "spiritually minded Christians," but their interpretive frames and modes of spirituality differ greatly. Messages encoded within religious narratives stemming from a common tradition diverge in the accommodation to modernity, creating a major religious and cultural cleavage between Born-again Christians and mainstream believers. In fact, a liberal-conservative theological distinction cuts across all the major faith communities today, making it necessary in any mapping of popular religious identities to distinguish between the large Born-again Christians constituency, and the more historic, mainstream religious identities. Both amount to large, quite distinguishable subcultures in the United States.

With modernity come even deeper disjunctions in religious experience than those within religious traditions. Unified experiences, or what philosopher Herbert Richardson once called the "felt-whole,"[51] do not come easily for an age caught up in sweeping cultural and religious changes. There are metaphysical believers whose traditions are identified more as spiritual than as religious, and who resist the "R" word because of its connotations of religious and cultural establishment. When asked, many say they are "spiritual but not religious" as a means of saying who they are and are not. Still others, like Vicki Feinstein, are searching deeply for a holistic perspective but might be said to be metaphysically homeless. The analogy to tourists has been made. Unlike the pilgrims Chaucer's tales remember—stories embedded in tradition—tourists

176

make forays into worlds, picking up souvenirs here and there, but stay on the move, never quite settling in or claiming any place as home.[52] In between these two extremes are many spiritual seekers trying to cultivate a mystical consciousness, that is, attempting to engage strategies of action in a deliberate and experimental manner. Spiritual experience for them does not so much derive from encoded sign and symbol; rather, it must be "formed" through learning and disciplined practice. People "work at" becoming spiritual through observation, imitation, instruction, shared practices, and regimes of exercises.[53] Members of the Baby Boom generation seem particularly receptive to strategies of "working at" becoming spiritual: often not very well grounded in any historic religious tradition and exposed to a "salad bar" of assorted teachings and techniques, they find it natural to weigh the possibilities.

In an age of widespread alternatives and conscious about their own spiritual identity, people honor their own creativity and take seriously their own leads. But it is the "spiritual entrepreneurs" who mainly rationalize choices and devise technologies, and who push ahead defining the spiritual frontiers. In keeping with the cultural toolbox metaphor, without the control of a religious monopoly or regulating institution, new combinations of religious elements proliferate at the hands of such entrepreneurs. The narrative task becomes that of finding a meaningful past and of cultivating a collective memory. Old pasts are reclaimed as in Wicca, or "new" mythical pasts created, as with much of the recent emphasis upon eco-spirituality. So important is this search for a collective memory, French sociologist Daniele Hervieu-Leger speaks of the "imaginary genealogies" that are created to establish a spiritual lineage.[54] As she points out, such creations—even the most eclectic ones—appeal to tradition, or selected aspects of tradition, mainly as a means of making claims upon origins and of legitimating themselves. Of course, much energy is expended by the individuals themselves because, outside the established faith communities, and in the absence of highly institutionalized beliefs and practices, spiritual searching is largely a private matter involving loosely based social networks and small groups. For this rather heterogenous population, the word *spiritual* is a basis of unity, invoked positively as a basis of self-identity, whereas the term *religious* is used often as a counter-identity for clarifying who they are not.

And for still others, neither description—the religious or the spiritual—seems to fit them very well. Even people whose experiences appear on the surface to be sacred may reject both when asked about their identities. Neither vocabulary—whether from a traditional religious script or from deep spiritual searching, externally or internally derived—conveys much meaning to them. "Flow" experiences come to mind of the sort psychologist Mihaly Czikszentmihalyi describes.[55] Such experiences carry one away in a rush of energy and excitement, a predictable re-action when one takes on a great challenge, be it climbing a mountain, listening to music, or perhaps even seeing a child overcome a disability. People report experiencing in such moments little distinction between self and activity, between past and present; through powerful, if un-namable experiences, they break through ego boundaries and into an expanded state of consciousness. What they experience are deeply inter-nalized moments of mystery, heightened self-awareness, and creativity as people who typically are highly individualistic, but without recourse to a widely shared language that would qualify as religious by most defini-tions. As judged by their vocabularies, they are truly the secularists of the present world.

Thus we arrive at the following juxtaposition of internal and external identities:

SPIRITUAL IDENTITY

	Yes	No
Yes	1a. Born-again Christians, including Evangelicals, Pentacostals, Neo-Penta-costals, Charismatics	3. Dogmatists, including Fundamentalists, Institutionalists, Moralists, Neotraditionalists
RELIGIOUS IDENTITY	1b. Mainstream Believers	
No	2. Metaphysical Believers Spiritual Seekers	4. Secularists

Labels shown here are those people often use themselves—some more so than others, of course. But the fourfold spaces are actually more important than the choice of labels within them. For it is around this intersection of inner-experiential and outer-institutional references that religious identities are narratively constructed; and, without some understanding of the array of possibilities, we cannot grasp the increas-ingly operative boundaries in contemporary culture. "Lived religion" presupposes some degree of balance between social-support structures and spiritual openness, or between groundedness and fluidity. Such a balance is less likely in spaces 3 and 4, where religion is either reified into a hardened system or rejected outright. By contrast, in spaces 1a, 1b, and

2, the spiritual dimension is more potent: there is greater interplay of the inner and outer aspects of narrative religious construction. In the American context, where religion is so deeply ingrained culturally and so broadly based within the population, this dynamic of freedom and structure, of spirit and form, is a crucial yet variable feature that cannot be overlooked in analyzing the current religious scene.

But of course, labels are not to be dismissed. They influence perceptions, give meaning, provide identity—all essential to good mapping. Even listing constituencies fitting to the spaces within the typology provokes further interest and questions. What are the subcultures? What are their distinctive social and cultural profiles? What religious and spiritual discourses characterize them? What particular spiritual quests drive them? And how are these quests narrated and embodied in practices? It is to these questions and a descriptive profiling of the emerging religious subcultures that we now turn.

✜ CHAPTER 6 ✜

Redrawing the Boundaries

*The act of describing the landscape and its landmarks will
not save souls or make all sad hearts glad. But it can contribute
to a sorting-out process that will be helpful to both
participants and observers.*
(*Martin E. Marty*)

M APPING THE religious landscape is, as Marty says, an "act" of limited
religious value, but one helpful to our understanding of religion's "sorting-out process." That process involves not just identifying newly emerging constituencies but naming them. By giving names to the religious
players on the scene at any given time, observers exercise power and
influence and contribute to the making of meaning, or what sociologists
customarily call the "social construction of reality."[1] Journalists, pollsters,
and commentators do so regularly, and often without worrying all that
much about the consequences of their actions; historians and social scientists are held to a somewhat higher standard of accountability for their
definitions, categories, and schemes. Not to overstate the latter's influence, the terminologies, statistics, and observations of scholars and
researchers especially as interpreted through the mass media and in the
public arena are absorbed within the religious communities themselves—still another example of the reflexive religious environment in
which we live. In the broader context of the sociology of knowledge, this
means that theirs is an undertaking not without consequences for participants and observers alike. If the making of meaning on the part of religious and spiritual entrepreneurs is serious business today, and inevitably has profound implications for people's lives, much the same holds
for the professional religion-watchers, commentators, and interpreters
who supply so many of the categories that feed into this larger social
process.

Categories as these are best judged on the basis of how well they
reflect the religious worlds in which people actually live. One way of
conceptualizing the property spaces of the typology from the previous
chapter is that of "tolerance zones," that is, as spaces in a pluralistic world
where people feel comfortable with one another.[2] Within such zones

180

people share definitions of reality, adhere to common moral values, and express similar emotions and feeling-responses. Tolerance zones may be likened to "subcultures," distinguished from one another on the basis of their values, styles, and symbolic boundaries. Subcultures may be thought of as "morally orienting collective identities which provide adherents meaning and belonging."[3] Because such subcultures involve both moral and religious content, distinctions among them can usually be drawn. Religious subcultures, or "socio-religious"[4] communities as they have sometimes been called, function simultaneously as communities, associations, and symbolic orders. People may belong to them in a deep communal sense or simply associate with them as they would with any other voluntary organization. They may identify with them symbolically and form moral and religious judgments about them, positively or negatively. Emotionally they involve attachments with varying degrees of intensity. Far more than just theology, or doctrine, or institution, socio-religious communities locate people in social space, defining them over against religious others. Keeping in mind as well the toolbox metaphor, subcultures provide resources for people to engage the world and to define themselves creatively in an ongoing, changing religious and cultural milieu. Symbols, customs, rituals, behavioral styles, theologies, and moral codes are all cultural tools for shaping a distinctive identity. Religious leaders and entrepreneurs engage such resources, of course, but so too do ordinary people. More than relying just on theologians and professional meaning-makers, people themselves are now playing a more active role in interpreting to themselves and to others who they are religiously. Increasingly, they are aware of the choices before them.

Our typology sensitizes us to the phenomenological worlds born out of the disjunctions of religious narrative and experience, or the life-spaces where, as anthropologist Clifford Geertz would say, people spin their "webs of significance."[5] Boundaries in this matrix of possibilities are relatively flexible, responsive to human agency in the formation of meaning, and subject to the ebb-and-flow of popular sentiment. Here we profile these newly emerging religious subcultures with these parameters in mind. For the various subcultures, we address three basic concerns: one, the social and religious demographics defining them; two, the emerging cultural and religious boundaries that shape their narratives; and three, reflexive engagement on the part of individuals and constituencies. Particular attention is given to the redefining and/or forging of new spiritual styles in keeping with the experiences and life-styles of the Boomer generation. While the description is at the level of

181

the subcultures, we give particular attention to the spiritual vanguard within each subculture and how it is engaging its own cultural and religious resources.

BORN-AGAIN CHRISTIANS

"Born-again" Christians are the most visible and recognizable of our religious constituencies. They also make up the largest constituency, roughly a third of all Boomers. Most call themselves "Evangelicals" or "Christians," which for many means they have had a memorable experience, or set of experiences, when they felt the presence of Christ in their lives; for some it is a code word, more a means of self-reference that has evolved over time than a specific moment when their lives changed direction. Still others, much smaller in number, prefer to call themselves "Charismatics," either Catholic or Protestant, or "Pentecostals" or "neo-Pentecostals." Size, visibility, a common discourse, and public recognition all make for a distinct subculture best described by means of the most inclusive of labels as "Born-again" Christians.[6] Personal faith, strong conviction, and, above all, a redemptive experience of salvation are defining features of the "Born-again" narrative. From the standpoint of narratology, stories about personal experiences become "enmeshed" in a larger, shared narrative of God's redemptive love. Stylistically, this particular narrative dates back to the 1950s and 1960s when Evangelical Christian movements sought a distinctive identity over against both religious Fundamentalism and religious liberalism, the "new religions," and secularism and amorality. Moreover, the unwillingness of vast numbers of Protestant churches in the late 1960s and early 1970s to welcome the Jesus People and other young Christians touched by the spiritual awakenings of the counterculture, forced many of them to look elsewhere for a religious home and left them with the impression of a rather cold and stodgy religious establishment. That impetus helped to lay the groundwork for their own networks and faith communities highly focused on personal and spiritual needs, and continues to find expression in a variety of ways, including the megachurch and popular interest in Jesus as a religious figure, in healing and support ministries, and Charismatic renewal.[7] No other subculture can claim as extensive and vigorous an institutional infrastructure.

This Born-again Christian subculture is remarkably diverse in its institutional affiliations. Slightly over half claim a conservative Protestant religious preference, but fully one-fourth are Roman Catholic and another 20 percent belong to one or another of the mainline Protestant religious communities. That almost half of Born-again Christians are outside of the conservative Protestant churches cautions against the use of denominational affiliation as a predictor. That so many Catholics identify with the movement underscores the large numbers of Charismatics and others who report having a religious experience, either within or outside of the Catholic community; it shows how much religious diversity exists among Catholics and that just knowing someone is "Catholic" (or "Protestant" for that matter) tells us actually very little. The religious backgrounds of the Born-agains are even more varied: 38 percent grew up as conservative Protestants (including Fundamentalist backgrounds), 27 percent as mainline Protestants, 28 percent as Roman Catholics, and the remaining 7 percent as Jews, some other faith, or nothing. Theologically the constituency amounts to a complex assemblage of traditions and subtraditions, distinct from one another in style and emphasis yet overlapping in doctrinal and moral formulations; it includes self-designated Charismatics, various types of Protestant Pentecostals, and many who simply call themselves Evangelicals, Pentecostals, or Charismatics without much grasp of the associated denominational (or non-denominational) heritages. A highly subjective religious identity meshes well with these secondary, institutional frameworks. What binds them into a transdenominational identity is a spirituality rooted in traditional Christian theology, but one reinterpreted in the twentieth century to combine the experience of a "personal God," or of a "personal relationship" with Jesus Christ, and Boomer culture and sensibilities.

"Born-again" spirituality thus has an affinity with an introverted self as articulated in recent decades in the broader American culture. As the followers themselves see it, it is a self in relation to God as described in the never-changing New Testament plan of salvation. Closer scrutiny, however, reveals an expansive self very much influenced by the wider culture. Books, music, witnessing, testimony, and ritual performance within the subculture all employ a rhetoric emphasizing that the individual who has directly experienced God may then discover the "real self." That this discovery occurs in a shared faith community is common but, by and large, the setting itself is secondary to the highly subjective narrative of an individual pretty much on his or her own, in a process of spiritual transformation. "Journey" and "recovery" languages keep the focus upon growth and self-development, thereby reinforcing a personal, psychological account of the meaning of salvation. This narration of self is

183

elaborated by recourse to psychocultural themes such as spontaneity, control, intimacy, and self-affirmation embedded within the culture, which define and make vivid rich dimensions of personal experience.[8] While such themes are prevalent in all the subcultures, what is distinctive here is the degree of enmeshment of such themes in symbolic religious language. Not to be overlooked in this respect is the influence of the mass media and the proliferation of small, informal social gatherings: about 20 percent of our Born-again Christians claim to have no involvement in any existing congregation, many of them saying that they watch an Evangelical program on television, participate in a house-church or some other gathering of believers, or that they are simply solitary believers.

Many report being "born again" at an early age, usually in their teen years or during college if they attended, or later around the time of marriage and having children. Striking is the overall youthfulness of the constituency: over half were born since the mid 1950s, the highest proportion of any of the religious subcultures in our analysis. Growing numbers of Asian Americans and Latinos are among this younger cohort. But despite their youthfulness, Born-again Christians are a "burned-over" population in the sense that many religious groups, including many differing theological brands of Evangelicals, have made appeals to them. Even now they encounter a mix of Evangelical styles and rhetorics, and considerable jostling among them for narrative control over the religious message. Evangelical media itself plays an enormous role in recasting the symbolic boundaries of the movement. Christian television networks and cable distributions, talk shows like the *700 Club*, and Christian soap operas help to solidify Evangelicalism as a national, indeed global, religious movement and to forge its more adaptive cultural styles. New genres of religious programming undergird a popular religious consciousness to a degree independent of, though not necessarily in opposition to, formal religious institutions. Through its use of symbols, beliefs, and values, the media speak to the malaise of modernity and offer the viewing audience a means of identifying with, and participating in, a religious option that is spiritually appealing. Television ministries especially cater to, and then further amplify, distinctions between the religious and the spiritual by encouraging people to "loosen up," to "explore riches," to "pursue" deeper understandings of God's presence in one's life, and sometimes within a context of entertainment Evangelicalism chiding religious establishments for their ritual formality and impersonalism.[9] Similarly, special-purpose groups help to redefine Evangelicalism by offering what Boomers particularly like—choice of religious causes and spiritual styles. Women's groups and minority caucuses, high school and college associations, programs for singles and for varying family types, organizations on behalf of self-help and social services, and occupationally based networks all continue to evolve, resulting in a tug-of-war over power and control within the Evangelical movement. What such groups have in common, in varying degrees, is that they work outside of denominational circles and introduce individuals of one congregation to those of another as well as to a larger community of like-minded individuals beyond both the congregation and the denomination. Networks like these give evidence of vigor and show how one after another niche of social experience is endowed with spiritual meaning, which has the larger effect both of strengthening bonds among similarly situated believers and of symbolizing to the larger world the comprehensiveness and flexibility of this remarkably multifaceted movement.

This pluralism of networks and styles makes for an Evangelicalism far different in style from that of a half-century ago. Its origins lie in the 1940s and 1950s, when as we have seen, moderate-minded conservatives who were embarrassed by the fractious, withdrawn, and anti-intellectual image of Fundamentalism began to distance themselves from its more extreme versions, and to shift the course of the Evangelical movement.[10] What they wanted was a more open, culturally engaging religious style, and a breaking out of the old Modernist-Fundamentalist framework that continued to define the parameters of religious conservatism. The neo-Evangelical movement shifted emphasis away from the "truth-oriented" posturing of an older religious conservatism toward a more "conversion-oriented" and/or "spiritually-oriented" faith, one denoting personal transformation, and the second an expressive, joyful, soulful mode of religion.[11] If being rationalistic and tough in demanding assent to doctrinal formulations characterize the old-style religion, personal assurance, inward joy, and spiritual presence are key traits of the new style. This shift set the neo-Evangelical movement on a different course and opened up possibilities for affinity with those claiming an experiential faith in other traditions. Social factors as well play an important part in redrawing the boundaries. Many college students in the 1970s and 1980s were exposed to this new style of Evangelicalism articulated in psychological idioms. Closely related was the expansion of higher education during this period. Higher levels of education in turn resulted in a considerable increase in the numbers of professionals and managers, many of them members of the "knowledge classes," and brought about an

185

altered social location for Evangelicals and Charismatics and with it, more favorable perceptions. Increased social mobility and middle-class standing opened the way to new, enhanced self-definitions.

In effect, Born-again Christianity for this generation underwent a process of cultural mainstreaming—with consequences for religious styles, social respectability, and claims on the wider culture. For example, when asked if the churches they attend are "in the mainstream of how Americans live and think today, or a distinct alternative to what most people think," two-thirds of the Born-agains we talked to chose the former. An older generation of Protestant Evangelicals may see themselves as over against the mainstream culture, but that is far less true for the younger ones who are more world-affirming and better positioned within that culture. Hard-core Fundamentalists and Catholic traditionalists, in contrast, are much less likely to think in these more accommodating terms, preferring instead to posture themselves in a more dogmatic, unrelenting manner, in opposition to dominant trends. Parallels are discernible within Catholicism. Over 90 percent of Charismatic Catholics insist that Church teachings should be in the hands of both the religious hierarchy and laypeople and not left just to the hierarchy, in keeping with a post-Vatican Council II spirit of greater lay involvement. The Charismatic movement, by unleashing deeply personal energies, has given rise to powerful democratizing trends within religion. For all these reasons, being Born-again, Evangelical, Charismatic, Pentecostal, or neo-Pentecostal does not carry for the Boomer generation the stigma that once gave all such labels a marginal status. Gone are much of the narrow-minded exclusivism and even some of the rigidly defined moral and symbolic boundaries that persist as stereotypes in the minds of many Americans about conservative Christians, characterizations quite fitting to Fundamentalists, traditionalists, and dogmatists but much less so for those espousing more popular-style, experiential faith. Within almost all conservative religious communities, there has emerged a greater internal pluralism across a fairly wide spectrum of issues—theological, moral, familial, and political.[12]

For Born-again Christianity itself, this shift in social basis did not come about without some loss of certitude and of a deeply ingrained culture—what sociologist James Davison Hunter calls a "loss of binding address."[13] Over the years of our panel study, many of the Evangelicals we followed moved often from church to church; others became inactive even though they claimed a church membership; and a surprising number claimed to be committed Evangelicals but said they were not, indeed had never been, church members at all. Greater variation in styles and institutional affiliations parallel a reconfiguring of Evangelicalism within the public culture. At the hands of this generation, Evangelicalism moved into the cultural mainstream and, consequently, its symbolic boundaries were redefined and sometimes blurred; there were increased negotiations among parties as to styles of Evangelical faith and "cognitive bargaining," a stance generally of accommodating faith and practice to modern life. In actuality, and also in some Boomer perceptions, Evangelicalism as a faith movement suffers from its internal pluralism, subjectivity, and incessant vying for narrative control among competing voices, and gives the movement as a whole, as one critic writes, "a sense of events-out-of-control, of confusion, disorder, and a constant instability of genres, borders, roles, and rules."[14]

But for all these reasons, "Born-again" Christianity is conducive to greater reflexivity. Mainstreaming and other democratizing trends have produced an epistemological shift of major magnitude: "Born-again" faiths are increasingly understood to be religious *options*. This in turn encourages a religious consciousness that resists impulses toward absolutism, particularly on the part of the better-educated and culturally sophisticated. Half of all Boomer Evangelicals agree that the religions of the world are all "equally true and good," and among the younger, upwardly mobile professional classes, the figure is even higher. While this need not necessarily imply a loss of commitment for Born-again Christians, it does signal a level of self-realization on the part of believers themselves about their religious commitments *as choices*, or as affirmations arrived at, whether consciously or not, though some degree of cognitive bargaining. It signals as well recognition of a range of possible interpretations within Evangelical Christianity itself. A Southern Baptist in Ohio, a college-educated engineer and committed chuchman, expresses a point of view in this respect that was fairly common among people with whom we spoke: "I firmly believe, and I have witnessed myself in many instances, that you can take two or three people, sit them down and study the same Scripture, and you'll get three or four different responses. Personally I believe it is meant to be that way. I think that everyone gets what they need, and we don't always need the same thing." Later in the interview, he avowed that we are all "looking for something" and that "we look until we find it"—a mode of discourse reminicient of the bumper sticker proclaiming "I found it," popularized some years ago by the founder of the Intervarsity Christian Fellowship. As it turns out, he was active in ICF during his college days, important to note since many of his generation received their understanding of Born-again Christianity under the influence of special-purpose organizations aimed at making Christianity compatible with education. Important to note as well, at least three cultural strands are interwoven in his comments: relativistic thinking with respect to biblical interpretation; a religious psychology of individual needs and experiences; and an optimistic, indeed, very American assumption that all such human needs will in time be met. Educated, upscale Born-again Christians no less than others of the religious mainstream espouse faiths shaped by this mix of cultural influences. The extent of the impact of such influences on the certainty of faith and conviction is an unresolved question. In the case of Born-again Christians of the Boomer generation, accustomed to so much pluralism, relativism, and psychologizing in religious thinking, it is the strong personal relationship with Christ that best sustains the commitment, which begins with a transformation through a personal relationship and is then sustained through social reinforcement of like-minded persons.

For the spiritual vanguard within this subculture, there is an emerging epistemology, or mode of knowing, grounded in the whole person, in both body and mind. Recall the Massachusetts woman described in Chapter 4, the one raised a "Fundamentalist, Bible-believing Christian," but who recently found a "more friendly Christian church" and discovered that Jesus might be imagined as different from the way she had always thought of him. Commenting on the help this new church setting had provided her in this discovery, she speaks of the powers of "perceiving" and "feeling" and underscores what psychologists have long said about the linkages between cognition, bodily sensation, and religious experience. This, too, represents a significant departure from an older-style Fundamentalism that focused faith around the revealed truth of the Bible, absolute truth requiring of its members unwavering commitment as a means of salvation. Spiritually oriented Evangelicalism, Pentecostalism, and Charismatic faith place less emphasis on salvation from guilt and sin, choosing instead, according to one commentator, "to magnify the accessibility and power of 'the Lord's intimate and constant presence.'"[15] In this process the gap between the natural and the supernatural breaks down, with the result that the body and the mind are brought closer together, the healing of both become much more central, and faith itself as a consequence deeply expressive. What is generated is a religious context in which, especially for people like this woman whose old religious systems and worldviews have lost their hold, the cohesion of faith, meaning, and experience lies, as theologian

Harvey Cox writes, "not in the system but in the person, not in the institution itself but in the people who draw on its resources to illuminate their daily lives."[16]

It is within the growing sector of "seeker churches" and "apostolic congregations"[17] that we find the strongest expression of this changing style of spirituality within the Born-again Christian community. Here are churches purposively trying to create dialogical contexts, settings in which people can deal with their questions and doubts and then present the Gospel in a cultural idiom that takes those questions and doubts into consideration. The whole person—body and mind—is presupposed as a starting point for religious conversation. Contrary to stereotypes roughly 40 percent of Born-again Christians, by our calculation, are open to a dialogical approach and an understanding of religious truth as experientially based. A surprising number of them actually identify themselves as "seekers," saying they believe in God but are not sure about organized religion (meaning churches as they have known them), or raise serious questions about the truthfulness of Christianity itself.[18] By far, most self-proclaimed Evangelical seekers are of the first type: they hold to some core religious beliefs, may even say their "Born-again" experience was a turning point in their lives, but for the most part they reject conventional churches and know very little about Christian doctrine and practice. They are surprisingly open to other religious ideas: a fourth of them in our survey report believing in the possibility of communicating with the dead, a third believe in reincarnation and astrology, and well over half say they believe in psychic powers. The doubts, uncertainties, and quests of the wider culture are very much reflected in their religious views, all of which makes for a population exploring a Born-again Christianity that looks markedly different from the earlier historical descriptions.

The decentralized, highly pragmatic setting of a growing number of churches presents this more open, seeking constituency with a new way of "doing church"—one that privileges open discussion, shared experiences, and attention to spiritual development. Here inquirers find a message in a culturally relevant medium and are more likely than in conventional churches to be "taught" than "preached to." It is a place where laypeople and small groups play a much bigger role in the processes of both discerning and disciplining faith. That these churches are listening to the people and giving them a chance to shape that tradition's future sends a strong message. It is seen as an accepting context, privileging direct access to the sacred and allowing for natural responses—bodily movement, feelings, healing, testimonies, visions, dreams, ecstasies, and other experiences often at odds with modern rationality.[19] Music is important not just in its lyrics, but for the ambience it creates where a religious leader can modulate the message to fit the mood, thereby creating an aura of openness and expectancy with regard to spiritual possibilities.[20] All this encourages assimilation into a religious fellowship, even with questions and doubts, making people feel they belong even before they are expected to profess belief; dialogue and opportunities for "working on" faith are valued, not rejected simply out of hand. Even the physical surroundings—often auditoriums and other neutral spaces rather than church sanctuaries, lacking visible religious symbols, and using screens for projecting culturally current lyrics rather than using hymnals—help to sustain an environment of informality, open-mindedness, and searching. The setting evokes fresh emotions, unlike people's reactions in other religious settings, and this is affirmed by what one woman who now attends a megachurch told us: "You just stand there and you clap, eye to eye with the screen, feeling what you're seeing." Her comment underscores the power of the visual dimension, and the extent to which ways of knowing and experiencing have for many people changed rather significantly. The fact that so many of these congregations play down their denominational background and distance themselves from any cultural baggage associated with it, opens up even more the possibility of creative religious responses.

To a considerable extent, then, Born-again Christians gather in settings where by design reflexivity and innovation are becoming institutionalized, where spiritual seekers interact with believers, learning from them and sharing similar experiences, and where believers are kept more honest in their faith by the seekers' questions.[21] This is a bold undertaking for religious organizations, yet consistent with the temper of the times and, probably, on the spiritual forefront as we move into a new century. While it is far from clear what this changing institutional context may imply for Evangelical and Charismatic communities, probably once such patterns are established there can be no real turning back without loss of many who insist on "growth" and "exploration" as an inescapable component of their spiritual—and Christian—journey. This in turn will encourage opportunities for forging new and changing spiritual styles, but not without tensions over boundaries between the truly "faithful" and the "seekers" in this more open, engaging context. It is unlikely, however, that the institutionalization of a concentric-circle model of commitment, with the faithful in the inner circles and with overtures to the larger seeker-sensitive circles, will disappear anytime soon. Evangelical fervor and a "post-Christian" culture, as many Evangelicals describe the situation, assure that such structures and strategies will continue to flourish.

MAINSTREAM BELIEVERS

Mainstream believers differ greatly from Born-again Christians, even if the label is something of a misnomer. People so described, and who frequently describe themselves this way, do not constitute a religious mainstream as judged by demographics or institutional vitality. Indeed, a case can be made for precisely the opposite: Born-again Christians are in important respects more the religious mainstream, and those identifying with the "old-line" or mainstream faiths are more on the religious periphery. Yet the social location of these latter is not so peripheral. First, when asked if they are in "the mainstream of the way Americans live and think," these are the people most likely to say yes—more than 90 percent agreeing. Even if they cannot say why or articulate clearly what they believe or who they are religiously, they see themselves as worthy of core cultural values and ideals closely linked to the American Way of Life. They resonate with a normative set of values, hopes, and dreams even if its religious components are at times blurred in their own minds. Hence their stories differ in significant ways from those of Born-again Christians: they are rooted more in family tradition and cast more in terms of old-style social identities and communal belonging. Socio-religious group attachments often reaching way back into the past are still valued; they particularly appreciate social connections and knowing who knows whom. On average, with their higher incomes, greater wealth, and superior family status, mainstream believers continue to enjoy a power and influence not yet fully enjoyed by most Born-again Christians.

Second, religious history is not unimportant: it provides continuity with kin and a level of community status most mainstream believers want to maintain. Religion is a dimension of social identity linking history and social standing. Furthermore, as we have seen in Chapter 4, there is a small but increasingly influential spiritual vanguard within these older religious establishments now creatively exploring faith traditions. For them, theology and heritage are important, as Lutherans, as Catholics, as Reform or Orthodox Jewish. More than just personal faith, religion for them is also a shared tradition. Mainstream believers who are active, or who have become active again, appreciate especially liturgy, sacraments, and meaningful worship experiences. There is a pride in heritage far greater than their level of church attendance would suggest.

Finally, negative reference is a factor. Many mainstream believers within the Baby Boom generation have grown up with relatives and friends who are Born-again, and for them the boundary—"us" versus "them"—is a basis of some importance for social and religious identification. Often they can better verbalize who they are not than who they are: they are *not* Born-again Christians. But who are they? When pushed, and not infrequently it takes some pushing, they draw on memories from their childhood and youth, of the historic faiths as mediated through their parents and grandparents. Frequently, they do not completely embrace that past but neither do they discard it. When directly confronted, they acknowledge what they really know, that the past is a part of them, and thus not to be cavalierly dismissed.

There are distinctions among the religious heritages, of course: among Catholics, Protestants, Jews, and others. But knowing only that someone is Catholic or Jewish or of a mainstream Protestant denomination is less salient for most Boomers than the distinction between Born-again Christians and the religious mainstream. This, considered along with the diminishing social and cultural differences between the major, old-line faith communities, allows the conclusion that in many people's minds there is a symbolic, rather unified religious mainstream. In fact, scholars since the 1970s have drawn attention to a religious mainstream in much this way, and many people appear to think likewise. From our research we discern what might be called a "second-order" of religious narrative construction: many Boomer Catholics, mainline Protestants, Jews, and even some Muslims speak as if they share, in varying degrees, a common "zone" of religious comfort and values. This is not to downplay obvious differences and tensions among them, but increasingly, what binds younger members within these traditions is a respect for differences, tolerance and trust, and a sense that whatever boundaries separate them are of less importance than those uniting them over against Fundamentalists, overzealous Evangelicals, and religious "cults." In part this symbolic unity rests on a similar social class standing. Middle-class Muslims such as Sadiq Khan in Los Angeles are assimilation-oriented and well educated; Khan, the owner of a profitable computer business, is quick to say: "I am an American citizen, I have many Christian and Jewish friends. We can, we must, get along as Americans." Similarly, a young generation of upwardly mobile blacks, sometimes called Buppies, are returning to churches and are at the center of the socio-economic restructuring of the black community. They expect a high quality of professional services and are pushing middle-class black churches toward mainstream status, strengthening ties with white middle-class churches while also distancing themselves from sectarian groups at the lower end of the socio-economic order.[22] Both the Muslim and black Protestant examples alert us to a reconfigured religious mainstream with new partners, undergirded by common economic interests and a culture of civility.

If we look at the demographic composition of "mainstream believers," we find that slightly over half are Roman Catholics, about 35 percent are Protestants identified with the old, established denominations, and the remainder are ex-Fundamentalists and burned-out Evangelicals, blacks, Jews, and assorted religious others. Catholics and Protestants, the two large groupings, set the tone for this emerging subculture. Over the past forty years, social attitudes on many issues—including abortion, once defined as a "Catholic issue"—have converged for the two constituencies. Shifts in religious affiliations between the two have become easier. Religious norms set by the Protestant majority consisting of hundreds of denominations and a climate of increased acceptance of other faiths encourage ease of movement among them. The mind-set of many in the Boomer generation, particularly among the better-educated middle class, is that if a religious affiliation sounds vaguely familiar and is not perceived as overly zealous, and certainly not as belligerent, fanatical, or "cult-like," then it is probably acceptable. It is a popular dichotomy that has emerged in thinking about religion, but one not surprising given the rise of so many diverse religious movements in their lifetime and a society where norms of tolerance and openness are deeply embedded in the culture. The cultural and religious boundaries have simply been redrawn, and widened to include within the religious mainstream groups like Muslims, who even a decade ago would have been suspect. The pace of religious change in this respect is astounding.

Moreover, within this sector of the Boomer population—roughly one-quarter of the total—the level of interfaith marriages is relatively high. This factor is of far-reaching significance, obviously leading not just to a change of religious norms but to enhanced religious and cultural assimilation. "When I told my father I was marrying a Jewish man I met at college," a Catholic woman in Ohio said, "my father wasn't all that happy, but the next day he said, 'Well, at least he's not Evangelical Christian.'" In an earlier era, one might have expected just the opposite reaction. But with the rise of large public universities and greater opportunities for students to meet others of different faiths, along with a more accepting mood in general toward interfaith marriage, the situation is changing. Already we see signs of a more hybrid mix of cultures originating out of such marriages, though acceptance of interfaith marriages does vary from one religious group to another. Since this topic is explored in greater depth in Chapter 7, we need not pursue it here except to observe that among middle-class mainstream believers the pace of religious and cultural assimilation is extraordinarily rapid. Among those with high levels of education, income, and social status, such marriages are not only increasingly accepted but looked upon often as opportunities for creative family-based rituals and celebrations, and this in itself signals a significant change of normative religious mood.[23]

Common experiences and concerns help to unify this reconfigured religious mainstream, again especially among its middle-class majority. Sharing roughly similar social statuses, cultural styles, and psychological stresses, mainstream believers are drawn to similar definitions of what they expect religion, or spiritual teachings, to provide for them. Religion encompassing therapeutic support and psychological adjustment is in considerable demand. Motivational gurus who write books on spiritual laws about material success or about relaxation, or ideally about how to achieve both with a single technique, appeal to those caught up in the fast lane. Managing the "self" and its emotions is a felt concern of many Americans and explains the widespread appeal of popular writers whose recipes for inspiration and well-being cut across faith traditions. Somewhat paradoxically, at a time when the needs of the self are very much on people's minds, ecclesiastical resources often seem either inadequate or beyond the grasp of many within this subculture. This in itself is a unifying experience of sorts for some who have come not to expect much in the way of spiritual resources from the congregations and traditions that historically shaped their identities. In no small part, the malaise afflicting the mainline churches follows from a loss of confidence that what they have to offer will make any difference in middle-class lives.

Mainstream believers on the whole have weak ties to religious institutions. Relationships with local churches, synagogues, and temples are in fact ambivalent: an overwhelming majority—84 percent—insist that one can be a "good Christian or Jew" without regularly attending church or synagogue. At the same time, even greater numbers of them say they would like to have a congregation nearby to meet whatever needs may arise, especially for baptisms, weddings, and funerals. This combination implies a need for some degree of religious belonging, even if only weak, and an attempt to be grounded while remaining fluid. It is also true that mainstream believers across faith communities often lack a clear and compelling religious vocabulary. For so long encouraged to keep emotion and intellect separate within the established faith traditions, many of them do not know where to turn in a time of greater discourse upon experience. Many opt for a softer language of the self but lack familiarity with historic theological words; in fact, often words they recall about religion, like *salvation* and *born again*, are avoided because of association with conservative faiths and popular television preachers.[24] Lack of a greater familiarity with religious language applies to both of the large mainstream constituencies—Catholic and Protestant. Mainstream Catholics and Jews share more of a communal religious culture than do most Protestants. Catholic piety and devotional life are more visually oriented to symbols, and Jews are bonded through history, the holocaust, and ties to Israel. Being more diverse institutionally, mainstream Protestants hold to a wide range of theological views, of moral and value commitments, of cultural styles. On almost any behavioral or attitudinal item picked from our survey, mainstream believers (and Protestants in particular) have a range of opinions usually greater than for most other constituencies—such as prayer in schools, abortion, gay rights, or physician-assisted suicide. Yet these differences among mainstream Protestants, huge as they are, are overshadowed by the broader demographic and cultural convergences among Protestants, Catholics, Jews, and increasingly Muslims, and especially among members of the middle class in urban areas. By and large, mainstream believers feel separate from both Born-again Christians and dogmatists whose worlds are too exclusively defined, and from metaphysical believers, spiritual seekers, and secularists whose worlds seem to border on the flaky or are seen as indifferent to religious values. Occupying a middle location between extremes, many mainstream believers hold that theirs is a position of practical reason and responsibility.

Important in shaping this new religious mainstream, also, are centrist forces within American life that push in the direction of similar moral and religious styles. Many mainstream believers fit the description of "Golden Rule" religion[25]—neither very cold nor very hot religiously, but mostly concerned with providing for their families, helping and caring for others, doing good deeds, being friendly and civic-minded, and living a good life. Tolerance and respect for people who are different and treating others as you would like to be treated are more honored than either strict adherence to doctrinal creeds or unrestrained emotions. A sense of fair play and abiding by the rules are terribly important, as reflected in the comment of a Presbyterian in California: "If you play by the rules, you can know that you are a good person and look in the mirror every day without shame." Rules make you good and blameless. Mainstream believers look on God much as they see themselves, as providing, protecting, caring, comforting, loving, law-abiding. Among Christians, Jesus is seen as both Savior and Teacher, Redeemer and Moral Exemplar. These believers are concerned about moral and religious instruction for their children, or at the very least they want them exposed to the basic teachings. They volunteer for causes and donate money where needed. Community and work figure prominently in their universe of religious meaning; they value personal happiness, material success, and the rewards of hard work. Faith has more to do with how life is lived in relation to family, friends, and community than ultra commitment to institutions or theological orthodoxy. Most say religion is important to them and that faith helps them get through life, even though, as one journalist concluded after spending a year as a participant-observer in a New England church, "most mainliners do not . . . know they have a story to tell."[26] Typically that story is so culturally diffused, if not lost in the cacophony of louder religious voices, that mainstream believers (or mainliners) often *act* as if they do not have a story even when, deep down perhaps, they know they do. Values they hold as they relate to getting along with one another and confidence in the goodness of people, combined with respect for a "quiet faith,"[27] serve as unifying bonds within the subculture.

But holding to a Golden Rule style of religion, as sociologist Nancy Ammerman points out, does not mean that mainstream believers are spiritually bereft. While they often lack a religious vocabulary that expresses very well their convictions, still, as she points out, they have not given up on transcendence.[28] Their views of God focus less on personal relationships and experiences as with Born-again Christians, and more on encountering the divine in human needs, social obligations, and in everyday challenges. For many, whether Roman Catholic, Protestant, Jewish, or other, living the good life, combined with acts of charity and caring about others, can be spiritually engaging, even if the vocabulary they use for describing such actions often borders on the generic. Public causes tap energies, often religiously inspired even if not identified as such. Certainly, the forces of modernity and secularity have greatly altered the role of these communities as custodians of the culture, but the residues of an earlier heritage seeking to bridge tensions in the wider culture are still present. Committed mainstream believers are still drawn to a widely encompassing religious narrative, the "public church"[29] model of faith and life. It is a model that takes seriously the broader connections to the culture and emphasizes, more than a "saving faith," an "ordering faith" at the center of life and emphasizes "not just 'the church in politics' but the church active in the mall, the market, the concert hall and gallery, the town meeting and academy."[30]

For those of the mainstream spiritual vanguard, like Sara Caughman, there is renewed attention to faith and its relation to the wider culture. Recall that she is a member of an Episcopal parish now in transition, one redefining itself and its mission to the local and global community. High on the list of priorities are programs and activities for working and career women, families, blacks, gay and lesbian groups, the homeless and needy, and those openly agnostic and searching for a faith. How to relate to this latter constituency—open-minded seekers—is very much a concern because some members of her parish are ex-Fundamentalists and burned-out Evangelicals, people who say they are looking for a spiritual style different from what they have known in the past. "I can't sit through one more shallow, rosy praise lyric," one formerly conservative Christian woman in Sara's church says. "I'm looking for something else." This particular woman is not all that atypical: born into a Catholic family, became involved in Campus Crusade for Christ while in college, joined several Evangelical churches over a period of eighteen years, and now reaching out for an alternative. Perhaps more than anything else, what religiously estranged Boomers exploring the mainstream faiths are looking for is acceptance, authenticity, and honest engagement with life. Often, too, for those on the way to renewed commitment in these traditions, there is a peculiar vocabulary problem. Well-known author and lecturer Kathleen Norris observes that many mainstream believers must discard, or "unlearn," the lingo encountered in religious communities before they can arrive at a richer religious vocabulary. Their dilemma is in one sense just the opposite of that of Born-again Christian converts. Whereas Born-again Boomer Christians have a personal language but must "work at" connecting with a viable cultural and religious past, those seriously committed within the religious mainstream search for fresh vocabulary but must "work at" distancing themselves from either an Evangelical past or even the older cultural and religious establishment in which many of them grew up. As a result, there is a growing variety of religious discourses and spiritual themes within the mainstream, a situation that affords rich opportunities but often poses obstacles for congregations. Agnosticism and doubt especially pose challenges for creative encounters with the wider culture.

As its record in the United States in the latter half of this century shows, mainline Protestantism often failed to build bridges across generations. Building such bridges is now a top priority. James L. Kelley, a staunch and long-time agnostic, offers some observations about the challenges now posed to religious institutions by doubters and skeptics who nonetheless search out the religious mainstream. Drawing off his experiences in an "open" church in Washington, D.C., where he says he feels welcome but not pressured to affirm any creed or congregational standard of faith, he offers the following prescription:

> Increased vitality in the church community and sensitivity to feminist concerns usually go along with diversity in membership. Diversity and vitality are sometimes accompanied by more democratic ways of running the church. When these elements coalesce, they form a church that might be variously described as liberal, progressive, welcoming, inclusive. I prefer the word "open" because it implies not only diversity of membership but also open-mindedness in matters of belief and a willingness to consider new ways of operating—the kind of church I might be interested in.[31]

More such "open" churches are now appearing, offering questers an alternative to both conventional mainstream religion and Born-again Christianity.[32] Both of the churches here mentioned—Sara Caughman's and James L. Kelley's—provide opportunities for engaging their theological traditions. There is openness in the sense of asking hard questions and in recognizing that lived religious narrative is itself open-ended, always evolving and ready to be revised. Both have sought to institutionalize narrative dialogue or encounter with, and conversation about, a broad repertoire of symbols, teachings, practices, and moral values as constituting religious tradition. Both churches are examples of a "participatory congregation,"[33] meaning that they are not trying to organize social programs and activities around a stable core culture, but rather to allow input from the bottom up to shape the changing rhetoric and agendas. This shift toward greater grassroots involvement parallels the rise of Boomers into positions of social power and influence, with their voice now heard in voluntary and community-based organizations. Religiously, having that voice means taking a greater role in drawing off a theological heritage and devising appropriate models of love, grace, forgiveness, and justice.

Such involvement is bringing new life to once-old, more authoritarian Catholic parishes. Boomer Catholics now involved in parishes, often after many years of inactivity, speak of how the church, its liturgy, and leadership have changed, 95 percent of them voicing approval of these changes. Growing numbers of these returnees, many of them women, now sit on parish councils and worship committees sharing decision-making responsibilities with priests about ministry and liturgy. Spirituality for these younger Catholics is defined largely in post-Vatican II terms, more egalitarian and ecumenically minded, deeply sacramental and richly imaged, yet also intentional and deliberative, and less linked to a particular state of life (lay, clerical, or religious) as historically defined.[34] The idioms of religious expression have greatly changed in the direction of the vernacular, shaped in part by the experiences and causes of the younger generations and by minority populations in particular. There is vitality particularly on the part of young and rapidly growing Latino populations, not just in the Southwest but throughout much of the country. Their numbers combined with great energy and embedded spiritual practices are revitalizing American Catholicism, and in ways likely to become even more pronounced in the years ahead.

It remains to be seen what normative styles will prevail in American Catholicism, but in urban centers across the country the flavor of its "theology on the ground" is clearly changing. The Euro-American center of this tradition fades as a new-style, multi-ethnic and multicultural church emerges. A theology of incarnation filtered through feminist and liberationist lenses yields increasing power among the younger ethnic generations, as voiced by a Chicana in California who speaks of "what Mary went through" as symbolic of oppressed women's struggles everywhere. For this young woman, Mary is a rallying religious figure for developing a more critical consciousness and praxis among Latinas. She and others like her, male and female, appeal to selected aspects of Catholic tradition to contest church teachings and practices that are deemed unjust, such as the barriers to women's ordination. Influenced by the lay renewal of Vatican II, feminism and gender battles, and minority ideologies, they look upon struggle as transforming and life-giving.[35] Based upon impressionistic evidence, a disproportionate number of these lay theologians—a young breed of *bricoleurs* in parish after parish using the cultural tools of the tradition to reshape it—seem to have been born after World War II. Important, too, is the changing demographic composition of the Catholic Boomer population itself, now considerably more Latino than two decades ago.

Young Jews are turning to the Kabbalah and to textual study, to a greater emphasis "on the practical implications of both for daily life and specifically for the life of ceremony."[36] More than just curiosity about mysticism or the Torah, the focus is on Jewish practice, observance of the mitzvot, and the *chavurot*. Books and guides to Jewish practice, many of them arising out of newly created fellowships, continue to draw the attention of Jewish Boomers and shape their spiritual sensitivities.[37] Organizations like Synagogue 2000 are devoted to transforming congregations into spiritual and caring communities through prayer, study, good deeds, and ritual healing, and using such disciplines and activities as opportunities for dialogue between Jewish tradition and Boomer culture. But more than just Jews, indeed, all major religious groups are consciously creating new rituals and organizing fellowships that allow for more participation and sharing of experiences and feelings. "Interaction ritual," as it is sometimes called, not only permits but encourages a creative connection between the stories of individuals and the larger religious narrative.[38] A diversified menu of small groups, contemporary and traditional worship services, and focus on a range of personal and public matters all help to create an environment where not only alternative styles are possible, but where clergy and laypeople alike must think through what types of program and services are appropriate. People must choose what lived religious expressions should be nurtured and celebrated, and how generally to be spiritually responsive in a religiously and culturally diverse world. Diversity and the necessity of decision-making force a degree of reflexivity on congregations and fellowships. It allows for people themselves to forge religious styles that are culturally current yet also theologically informed or, as a United Methodist minister in California told us, "to retain tradition and depth of good theology."[39]

Are many mainstream believers looking for such congregations? Proportionately no, but the fact that roughly 40 percent of them favor exploring spiritual teachings over sticking to a faith suggests there is a considerable reservoir of interest and energy ready to be channeled by creative religious leaders. Mainstream religious communities are potentially resourceful, but they do face severe challenges. A third of them say that God is found within themselves and that religious structures may not be all that necessary. Another third are only weakly committed to religious institutions and deeply torn in their loyalties and obligations. Hence many churches and synagogues are caught between two opposing pitfalls—if they close themselves off to seekers they lose potential members, as well as long-time members who may want a more self-engaging spirituality, *yet* if they lean too far trying to engage seekers and alienate more traditional believers, they risk losing their most solid supporters. Much depends on the relatively small vanguard who are deeply committed to religious practices as a means to spiritual growth. If they can find sufficient space to forge a vision combining spiritual resourcefulness and institutional commitment, there is some promise of revitalization, but as a minority voice within mainstream religion and the larger religious economy.

Several observations can be drawn about the mainstream vanguard. First, the truly sustainable quest on the part of the vanguard is not just within the self, or even outward from the self, but primarily an exploration into the depths of traditions and practices. Mainstream American spirituality is self-consciously metaphoric; it thrives on the knowledge that ultimate truths reside not in literal interpretation of texts or in lifeless tradition, but in open and honest encounters between people and religious stories informed by tradition. Central is the religious imagination, comprising stories of God, as handed down from the past and as experienced in everyday life. Mainstream believers, more so than some others, understand and appreciate religious narrative as open-ended and generally accept the messiness of life—its struggles, pains, and joys—and even try to discern the divine in its midst.[40] Some are now discovering the richness of their own faith traditions and surprising themselves often with what they find, that is, teachings and role models that were hidden to them but relate to their lives. Even the old language has a mythic power that surpasses expectations. They recognize as true what is said of the theologians of the early church, that their writing is "remarkably vivid, energized by metaphors so grounded in earthly reality as to still be effective after more than a thousand years."[41] The challenge before the mainstream is to reclaim those earthly realities, to keep their discourses grounded in metaphors open to fresh interpretation, and to keep spiritually alive through meaningful practices and to ward off tendencies toward hardening into rigid forms and interpretations.

A second observation is that as mainstream believers reclaim their traditions, they discover how resourceful their heritages are to one another. Progressive Catholics and mainline Protestants discover the "merits of borrowing" from one another in exchanges over liturgy, in notions of the church as the "People of God," in the use of the lectionary, and in the introduction of vocabulary from Buddhism and other meditative traditions into their rhetoric about spirituality.[42] The spiritual movements within Judaism are becoming more comfortable, as Tamar Frankiel points out, with a panentheistic concept of God alongside the personal God of Christian tradition.[43] There is crossing of religious and cultural boundaries in the popularity of such figures as Gandhi, Martin Luther King, Jr., Simone Weil, Dorothy Day, Mother Jones, Thomas Merton, Elie Wiesel, Rabbi Abraham Heschel, the Dalai Lama, and, more recently, Václav Havel. A new cataloging of saints offers role models in areas of peace, justice, ecology, and spiritual grounding. Whatever else these figures stand for, their lives and writings help to generate a metaphoric language that speaks to widespread concerns for spiritual growth, authenticity, and hope. Debate over these and other such figures raises consciousness about issues people now face and encourages the pursuit of common visions and values, sustained by prayer, meditation, study, and other practices. Such exchanges underscore Havel's own comment about *consciousness* preceding *being:* though visions and values may now be largely inchoate and not fully formed, they may yet become better crystallized.

Finally, despite appreciation for wisdom and examples from other sources, those in the spiritual vanguard within the mainline traditions know they must create their own distinctive spiritual styles. They see themselves in a position of forging spiritual styles that honor heritage but lend themselves to improvisation and straddle between Fundamentalist and Evangelical Christian teachings, on the one hand, and the more open, do-it-yourself spiritualities of the contemporary religious marketplace, on the other. Rather than be swallowed up by either alternative, they seek to rebuild a spiritual life drawing off their own shared religious resources. In fact, their forays into other traditions and explorations into spiritual alternatives often result in greater clarity about, and appreciation for, their own faith traditions.[44] The more they explore their own traditions and others, the more they realize that what finally justifies their distinctive niche in the American religious economy is that it offers a sanctity compatible with life in the world amidst its complexity, tensions, and paradoxes. If there is one thing that unites the spiritual vanguard across the mainstream traditions, it is this hope and challenge. As example, historian Ann Taves describes the changing mood among Christians across traditions as they are pulled together:

> For progressive Catholics and mainline Protestants, "Christian spirituality" is . . . a very positive word, precisely because it holds a variety of conflicting connotations in tension. It holds tradition and depth in tension with ecumenical and inter-religious openness and a desire for institutional renewal and reform; corporate belief and practice in tension with the immediate and explicit experience of the individual; the contemplative prayer of the monastery with committed action in the world. For Catholics, it signals a new emphasis on the spiritual equality of the people of God, regardless of vocation, in the wake of Vatican II and, for liberal Protestants, an escape from the narrow confines of the piety of Protestant evangelicalism.[45]

METAPHYSICAL BELIEVERS AND SEEKERS

The most diverse of our religious subcultures, metaphysical believers and seekers come in all stripes, identifying themselves as Neo-Pagans, Wiccans, goddess worshippers, Zen Buddhists, Theosophists, nature-lovers, feminists, holistic people, New Agers, spiritual people, "followers" of various spiritual masters, "seekers," and many without a name for themselves, or who in some instances shift from one name to another so frequently it depends on which day you ask. Over the eight years from the time we first talked with our respondents until the second or third interview, less than a fourth called themselves by the same name. A considerable number of people in this category admit when questioned to being seekers but are not likely to voluntarily identify themselves in this manner. Our definition for this category—rejecting a religious identity but affirming a spiritual one—broadens the category beyond those who might readily identify themselves as part of any particular tradition or movement. It includes feminists of an amazing variety who have broken with organized religion and who tend not to call themselves seekers, yet for whom spirituality clearly implies an indwelling of the sacred. It also includes people influenced by the nineteenth-century New Thought and metaphysical traditions who, when queried, are likely to think of themselves as metaphysical believers. Our category is also broader than what usually passes as New Age. While the popular media lumps a great variety of people under this rubric, relatively few people we talked with actually use the term to identify themselves; more did in fact in the late 1980s than in our second survey during the mid-1990s. And to add to definitional complexities, there are those who adamantly reject the New Age label. Thus the 14 percent of our sample we describe as metaphysical believers and spiritual seekers make up an extraordinarily heterogeneous subculture—even in terms of their own self-designations and identities, not to mention the great variety of beliefs, values, and ethical commitments they hold. Obviously it is difficult to generalize about so varied a constituency described by one researcher as an amazingly "large, amorphous, poly-traditional, spiritually-oriented national or global community."[46] Our term for this subculture combining two overlapping strata, admittedly a bit cumbersome, is simply Metaphysical Believers and Spiritual Seekers.

To complicate things even further, the spiritual impact of this subculture is even bigger than statistical estimates would suggest. There is a boundary problem considering that many people who are affiliated with a church, synagogue, or temple embrace teachings, practices, and sensitivities derived from this broad movement—like Karen Potter, the Southern Baptist-turned-feminist, who holds to spiritual teachings derived from theological and metaphysical sources that are greatly at odds with the faith in which she was raised. One national survey finds roughly one out of five Americans looks upon faith as a deeply private matter, saying that the Ultimate is intermingled with the self, and these Americans are themselves focused more on spiritual consciousness than on conventional ritual or practice.[47] It seems reasonable to conclude that among so sizable a population many of these people, of whom a good proportion hold church memberships, draw inspiration from a great variety of sources. In a world of disembedded symbols and teachings, it becomes increasingly difficult to identify their sources with accuracy.

A related development that complicates any simple accounting of spiritual trends is the growth in the number of Americans who say they hold to a nonpersonal conception of God. A Gallup poll as far back as the mid 1980s reported a third of Americans holding to such a view.[48] If we can interpret these survey findings as indicative of a spiritual resurgence and/or changing conceptions of the sacred, then the evidence of a spiritual shift mounts into a fairly large popular base. It is quite apparent that ideas, beliefs, and sensitivities originating from a grassroots spirituality are now rather widely diffused in American culture as a whole—

including within the churches, synagogues, and temples. Our own evidence of the ease of movement among Boomers from one religious and symbolic frame to another, plus the tensions inherent in trying to be experientially fluid while simultaneously grounded within some type of religious framework, makes for a strong case for its diffusion. As one sociologist commenting on the cultural mood in the United States recently put it: "The New Age phenomenon surrounds conventional religion like a cultural fog bank, almost completely lacking in large-scale organization but giving the fringes of faith a mysterious appearance."[49] Certainly for both the Boomer mainstream and Born-again subcultures, that mysterious appearance of faith is readily apparent as judged by the infusion of New Age (or what is increasingly called "New Spirituality") beliefs and sensitivities.

With respect to religious backgrounds, the subculture is almost as diverse as the current spiritual pursuits of the people who make it up. A majority were raised as conservative Protestants, a fourth as Catholics, and the remainder as liberal Protestants, Jews, and nonaffiliates—almost as if they were randomly drawn from a cross section of the United States. This in itself is an important observation. Whatever the nature, or quality, of the spiritual ferment at present, it touches much of this country. The widespread diffusion results partly from its subtlety. People often do not so much abandon old beliefs and symbolic frames from childhood and youth as modify them to fit a seeker mentality. Elements of belief and practice easily mix and match as circumstances change. There is more of a clean break in conventional patterns of religious participation. Two-thirds of the subculture as defined here feel that the spiritual part of religion has been lost in organized religion. These same people tend to have dropped out of active participation in a church and tell stories— often horror stories—about their experiences. Many feel their needs went unmet; they disagreed over certain practices or beliefs; and occasionally they reported being abused. Of all our constituencies, including secularists, they bear the deepest wounds from earlier experiences in organized religion, particularly in Catholicism and Protestant Fundamentalism; most in fact did not drop out as a result of indifference or loss of habit, as is usually the case with Boomers, but have specific reasons for having done so. Not surprisingly, many of them turn to small groups, workshops, and informal gatherings to tell their stories. A third of them, second only to Born-again Christians, report being in support groups where they can share experiences and receive spiritual support from others like themselves.

Alienation from religion is a key factor contributing to the search for a new spiritual identity. A man in North Carolina who had joined a twelve-step support group consisting of ex-Fundamentalists told us, "First, I had nothing to do with religion for a long time, then after that I started looking around at other groups, some really way out, but knowing that I would never, never go back to Assemblies of God." Both his choice of words and the tone in which he spoke made clear the depth of his feelings. Often in people's stories, "leaving religion" carries overtones of an exodus and the hope for a promised land, a play on a trope deeply embedded in the religious consciousness of Americans. It is a play also in keeping with the pattern of disengagement and reengagement so common in religious life, but which in this instance is expanded to maximize opportunities for spiritual searching. More than just a cognitive shift or a change of religious identification, what is usually central is a working out of feelings about oneself, of clarification and self-assertion. Clearly, too, the support groups and social networks to which many metaphysical believers and seekers belong encourage a break with old religious lives and a setting out on new spiritual adventures. Dogma, fixed beliefs, and routinized practices are seen as obstacles to personal transformation. Those wounded or feeling overly contained are told it is good to leave behind whatever is boxing them in, that nothing should stand in their way of cultivating self-esteem and positive images of themselves. People deserve better. Individuals not only share their stories, they recreate them incorporating input from other people, workbooks, and guides; the result is a larger, corporate narrative of who they are and of the defining moments of their lives. Not infrequently their shared hostility to the term *religion* becomes a positive, defining factor shaping an alternative identity. Metaphysical believers and spiritual seekers receive a great deal of reinforcement, from empathetic others, in their accounts of bridge-burning experiences in search of their own well-being, encouraged in what has been termed somewhat uncharitably a "quest for self-gratification."[50]

Not all have bridge-burning experiences, of course. When asked about spiritual matters, some seekers will, if pressed, acknowledge that their religious pasts—as Catholics or Protestants—still has a hold on them or they try to avoid the possibility simply by saying they have no religious preference. Catholics often continue as cultural Catholics even after moving away from the Church, similar to Jews who share a religiously based culture but are not ritually observant. To claim no religion is also partly a function of the way questions on religious preferences are asked in surveys and polls. Options allowing for more discriminating religious and spiritual choices are seldom available, when, as is typically the case, researchers and pollsters simply ask, "What is your religious preference—Protestant, Catholic, Jewish, Other, or None?" Sometimes people draw on conventional religious labels but modify them ("ex-Catholic," or "grew up Episcopalian but have my own beliefs"). They are fiercely independent in their thinking and hold to an optimistic view of human nature. Two-thirds say religious labels are not very important and half have switched religious or spiritual groups twice or more. Eighty percent say one can be spiritual without organized religion; 97 percent insist that in religious matters a person ought to think for oneself and not necessarily follow the teachings of any one religious tradition; and 98 percent say, "If one believes in oneself, there is almost no limit to what one can do."

Both the crossing of preexisting religious boundaries and affirming confidence in oneself and one's own choices come rather easily. They weave life-stories linking biography and religious tradition, looking forward into the future with utopian hopes and expectations and backward to nineteenth-century and earlier spiritual foundations. They claim access to spiritual truths and experiences other than by institutionally prescribed means and often create for themselves combinatory or pastiche spiritual identities. Indeed, of the hundreds of people we interviewed over a period of ten years, those most excited—and frequently the most articulate—about their spiritual lives were those who fashioned hyphenated identities such as vegetarian-Unitarians, eco-spiritualists, or the like. The deliberate, self-conscious construction of a religious identity drawing from a variety of sources reaches its apex within this subculture: eight out of ten say it is more important to explore religious alternatives than to stick with a particular faith. They are the most fluid in outlook of all the religious subcultures, with little discernible drift into wanting greater fixed religious positions even as they age. In this respect, they defy life-course stereotypes that presume that as people age they either return to the traditions in which they were raised or settle into a firm religious commitment.

There is a remarkable parallel between people's spiritual lives and their social experiences within this subculture, pointing to a degree of rootlessness, or perhaps as more favorably viewed, considerable adaptability to a world of shifting social realities. Sixty percent are unable to name an ethnic heritage for their families of origin, and those who can name a heritage tend not to have close attachments. In terms of friendships and stable social networks, they are the least socially embedded of all our constituencies. They pride themselves on their survival skills, both socially and spiritually, and like thinking of themselves as a spiritual vanguard, as innovators of a new movement that in the long run they believe will have global consequences. Even for those, and there are many, who do not think of themselves as necessarily a part of a solidified New Age or New Spirituality movement, those very labels serve as a symbol and vision of, and hope for, not only personal but social and cultural transformation in the future. Of all the religious subcultures, they are the most optimistic about a new world in the making. When asked about this new world to emerge, respondents usually affirm a simple degree of optimism without much clarity as to how this will come about except through the power of mental constructions.

Metaphysical teachings, of course, encourage an expansive self and collective hope. Gnostic and theosophical teachings, referred to in an earlier time as Theosophy and New Thought, posit an energetic world of movement between spirit and matter. "To be spiritual, in a metaphysical universe," writes historian Catherine L. Albanese, "is to unblock the door and to let the waters of life flow through. To put the matter in more contemporary language, it is to be sensitive to subtle energies and to respond to them with openness and delight."[51] Philosophically, as well as practically, the effect is to produce a spiritual style that dissolves old boundaries and facilitates; in rhetoric now increasingly common, the possibility is held out for "crossovers" from one religious genre to another, allowing for combinations and creation of a more full-fledged, expansive metaphysical theology. Old dualisms (body/mind, matter/consciousness, thinking/feeling) considered a product of an outmoded Enlightenment worldview are abandoned in favor of kinetic and holistic conceptions. Matter is a form of energy, but advocates in this tradition expand this distinction and add consciousness, arguing that matter, energy, and consciousness all make up a single continuum.[52] Likewise, Western rationality comes in for serious critique. Reason is one source of knowledge but there are others, and some sources are regarded as superior to reason because they are held to be immediate, more personal forms of knowledge, more intuitive and self-authenticating. Ultimate reality is beyond reason, at best encountered in an intuitive experience that cannot be reduced to words. Highly committed to a synthesis of ways of knowing and understanding the world and forces within it, followers within this tradition are hopeful that in time a unity of religion and science will prevail. Almost three-fourths of metaphysical believers and seekers, more than for any other subculture, think that conflicts between religion and science are likely to be resolved in the future. New Age and metaphysical publishers help to create optimism about this prospect, not just through books brought out again by Gnostics and theosophists from the past, but by contemporary writers on science, alchemy, popular psychology, and self-help philosophy. Consequently, emerging at present is a transformed Gnosticism in publications and on the Internet, now held up and celebrated as basis for both a monistic worldview and an optimistic conception of human nature.[53]

This optimism about an expansive self—"radical fluidity," Robert J. Lifton would say—arises out of a philosophy of self-reliance and of unending quest. When asked about personal and social influences that had most shaped their lives, metaphysical believers and seekers are the most inclined of all our constituencies to credit strong "will power" and "new insights" gleaned from their own experiences as decisive. They tend to view themselves as masters of their own fate. God as a personal being is not singled out as having a great deal of influence on them; many of them actually do not believe in a personal God. Consistent with an emphasis on the self, they are also far less likely to attribute influence to social, economic, and political realities. Generally, metaphysical believers and spiritual seekers pay relatively little attention to the social nature of human experience and tend to lack a language in which to describe social influences on them personally. "Luck" is recognized as a shaping influence, more so than "power" in society or even family "upbringing." Since, according to their worldview, the established patterns of society foster rational and dualistic worldviews and thus inevitably leave an imprint on the ego, the solution is to escape social influence and to find the deeper self within the individual—in "a space beyond conditioning."[54] It is finding this space that ultimately shapes personal narratives as told within this subculture. Under conditions of fluidity, keeping a personal narrative "going" becomes a task, and for these believers and seekers what keeps the narrative "going" is the high level of optimism and hope that they can indeed escape social influence.

Those narratives are typically a product of boundary-crossings. The combination of Eastern views on reincarnation and the optimism found within the metaphysical traditions offers many followers a space beyond conditioning. "Whereas in the East the reincarnation model ultimately proves the illusory character of the self, the Western innovation turns out to secure the self," writes commentator Lars Johansson, noting that this latter may be a peculiarly modern impulse. Reincarnation is not a curse but is welcomed in the modern Western world precisely because it offers another chance. Of course, interpretations about reincarnation, and views of Eastern spirituality generally, are a reconstruction stylized to the Western context. Johansson goes on to observe: "Drawing out the implications of this in relation to MacIntyre's concept of selfhood, in which self-identity is related to an individual's narrative that links birth to life and death," one can "see the attractiveness of an extended narrative where the self gets numerous chances to actualize itself."[55] Here we have a basis for understanding the popular appeal of metaphysical narrative. Within its framework the self becomes fully unbounded, transcending all social contexts, and is capable of uniting with the universe as a whole. Spiritual evolution encompasses no less than a cosmic journey with the self's potential for transformation plotted on the highest plane imaginable.

So much emphasis on personal identity and transformation distinguishes contemporary metaphysical spirituality from that of the nineteenth-century.[56] The body is especially symbolic and central, particularly for feminists. "We have plucked, shaved, veiled, corseted, sanded, lifted, and siliconed our bodies as we learn to objectify them and ourselves," as one feminist writer puts it, noting the alienation many women feel with their own flesh, and the necessity of redrawing the boundaries surrounding the body and its meaning.[57] A radical stress upon bodily experience as a basis for knowing encourages a proliferation of terms and vocabularies concerned with personal transformation and embodiment. Languages of "energies," of "inner voices," of "vibrations," of "*chakras*," of connections to the "elemental forces" of the body and of the universe replace theistic concepts and belief in a personal God. The task is to get in contact with this deeper self, to tap the enormous resources that lie within but, for whatever reason, are presently blocked to one's intuitive sensitivities. "It's about energy, feeling your own energy," one woman in California told us, "and if you know where the energies are and how to open up to them, you can learn about your life, put things together, discern its meaning just for you." Hers is a very different mode of speaking from that found within Christianity, or any other religion that affirms a transcendent God, yet it bears some resemblance to Christian talk about "where the Spirit leads." Energy, like Spirit, offers a way of pulling disparate things together and of keeping open the possibilities of mystery and self-transformation. Paradoxically, metaphysical language, as one commentator correctly observes, is rather abstract and ambiguous yet is easily learned and quickly put into use as personal philosophy. Openness and flexibility are qualities that make it an easy fit to almost any individual's life. In this respect "its philosophical and theological thinness is an asset rather than a liability."[58]

For intensely minded seekers, reflexivity is enhanced by both the fragmented worlds in which they live, and by their preoccupation with experience as self-authenticating. Concerned about not being bound by arbitrary limits, seekers are wary of structured communities and tend to have weak attachments to them. Sixty-one percent say, "People have God within them, so churches aren't really necessary." Of all our constituencies, they are the least likely to say they "feel close" to any religious group. Their group experiences are limited largely to small support groups and workshops, lectures, the circles of New Age bookstores, festivals, and informal social networks; some in large urban areas turn to metaphysical congregations, but most do not rely on worshiping communities as traditionally structured. Within the small groups, workshops, and social networks, there is considerable fluctuation in levels of participation. Fee-for-service is a common practice, which encourages separation of the product from the producer: there is less of a generalized, totalistic commitment as found within traditional faith communities and instead, more selective, individually initiated exchanges. Individuals pursue a particular service (specific topics on lectures, tapes, videos, or books) with regard to some spiritual theme, pay for it, and then "work" at incorporating its meanings directly into their lives without much assistance from an authority or communal involvement.[59] As a general rule, metaphysical believers approach religious questions with an openness to new, unfolding possibilities and with a mind-set of following their intuition in a direction of greater self-expansiveness. If this means leaving behind an old network or group in favor of a new one, or just leaving the network or group behind temporarily, so be it. Frequently participants feel they must, as anthropologist Michael F. Brown says, quoting a person he interviewed in a workshop on channeling, "step outside the organizational frame of mind," even if for a short period of time. "As soon as I made that choice," he quotes the interviewee as saying, "I felt the expansion."[60]

Self-expansiveness has its vulnerabilities, of course. Aside from a resistance to institutionalization, it generates varying notions of the sacred and encourages an incredibly disparate mix of teachings and practices. Both metaphysical believers and spiritual seekers look on the sacred as more impersonal than personal, as immanent more than transcendent. Next to secularists, they are the least likely to think of God in the traditional conception as Father, and hold instead to a vast array of feminine

211

and androgynous imageries, to panentheistic notions of the sacred permeating all things, and to more abstract conceptions such as "Higher Power" and "Unifying Presence." Talk about the sacred, the divine, or God can be rather vague and ambiguous; seekers especially are content to let such terms go largely undefined, sometimes even preferring to celebrate the mystery that goes unnamed.[61] Being neither bound by creed nor theistic in perspective, they speak far more convincingly of the energies found within the universe, or of the self in relation to the God-presence—or more likely, the self *as* God-presence. There is a corresponding disparate collection of beliefs, practices, stories, genres, and experiential frames, a mix of elements making possible one after another metaphysical configuration. Female and androgynous imageries of the divine mix freely with astrology, reincarnation, and psychic powers. Interest in the paranormal blends with prayer and belief in eternal life. Eastern religious ideas, macrobiotics, and humanistic psychology with its concern for healing and relationship therapies come together in talk about changing forms and patterns of energy. Angels, near-death experiences, and even UFOs and invasion by aliens seem every bit as real to many seekers as belief in the resurrection of Jesus Christ from the dead. Spiritual mediums and voices from the ancient past like that of Ramtha, the mysterious 35,000-year-old entity, seem just as persuasive, if not more so for some seekers, as sources of enlightenment today as the more conventional priests, rabbis, and pastors. If indeed, as we have said, the protean self seeks simultaneously to be fluid and grounded, then most certainly we see it in its most boundless and multiple forms in this subculture.

Dogmatists and Secularists

Having profiled the three spiritually minded constituencies, we turn to the two remaining subcultures—dogmatists and secularists. Dogmatists, who say they are religious but not spiritual, make up 15 percent of our population while secularists, claiming to be neither religious nor spiritual, account for 12 percent. By definition, dogmatists—known as Fundamentalists, moralists, neo-traditionalists, or ritualists[62]—tend to be rigidly religious, some might say Pharisaic, concerned more with the external forms of religion than with its spirit. Tradition for them is largely bounded by encrusted institution and frozen in a nostalgic past. Religious narrative takes on a formulaic character and becomes rather lifeless and closed. Secularists, as we would expect, are the least religious as conventionally defined, though they are more "ir-religious" or "a-religious" than really antireligious; religious agnosticism and indifference are far more common even among secular Boomers than hard-core atheism. Tradition for them often seems distant, or of little personal relevance. Some are religious in a privatized sense, but for the most part their religious stories are attenuated and vague, and largely of their own making. Thus the two constituencies are somewhat polar opposites: dogmatists see secularists as infidels, traitors to God and the nation, irresponsible and often immoral in their attitudes and behavior; secularists see dogmatists as Bible-thumping fanatics, insensitive to women and minorities, who, if given half a chance, will impose their morality and religion on them.

Looking at the descriptive profiles, it is not surprising why the two constituencies would view one another in this way. Secularists grew up much more positively influenced by the 1960s than did the dogmatists. Secularists, in fact, were the most influenced of all the subcultures as judged by our research: they were involved in more protest activity and embraced countercultural values to a greater degree than did the others. Dogmatists were reactionaries to those cultural changes, led to create a fortress mentality of resistance and of intensified moral and religious boundaries. Dogmatists have less education, typically only a high school or two-year college degree, and by and large are aligned with the values and interests of the old business class; in contrast, secularists enjoy higher incomes, hold more professional positions, and are far more likely to belong to the new "knowledge class." Dogmatists are politically conservative, many of them in fact alienated by the existing two-party system and feeling unrepresented; secularists are political liberals, and particularly so on lifestyle issues. Dogmatists cluster in suburbs and small towns, secularists are more evenly distributed but are disproportionately found in large cities.

Their religious backgrounds differ. The great majority of dogmatists grew up as either Catholic or conservative Protestant and still identify with these faith traditions. Six percent were raised in homes with no religious affiliation—historically, a recruiting ground for conversion to conservative faiths. Overall, their biographies show loyal commitment to their churches from the time of their young adult years to the present. They are the most frequent church-attenders currently of all the subcultures (51 percent are weekly attenders). But, as we would expect for secularists, their religious backgrounds and styles are strikingly at odds with those of the dogmatists: 8 percent Jewish, 20 percent Catholic, 16 percent conservative Protestant, and a whopping 56 percent mainline Protestant. Over the years they have moved in and out of congregations often with long periods of lapse, and not infrequently have switched from a mainline Protestant church to another denomination, maybe even explored other spiritual alternatives, before dropping out altogether. Eighty percent say they hardly ever or never attend religious services of any kind at present. To the extent we can speak of their religious narratives, they are punctuated by serious doubts, bad experiences, and considerable indifference to religious institutions; secularists are often fairly inarticulate about what they really believe, but when articulate offer mostly accounts of a negative narrative and of how they came to their own secular views. For whatever reason, they have for the most part worked themselves out of a religious frame of reference and, to a considerable extent, out of any meaningful language in which to talk about faith and spirituality. It is hard to dispute Peter Berger's observation that mainline churches serve as "*schools for secularity*," or "way stations for people heading out from *any* religious affiliation."[63]

Both subcultures are the fallout from the raging storm known as modernity; one led to dogmatic defensiveness of religious tradition, the other to secular indifference. Even friendships and social networks differ: a majority of dogmatists say that many of their friends are of the same ethnic group (for Catholics, mainly Irish; for Protestants, mainly German); almost as many say they feel close to their religio-ethnic group and that their friends know one another; and nearly a half say many of their closest friends attend the same church. Religious group ties are dense and encapsulated, turned inward upon themselves. They attend religious services frequently and it is important to them that friends attend religious services. Of all the constituencies, they are the most likely to endorse worshiping with others as opposed to worshiping alone, and the least likely to think that one can be a "good Catholic" or "good Christian" and not attend religious services. By and large, secularists fall out at the other extreme: fewer of their friends are of the same ethnic group, with 43 percent admitting they "don't know" their own ethnic background; ties among friends are much less dense; and remarkably few claim to have close friends attending any type of religious congregation. Aside from occasional rites of passage within a religious community, religion is for the most part something deeply personal, outside of a religious gathering. Two-thirds say they prefer to worship alone than to worship with others. Only a small minority say they care if their friends attend church.

Thus what we have are two quite distinct social enclaves with congregational worship overlapping with kin and friendships for dogmatists, but not so for secularists. As sociologists using Christian terminology often say, there are two cultures in the contemporary United States—the "churched" and the "unchurched"—for the most part, structurally separate from one another.

The practical consequences of this structural separation are considerable. For dogmatists, close attachments to religious communities comprise the social mechanism sustaining meaning systems, for which there really is no analogue for secularists, who are inclined toward a monarchical conception of God (king, lord, judge, lawgiver) with its related images of domination and subjection.[64] God, pictured almost uniformly as male authority, is seen as the governing influence of their lives. They affirm, in large numbers, literal belief in the Bible, in the devil, in an afterlife. Jesus is typically thought of as shepherd who takes care of those loyal to him. They are much more likely than any of the other subcultures to believe that a child is guilty of sin and to disagree with the statement that "all the great religions of the world are equally true and good." They take a dim view of human nature and prefer to think of moral issues as clear-cut, either right or wrong. Secularists, on the other hand, hold to a vast array of popular-based divine imageries, some quite conventional, but most their own creations; one-half say "God is within you, so churches aren't necessary." Ninety-four percent say one should think for oneself on religious matters and look on one religion as about as good or true as another. Well over two-thirds agree that God might be thought of as a "Higher Power." Still, over half say that God, however conceptualized, is involved in their lives; almost half report reading the Bible occasionally; and 40 percent claim to pray daily and say grace at meals. Many are curious about religious and spiritual matters and read, often quite widely, on the subject—especially top-selling books. When asked what were the influences that shaped them when growing up, they are the most likely of all to say the characteristics they were born with, thus attributing to genetics—not God, society, luck, the way they were brought up, or even their own will power and personal insights—why they are as they are today.

Hence, our social and religious profiling of the subcultures—the *dramatis personae* of an emerging and realigned religious landscape. Important though the dogmatists and secularists as polar opposites may be, of greater significance is the larger map of all five subcultures, all of which are in an evolving process of identity-formation and redrawing of

215

boundaries in the contemporary cultural environment. Three of the subcultures are in the throes of spiritual ferment or reawakening. Involved is a sifting and sorting along new social and religious lines, and a major reconfiguring of moral and religious values. Born-again Christians, mainstream believers, metaphysical believers and spiritual seekers, dogmatists, and secularists are more than statistical aggregates; socially, culturally, and religiously, they are embodied constituencies, increasingly conscious of themselves as major players on the religious scene. Their meaning systems, religious practices, and social and organizational attachments are patterned, increasingly, along the lines here described. But what about the connections of religion and family, or the changing links between these two closely related institutions? To what extent, and how, does family structure play into this changing configuration of religious subcultures? And also, in what ways is the changed family structure of our time increasingly a structural basis on which these religious subcultures rest? These are crucial questions discussed in Chapter 7.

Realigning Family and Religion

As the family goes, so goes the church.
(*Penny Long Marler*)

O F ALL THE CHANGES in American religious life since World War II, perhaps the most consequential in the long run has to do with religion and family. Historically, the two institutions have enjoyed a mutually supportive relationship: religion provided legitimacy for marriage, as well as support and guidance strengthening family life; and, in turn, families as the primary units of society functioned as an extension of the religious community, inculcating its beliefs, values, and practices. In the case of the United States, religion and family have long been viewed as working together in a voluntary religious order to ensure the maintenance of beliefs and values in society through moral and religious socialization of the young. At stake is the transmission of the religious heritage itself. Put into narrative terms, families are the settings where great stories embodying trust, respect, love, honesty, integrity, fairness, responsibility, and other values are shared and practiced. Here children first learn what it means to belong and to be loyal, to relate to others, to share in ritual practices, to celebrate the values of families and loved ones, all crucial to personal identity and social life. Here parents not only teach moral virtues and faith but model them, setting examples that children may follow. We might even go so far as to assert that the link between parents and children rests to a considerable extent on storytelling itself. Underscoring this very point, philosopher Alasdair MacIntyre writes:

> It is through hearing stories about wicked stepmothers, lost children, good but misguided kings, wolves that suckle twin boys, youngest sons who receive no inheritance but make their own way into the world, and eldest sons who waste their inheritance on riotous living and go into exile to live with swine, that children learn or mis-learn both what a child is and what a parent is. What the cast of characters may be in the drama into which they have been born and what the ways of the world are. Deprive children of stories and you leave them unscripted. Anxious stutters in their actions as in their words.[1]

217

But what happens to storytelling when families must compete with peer groups and the media? Or when families lack coherent stories? Or worse still, when families are settings for abuse and family members are led to doubt, if not outright reject, the love, respect and values of spouses or parents? Obviously, changes in family and religion over the past half-century have complicated the storytelling, leading as MacIntyre says to children who are "unscripted," known by their "anxious stutters" in actions and words. The very definition of what constitutes family is itself up for debate and what was at one time looked on as a normative, mutually supportive relationship for religion and family is hardly so anymore. For many people having grown up in an era of rapid social change, "family" seems less of a stable social unit than a maze of alternative arrangements and uncharted experiences. So swiftly have these changes in gender roles, marriage, family, and organization of personal lives come upon us, that many Americans feel a good deal of unresolved tension and lack of clarity in their roles as lovers, spouses, and parents. Not surprisingly, there has been much inflamed rhetoric about "family values" and the rise of family-based ideologies in recent decades. So much flux, too, fans a good deal of lingering nostalgia for a 1950s-style, Norman Rockwell United States where family life is thought to have been better ordered. Imageries of warm, happy families centered around a working husband and father and a domestic wife and mother and of a close, cozy connection between family and faith live on in the minds of many people despite family sitcoms on television and an avalanche of demographic information portraying a world with little resemblance to that not-so-distant past. Moreover, such imageries perpetuate, as sociologist Penny Long Marler points out, a "nostalgic church," one lost in the 1950s, she says, caught between family fiction and family reality.[2]

John McRae, our Catholic-leaning respondent from Ohio, is caught up in this nostalgia. When he talks about his childhood, he remembers Christmas holidays, gift exchanges within the family, loving parents. His nostalgia is further compounded by experiences in his first marriage: a painful divorce, separation from his child. But he is not completely caught between family fiction and family reality, for he knows fully well through personal experience the current realities of marriage and divorce, and that his world can never be the same as that of his parents. Nor would he want to turn the clock back to an older style of family life, since he knows that not all was well in his parent's marriage. He is also committed to a more egalitarian marriage and nurturing family where husband and wife, and parents and children are sensitive to one another's needs. On the surface he seems remarkably well adjusted in his transition in both family and religion, even if at a deeper level his emotions are not fully resolved. "I grew up on *Leave It to Beaver*," he says, "but live in a *Thirtysomething* world." Only a quarter-century separates these two worlds, but experientially it is a huge leap. Now he hopes to work out those emotions and to get his intimate relationships in sync with his deepest feelings about himself as he prepares for a new marriage.

His story is illustrative of the changing context of religion and family at several levels. Most apparent, given the extent of lifestyle pluralism, is that the connection between the two institutions is structurally fragile, and increasingly diverse and unhinged. People understand this to be the case today, although interestingly, John McRae draws heavily on media-created imageries in locating himself in a world of family realities. Perceptions of family, and by extension, those of family and religion, are for many in this generation deeply influenced by the media. Quite possibly, too, media construction accentuates the gap between family fiction and family reality not simply in the direction Marler speaks of, but in an *opposite* direction as well—overlooking couples and families who actually are religious and exaggerating in television and film those who are not. Given these mixed influences, the resulting confusion and uncertainty about the expectations of family and religion further reinforces a view of the family as a perplexing maze. Nor has scholarly research contributed as much as it might in clarifying relations between these two institutions. Studies on the family seldom give attention to religion, and those that do often overlook the realistic patterns of families. Far more attention is given to the contentious rhetoric surrounding family values than to actual structural realignments of family and religious communities. Even the most informed discussions on the restructuring of religion and society in the United States since the 1950s give amazingly little attention to family-based changes.[3]

In this chapter we address more forthrightly the religion and family nexus, particularly how such changes relate to the religious subcultures as profiled in Chapter 6. How important is the family connection for religion? More precisely, to what extent are the family changes of the past fifty years a source of religious changes? And in what ways do these new family structures serve as carriers of one or another of the religious subcultures we have identified? The focus here is the evolution of family patterns and the realignments of family and religion, leaving for Chapter 8 attention to the symbolic crusades over gender, family, and other aspects of the so-called cultural wars. We must examine the "religion and family connection" at both levels: first, as an instance of demographic and structural change within American society; and second, as a setting for moral and ideological debates currently. Without some attention to both, we cannot comprehend the full range of cultural changes underway or speculate in an informed way about where religion may be headed in the coming century.

REALIGNMENTS IN THE MODERN PERIOD

From our perspective in year 2000, two things are clear about the 1950s, a period often remembered as a golden age for family and religion: it was an aberrant decade for both institutions, and it also marked a turning point in the way these two institutions related to one another. Both institutions had long been caught up in the structural shifts of modernity and advanced capitalism and were on a trajectory that would lead to further changes. An older Protestant culture stemming as far back as the Reformation had shaped a "bourgeois family" built on notions of individual autonomy and the role of the family in preparing individuals capable of taking responsibility for their own lives. It was a model of the family as a social unit positioned well for relating individuals to the larger society. It was also a model of family and religion as two institutions working closely together. Especially in the mid- to late-nineteenth century in the United States, this model came to be more normatively defined, the presumption being that since children were born into a religious family they need not be converted, only nurtured in faith; hence religious socialization was the responsibility of the family. Austin Phelps, the nineteenth-century Congregationalist minister, idealized this institutional arrangement when he wrote, "The family is the nursery of faith and the church is but the family on an extended scale."[4] But already in his day social and economic forces of an industrial age were set in motion which in the course of time would place considerable strains on such an arrangement. Economic production was shifting away from the home, eroding structural supports that had kept the family intact. Public and private realms of people's lives were being pulled further apart. Life expectancy was on the increase, giving people extended years for an active life. Men were enjoying greater autonomy in work; women found that their traditional role as homemaker was being "pared to the chores of housework, consumption, and the cultivation of a declining number of progeny during a shortened span of time."[5] These were all massive social structural shifts driven by the momentum of modern capitalism, and which have continued to unfold in the twentieth century. By the 1950s the incongruities of social realities and religious fiction were reaching a breaking point, even though *Life, Look,* and other popular magazines continued to carry articles and pictures depicting an older normative pattern of family and church.

The 1950s kept these incongruities invisible in many ways. As we have already seen, the generation born in the late 1940s and 1950s was widely exposed to religion at a young age. Nine out of ten of the people in our survey reported attending regular religious services when they were 8 to 10 years old. Great numbers of them were baptized and attended Sunday School. Many we spoke with fondly remembered joining with their families in religious activities. As judged by self-reports, they were as involved in churches, synagogues, and temples as any generation born in the twentieth century.[6] They were perhaps more involved: when they were children popular interest in religious values and participation had reached an extraordinarily high level. It was an expansive era when new churches and schools were under construction, when white middle-class Americans were buying homes and moving to the suburbs, when the new medium of television disseminated middle-class hopes and aspirations to an increasingly national audience, and when it was generally assumed that parental values and religious identity would naturally pass from one generation to the next. Landon Y. Jones, writing about the world into which the Baby Boomers were born, summed up the situation by the title of his book, *Great Expectations.*[7] No generation, so it seemed to many middle-class Americans at the time, had been launched with so much promise and opportunity.

The links between religion and family themselves appeared still to be intact and unchallenged. Religion was flourishing, and so too were nuclear families and an ideology of family togetherness, particularly within an expanding white middle class. Postwar affluence and new homes in the suburbs encouraged wives to stay home and devote themselves to mothering. People were marrying, forming families, and having more children than in the previous decade. What was deemed to be a return to normalcy after years distraught by war encouraged a symbolic affirmation of God, motherhood, prosperity, and the American Way. On the surface, the culture was sufficiently homogeneous that *Life* magazine could portray it as a singular, unified way of life. Public intellectuals spoke to large audiences drawing upon the resources of faith traditions and making a case for how religious and national symbols blended into a common purpose; cultural unity was such that "religious discourse could still be taken as normative for understanding, and critiquing, the political process or society generally."[8] What had come to be called the "Judeo-Christian" tradition during this period, with its overtures to national unity, shared morality, and civility, enjoyed considerable appeal. Popular books like Norman Vincent Peale's *The Power of Positive Thinking*, Catherine Marshall's *A Man Called Peter*, and Fulton Sheen's *Peace of Soul*, along with such films as *The Ten Commandments*, all helped to create a climate in which traditional moral sensibilities, the nuclear family, and practical bourgeois faith seemed wholesome and suitable for just about everyone. Close symbolic ties between family and religion lay at the heart of this normative faith and found expression in the popular slogan at the time asserting that "the family that prays together stays together." While more a slogan than a reality even then, its popularity arose out of a widespread ethos that sentimentalized the home and regarded child-rearing as an opportunity for passing on the family's faith tradition, and allocated the responsibility for all this largely to women. Even as late as the early 1960s, views on family, gender, and church as found in religious magazines and pastors' manuals suggested an intertwining of roles and institutions that seemed to have changed little from as far back as the 1930s and 1940s.[9]

Yet as we all know, things were not well with either institution. Deep fissures within the culture were waiting to erupt in the 1960s that would fracture an easygoing, white, bourgeois world. All along family symbolism and religious participation had rested on a fragile bond. Shaped in no small part by apocalyptic Cold War fears of Communists and a dogged technological race to the moon and outer space, family and religious symbolism were drawn together in what amounts to, as one commentator writes, "a last-gasp orgy of modern nuclear family domesticity."[10] But beneath the sentimental gloss the 1950s placed on women and domestic responsibilities, forces were well underway undermining the family as it was idealized at the time: divorce rates were climbing; women were beginning to move into the labor force as levels of consumption increased; tensions were mounting among women who felt unfulfilled, if not oppressed, in their roles as housewives; nonfamily households that looked very different from those portrayed on television were on the rise. The birth-control pill and the women's movement that soon followed spelled doom to the old domesticity and, in retrospect, as viewed now from an era of greater freedom and gender equality, the 1950s was smoldering, ready to burst into flames. One commentator writes, it was "an era of suppressed individuality, of national paranoia, and of largely unrecognized discrimination against minorities, women, the poor, foreigners, homosexuals, and indeed most of those who dared to be different—the era that came to an end with the onset of the '60s was a time waiting to explode."[11] And after that explosion family life would never be the same again, nor would many Americans want it to be the same, despite continuing nostalgia for a world that never really quite existed.

If the situation for families changed drastically and quickly, much the same happened with religion. The positive and hopeful situation for normative faith and public life that existed in the early 1960s faded rather abruptly within a ten-year span. So staggering were the shifts in religious mood, Protestant church historian Sydney E. Ahlstrom, who in 1960 foresaw in the making a theological "renaissance unparalleled since the age of the Reformation," looked back on that resurgence of Neo-orthodox theology in 1970 as little more than a "layer of dogmatic asphalt" over "the old claims of scientific and historical investigations."[12] It was a shallow mix destined not to hold. Once this dogmatic layer had cracked, as sociologist Benton Johnson observes, theological and intellectual currents broke loose, truly signaling the collapse of an older Protestant culture and the emergence of an unprecedented religious pluralism. Very much at stake was the religion and family connection itself, as it had been modeled by the white middle-class United States—and thus taken to be worthy of emulation by others. Johnson writes:

> The totally unpredicted cultural revolution of the 1960s had profoundly reshaped the religious landscape. The revival following World War II was only a memory; the institutional church was under attack as irrelevant; conventional moral codes were being overturned; and the "WASP [white Anglo-Saxon Protestant] ascendancy" in national life was being challenged by radical students and black militants. As for the theological renaissance, that, too, was history. Theology had turned critical and destructive and was undermining the very foundations of the Christian faith.[13]

Of all the moral codes overturned, none were shaken more than those dealing with sexuality, gender, and family life; and of all the critical theological issues raised at the time, none generated more heated debate than the liberationist movements of feminists, racial minorities and, somewhat later, gay and lesbian lifestyle constituencies. It was not so much that the foundations of Christian faith were undermined, as Johnson says, as the "double message" that had long been embedded within American Christianity was blantantly exposed: teachings associated with the white, patriarchal bourgeois family and its morality, on the one hand, and religious teachings that held up other ideals as a basis for social morality, such as freedom, justice, and equality, on the other.[14] Therein lay an enormous abyss of discrepancies and unresolved boundaries. Whatever older cultural consensus on family and faith might have existed was now greatly shattered, and a new era of contestations over symbols of God, theology and ethics, definitions of the family, and sexual orientation had begun in earnest.

What is important about all this from the standpoint of the Boomer generation is that these momentous developments coalesced in its formative years. Boomers grew up in a climate when an old order of family and religion came unraveled and debates raged over what shape the new order would take. They entered into adulthood greatly divided, some celebrating this new emancipation from religiously legitimated sexual and family norms, others defending a traditional order thought to be divinely ordained and worthy of preserving. Far more divided than the stereotypes of their youthful, countercultural years would imply, Boomers would find little common ground except respect for personal conscience and "inner feelings" as arbiters of moral judgments. In some respects the situation has not really changed all that much: individuals may have firmed up their ideological positions, even switched positions or buttressed their views with stronger religious commitments, but the moral issues surrounding sexuality, family, and lifestyle choices, and the religious symbols they invoke, continue as a wedge dividing them in roughly similar numbers.

RELIGIOUS SOCIALIZATION

For a generation so caught up in turmoil, one wonders about the lasting impact of parental influence. Family sociologists point out that as a child ages the influence of the family of origin wanes in relation to other influences. Historical events, crises, and the moral and cultural ethos during the formative years of any generation play a big part in shaping its outlook and sensitivities, often overshadowing earlier influences of the home. Yet folk wisdom has it that "as the twig is bent, so grows the tree"— that is, family influences on children are subtle and lasting.[15] What children have modeled before them carries over into adult life. With Boomers, research demonstrates that two sets of influences—childhood religious socialization and the countercultural values of their adolescent and teenage years—would compete with one another, making for a complex and even more nuanced pattern of socialization.[16] In our own survey, we find that those whose parents were active in a congregation or some type of religious activity during the years when they were growing up are themselves now more religiously active as compared to those who had inactive parents. Sixty percent of those whose mothers were weekly attenders at church, synagogue, or temple back then now report attending at least once a month. Religiously active fathers had an influence: 54 percent of those whose fathers were weekly attenders back when they were growing up now attend religious services once a month or more. Much the same holds for current involvement in small groups. Those with religiously active parents in the earlier years are more likely now to join Bible study, prayer, and spiritual support groups. There is also a consistency effect. If *both* parents were religiously active *and* in the same faith, Boomer children were less likely to have dropped out of attending church, synagogue, or temple when growing up. Consistent religious socialization, that is, influences reinforced by both parents, had a lasting impact. But much also depends on religious tradition: those who were brought up in a conservative religious environment with stricter moral values and behavioral norms are less likely to have wavered in their own faith, with or without parental support; but parental support plus strict tradition created an even stronger influence. Conservative theology and faith, combined with strong social networks and the support of parents, provided social and symbolic reinforcement in a world of conflicting and competing influences.

Yet even so, parental influence was moderated by countercultural influences. Those most exposed as children to the radical cultural changes of the era show lower levels of involvement in religious activities and acceptance of orthodox beliefs, as measured by conventional Judeo-Christian indicators. Even if their parents were highly religious, countercultural influences eroding religious influence are evident. These wider influences were greater within the more liberal and moderate faith traditions where the boundaries of religion and culture are less clearly drawn. Conversely, exposure to the counterculture as opposed to being highly sheltered from it correlates with various indicators of spiritual quest: with interest in exploring alternative religious teachings, with curiosity about the meaning and purpose of life, and with a greater likelihood of defining oneself as "spiritual" rather than as "religious." In fact, antiwar protests and drug usage show a relationship, though a relatively weak one, with a continuing spiritual interest in adulthood. Among those who dropped out of active religious participation for an extended period as teenagers or young adults—no matter the faith traditions—parental religiosity seems to have had little effect on whether or not they have ever returned to active involvement. If, and to what extent, there was a qualitative break with historic patterns of religious socialization, that is, Boomers compared to previous generations, is a matter of some debate; however, the peer groups, television, assassinations of national leaders, and cultural climate of institutional distrust in their younger years unquestionably left a distinctly different and lasting imprint on their beliefs, values, and outlook.

But how does all this play out for the five major subcultures described in Chapter 6? Breaking out the religious constituencies in this way, we find that two of the subcultures—Born-again Christians and religious dogmatists—were the most influenced by early religious socialization in their families of origin. This is in keeping with the strong views about family within conservative Christianity and its rich symbolic resources for sustaining each and every believer. Surveys reveal that 60 and 59 percent of the two constituencies, respectively, report having mothers who were weekly attenders when they were growing up. Fewer say their fathers were weekly attenders. On a variety of beliefs and practices, there is evidence of parental influence: those who had at least one parent who was religiously active are more likely to say they "definitely believe in God," to regard Jesus as a caring Shepherd, to say grace at meals, to read the Bible, and to return to active religious participation if they have ever dropped out. Those with both parents religiously committed are even more likely to affirm or to do these things. Clearly, strong childhood religious socialization and parental role models make for lasting influences in these subcultures. By contrast, the religious links with parents are weaker for both mainstream believers and metaphysical believers and seekers. Because the meaning systems for these individuals are less contained by strong religious sanctions, practices, and symbolic formulations, it is reasonable to assume that other influences (peer groups, friends, spouses) had a stronger influence on them. Secularists grow-

ing up experienced a combination of influences shaping their worldviews: weak childhood religious socialization, intensive exposure to the
counterculture, and often bad experiences with organized religion.
Thus we observe a pattern of religious socialization that might best be
thought of in terms of a gradient: a religious script is more easily transmitted from one generation to another where there is strong parental
influence and the reinforcement of a religious environment, less so in
more moderate to liberal religious environments, and still less so for
secularists. Inherited faith is more likely in an environment of strong,
coercive moral and religious norms and distinct idioms of religious expression. Religious transmission, like cultural transmission more generally, rests on institutional reinforcements, embedded social networks,
and shared and meaningful religious vocabulary that can be passed
across generations.

By no means is this surprising when we think of religion as a symbolic
resource, although it is possible that people with religious parents are
more prone to remember selectively and, perhaps, to exaggerate the
devoutness of their parents. We heard anecdotes about the religious examples their parents had set for them, particularly among Catholic traditionalists and Protestant Fundamentalists and Evangelicals. Even formerly religious liberals who had converted to more conservative faiths
often spoke of devout parents. This points once again to the role of
"symbolic families"—broadened to include not just media-constructed
imageries, but those that people create about their parents or other
members of their families. Given their strained relations with religious
institutions, Boomers are inclined to personalize religion and to see in
significant others either a religious model for themselves, or one they
admire but would not try to emulate, or one to outright reject. Depending on the subculture involved, a person defined as "religious" can evoke
a range of imageries and responses: as a faithful believer in God and
loyal churchgoer, a good and caring person, someone who is spiritual,
an authoritarian who will impose morality and faith upon others, or one
who appears not very spiritual as this term has come to be popularly
defined. True as well, individuals creating their own definitions of religious meaning interact with a wide variety of symbolic resources: not just
the scripts, practices, beliefs, and customs afforded by a religious tradition but exemplary role-models in actual life or in mediated worlds,
people as they are or as imagined to be or once to have been. Negative,
not just positive, reference is involved as well—as when one Protestant

Fundamentalist we interviewed said sadly about his own father, "he wasn't much of a Godly man; in fact, I try to forget him and follow the teachings of the Bible as best I can and try to do better." Whatever the extent of nostalgia and selective and exaggerated memory, all this underscores the considerable power and significance of a constructed, even idealized, family lineage for the transmission of religious identity. In the context of modernity and its unsettling influences, family-based religious narrative, "real" or "imagined," still functions as a stabilizing and boundary-defining mechanism. Sorting out the influence of parents themselves and that of other sources thus becomes much more difficult in an age of constructed realities, though not necessarily any less significant. Family Web pages on the Internet and recent attention to genealogy on the part of Boomers signal the significance attached to family and efforts to sustain a common family heritage.

Relations with Family of Origin

Religious groups in the United States differ greatly in their teachings about child-rearing methods. The Catholic Church, the Mormons, Orthodox Jews, Muslims, and the Seventh Day Adventists are, in their official teachings, fairly strict about how children should be raised; in contrast, most mainline Protestant denominations emphasize family nurture and life-experiences as learning experiences more than rigid teachings and practices for children. Yet what believers themselves think about child-rearing and parent-child relations in their faith tradition is something else again; in these matters, as in others, they may or may not adhere to what is held up as a normative standard. Furthermore, as presumed throughout this book, the post–World War II culture had a considerable leveling effect across faith traditions on child-rearing methods and family dynamics. Those traditions once known for their emphasis on authority and obedience faced the same cultural changes as did other, more liberal and lenient traditions. Hence we asked our respondents about their family experiences when they were children and sought to find out directly from them how they remembered relations with parents. Despite the potential bias resulting from the selective memory involved, this is a far more reliable approach to this subjective dimension than drawing inferences from affiliations or the formal teachings of religious groups.

228

We inquired into how "close" people were to their parents when growing up as well as about child-rearing styles. With the first, we wanted to know about the warmth and quality of their relationships as they remembered and perceived them many years later. Dogmatists, it turns out, did not have particularly close relations with their fathers, and rather mixed relations with their mothers. Born-again Christians, however, report closer relationships with both their fathers and mothers—indeed, the closest of relations with their parents of any of our subcultures. Often they spoke of "warm" and "caring" mothers; they had less to say about emotional ties to fathers yet clearly felt close to them. Though their social and religious backgrounds were diverse, what seemed to be a common denominator for Born-again Christian converts was a family of origin where parental relations were supportive even if a strong religious heritage was lacking. Interestingly, whether for this reason or not, Born-again Christian imageries of God seem to reflect a close and warm contact with a mother: 21 percent, higher than for any other subculture, say they can imagine God as a mother. In our conversations with Protestant Evangelicals and Catholic Charismatics, soft, feminine imageries of God were frequently voiced. Over time there appears to have been a softening of God-imageries within this subculture. This is in striking contrast to the views held by strong-minded traditionalists and Fundamentalists, no matter whether Catholic, Jewish, Protestant, or anything else. These latter, far more oriented toward patriarchal authority, stress order and hierarchy in relationships and are much less flexible in their imageries of the divine. Seventy-two percent of dogmatists prefer thinking of God as a father, and only 6 percent imagine God as mother. Whereas these latter hold to a rigid, monarchical conception of the divine as lawgiver and judge, Born-again Christians tend toward more personal, affectionate views of God as love and Spirit.

Conceptions of human nature vary as well: dogmatists are very likely to look on a newborn child as already guilty of sin, but Born-again Christians are far less inclined to do so. Emotional ties between the generations play less of a binding role for dogmatists than a cognitive world in which all things are presumed to hang together in a stable, well-ordered way, or as Lester Kurtz has written, "In the patriarchal Judeo-Christian tradition, the structures of the cosmos and the family typically reflect each other: the father who presides over the family mirrors God the father in control of the universe."[17] This is a model of authority some Protestant Evangelicals and Catholic Charismatics share, but because the latter attach far more significance to a caring, highly personalized and affectionate God, their religious world reflects a more delicate balance between feminine and masculine qualities. Traditional family symbolism, most notably that of God-as-Father, while not rejected by Born-again Christians, tends to be reinterpreted in keeping with contemporary cultural belief about the importance of greater mutuality in relations of love and intimacy and emotional ties as a means of uniting families.[18] Here would appear to be a growing, and increasingly significant, cleavage resulting in two distinct subcultures. Increasingly, researchers and scholars who overlook this divergence of imageries and conceptions between these two sectors of religious conservatism—mainstream Evangelicals, Pentecostals, and Charistmatics making up one, and Protestant Fundamentalists, Catholic traditionalists, and some Orthodox Jews the other—fail to grasp some powerful currents flowing at the grassroots level and spin a certain amount of statistical fiction by treating them as a singular monolith.

Interesting, too, are patterns for metaphysical believers and seekers. They are the least likely to report close relations with their mothers, and next to the least to report similar relations with their fathers. With regard to child-rearing styles, it turns out that metaphysical believers and seekers have had the most rigid backgrounds of all the subcultures. Interview material supplements the survey evidence on this point: disproportionately, metaphysical believers and seekers appear to have grown up in families that lacked warmth, were highly controlled and demanding, and did not communicate easily. "We couldn't talk about religion when I was a child, we were told what to believe and do. . . . Only after I grew up and left home did I have a spiritual awakening," a schoolteacher in Ohio told us. Whether this absence of close ties combined with rigid parenting, poor communication in families, and childhood disruption had anything to do with their espousal generally of a greater number of nonpersonal views of the sacred later in life is speculative, but the empirical patterns here uncovered warrant this hypothesis. Generally, as a constituency, they stand out for their rejection of male, patriarchical imagery of the divine and for their embrace of alternatives.

Some commentators argue that a permissive family background encouraged religious experimentation and a more open attitude in matters of faith and morality on the part of this generation. Permissive child-rearing philosophy of the sort associated with Dr. Benjamin Spock is often singled out as undermining old religious styles and as contributing to more cognitive flexibility. The first edition of his *Baby and Child Care*, the how-to manual whose optimistic credo ("Trust yourself. You know more than you think you do") that helped shape a new world of parenting, came out in 1946 and would become the best-selling book of the twentieth century, second only to the Bible. It redefined traditional patterns of transmitting values from one generation to the next, encouraging greater self-sufficiency on the part of post–World War II parents and, in general, a more egalitarian and pragmatic outlook. Thirty percent of the Boomers we talked with said their parents were permissive with them, as compared to 69 percent who claimed a rigid family background. Spock's book was influential but perhaps not as much as folklore would have it. Forty percent of mainstream believers, more than even for secularists, report growing up in a "permissive" or "very permissive" home. Predictably, this child-rearing philosophy reinforced family symbolism in the early years of their lives—open, accepting, caring, negotiable imageries of God—undergirding religious styles that have remained with them. It turns out that an equal number of mainstream believers and Born-again Christians (56 and 57 percent, respectively) say they can imagine God as a father. Mainstream believers tend not to hold beliefs about God as firmly and as emotionally as Born-again Christians and are less hierarchical in their conceptions but in actual gender-based imageries their views are not all that different.

Striking is the comparison of the two religious subcultures, the dogmatists and metaphysical believers and seekers. Both report rigid family backgrounds, yet their current spiritual styles are so very different. Without too great an emphasis on child-rearing itself, it should not go unnoticed that rigid upbringing is associated with both outcomes. It appears that authoritarian family backgrounds with expectations of obedience and loyalty in the post–World War II cultural climate produced a deeply felt ambivalence resulting in two, quite alternative paths: one, leading to a strong reaffirmation of those values on the part of conservative dogmatists, and two, a break with that past and to greater spiritual freedom as in the case of metaphysical believers and seekers. As one commentator quite perceptively observes: "Human inheritance is both blessing and curse. And in religious inheritance this paradox is acute. For many of us religion is heavy baggage."[19] In authoritarian child-rearing patterns, we see evidence of that religious paradox. For some people, child-rearing of this sort is a mechanism of cultural and religious continuity that operates fairly smoothly, but for others it can be heavy baggage resulting in resistance, if not outright rejection. For a generation brought up in an era of so much cultural discontinuity, of numerous and conflicting influences shaping their religious sensitivities, it is not surprising this paradox continues to be played out, and at times dramatically, among its members.

BOOMERS AS PARENTS

Like generations of parents before them, when the Boomers had their own children they were concerned about their moral and religious socialization. In our 1988–89 survey, 60 percent said their children's religious training was "very important," another 32 percent thought it "somewhat important," and only 8 percent were indifferent or unsure about it. Whether this distribution of responses at all resembles what might have existed in an earlier time, we simply do not know. Significant, however, are the more diffused egalitarian values bearing on the decision whether children should attend religious services and activities. About three-fourths of Boomer parents insisted that they should be the ones to decide, but fully a fourth said the children should be allowed to. The more egalitarian values are not limited to the more casual mainstream believers or to metaphysical believers and seekers who have rebelled against their authoritarian religious pasts; rather, these values are widely diffused among the urban, better-educated young adults and spread about equally across religious constituencies except for dogmatists, who are predictably narrow-minded in such matters. That Born-again Christians differ not all that much from mainstream believers—the two large subcultures accounting for almost 60 percent of all Boomers—on this rather important question of passing on the religious tradition to their children signals, again, a convergence of attitudes and predispositions of some potential significance. It points to a much closer pattern of relating to religious institutions now evolving for two constituencies, often depicted as so very different, than is generally recognized both in the media and by scholars. What it foretells is a homogenizing of religious views in a redefined religious middle, as a result of the trend toward extending individual autonomy in religious matters to all persons, including children and young people—a theme we come back to in this and subsequent chapters.

As described in my *Generation of Seekers*, many parents returned to church, synagogue, and temple when their children were young. Large numbers of them had dropped out as teenagers, but as their children reached school age they returned. When asked about why they did so, often the response was simply, "I care about my children" or "I want them to know about God." Even irregular churchgoers became more active as their children reached school age. Boomer parents were not all that different in this respect from parents in previous times, except probably that more of them had dropped out and could return. Research dating back to the 1950s shows children as a major influence on parents in choosing a congregation—even more so than location, the priest, rabbi, or pastor, or the particular denomination of which it is a part.[20] As we saw in Chapter 4, ten years ago large numbers of Boomers were in their late thirties and early forties with young children, and hence much media attention was given to a "return to religion." Our data showed the presence of school-age children especially to be a factor in that return. *Newsweek* magazine went even further in 1990 proclaiming children as the dominant factor on its cover—"And the Children Shall Lead Them: Young Americans Return to God."[21] Yet, as we also saw in Chapter 4, our second round of interviews showed that many who at one time did return to organized religion had dropped out again or were less involved than they had been when we first talked to them. Even some institutional loyalists, those who had never dropped out of the churches, synagogues, temples, or mosques for any extended period in their adult lives, were becoming less committed. More than just a trickle, the statistics pointed to a declining mode of institutional involvement for many. Described was a fluid situation of people moving into and out of organized religion—a circulation not of saints but of people whose spiritual interests and faith commitments ebbed and flowed.

That being the case, the question arises: if the parents' return to religion was a result largely of the presence of school-age children, do they drop out later when those children grow up? Based on our survey results, the answer appears to be yes. Parents with children up through the teenage years were, and still are, more likely to attend worship services, but as their children have aged and moved out of the household religious participation has declined somewhat. Twenty-seven percent of those with children 20 years of age or older report attending religious services once a month or more as compared with 38 percent of those with children 6 to 12, and 40 percent for those with children 13 to 19. This pattern of increased, then decreased religious involvement so closely associated with the age of children raises the possibility of a major generational change. Previous research has found that frequency of religious attendance for parents increases with children and then levels off into a stable pattern after children reach adolescence and declines after middle age—particularly for those over sixty years of age. But with Boomers the declines in religious involvement seem to be setting in at an earlier phase in the life cycle. Thus there is some reason to regard the return to organized religion as heralded in the early 1990s as just a temporary phenomenon for the sake of the children, and not really a lasting return. If our evidence on this point is indeed generalizable, there is a basis for thinking that a culturally grounded perception of organized religion as a "service agency" for meeting individual needs is becoming more pronounced—adding childhood religious instruction to a list of services, such as marriages and baptisms, that has long been sought after and provided by religious institutions. If true, that marks a significant shift in normative patterns for families and religious institutions.

Is there a liberal-to-conservative theological gradient involved in this pattern of parents dropping out as they move beyond the child-rearing phase? It might reasonably be argued that because mainstream believers had parents who were greatly influenced by the more permissive values in rearing children and tend generally to be less bound to traditional norms of moral and religious duty, that they would be the ones most likely to drop out. But the situation is not that simple. Greater numbers of religious conservatives (Born-again Christians and dogmatists) are likely to be regular attenders at worship services when young children are present, but proportionately, they too are dropping out as their children grow older at almost the same rate that applies to mainstream believers. The conservatives have somewhat higher levels of returning after dropping out, and repeated cycles of leaving and coming back, as children spaced over a span of years themselves age, but the differences across the subcultures are not statistically significant. Since these three religious constituencies account for three-quarters of our entire population, there is basis for generalizing: *for a large proportion of Boomer parents, reduced religious participation follows as their children grow up and take responsibility for their own lives.* Reduced involvement on so widespread a basis and frequently in midlife would seem to point to a weakening of institutional religious commitments and of the role of institutions in the process of intergenerational religious transmission. With regard to the other two religious subcultures—spiritual seekers and secularists—they take their children to religious activities outside the family much less to begin with, and therefore there is less of a detectable pattern of religious involvement varying in relation to the life cycle as a whole.

234

MARITAL-STATUS AND FAMILY PATTERNS

No generation is better known for its marital and family trends—for co-habitation, for marrying less, for marrying later, for having fewer children, for creating new types of families, and for spending less of their lives in family households. In addition, no set of social changes are better known than those that have come about with regard to the so-called nuclear family. In 1970, 40 percent of Americans lived in nuclear families with children present under the age of 18. By 1990 that percentage had fallen to 26.3, almost a fourth of which are stepfamilies, sometimes called "blended families."[22] The implication is obvious: people now move in and out of relationships more. People move in and out of families almost as much as they do in careers and differing types of work; reflecting upon the social and psychological consequences of greater longevity combined with this new openness to the formation of relationships, social scientists Barry A. Kosmin and Seymour P. Lachman write, "There are more transitions as people form, dissolve, and re-form households and families" than was true for older generations.[23] Life cycles follow less of a predictable script and must be rewritten as new types of family formations proliferate. This is true particularly for that sector the U.S. Census Bureau defines as "nonfamily households," consisting mainly of gay and heterosexual cohabitors where no recognized marital or blood ties are involved. Of course, for all types of families official data fail to capture the enormous challenges and dilemmas resulting from so much change in family life: the continuing evolution of lifestyles and gender roles as they affect the formation of marital unions, disputes between parents over custody of children, tensions among children in blended families, the frustration many parents feel in dealing with children with addiction and other problems, the rearing of children by grandparents in many instances. Recent efforts at organizing parenting classes devoted to helping parents learn basic skills and assume responsibility for their families are responding to the high level of frustration and stress that many parents feel today. Hidden behind the rhetoric about "family values" even among conservatives, is a great deal of fear and worry within families about their own well-being.

Implications for religion are considerable, making Penny Long Marler's dictum "as the family goes, so goes the church"[24] all the more prophetic as we move into the twenty-first century. The decline of the traditional nuclear family may foretell declines in congregational participation. Levels of religious participation continue to be higher for such families. The family types currently growing—singles, divorced and separated, and the so-called nonfamily households—show lower levels of involvement in, and support of, organized religion, though by no means less personal faith or spiritual well-being. People in these family situations are more likely to hold to privatized or family-based religious views largely unrelated to congregations, or to identify themselves simply as religious "Nones." In the eyes of many Boomers who make up these new households, conventional religious congregations look like bastions of traditional familism and heterosexual culture. If this growth in nonfamily households continues into the future unabated, with the resulting religious trends, the link between organized religion and marriage and nuclear family will become ever more apparent. That will be a major structural development in the reconfiguring of family and religion, with enormous consequences for childhood religious socialization and institutional affiliation for a sizable proportion of the population.

Particularly among Euro-American Boomers, the nuclear family is a carrier of traditional religious styles. Mainstream believers are more often married and living in a nuclear family than any of the other religious subcultures. This demographic reality is at odds, of course, with much rhetoric of the past decade linking conservative faiths and the family. Yet the fact is that for liberal religious groups marriages are more intact than among the more conservative faith communities. Eighty percent of the mainstream believers we surveyed are married, higher than for any of the other religious constituencies (excluding secularists), including Born-again Christians at 70 percent. These demographics should come as no surprise considering that mainline Protestant and Catholic churches have long been strongholds of heterosexual couples' culture and traditional familism. Dating back to the fifties when *McCall's* magazine settled upon the word *togetherness* and the Methodist magazine *Together* reached a high circulation, the values formed, expressed, and reinforced within the family were closely identified with these churches.[25] Still today, the demographic composition resembles that of the past: the white middle-class church is made up, largely, as Marler points out, of older empty-nesters and widowed persons, a "fifties' *family residue*," as she says.[26] Memories of an older conception of family life live on among these older members, of times when congregations were filled with children and young people, when their children got married, when in happy times and crises families were drawn together. And for many Boomers as well, these institutions are identified with a Norman

Rockwell portrait of a happy family, lingering on in their nostalgia. John McRae's nostalgia referred to at the beginning of the chapter is not all that uncommon: many Boomers still remember the church of their childhood. Mainstream believers particularly, for some reason, offered more comments in the interviews signaling a gap between family experiences as they remembered, or imagined them in the past, and the present realities of their relationships. However, this gap is real to the great majority of Boomers.

Marler observes there are "new" Boomer-age traditional families who share values similar to those of older families, the major exception being they are less likely to view the church as an extended traditional family. More consumption-oriented in their religious choices, these younger mainstream believers become involved in religious congregations more out of concern for themselves and for their children, and much less out of duty to the institution, which used to be an important motivation. But the fact that they do bring the children, or are involved for whatever reason, is not to be overlooked. A fair number of them have not been in a church or synagogue since they themselves were quite young—so they carry religious memories that in some ways do connect with the culture of the mainline institutions. As parents they are concerned about bringing up their children in a wholesome atmosphere. They return to these old established churches in part because they are looking for "family talk," a discourse driven by rich memories and connections to the past and, hopefully, a basis for present and future parent-child conversation; as religious consumers they look to programs and activities reminiscent of their own past.[27] And in keeping with a consumer mentality, these same parents easily fit the pattern of dropping out of active participation once they are done providing for the children. Yet for some the symbolic links between family and religion become a basis for renewed exploration of and commitment to an enlivened faith. This was particularly true among people we interviewed in the American South.

Social status should not be overlooked as a factor in the religious choices of mainstream believers. Particularly for those of middle-class standing, family status is often deeply interwoven with religious consciousness. Second only to secularists, they are highly active in voluntary organizations and social clubs, and highly involved in community and neighborhood activities. Membership and involvement within a mainline church or synagogue, more than just a religious affirmation, carries status and, to some extent, "social capital"—opportunities for making contacts, establishing friendships, building networks. More so than for any of the other subcultures, mainstream believers agree with the survey item, "Being a church member is an important way to become established in a community." Congregation and social status remain symbolically linked in their minds. Even for the religiously inactive, an institutional religious affiliation has drawing power. Extended families gather for holidays and for rites of passage, further solidifying symbolism of family and religion among those for whom family standing is a key determinant of who they are and of how they see themselves. What has changed in mainstream religious affiliations is an expanded "tolerance zone"—religiously and culturally.[28] The blurring of theological and cultural differences among the old Protestant religious cultures and growing numbers interacting socially across Jewish-Protestant-Catholic lines—for reasons of intermarriage, business and careers, friendship patterns, or whatever—open up a greater range of family-linked social and religious connections. "Family" history and status, like religious history and identity, is to some extent constructed to fit the occasion, as when a Jewish man we interviewed says that he introduced his Protestant fiancée to his parents as a "Presbyterian whose father is a physician in Denver." Religion and social standing fuse into a singular identity, so much so it is impossible to sort out the relative weight of the two components in the status dimension. Golden Rule religion has such a quality about it, where faith is bolstered by, and often inextricably bound up with, status considerations, and vice versa. Secular interpretations of American culture often overlook this persisting religion-and-status nexus and thereby fail to detect religion's subtle influence in this instance.

Marital-status patterns for religious conservatives—for both dogmatists and Born-again Christians—actually mirror American society as a whole more closely than do any of the other subcultures. Twenty-two percent of the dogmatists and 23 percent of the Born-again Christians are divorced or separated, and 9 and 7 percent, respectively, have never married, close to national averages. Only 14 percent of mainstream believers are divorced or separated and 6 percent have never married. Many Born-again Christians are single parents, more so than for mainstream believers. It is these demographics that occasion the efforts of Evangelical Protestants to provide programming and activities for a wide range of family types—for singles (which can now mean "previously married"), single parents, blended families, dual-career families, and other such subgroups. Far more so than the mainline Protestant and Catholic churches, Born-again Christian communities successfully target these contemporary permutations of family as social niches for specialized

238

ministries. This helps in creating a user-friendly impression of Evangelical churches, and in explaining the marital-status demographics of these churches. Sam Wong and his wife met at an Evangelical singles' function, which left him with the impression that the Vineyard Fellowship of which the two of them are now a part was sensitive to "building relationships," an observation also shared by many other participants as well as scholars who have studied these churches. The strong emphasis Evangelical Christian churches place on a "relationship" with Christ provides an analogy to human relationships and a strong basis for appeals to building strong marriages.[29]

For metaphysical believers and seekers and for secularists, the proportions divorced, separated, or never married are even higher. Almost a third within each of these subcultures belong in these nonmarital categories. Also, among metaphysical believers and seekers fully two-thirds are female. Our interviews suggest that disillusionment as a result of an unhappy experience with a mainline or Evangelical congregation is often a factor helping to swell these demographics. Many of these people left the religious tradition in which they were raised or otherwise affiliated with as young adults to explore spiritual alternatives or simply have abandoned religion because of, among other things, a feeling of rejection due to divorce, separation, or lifestyle. Aside from the unfortunate cultural stereotypes associated with these lifestyles as found in many conventional congregations, often there is a withholding of openness and warmth people easily detect. Though this atmosphere may be gradually changing, a surprising number of the people we interviewed say they feel unwanted or pressured to accommodate older religious and moral styles that often seem out of keeping with their lives.

WOMEN IN THE WORKFORCE

The entry of women into the workforce has had, quite predictably, a major, long-term impact on the religion-and-family connection. By the mid 1970s, well over half of women in the United States under 55 were in the paid labor force. In the next decade and a half, employment rates essentially doubled as large numbers of women in their twenties and thirties moved into the workforce. By 1990, among white women, 70 percent were employed at least part-time; over 40 percent of all mothers whose children lived with them were employed full-time. Among married women in 1996, 77 percent with school-age children were working outside the home or looking for work; for those with pre-school-age children the figure was 63 percent—five times higher that it was in 1950.[30] Postponed marriages, fewer births, expanded childcare facilities, and increased career opportunities for women have resulted in a cultural redefinition of motherhood and the rise of the two-income family. Whereas at midcentury the more a man earned, the less likely his wife was to work outside the home, by 1970 that pattern had reversed, and wives of middle-income men were now more likely to be employed.[31] That reversal continues to work itself out as more and more couples rely on two incomes. And by any reckoning, significant transformations within the family stemming from these shifts in employment and income will continue to unfold. Indeed, the radical realigning of work, family, and religion now underway is unparalleled in modern American history and bears enormous and as yet not fully fathomed implications for religion—changes all the more staggering considering that so much has happened already within the span of a single lifetime.

How women's employment is reshaping religious commitment is far more complex a matter than it might first appear. Much research is addressed to the situation, and even over the course of my research and writing this book the focus became sharpened somewhat. At the time of our first survey, it was clear that differences in religious attitudes and behavior between men and women were declining, for cohort after cohort born in this century, and notably so for those working full-time. That is, the religious patterns of career-oriented and working women were beginning to look more and more like those of their male counterparts. On the question of women working, the results were mixed: women working full-time outside the home were not appreciably less committed in "public religiosity," that is, to religious attendance and congregational membership, than were women not in the labor force or who worked only part-time. These same working women were actually slightly more committed to "private religiosity," or believing in God and recognizing spiritual influence on life, than other women; they also showed somewhat less interest than the other women in "family religiosity," as determined by the extent of concern about religious training for young children and seeing to it that young people are involved in religious activities.[32] But in our later interviews, the patterns were in clearer focus and changed somewhat. Personal faith and spirituality were, if anything, encouraged by careers and work opportunities, though religious membership and participation to a lesser extent. The disjuncture between the public and private aspects of religion had become more evident in keeping with the mounting pressures of the workplace. This difference in religious style was especially true for married women who worked full-time. These women, and even their husbands, were less likely to be actively involved in congregations and religious activities than women who were married but did not work outside the home. Impressionistic evidence suggests that their children were less involved religiously as well. Our observations fit with sociologist Bradley Hertel's conclusions: "The lower level of membership, attendance, and religious identity of men and women in families in which the wife works full-time may in turn—and probably does—lead parents to place less emphasis on religious training for their children. If so, then the work-related declines in married women's involvement in religion may impact negatively on the long-term future religious involvement of their children."[33]

But patterns do vary somewhat by subculture. Even within the conservative religious sector there are noticeable differences. Among dogmatists, full-time working women remain as committed to religious organizations as do housewives, but not so with Born-again women who work. Born-again working women attend religious services less frequently and participate in fewer congregational activities than do their more conservative counterparts. Moreover, greater numbers of Born-again Christian women are now working. Fifty-nine percent of Born-again women are full-time workers, not that far behind mainline and secular women, at 64 and 66 percent. Growing numbers of them in the workforce puts added strain on institutional religious duties. Born-again working women, not unlike other working women, find it increasingly difficult to carry out the demands and responsibilities of a full-time job or career while at the same time participating as usual within their churches. Yet interestingly, Born-again Christian women working full-time are no less likely to pray, to read the Bible, or to say grace at meals than housewives. An accommodation to the realignments of work and family appears in the making: because of time constraints, these women try to compensate within the family for what has become more difficult to accomplish within religious organizations. Feeling that they should take their faith seriously, and concerned about their children, they express themselves in this more focused way. "I can't always go to my church services, even though I try," a Charismatic Catholic woman in North Carolina working full-time told us, "but I sit down with my children at night and we read stories and I try to tell them about God. I try to do my part." For such women, working and being away from the family during the day results in a conscious effort to give children attention, to engage in religious practices and infuse family life with religious and spiritual values.

By comparison, there is less evidence of such focused attention to family matters and to teachings and rituals among working women in the mainline subculture. Here the women express concern about children and family but take less initiative to actually do things with their children. However, differences between the Born-again and mainline subcultures for working women are not huge and should not be over-interpreted. Among metaphysical and seeker women who work, there is considerable concern for children and initiative—if they have children—almost as much as with Born-again women. With regard to prayer, Bible reading, saying grace at meals, and attending to children's spiritual questions, women seekers, working or not working, also come close to matching Born-again women. They too are remarkably creative in devising family rituals and quality moments filled with spiritual meaning, aided by a readily available supply of do-it-yourself manuals from bookstores and on-line services. If we consider these additional, tailor-made family rituals that metaphysical believers and seekers are particularly adept at cultivating (for example, mother-daughter and father-son celebrations, establishing family altars, improvising marriage vows), clearly these women lead the way in creating and instituting new religious rituals within the family. In this respect the family emerges as an arena encouraging, indeed calling for, religious innovation on an unprecedented scale.

By far, however, the greatest impact on organized religion resulting from the entry of women into the workforce relates to religious "volunteering." Historically in this country, women were responsible for the bulk of service activities within Christian congregations, and to a lesser degree within Jewish congregations. But as Boomer women moved into the workforce, they had less time to do traditional church work and, more importantly, they now look on such work very differently. Unlike an older generation of women who functioned in congregations as a cadre of workers ready to do whatever was needed in a gender-defined religious world, such as preparing and serving meals, teaching Sunday School, and fund-raising, these younger women are more prone to look to activities that extend their own spiritual fulfillment and allow them to use their own particular talents or professional skills. They adopt a more "individualist" approach to service work, choosing what they want to do, when, and how; essentially they find ways of meaningfully investing themselves in voluntary activities and groups rather than simply being on call when needed.[34] In so doing, they are redefining religious roles for women, and also attending to their own spiritual nurturing. In redefining roles they engage in a creative activity, drawing on their own experiences and reappropriating symbols, teachings, and practices from religious traditions to illumine those experiences. Spiritual nurturing, of course, is what is more immediately sought. This changing pattern of religious involvement for women is apparent in the popularity of small groups, be they self-help or special-interest groups, dealing with personal concerns like divorce and single parenting, or the juggling of work, marriage, and family on the part of married working women. High on the list for working women are small groups described in our survey as "spiritual" and "support"—almost equally so among Born-again Christians, mainstream believers, metaphysical believers and seekers and, to a lesser extent, secularists. Dogmatists, both women and men, rely far less on such sharing groups.

INTERFAITH FAMILIES

Another important trend in family patterns, spearheaded by the post–World War II generation, is the growth in mixed-faith marriages and "blended families," where children of previous marriages and often diverse faith backgrounds are drawn into the same household. While mixed marriages were hardly uncommon in the past, there were fewer of them, not only because of religious pressures but as a result of one spouse "switching" to the faith of the other. Relatively high levels of religious switching (25 to 30 percent for the American population at large), often at time of marriage, served to maintain religious homogeneity within the family.[35] Cultural norms prescribed religious homogeneity for families, especially where there were children. Parental pressures often encouraged conversion by one spouse as a means of creating families in which children could grow up in a shared religious environment. Today that normative context is vastly different. There is still considerable religious switching, but the larger cultural forces of rampant individualism, high levels of divorce, greater gender equality and increased entry of women into the workforce, weakened influence of parents on children, and the reconstituted religious communities we have described, all make for a context in which interfaith households are much more common. Based on the huge National Survey of Religious Identification in

243

1990, which allowed for a thorough analysis of interfaith family trends, those conducting the survey comment as follows:

> Today's couples have more economic independence than the teenage bride and groom of the 1950s. In addition, the individualism in our society conflicts with the notion that third parties should interfere in a couple's marriage decision. With people increasingly assertive concerning their own experiences and ideas, one would naturally expect them to be less willing to give up their own religious identity. Moreover, in these pluralistic times, we would expect partners to be more respectful and, therefore, more tolerant of their spouses' religious differences. In addition, the ecumenical atmosphere generated by religious bodies has created an acceptable milieu for religious compromises.[36]

In this milieu of religious compromises, a variety of configurations are emerging for interfaith households. Individual choice in religion is highly valued, and especially so where the partners come from differing religious backgrounds and are in second or subsequent marriages. Religious choice is very functional for these households, minimizing conflict between marriage partners and among children brought into the families through divorce and remarriage. Pressures in the direction of privatizing religious belief and behavior obviously mount.

That the link between parenting and religious observance and participation as traditionally conceived becomes weakened for mixed-faith and blended families seems fairly obvious. Consistent religious socialization is undermined. Religious involvement typically is lower. On virtually all traditional religious indexes—religious membership, congregational participation, orthodox beliefs, religious observance within the home, and religious training for children—levels for religiously mixed households are lower. Rare is any survey measure that yields counter-results. Journalistic evidence also reports situations where children are often forced into making stressful decisions, or have to choose between their mother's or father's religion, or feel caught between two worlds and often "not as good as their all-Jewish or all-Christian cousins."[37] In one reading of the situation, such families represent the triumph of a diffused cultural and religious individualism that greatly weakens possibilities that families of the future can be transmitters of a strong, unified religious culture from one generation to the next. The interfaith household is both a product, and increasingly the carrier, of this diffused complex of values. Passing on anything identifiable as a distinct religious heritage from one generation to the next simply becomes more unlikely.

Yet another scenario keeps open the possibility of new and creative religious developments. Just as with changing family forms, there may be innovative ways of responding religiously within interfaith families. Sociologist Judith Stacey, for example, speaks of "recombinant families," pointing to how mixed-faith, often divorce-extended families are now developing new gender and kinship strategies. White, middle-class families specially, she argues, are the chief beneficiaries of these newer strategies and can learn further from African-American, Latino, and white, working-class families about extended and fictive kin support groups. The growth demographics of these latter constituencies assure that whatever family forms these latter populations develop, they will be influential in the wider culture. It seems reasonable to expect religious innovation and strategies, along with adaptations; indeed, Stacey's own analysis of Silicon Valley families documents how the religious and the familial cultures draw on one another. And the patterns she points to are very much in the mold of "recombinant religions." She finds that working-class women influenced by the feminist movement turn to both Evangelical Christianity and metaphysical traditions and draw on their resources for inspiration and strategies. Boundaries between the various meaning-systems are permeable, and innovative configurations follow. According to Stacey, the religious resources even within Evangelical Christianity can and do—under certain conditions—sustain family reforms such as more egalitarian marriages, gender bondings, and resourceful cross-generational relationships. All are creative responses to the considerable challenges now facing interfaith, or actually sometimes multifaith, families. For such families, religion is often understood as a resource, and is not to be looked upon in narrow sectarian terms.

Similarly, we uncovered creative responses to mixed-faith families particularly among Born-again Christians, mainstream believers, and metaphysical believers and seekers. Dynamics of such households vary enormously and make it very difficult to generalize about specific patterns fitting to the subcultures. Often the most religious parent, a mother or father in a heterosexual union, sets the spiritual style, and all or some family members join with that parent in observances, while at the same time respecting the faiths of other members. This makes for a dominant family faith of sorts but in dialogue with other faiths. Dogmatists have the most difficulty doing this without creating serious family strain; Born-again Christians do so more successfully, in part because so many of them already live in mixed-faith households and have learned norms of tolerance and civility. That may appear to be at odds with popular perceptions, but because Protestant Evangelicals, Pentecostals, and Catholic Charismatics hold so strongly to a personal faith, they often find themselves in family contexts where spouses, parents, and children live amicably without holding to a shared religious outlook. Large numbers of second marriages and blended families within this subculture likewise bolster the possibility of mixed-faith families. When we asked respondents in our survey if their families shared the same religious views, Born-again Christians were the *least* likely to say yes, 58 percent as compared to equal proportions, 78 percent, for mainstream believers, metaphysical believers and seekers, and dogmatists alike. Secularists, it turns out, constitute the most homogeneous families, with 89 percent in response to the question saying their families share similar views.

But there are other strategies. A second is more multireligious: families create an environment in which they can have a Seder one night and Easter dinner the next day, or skip one in favor of the other. Pragmatic and somewhat free-wheeling, people in this context try to fit rituals to family occasions and to deal with questions as they arise; parents take on a pro-active stance dealing with religious differences and affirming that religious teachings and practices—even a mix of them—are all to be valued. These families forge new traditions of sorts deciding what is appropriate from the resources at hand. "Sometimes, if you don't give children a religion, they end up believing in nothing. So we've sort of created our own traditions. After a while, you learn to adapt and compromise."[38] A third, somewhat more disciplined response is to observe in a stricter fashion practices from differing religions, as when a Catholic-Jewish couple we spoke with attends a Passover pageant with their 5-year-old son but also talks to him about the meaning of Easter and Christmas. Both sets of grandparents in this instance have strong convictions that prod the parents not to choose one faith over the other, and certainly not to meld them into a watered-down, random mix, but to expose their son to both traditions in as much fullness as possible so that he might someday make a choice. "It forces us to think about religion—why this ritual, why this belief—in ways we never thought about before," comments Harold Epstein, who is determined, as a Jewish father, to instruct his son in his heritage, but is also concerned that Cheryl, his Catholic wife, have equal time to teach about hers. Yet a fourth pattern we observe are gender-based rituals and celebrations, particularly among metaphysical believers and spiritual seekers. The focus is upon rituals such as those between mothers and daughters and, to a lesser extent, between fathers and sons. Family as a unit becomes less a basis for spiritual unity, with energies channeled instead into creating stronger relationships between some of its members. The goal of cultivating bondings between parents and children of the same gender is usually explicit.

Religious strategies—like kinship strategies—continue to evolve, and those we observed are still too fluid and inchoate to describe in much detail, much less to comment on extensively. Partners in mixed-faith marriages can be very serious in what they are trying to do religiously within the family; many are less so and seem to get through their daily lives without much attention to such matters. For those partners who are serious, tolerance and respect for religious differences are cherished values they teach their children. Because the mixed-faith family is a setting for an experiment in pluralism in which emotions are closely bound up with relationships, but where authority, especially for the parent not linked by blood, can be weak, it is a context that can, and often does, produce family tensions. But it also encourages a degree of reflexive inquiry into religious matters. "I worry about my wife's teenage daughter," a Los Angeles insurance executive told us. "She doesn't know much about this new religious movement she's hooked up with. I got books on it, studied it, talked with people about it, and even after all that and comparing it with Catholicism which I know best I don't know what to think." His words bespeak more than just desperation, but also what can result from serious faith encounters within a family: they may arouse interest, curiosity, and even clarification about religious alternatives, but whether any of this results in an increase of religious commitment itself is an open question. Nor do we know much about religious commitments for the long run. The Boomer generation is the first to deal with mixed-faith households on so large a scale; it will probably take another generation, with their experiences and better-crafted responses to the situation, before we can determine fully the religious consequences of such family arrangements. As in so many other realms, Boomers are pioneers experimenting with family formations.

INDIVIDUAL AUTONOMY, FAMILY, AND RELIGION

More broadly, we must address a theme that runs throughout this book—individualism and narrative—and ask the following questions: given all the various types of individualizing influences on the contemporary family, should we continue to think of families as genuinely sharing common religious beliefs and values? Or has individualism so invaded the family as an institution that we should think of its members as making decisions about religion largely on their own? Even posing the questions implies a great deal about the changing circumstances for the two institutions. From the early 1960s to the present, the culture moved rather quickly from a situation where there were observable differences in family styles along religious lines to one in which these differences have greatly disappeared. Euro-American Catholics, for example, who as recently as forty years ago were known for their largely ethnic-based family practices and values, by now have generally absorbed the values of individualism historically associated with the Protestant traditions.[39] In the intervening years, both institutions—family and religion—evolved in the direction of accommodating values of autonomy, choice, and privatism. While religion in the United States was in principle a matter of choice, it was not widely viewed as one to be exercised *within* the family; as the basic unit of society, and therefore responsible for the socialization of the young, the family as normatively defined should remain the primary transmitter of cultural and religious values. But in the contemporary context, families function less in this role and religion is bound by less of a normative standard. Both family and religion are highly privatized. Consequently, attachments to both institutions are in a process of reorientation just as alignments between the two themselves are undergoing a transformation.

In order to get a better grasp of the impact of individualism within the family context, earlier in the first survey we asked our respondents: "Is it important to you to attend church/synagogue as a family, or should family members make individual choices about religion?" Responses to this question showed them to be split almost down the middle: 55 percent answered that it was important to attend as a family, and 45 percent said family members should make their own choices. Knowing of no comparable data for an earlier generation, we cannot determine the extent these responses may differ, but by any calculation the proportion taking an individualist perspective is significant. The 45 percent figure is high—probably higher for this generation than in the past. A "shared religious" family is still the majority ideal, but not by much. Though just a single question, it was worded well and proved to be a good predictor of a major normative cleavage within Boomer life. Whereas those holding to the shared religious perspective on the family emphasize duty and social obligation, especially parental responsibility to children, the more individualist-oriented are much more likely to make religious decisions based on personal need and their own search for meaning and self-expression. The contrasting perspectives express two differing character types within contemporary society, whose views are increasingly sustained by quite differing phenomenological worlds and social structural realities. Increasingly, norms of religious individualism affecting families and their worlds are sustained largely around two basic social structures: the workplace and family type.

The professional and career-oriented classes lead the way in individualist orientations toward religion. For them, autonomy goes with their work and greatly influences personal identities. Working Boomer women increasingly hold religious views and engage in religious activities similarly to those of men. Single men are more independent-minded about religion than single women, but differences here appear to be declining. Cohabitants, the divorced and separated, both male and female, are understandably inclined in this direction. But the family factors that clearly predict otherwise are marriage and parenthood: those with children, especially as they reach school age, favor family norms of religious participation. Two-thirds of all who want a shared faith are two-parent families with children. Only 19 percent of married working women without children and 39 percent of married working men without children favor a shared family faith, but 55 percent of working mothers with children and 68 percent of working fathers with children do so. Clearly, marriage and the presence of children take precedence over work as the stronger influences shaping religious norms. Becky Johnson, John McRae's fiancée, provides an example: she works full-time and, while not yet married, anticipates shared religious experiences with her partner (and his son when he visits) and looks forward to starting their own family, hopefully a religiously cohesive family. Family life is important to her. It is her wish that John convert to Catholicism but she does not know whether he will. In the meantime she is content to continue participating in the small Eucharist community where he feels comfortable. Her decision in this respect is not all that uncommon: many young Boomers find themselves in her situation, wanting to deal responsibly with a mixed-faith relationship without jeopardizing it. Family life is valued—indeed, more so now than it was even a decade ago. People are concerned about teaching spiritual values within the family. Even where family-based religious activities may be temporary, relating largely to child-rearing, for the most part the memory of these years is greatly valued and treasured by parents.

The greater difficulty in sustaining family-based rituals and activities relates of course to divorce. When divorces occur, ruptures in religious routines almost inevitably follow. Attachments to religious institutions become strained. Children are often caught between their parents' religious inclinations. Parental perspectives on religion often become more individualist after divorce, a scenario also found in blended-family arrangements where pragmatic considerations override more idealistic hopes for the family. The success of marriages and of family members with mixed faiths in finding common religious ground thus become key factors in sustaining and promoting religious values for children. There are other considerations, too. A shared religious culture, to a lesser or greater degree, is more likely for families having close and supportive emotional ties; for those who at least engage in simple rituals like saying grace at meals or lighting candles on holidays and are willing to talk about it; for those involved in organizations and service activities within the community; for families with similar-minded friends and extended family nearby; and for families who like to discuss religious as well as other topics within the family, and to read stories to children. In pollster Daniel Yankelovich's terms,[40] in families where there is an "ethic of commitment," where sharing is honored and its members' personal views respected, there is more of a chance of shared spiritual values.

With respect to our religious subcultures, two patterns here are worthy of note. Mainstream believers are the most likely to espouse a traditional, family-based religious style, which is unsurprising. Recall that more of them are in intact marriages and, as we have seen, the family-and-religion connection is of symbolic significance to them. The Golden Rule religiosity so common within this subculture places great emphasis on relationships, and on the links between family and tradition. Family symbolism is deeply embedded in all the major religious traditions, but it is reinforced by the fact that religion in the United States, as a voluntary association and activity, is so closely identified with family and community. Wanting a shared family experience, including a shared faith, more than just a religious motivation, arises out of a deep concern to preserve family tradition. A second pattern we observed is that metaphysical believers and spiritual seekers have relatively low levels of concern about families sharing a spiritual tradition. Since so many of them are single and/or single parents, divorced or separated, or experienced in diverse family situations, this more individualist approach to religion is understandable. Where there are intact families with children, family rituals and celebrations are not at all uncommon; indeed, as already

250

pointed out, they can be quite creative. But family-based practices themselves are overshadowed in a subculture characterized by so great a variety of spiritual teachings and where so much attention is focused on the
individual's own search for metaphysical truth.

More broadly, the picture that emerges for family and religion is one
of structural changes, fluidity, and boundary-crossings. The mixed-faith
household is the most blatant example, but the list of examples is much
longer. Historically, Americans crossed boundaries of religion as they
adjusted to social mobility, and now they do so as they accommodate an
openness to sexual orientation and shifts in family formations. People
move in and out of religious involvement over the course of their lives,
many becoming more involved in phases such as child-rearing and less
so in others; Evangelical gender-based movements like Promise Keepers
and Women's Aglow Fellowship mobilize men and women, respectively,
out of old cultural roles and into exploring new ones with subtle realignments of power and identity. Other developments are even more paradoxical: mainline Protestant, Catholic, and Jewish congregations are
open theologically to family diversity yet on the whole are bastions of
familism and heterosexual culture; Evangelical Protestant and Charismatic Catholic congregations posture for traditional husband-and-wife
families yet are made up of great numbers who do not fit this family
form. Except for secularists, there is within all the religious subcultures
considerable concern about both family and religion, yet how to connect
these two institutions in mutually supportive ways remains, for many people, more a hope than a reality. So much flux on the religious scene
need not be considered a weakness but may actually anticipate the creative restructuring of sharing arrangements by partners in marriages and
sexual unions, and by parents and primary caregivers.

If we expand the perspective to look seriously at the triad of work,
family, and religion, there are added complexities, but also new potential. Businesses and corporations are addressing issues of employment
and parenthood. Pregnancy leaves, on-site day care and kindergarten for
young children, lactation-support services, afterschool care for older
children, facilities for exercise and family recreation, flexible work
schedules, are all far more common now than twenty years ago as a result
of the entry of Boomer women into the labor force. The corporate
workplace is also emerging as a setting for Bible study, Torah study, Is-
lamic study, and Buddhist meditation. Marketplace Ministries, Fellowship for Companies for Christ International, Chabad Lubavitch and
other such newly developed organizations cater to religious concerns on

the job, giving attention to ethics, spiritual well-being, diet and health, dress, family responsibilities, even family finances. Other entrepreneurs bypass talk about religion and choose instead to organize seminars on spirituality in the workplace, and speak of individuals and corporations as sharing goals and accomplishments. Explicit attention is given to the intangible dimension of life, in personal and family life as well as on the job. This surfacing of religious and spiritual concerns in the work arena suggests an unleashing of creative energy, leading one commentator recently to conclude "People are not only embracing religion in different ways, but also have become more comfortable in the public expression of their faith."[41]

The changing patterns of work, family, and religion may be even more radical than what we have as yet envisioned. A recent study of an American corporation finds people caught in a work-family squeeze, one in which they suffer an emotional toll as a result of working longer and feeling stressed at home. That in itself is hardly news, but in its analysis of the reasons for this the study exposes far deeper structural strains than those hitherto generally recognized. Once a "haven in a heartless world," the family carefully marked the boundaries from the outer world that was cold and competitive and thereby gave space and sustenance to people's lives, but now the family faces serious complications of its own. The conclusion is that the emotional magnets underlying work and family may themselves be in a reversal process, with family life becoming more regimented and governed by time pressures, and the workplace looking more like a surrogate home with its emotional and even spiritual support structures. Arlie Russell Hochschild, the sociologist, proposes that both working wives and husbands may be more sustained by the emotional culture of the workplace than that of the family, in which case "a tired parent flees a world of unresolved quarrels and unwashed laundry for the reliable orderliness, harmony, and managed cheer of work."[42] Hochschild's portrait is but one of Americans and their current institutional attachments, but as a portrait of where corporate culture may be headed, it raises some vexing questions.

With so many reconfigurations of work, family, and religious patterns, this generation is deeply caught up in the ideological debate and opposing moral visions engulfing the nation as a whole. The structural changes in American society underlying work and family life are creating widespread strains and anxieties. These changes, combined with the rampant culture of individualism and expanding pluralism, are also generating a great deal of moral and religious rhetoric—the so-called culture wars—

over moral standards, the family, the environment, and religion's public role. How are people to balance their commitments to work and the pursuit of material values, but also to themselves and their families? What should be the right balance of individual freedom and family responsibilities? Are all types of families equally suited for raising and caring for children? How far should Americans go in tolerating alternative lifestyles? And should religion have a public role shaping moral standards and values? These questions are all being widely debated by the public and certainly deserve further inquiry.

✣ CHAPTER 8 ✣

Moral Vision and Values

In the main drift of religion the theological and liturgical and
contemplative move into the background . . . The penumbra of
beyondness, absoluteness, and mystery fades away, and leaves—as
the core of what Americans think religion to be—the moral.
(*William Lee Miller*)

By its very nature spiritual life is transformative of all life.
(*Louis Dupré*)

Public life in the United States at the turn of the century poses something of a paradox: there is continuing rhetoric of a "culture war" implying that the nation is deeply polarized over values, beliefs, morality, and
lifestyles, yet there is also a questing mood, a ferment, a search for a
deeper spiritual life that seems at odds with anything labeled a "war." If
the first rhetoric rests on a binary conception of the social order, "us"
versus "them," conjuring images of social division and conflict, the second is much softer and unifying, resonating with personal and social
well-being. One has an ominous tone of belligerence and irreconcilabil-
ity; the other conveys some hope about the possibilities of a transformed
self and society. But what are we to make of such alternative views? Are
we to assume the "culture wars" model accurately describes the way
Americans born after World War II think and behave with respect to
moral and ethical issues? That despite whatever religious and deeply
spiritual values they may hold, what really matters is their moral values
and ideologies? Or is the "culture war" model overextended? And what
about spirituality? Is the spirituality we have described a unifying or divisive force? And is it sufficiently grounded and robust enough to be
"transformative of all life" which, according to Yale philosopher Louis
Dupré,[1] is the test of genuine inwardness, or is it so self-absorbed and
circumscribed that its influence barely extends beyond the person? All
are serious questions, yet ones we must grapple with if we are to appreciate the nuance, and indeed ambiguity, of the moral and religious situation currently. Nor should we assume that one conceptual model need
be correct, and the other incorrect. For once we move beyond the static

254

descriptions of religion in this country as "pluralism," as "denominational order," or as a "mosaic" of faith traditions and communities, it becomes apparent that no one model describes adequately the dynamic and perplexing features of American beliefs and values. Sociologist Peter Berger once avowed that religious life in the United States resembles that of a little secular Sweden superimposed upon a vast religious India[2]—the substance of which we need not debate here, but as a metaphor it obviously emphasizes tht ours is a thick and multilayered religio-moral order. Not only does religion in America resist a permanent outline over time; it is not reducible at any one time to a single outline.

CULTURE WARS?

William Lee Miller's observation about the moral core of American religion is compelling at a time when the moral fabric of the society is deeply torn, and religious and political voices in the public arena speak to those pulls and tears.[3] Hearing so much as we now do from pundits, politicians, and preachers about gay rights, families in crisis, declining civic engagement, and loss of moral character in political leaders, Miller's comment seems even more appropriate now than when his words were written at the end of the Eisenhower years. Since the mid 1970s disputes have flared over abortion, pornography, school prayer, women's rights, and homosexuality, exposing deep-seated ideological and lifestyle conflicts, somewhat reminiscent of the theological split between modernists and Fundamentalists earlier in this century. However, the difference in this latter period is that controversies are more explicitly focused around moral values and lifestyles. Highly charged issues of the past two decades have divided religious denominations and faith communities, captured widespread public attention, and led to the rise of many new special-purpose organizations, taking up one or another cause and stirring up a great deal of popular support. Particularly on the conservative side, the rhetoric has been noisy and forcefully targeted against trends considered threatening to the country; indeed, conservative funding in support of a battle over moral ideals in the early 1990s reached staggering proportions.[4] Patrick Buchanan brought the notion of moral warfare to the country's attention in his declaration of a "war for the nation's soul" at the Republican National Convention in 1992, the same year Vice President Quayle gave his famous speech on "family values." Throughout the decade much the same call to battle was voiced, as sociologist

Rhys H. Williams observes, "by such 'cultural warriors' as Rush Limbaugh, William Bennett, former secretary of education, and James Dobson, director of the interest group Focus on the Family."[5] The very fact that these five diverse leaders and opinion-makers—a presidential candidate, a vice-president, a radio talk-show host, a cabinet member and successful author, and a popular Evangelical psychologist and family advocate—were drawn together around a moral vision for the country, despite differing social and religious backgrounds, attests to the powerful force of moral and religious ideology. No coverage of the current moral climate in the United States is adequate without serious attention to these forces.

Among social scientists, the chief proponent of a broadly based cultural and political conflict is sociologist James Davison Hunter who, in 1991, published *Culture Wars: The Struggle to Define America*. Later, in 1994, Hunter wrote another book with an even more ominous-sounding title: *Before the Shooting Begins: Searching for Democracy in America's Culture War*. Hunter sees the country ideologically divided into two major camps, the "orthodox" and the "progressives," and Americans generally involved in a struggle that cuts across social classes and cultural realms. Religion is seen as very much fueling this national debate, but the struggle finds expression widely in many institutional sectors—in education, in media and entertainment, and in the arts. As the argument has it, older religious divisions such as those between Protestants and Catholics and between Christians and Jews are now superceded by a conflict that cuts across them—between religious traditionalists who believe in God as traditionally defined in Western religious heritage and religious modernists, agnostics, and secularists who take a more relativist, socially constructed position with respect to moral values and religious truth. All other bases for division within the society—economic and noneconomic—are eclipsed by this singular cleavage, which is all-encompassing, so the argument goes, because it arises out of differing sources of authority and moral truth, whether in a transcendent source beyond society, as with the orthodox, or in reason, culture, or authority of the self, as with the progressives. At bottom is an irreconcilable basis for making truth-claims. Because these differences function at the level of competing "moral visions" and "worldviews," again to cite Rhys H. Williams, in this instance commenting on Hunter's position, "they do more than just shape our moral, social, and political ideas, they also mold our very perceptions of reality . . . our sense of how the world 'should' be *and* how it in fact 'is.'" Hence, there is little ground for any real negotiation and compromise: the nation is seen as caught up in an inevitable struggle over moral values and ideologies that are incommensurate with one another.

The specific issues contested are mainly abortion, sexuality and family values, gay rights, welfare reforms, and the public role of religion in American democracy. According to the "culture war" thesis, the views of Americans on these quite differing cognitive and lifestyle domains are relatively consistent. Because moral questions are now so salient and cutting-edge, they generate a consistency of responses, which, moreover, not only fall on some continuum between orthodox and progressive but are said to cluster at the extremes of the continuum. Culture war conjures up imageries of battles, bombshells, and bloodshed, of groups mobilized for action and locked in intractable conflict. Less belligerent imageries—but still warfare—are perpetuated in interpretations of American religion as divided into two conflicting camps: religious conservatives and religious liberals, fanning the theological rift between opposing parties that has shaped much of twentieth-century thought. The severity of this rift is underscored by scholars who point to ways the nation's major denominations and faith communities are themselves internally split. Of course, the bombing of abortion clinics and public statements by religious bodies on moral and lifestyle issues further substantiate these perceptions. Commentators on religion and public life seize upon these events, exaggerating the gap between religious liberals and progressives on the one hand, and religious conservatives and reactionaries on the other. And the media portray this religious and cultural divide often in grim terms, as a full-fledged battle between organized and warring parties, and the country as on the brink of impending doom. At the hands of the media, culture-war rhetoric easily becomes transformed into an *explanation* of why Americans are so polarized in their outlook. Popular commentary in political campaigns, in the press, and on television talk shows drawing off religious symbols and beliefs reinforces notions of a country deeply caught up in a struggle over its soul. In this climate of divided opinion, the notion of a "culture war" can take on features of a self-fulfilling prophecy, that is, perceptions are reinforced to the point they appear as social realities.

Though a thesis applied generally to American life, the issues over which the alleged war is fought resonate with the Boomer generation. Abortion, sexual ethics, changing family patterns, and new lifestyle enclaves are all issues arising out of the 1960s, or more properly put, the way in which these issues are now framed very much bears the imprint of these earlier cultural confrontations. The Boomer generation is the cultural avant-garde that broke with old patterns and forged new ones. They are also well-represented—perhaps overrepresented—among the intellectual elite, community and religious leaders, and politicians who now shape conversation about these issues. After all, it was Vice President Quayle, a Baby Boomer, who ignited so much controversy in his "family values" speech some years ago when he cited the *Murphy Brown* television series and the lead character's decision to have a baby out of wedlock. The television program mirrored the lifestyles and family disruptions of many middle-class, career-oriented Boomers. In particular, it crystallized attention to the emerging reality of out-of-wedlock births in the white middle-class United States, that sector that easily becomes a lightning rod sparking controversy—as was true with drugs in the 1960s—when behavioral styles thought to be restricted to minorities or the white underclass are discovered to have diffused across racial, ethnic, and social class lines. Over the next several years, President Clinton, another Baby Boomer, engaged the debate on family issues emphasizing the problems of teenage pregnancies, out-of-wedlock births, and absent fathers.[6] Clinton agreed with much of what Quayle said even as he disagreed in advocating a greater role for government in trying to solve the problems. As a result, the national debate that had earlier been highly divisive shifted in the direction of greater consensus. What had been a conservative political crusade was coopted to a considerable extent by the Democratic party and turned into a national issue. Family concerns became defined less in partisan terms and were increasingly voiced by many Americans—certainly not just by Baby Boomers. By 1995–96, when we conducted our second survey, family concerns were at the top of the list. On two topics especially—casual sex and using drugs—the Boomers were decidedly more conservative than they had been in 1988–89. By no means does this suggest that these issues no longer divided the generation, nor should we exaggerate the return to more traditional moral values, but much of the highly charged, inflamed rhetoric did subside and liberals and conservatives were beginning to talk to, rather than at, each other. In 1996 Hillary Rodham Clinton brought out *It Takes a Village: And Other Lessons Children Teach Us* and Dan Quayle and Diane Medved published *The American Family: Discovering the Values That Make Us Strong*, two books hardly agreeing in either diagnosis or prescription but that helped to set the terms for more recent, and a more widely based, discussion on family, with attention particularly to the absence of fathers and the well-being of children.[7]

But clearly, this movement toward a more common ground became clouded with the crisis of the Clinton presidency in 1998. Clinton's sex scandals and particularly the Lewinsky affair opened up the debate once again about the 1960s and the moral values stemming from that period. Feeding much of the fervor to impeach and oust the president was the conservative belief that he embodied almost everything that went wrong in that fateful decade: sexual and lifestyle freedom, abortions on demand, avoiding Vietnam, greater moral relativism. The culture war that had gripped the nation for thirty years came to a head and, as a result, rancor and animosity invaded Washington producing a "politics of personal destruction" on a level seldom witnessed. However, polls tapping the opinions of the American people showed the politicians to be out of step with majority sentiment. Even amid something of a return to more traditional values as the Boomer population was maturing, this generation, and the nation as a whole, did not seek to turn the clock back to a pre-1960s world. Rather, most Americans denounced the president's behavior, yet rejected the view that his offenses constituted grounds for justified removal from office. What the public response seemed to signal was a pragmatic moral consensus that recognizes the importance of moral ideals but acknowledges human frailty and is tolerant of human imperfection. Americans were ambivalent over whether the alleged sexual activities in the White House were public or private matters, but the distinction itself was judged to be one of some importance in making moral judgments. For Boomers the distinction had long been sacrosanct, supporting the view that in sexual and lifestyle matters privacy must be maintained. Americans below the age of 52—that is, Boomer and younger—according to a CNN poll were more likely than the rest of the population to look upon sex as a private matter, yet were about equally perplexed about whether to define the White House as a public or private setting.[8] This legacy of Boomer culture regarding privacy, and looking upon sexual acts of consenting adults as private, appears to have helped to create a more open and honest moral climate for the nation, much to the dismay of conservatives like William Bennett, who during the Clinton episode often asked why there was so little moral outrage. More so than provoke outrage, the president's behavior punctured pious moralisms and called into question the motives of his adversaries.

Where all this might lead as to moral posturing in the future is an open question, but at this time the more moderate grassroots voices appear to have prevailed. Politics in Washington aside, what the Clinton episode demonstrated was that for all of its reality and rhetoric, the notion of a culture war also has its limitations. Neither the nation nor the Boomer population in particular is as polarized as it would suggest. Furthermore, there is something deceptively simple about so encompassing a thesis as "culture war," especially when we consider the full spectrum of issues before the country at the turn of the century. Debate on abortion, family, marriage, gay rights, and religion's public role in the United States seems to have moved in the mid-to-late 1990s toward a new centrism, and one that will not easily be diverted by the Clinton controversy. Social scientific evidence on mainstream American attitudes and values show solid movement in this direction and caution against any wholesale endorsement of culture-war theory. A brief summary of the research evidence on the theory will help to set the tone for the remaining discussion of this chapter.[9]

First, a growing body of evidence fails to substantiate the assumption that opinions, values, and attitudes in the United States at large fall out on a single continuum as culture-war theory implies. Research points to at least two major axes along which people's responses to controversial issues are distributed: items of an economic and political kind fall out one way, items pertaining to morality and lifestyle fall out another way. This in itself complicates the notion of a singular basis for culture war. That we would expect consistency in attitude formation is itself more a rhetorical construction than a reflection of the actual views of Americans.

Second, the research repeatedly shows that views of Americans are not as polarized as the culture war thesis suggests. Surveys and polls find a large moderate sector of the population who fit neither of the strong ideological clusters of "orthodox" or "progressive." Americans typically are propelled toward the middle on social and political attitudes. Since as far back as the 1970s, in fact, there is little evidence of any dramatic increase in social-attitude polarization on most of the burning issues of our time, with the one exception of views toward abortion.

Third, to the extent there is a "culture war," it is more something staged by intellectuals and cultural elites than by ordinary Americans. Conservative and liberal ideologues spar with one another generating a great deal of rhetoric, but this often gives false impressions and exaggerates the actual extent of the cultural divide. The rhetoric of special-purpose groups is targeted to mobilize and to create a belief that opinions are polarized and reform movements are organized ready to address the situation. "The antagonisms between movement 'elites,'" as has been pointed out, "are not necessarily reflected among either rank and file members or the great unmobilized mass—as the elites themselves know full well."[10]

Fourth, national surveys and polls find greater disparity in beliefs, moral values, and opinions than do ethnographers who study local communities. Because survey items are typically framed to force people into making choices between extreme positions, they easily give the impression that people disagree more than they really do. Yet when people are asked about their views in greater depth and have the opportunity to qualify what they actually think, caveats and all, support for extreme positions is usually less substantial. But there can be the opposite bias: ethnographers looking at selected communities without benefit of representative data for the whole country risk concluding there is more consensus and religio-moral unity than actually exists.[11]

And finally, there is the question of whether the moral disputes of our time arise out of a crisis of faith. Often a direct, behavior-follows-belief connection is assumed: a strong theistic faith should result in conventional moral behavior, whereas absence of such faith will result in its erosion. And yet the connection between belief and behavior is not so simple. It is not at all obvious that moral and religious rhetoric corresponds to moral behavior; and also, reflexive spirituality of the sort we have described may encourage a variety of "strategies of action," or what might appear as inconsistent behavior depending on circumstances. Strategies may or may not establish direct links to belief in God or the sacred, and many vary from one religious subculture to another, even from one moral issue to another. In short, given a complex, multilayered American religious terrain, we should not expect patterns of religion and moral culture to be very neatly ordered, much less to conform to some simple or rationally consistent conception of how belief systems ought to work, or with what social realities they should correlate.

ABORTION CONTROVERSY

For Boomers no controversy has been noisier, or more drawn out during their lives, than that over abortion. The issue has been the subject of extended debate, no topic stirring more passion, especially among the women of this generation; in fact, *Roe v. Wade* symbolizes for many the struggle for lifestyle and reproductive freedom. Abortion was at center stage galvanizing conservative moral and religious sentiment during the 1980s and into the 1990s, a time when much political discourse was preoccupied with the controversy. The war metaphor was commonly invoked in discussions on abortion and continues to be invoked, as evident in the flow of new books with "war" in their titles.[12] Yet the alignments of Boomers and other Americans on this issue, then and now, defy easy generalization, partly because they—like other Americans—are deeply conflicted: when asked in 1988–89 if abortion was ever morally wrong, 25 percent said always, 18 percent usually, 48 percent sometimes, and less than 10 percent said never or were uncertain. Since then views have solidified somewhat but the generation remains highly divided. It is also true that Boomers especially do not easily fit the usual liberal-versus-conservative categories of social and political ideology. Their indifference to political parties and suspicion of authority earlier on in their lives predisposed them to approach divisive issues from multiple frameworks. Concern about personal space and privacy, an example already alluded to, is one such framework: individual freedom and choice are neither really conservative nor liberal. And on a range of issues—gender roles, marriage, whether to have children, parenting—surveys and polls since the 1980s show them to be greatly concerned to preserve privacy over against the invasions of their space by government, corporations, and any other large-scale organizations. Privacy is a widely shared value, and one that blurs ideological differences except at the extremes.

At the time of our first survey, 59 percent of Boomers led other Americans in insisting that women should be able to obtain an abortion "regardless of reason." Over the past fifteen years, their support for this position has declined slightly, but they still set the pace on the pro-choice position. Their wish to preserve privacy and space pushed the national debate on abortion rights, though not necessarily the religious debate, in the direction of specifying conditions under which abortion should, or should not, be legally available. Here is an instance where the polls themselves may have made a difference: by offering a broader range of favorable options in polls and surveys, they have helped to mold a more reasoned, subtle position people might take on this issue. Except for the religious right for whom there is no budging, most Boomer Americans arrived at, or continue to negotiate, positions more in the mid-range of circumstances than at the extremes of the spectrum; 38 percent of the people we talked with at the time of the first survey indicated in fact they had changed their mind on this issue in the past few years, which means that there is a good deal of volatility and unpredictability in attitudes. In other areas, too—women's rights, the environment, health care, and education—progressive politicians recognize that these do not necessarily fall squarely on one or another partisan side. Hence, politicians can mold opinion, and not just by taking extreme positions but through careful and negotiated framing of issues, posturing so as to be responsive to individual concerns about freedom, yet socially responsible and accountable to the public.[13] Pollsters and politicians in this past decade have catered to a populace somewhat more open to centrist positions generally. Coming out of the Reagan 1980s when views on abortion and other issues were more polarized, the early 1990s were a time of dramatic increase in the proportion of ideological liberals, from 35 percent in 1985 to 49 percent in 1993, and a corresponding decline in the number of ideological conservatives, from 28 percent to 17 percent during these same years. Boomers were growing somewhat more conservative as they aged, but this was moderated by a shift in national mood. Demographically, too, more young people are found among liberals than among moderates or conservatives, which means that growing numbers of older, moderate-minded Americans now align themselves with Boomers and others still younger in ideological stance. All this has helped to create a more informed and calculating public with regard to views on abortion, and certainly countered trends toward clear-cut, unmistakable divisions with "whole armies itching for battle."[14] This more pragmatic trending for the society as a whole, combined with savvy political framing of major social issues before the nation—indeed, the two inextricably get fused together—augurs for a more variegated picture of Americans and their ideologies. And in this regard, our typology of religious subcultures once again proves to be quite useful.

As improbable as it may seem, there appears to be a melding of views toward a middle ground including large numbers of Born-again Christians, who see themselves as increasingly caught between narrow-minded dogmatists who refuse to give in at all, and open-minded secularists for whom moral principles are unclear.[15] Listening to the rhetoric of many Born-again religious leaders, one would not draw the conclusion about any melding of views but, as noted above, the voices of the people and those of their leaders often diverge. This changing configuration of popular views is best shown in responses to an item asked in both our surveys, in 1988–89 and 1995–96: "Should a married woman who doesn't want any more children be able to obtain a legal abortion?" Framed so as to push the issue toward its outer limits, the item taps the extremes of responses to feminist ideology. Forty-six percent of all our respondents said yes in the first round, 44 percent in the second round—a slight decline hardly unexpected due to the aging of the generation. With regard to the more recent survey, the subcultures break out as follows: dogmatists, 31 percent; Born-again Christians, 48 percent; mainstream believers, 50 percent; metaphysical believers and spiritual seekers, 51 percent; secularists, 56 percent. Striking is the broad middle of affirmative response among Born-again Christians, mainstream believers, and metaphysical believers and seekers. We did encounter some strong negative voices among Born-again Christians, even some obnoxious ones, as well as a few from the other two constituencies. But more often than not, in the extended telephone interviews members from all three groups used their own distinctive vocabularies—be they religious, feminist, or anything else—to express their reasons for the position they hold and made frequent recourse to phrases like "you really want to know my personal opinion?" or "in all honesty what I think is . . . " Given a chance to sort out layers of opinion and feeling, often the final response to the question—yes or no—came with caveats about a womans's specific circumstances, and especially so when those polled were asked what they would do in the situation of that woman. Without engaging a conversation on abortion, it is easy for a researcher or observer to arrive at premature conclusions about another person's actual feelings or outlook; and considering that often these latter do not always go together, people can be deeply conflicted in their moral views. Yet despite differing rhetorics, theologies, and worldviews, what this large middle does share is appreciation for a religious and spiritual narrative of life and recognition, increasingly, that they should be led in moral decision-making by what is the *loving* thing to do. What this often boils down to is awareness that they should carry on a dialogue within themselves in search of a caring answer appropriate to their situations rather than rely on a rigid ideology or some external moral code.[16] Of course, the way that questions on abortion are framed, the use of symbolic and charged language, even the tone of the interviewer's voice, all bias responses and filter people's feelings and expressions of love. The point simply is, given our most careful efforts at sensitive listening and framing interview questions, we conclude that controversy over abortion is on the wane, even more than we expected, in the emerging cultural and religious middle.

To be sure, Protestant Fundamentalists, Catholic traditionalists, and other types of dogmatists are not a part of this emerging middle. They

best fit Hunter's conception of the "orthodox" and hold to a more literal, monarchical conception of a God who relates to people as subjects
and stands over against the world. They look on abortion as a violation
of God's laws; on sex and sexual ethics with some suspicion, as visibly
apparent in the controversy over President Clinton; and look on women
rather narrowly as bodies and emotions and, therefore, in a very real
sense, in need of control by men.[17] Between them and the secularists,
there is of course a huge disparity in moral and religious views. Listening
to those on each side of this major divide, one hears much anger, blame,
mistrust, and irreconcilable differences of worldview. The two sides disagree over abortion but also over other more basic aspects of the nature
of social reality itself. They differ in conceptions of how the social world
hangs together; in moral logic for addressing personal and social issues;
in views of marriage and institutional structure; and in what constitutes
final authority over human life. As communication theorists are prone to
say, the two are locked into incommensurate discourses over moral orders and are thus seldom able to rise above their own rhetorical resources.[18] As of yet, no resourceful vocabulary allows for effectively communicating across this cleavage. The culture war alleged to exist does in
fact exist in these quarters, and most especially so among elites giving
voice to these constituencies. Among rank-and-file dogmatists there is
more of a sense of warfare than among secularists. Dogmatists currently
feel besieged by secular surroundings, although fifteen years ago it was
just the opposite when secular humanists, as they were then called, felt
prevailed upon. But that war must be seen as dividing the ideological
extremes of the contemporary United States, and not one that is seriously splitting the cultural and religious middle now shaping much of
public opinion. Generally, the debate on abortion is less raucous at
present than it was even a few years ago and is now somewhat overshadowed by controversies over gay rights and expanded public debate over
family issues.

FAMILY DEBATE

One of the clearest indications of a changing debate over family issues is
heard in the moderating voices of Born-again Christians during the
mid-to-late 1990s concerning women working outside the home. Even
within the Christian Coalition, the conservative religious movement,

rhetoric cooled a bit. It could be said that Born-again women are "catching up" with others swept away in the trend toward dual-wage earners within the family, yet in another sense they are at the forefront of religious change and pragmatic decision-making. It is a shift in keeping with social predictions. With increased education, rapidly changing gender roles, upward mobility and a more solid middle-class status, high divorce rates and fragile marriages, expanding financial needs of families, and shifting cultural and religious orientation for this population over the past quarter-century, we would expect both the movement of Born-again women into the workforce and greater acceptance of it. Even by the early 1980s, research conducted with Evangelical college students foresaw these trends, observing back then they were drifting toward greater gender equality and were more liberal in their views on changing roles for women than for men. Only a third of young Evangelicals at the time agreed with the statement: "Though it is not always possible, it is best if the wife stays home and the husband works to support the family."[19]

As Born-again women moved into the workplace, they accommodated views from the wider culture—but not without psychological strains or the need to redefine personal religious views. For many conservative religious women, there is a gap between their "idealized" view of themselves as the good wife and mother who does not work outside the home and the practical realities of their families' financial needs. Rising costs of living combined with expanded consumer expectations have only intensified this cognitive dissonance. But it is also clear that increasingly for Born-again Christian women of this generation who are educated and committed to more egalitarian social and religious beliefs, there is less of a gap. For married Born-again women, in fact, knowing if they hold to traditional versus egalitarian ideals about marriage, family, and work is a better predictor of female labor-force participation than church teachings, husband's income, or even the presence of preschool children in the home.[20] That is a substantial shift over the past two decades catapulting women—not their husbands, their children, nor the church—to the center of decision-making. If Martha Wong (Sam Wong's wife) is any indication of trends, commitment to egalitarian ideals not only finds growing expression within the Evangelical community but is increasingly played out in subtle, interpersonally negotiated ways. Evangelical ideology about women, home, and work is one thing but actual practice as found in everyday life is quite another, as evident in her response when we asked what her husband thought about her working in a full-time job:

Good? Well let's say necessary. I have to work. We couldn't survive if I didn't. Maybe God doesn't want it that way but that's how it is today . . . paying the bills and living. The Bible doesn't say a woman shouldn't work. What the Bible says is that the husband is the head of the household, but things are a lot more complex now. God wants us to survive, I'm sure he does.

"What do you mean when you say the husband is the head of the home?" the interviewer asked in a follow-up. To which she responded:

He is the spiritual leader. A man is responsible to his wife and family. He must assume that responsibility, it is what is expected of him.

"In charge of economic matters and making decisions, too?" the interviewer persisted. To which she had this to say:

We talk about these things, make decisions together. He is spiritual head of the family but we share a lot. He listens to me, appreciates what I have to say, and I appreciate what he thinks. It works out.

Unresolved tensions exist, but they have arrived at a pragmatic moral consensus. She herself recognizes the tension between the traditional ideal of the wife who does not work, consistent with a patriarchal view of authority within the family, and both women's wish to work and the sheer necessity for both marriage partners to work. Awareness of the tension is a first step toward its resolution. As with cognitive dissonance of any kind, it pushes toward a solution—which for educated, Born-again Christian women in this instance means, more and more, the reformulation of religious beliefs and rationales to fit the realities of work and family. Important to observe, while she acknowledges her husband as head, she redefines his headship as having less to do with judgments over economic matters and more with "spiritual" authority. In this way she enhances both her own role and that of her husband but in very differing ways, elevating hers to a greater level of equality in decision-making over economic matters and investing his with broader but somewhat vague responsibilities for the well-being of the marriage and the family. Involving more than just religion, this is about the redrawing of boundaries bearing upon power and gender equality, family dynamics, and leveraging men to become more accountable as husbands and fathers. Here clearly is an example of a new "strategy of action"—of women redefining roles and relationships and of adapting their Evangelical faith around new behavioral styles. Other researchers have called attention to this creative use of religious resources on the part of conservative women reconstituting the meaning of their marriages and to the rise of a "symbolic traditionalism"[21] now replacing a more literal, hierarchical one as the operative religious principle governing family life.

Another observation in this situation has to do with the language Martha Wong uses in "resolving" her working. She appeals to conversation within the marriage, to making decisions together, and to mutual respect. The egalitarian marriage where partners talk on the same level with one another and share decision-making is held up as an ideal rather than the stereotypic conception of a biblical pattern of male authority so often presumed to characterize religious conservatives. Even in our earlier 1988–89 survey we saw evidence of this egalitarian ideal emerging among religious conservatives, and of an expanding gap between Born-again Christians and dogmatists. At that time we asked respondents about the following statement: "Some equality in marriage is a good thing, but by and large the husband ought to have the main say-so in family matters." Forty-seven percent of Protestant Fundamentalists and traditionally minded Catholics agreed, but only 27 percent of Protestant Evangelicals and Charismatic Catholics, 20 percent of mainstream believers, 21 percent of metaphysical believer and spiritual seekers, and 8 percent of secularists. The egalitarian marriage as an ideal is deeply embedded in middle-class American culture and the pressures of the workplace push in this direction for all people. But striking even then was the extent of egalitarian sentiment within the Born-again Christian community: it underscored how religious views of marriage and family within this constituency were increasingly informed by an egalitarian ethic stemming in no small part from a diffused feminism, a widespread democratization of intimacy and values in modernity, and by secular, pragmatic considerations families face. Like many other Americans, they are drawn into "Golden Rule" religion of the sort we have already described, a religious style based more in everyday experience and practice than in creed or absolute moral principles. Caring between spouses, relations between parents and children, and close ties between families and friends are all vital aspects of this moral style, arenas really for faith-based moral commitments. Simultaneously, as forces push toward a more centrist position on gender-based egalitarianism, the larger effect is a reconfiguring of the boundaries of religio-moral community, and thereby an expansion of the cleavage between the growing middle ground and the dogmatists.

But what lies behind this force? There must be something more than just an economically driven, highly secularized version of an equal-partners marriage. As underscored in other research, Golden Rule religion is not a rejection of orthodoxy, a watered-down version of true religion, but "a different orthodoxy," with its own integrity deeply rooted in good deeds, in valuing relationships and fairness to others, in caring practices.[22] Such religion is quintessentially American and, as William Lee Miller says in the introductory quote to this chapter, moral-behavioral at its very core. Still, though, we must ask, Why this trend at this time? My interpretation is that a deeply moving spiritual undercurrent is involved, something powerful in its own right: *Boomers, whether Born-again or not, increasingly accept the principle of mutuality in love and marriage.* Both their aging and the ethos of the times contribute to a greater acceptance of this principle, one that not only reorders gender roles and family life but opens up dialogue about self-images and relationships. Evidence suggests that among spiritually minded people, models of love and intimacy are likely to be bound up at a very deep level with divine images.[23] To be sure, people may have a higher regard for mutual love than they actually demonstrate in their behavior, but still it is mutuality, and not the self-sacrifice that was honored more in an earlier age or even self-fulfillment as often celebrated by many Boomers in their youth, that is now the dominant model of love and marriage certainly for this generation, and perhaps for Americans generally. Moreover, as recently uncovered in a survey sponsored by the Religion, Culture, and Family Project at the University of Chicago, people who have had spiritual experiences are far more likely to value self-giving in loving relations, be it the stronger version of self-sacrifice or the milder version of mutuality. And consistent with our argument, various religious measures—the "importance of religion," experience of the "presence of God," "Born-again experience," "mystical experience"—all correlate with self-giving and conceptions of a good marriage or intimate relations.[24] Within the context of intimacy, marriage, and family, spiritual sensitivity flourishes; committed relationships generate openness and an ethic of sharing that spills over. Increased reflexivity is encouraged as well, as partners to marriages and relationships come to appreciate one another and their distinctive narratives. This opens the way toward shared religious stories and a reworking of those stories in light of one another with the potential of transforming relationships and families into more supportive and nurturing microcosms.

269

Issues of love and intimacy, of course, extend well beyond nuclear families. Recognized are the growing numbers of single families, blended families, cohabiting couples, and same-sex families, and the distinct challenges each of these arrangements faces in the living out of an ethic of mutuality and caring. A major challenge is openness and honesty about intimacy and its relation to authentic faith and spirituality. For most Boomers the term *family* evokes a flexible image even as politicians and religious leaders speak of the "traditional nuclear family" as normative. Herein lies a significant gap between definitions of the "ought" versus what "is," a gap widely recognized but more egregiously apparent within some religious subcultures than others. For example, religious rhetoric and actual behavior are particularly at odds within conservative faith communities. Leadership in these communities regard all the new family forms more or less as deviations from the divinely ordained nuclear family, even though the actual beliefs of their Boomer members bear little if any relation to actual levels of divorce and living arrangements, to keeping in contact with parents, or even to involvement in their own children's education. Idealized religious rhetoric within these communities is one thing, statistics on divorce, family abuse, and concern for children are quite another.[25] The gap is slightly less for Born-again Christians than for the more rigid dogmatists, but both are caught up in fiction and hypocrisy. Though not particularly traumatizing, increasingly it is recognized by a growing number of perceptive believers; as such, pressures are mounting in the direction of greater openness and honesty. Such a gap between belief and family-based practices is considerably narrower for the other religious subcultures.

Of all the current issues, same-sex unions are by far the most controversial for Boomers as a whole. By and large, heterosexual Boomers hold to a principle of lifestyle diversity, including that of sexual orientation, and defend the rights of gays and lesbians to live as they please. Few would question such a basic right. However, when questioned about blessing homosexual unions and raising children, they tend to draw the line. "I don't care how a person lives, that's their right, married, not married, gay or straight, but a child ought to grow up with a mommy and daddy," a Catholic man in Massachusetts told us. "It can't always be, but it ought to be." The moral logic usually based on a human right to choices falters on the issue of extending homosexuals full-fledged legitimacy as family units. Here the distinction between dogmatists and Born-again Christians, or for that matter between any of our constituencies except for metaphysical believers and seekers, makes very little real difference. No matter how we sort out the populations religiously, by denomination and faith community, by level of religious activity, by religious upbringing, we find no statistically significant differences in the aggregate in degree of liberality toward homosexuality. Metaphysical believers and seekers are far more open and accepting than others, many themselves acknowledging that they are gay or lesbian. The small number of gays and lesbians we interviewed see themselves as pioneers forging new expressions of love and mutuality, of building relationships and family-support systems in whatever subcultures they happen to be. Religious communities increasingly are settings in which these issues are openly discussed and addressed, particularly in congregations of the Metropolitan Community Church and in those mainline parishes and congregations that have declared themselves as open and affirming and willing to bless gay unions.

Overall, what we observe is a broadening of the family debate—toward greater attention to loving relationships of whatever kind, to absent fathers whether physically or emotionally, to continued gender inequality and the poverty of single-mother families, to parenting and the well-being of children. Economics remains high on the list of concerns, but now added is a greater sensitivity to interpersonal bonds between spouses and between parents and children, and to the resourcefulness of individuals in building bonds that are emotionally and materially sustaining. Of no small significance is the attention given to gender bonding and its own distinctive resources. The all-male Promise Keepers and its female corollaries like Women of Faith capture attention with their large rallies, but with strikingly diverging dynamics: men are urged to assume responsibilities to wives and children, and women find strength in deepened connections but also a degree of liberation, a breaking out of old bonds. Part inspiration and part therapy, such movements appeal to conservative Boomers caught in the aftermath of a feminist revolution and for whom gender roles and identities, and even abortion and homosexuality, are increasingly open to discussion.[26] Less newsworthy but by no means unimportant are the energies expressed by ordinary people in their relationships, and their efforts at resolving old conflicts or improving the quality of their lives together. People are drawn to gatherings that offer opportunities to share real-life stories, allowing them to express their deepest emotions and human connections. An example is a young African-American man we met who spoke in an all-male setting in a Los Angeles church about how his life had turned around as a result of a little homeless girl on the street who asked him, "Will you be my daddy?" An absent father of four, he tells of being so moved by this encounter with the young girl, he looked up his wife and family and began to offer at least limited child support. It led him to participate in a program on "Fathers and Sons/Sons and Fathers: Empowerment through Exploration of Relationship," which is but one example of what is happening in many congregations, and especially among men of this generation concerned about "working out" emotions often reaching far back into the past and of mending relationships with spouses and children currently. "Relationship stories" comprises an emerging, new genre of testimonial forms.

If there is a concern that increasingly stands out across faith communities, social classes, and family situations, it is the well-being of children and the responsibility of parents to them.[27] Long known for their insistence on personal choice and lifestyle alternatives, members of this generation have by the mid 1990s, however, become more vocal about building good environments for children than defending parental freedom. How are children best served by families? How can mothers and fathers become better parents? How can kin networks, friends, and religious communities assist families? When *Newsweek* magazine carries on its cover a picture of a baby with a by-line, "Do Parents Matter?"[28] clearly the debate over children and the role of parents has moved from academia to the public arena. The debate encompasses a wide sector of contemporary society, for African American, Latino, and other minorities faced with drugs and violence in inner cities and for white, middle-class suburbanites who have similar concerns for their children. To some extent, Boomers now find themselves bonded anew around the concerns of children and responsible parenting; yet they often feel they do not get much help and support from agencies and institutions—including religious institutions—outside of their own immediate families. Participation in parenting classes and the rapid growth of mentoring programs in cities both reflect this desperate need for help.

Partly as a result of social scientists, politicians, and religious leaders who have led the way in shifting the debate on the family toward greater concern for children, single parenting, and emotionally detached fathers, religious lines are now drawn differently than they were even six or eight years ago. Dogmatists, Born-again Christians, and significant numbers of people scattered across all the subcultures, religious or secular, openly speak about two parents (a mother and a father) as being better for children than one parent, and how as a society we must encourage and assist intact families. High levels of dropping out of school, teenage pregnancies, and delinquency are frequently cited as consequences of homes lacking two parents. Strong arguments on behalf of intact, husband-and-wife families for raising children are voiced not just from the pulpit, but by special-purpose groups, family institutes, and popular writers and radio psychologists like Dr. Laura Schlessinger. These voices tend to endorse as well tough parenting in response to what is judged to have been an overly permissive generation. Discipline and less worry about self-esteem are called for, as this more conservative movement would have it. At the same time, many mainstream believers, metaphysical believers and seekers, and secularists who are single parents or in nontraditional families or, as is increasingly the case, have grown children in these situations, say equally forcefully that the quality of relationships, not the family type itself, is what really counts, for both adults and children. Healthy people are those who respect themselves and others, they say, qualities best engendered in children by loving and accepting parents, not by punishment and authoritarianism. What is needed, they argue, are better social supports and services aiding single parents and a more open, tolerant atmosphere toward nontraditional families. Metaphysical believers and spiritual seekers especially are concerned about gender issues and quick to criticize the nuclear family as an ideal and often welcome a loosening of conventional morality and family structures regarded as oppressive to women. Aside from homosexuality, this debate over family type and parenting is what most divides the generation at present. Yet even the tone of the debate is changing as growing numbers are shifting away from excessive freedom and the pursuit of individual fulfillment on the part of parents toward a more balanced concern for the emotional needs and nurturance of children—a trend increasingly encouraging to the two-parent family as an ideal for raising children, but in a context of recognition and tolerance of other family arrangements.

Elites argue and pass judgments on these matters and of course are influential shaping public opinion. But at the grassroots level, conversations are driven more by everyday realities than by firm ideology. For most people the debate has far more to do with the situations their families are currently facing, with meeting their needs and aspirations, with how they can resolve tensions over ideals while at the same time finding workable solutions within their financial capabilities. People tend to judge others by their behavior but evaluate themselves largely in terms of their intentions, and by how well they find satisfactory solutions to life's crises. In effect, what we observe at the turn of the century is an expansion in "coping strategies," creative approaches to forming human relationships and of balancing conflicting demands between family and workplace. Faced with these challenges, religion becomes an important symbolic resource from which to draw on ideas, teachings, symbols, and rituals that aid in developing a model of family life and survival in a given circumstance. There is no one model, only that which makes for creative responses in different situations. Sociologist Kathleen Gerson aptly sums this up when she writes: "The complex landscape of emerging family patterns defies generalizations about either the decline or persistence of American families. Instead, men and women are developing 'multiple strategies' and contradictory directions of change to cope with the contrasting dilemmas they confront."[29]

WORK, MONEY, AND THE AMERICAN DREAM

Many within this generation feel they have been both blessed and cursed: blessed because in their lifetime they have had more opportunities for education and better-paying jobs than did their parents, but also cursed because no matter how hard they work or succeed in jobs and careers, life continues to be pretty tough. More than just the sentiment of those having suffered from corporate downsizing early in their careers or who for whatever reason have had to scale down their material expectations, this mix of feelings is expressed by solidly middle-class, upscale professionals. "I thought the world was mine when I was 22 graduating from the University of Alabama, I got a good job and made good money," Barny Stauffer, an electrical engineer living in North Carolina, tells us. "But now at 48," he continues, "I'm still doing allright but we struggle, just trying to stay above water, one month away from not making the house payment." Both he and his wife have good jobs and have recently bought a half-million-dollar home and horse barn in an upper middle-class suburb; by any economic index of income, status, or home ownership they are among America's affluent. Yet to hear him, they are stretched financially to the limits. In addition to a huge house payment, "there's swimming lessons for the kids, the two cars, the life insurance, and all the other things we seem to want, and don't forget Shari, now 15, only three years away from college. Saving for college—forget it!" While his comment registers a rather characteristic American reserve, even ambivalence, about acknowledging success, or the enjoyment of success, still it expresses something more deeply frustrating. A theme we heard voiced many times might be phrased as follows: people feel they are working hard, striving for the American Dream, yet sense they are living on its edges and are insecure in their achievements. What would resolve his unease? More income? Less work? A smaller mortgage? Greater happiness and less stress in his life? Certainly, the old cultural narrative of how hard work will lead to financial success, social stability, and a good life, both for oneself and for one's family, seems not to be working as many thought it would; it appears to have become more a source of frustration than a recipe for success and happiness. The frustration reaches into other aspects of their lives, affecting levels of satisfaction within jobs and careers, creating tensions within families, and raising levels of stress.

The sources of this dilemma extend into the American past, much prior to the Boomers, of course. Historian Loren Baritz describes the cultural definition of the "good life" involving rising expectations and the acquisition of things, a dominant force within the culture as far back as the twenties. He also observes the somewhat twisted logic on which the new world of consumption would make its case: contentment prevents happiness. Already the American Dream had become captive, through mass advertising, to what he calls "the wonderful world of dissatisfaction," the notion that discontent with one's life and possessions will motivate a desire for something better, the dream of a future that will be brighter than the present. Ever since, then, he argues, Americans have been on a course of wanting more than they presently have, of wanting the newest and the latest things, *and* of wanting—but often not finding— a resolution to their own dissatisfaction.[30] This unresolved dissatisfaction is a paradox acutely felt by Boomers, arguably more so than for any other generation of this century. Brought up on television, heirs to the postwar affluence, and strategically targeted at every stage of the life-cycle by mass advertising, their appetites were, and still are, saturated by an ethic of consumption. The Yuppies of the 1980s did not really disappear, but rather it became less fashionable to talk about material acquisition and success in the post-Reagan years. Ironically, the Clinton years have been even better years for the vast majority of Boomers caught up in the pursuit of the "good life." But now in their middle years, many once known as Yuppies and even more who were not, are feeling they are the victims of a vicious cycle—of wanting more in order to find a happiness that itself is premised on getting still more. Many complain about having to work so much and of having so little time to spend with families. They recognize the importance of leisure and quality time but say they are unable to enjoy it as they had hoped. Pressures of earning a living and paying the bills occupy their time.

Are they and other Americans really caught in a vicious cycle? Is it at all possible to break out of it? These are not the questions of sociologists but of ordinary people as they think more and more about their own health and happiness, the importance of family life, community service and volunteering, and their own deeper spiritual needs. They are asking the questions, but in reality the old cultural habits they and so many other Americans hold to are not easily thrown off. "I'm not old enough to retire yet," says Barny Stauffer, the North Carolina electrical engineer, "but something's got to give. Either we ought to make more money or spend less, have more or have less." He knows there is no quick fix, no easy resolution to the tensions and pressures that follow from the frantic pursuit of material success and getting ahead.

This dilemma, felt by so many overextended Americans, is rooted in a complex and paradoxical cultural formation. The great majority, 91 percent in fact, within this generation feel there should be less emphasis on money and material things. Money, that is, wanting more of it and more of what it buys, is understood to be at the heart of the problem. People are quick to say money will not buy happiness, yet they are not really persuaded by their own argument. Certainly, it is not that they want less money; most want more. What is problematic is not money itself but the social meaning and significance attached to it. In this respect Boomers echo a deeply embedded cultural orientation derived from an ascetic moral tradition: they know that so much attention to status and outward appearance is self-corrupting. Yet when asked if there should be less emphasis on working hard, only 22 percent agree. Those agreeing think that less work would open up more time for family and leisure, redress an imbalance they feel in their lives. For the vast majority, however, the work ethic is alive and well. Secularists, more so than any others, think there should be less emphasis on working hard, but overall the differences among the subcultures are negligible. But why such discrepancy between views on money and material things, on the one hand, and the importance of working hard, on the other? The electrical engineer we interviewed offers a clue. When asked if he had considered selling the house, buying down, maybe working less, he pauses and then says, "Well, maybe buying down, that is a possibility, I suppose, but not working less. I'm committed to my work. It's what I do, it's me." While both the question and his answer have a hypothetical ring about them, what is clear is that his work is vitally important to him. He derives from his profession an identity, a conception of self, that at this juncture in his life he could not imagine willfully abandoning. Money and work have to do with two differing realms: he would possibly consider less money along with reduced financial obligations, but not less work and hopefully not different work. Work, especially for middle-class Americans, is associated with a set of cultural meanings and responsibilities bound up with a conception of self, such as family obligations, social standing, and peer approval in the workplace, whereas money is seen as mundane and corrupt, utilitarian and neutral as far as other values go. It is the money part, of getting and spending and building up huge indebtedness, and not work itself, that is out of personal and family control, and resulting in much discontent. Behind this dichotomy lies a larger, culturally framed "decoupling of work and money," which makes it difficult to resolve contradictory views about money, and even more so to restore a meaningful moral discourse about the relations between work, money, and material possessions.[31]

Yet it is not that moral discourse is totally eclipsed, or that work values and opportunities are themselves irrelevant. For those who aspire to it but are unable to experience the "good life," other factors moderate their views on money and work. For Luis Lopez, who has only a part-time job in a welding shop in East Los Angeles and belongs to a Latino Pentecostal church, keeping food on the table for his wife and baby is the highest priority. Thirty-eight years old, he has lived in California and New Mexico for the past eleven years. Asked about the American Dream, he replies: "I don't know about that." If it is to happen for him, he must go back to school and obtain skills; right now he has no immediate plans to do so; he simply wants his family to survive. He hopes he will not have to return to Mexico. A lack of education, a decline in the number of available blue-collar jobs, the upgrading of skill levels in advanced capitalism, and competition among unskilled laborers in urban areas all work against Lopez and his chances of upward social mobility. Not unlike other unskilled "new immigrants," he faces a severe challenge in finding a job that pays enough, and on a regular basis, to support a family. His Evangelical faith offers compensation for his hardships and gives him something to keep him going, particularly on days when he wonders why opportunities in the United States are "not like I'd thought they'd be." Right now he and his family receive clothes, medical assistance, and parenting training from the church. But he knows that the future for him, as for thousands like him, is uncertain and probably not very promising.

The life situations for these two men—an affluent electrical engineer living in a gated community and a part-time Latino employee in a welding shop struggling to pay the rent—are so strikingly different, yet both are caught in traps beyond their own making. For Stauffer, the trap is that of having fallen into believing that the self, if surrounded with enough materially, would find the happiness it sought; for Lopez, the trap is that of being overwhelmed by social and economic forces, and unable to amass the material resources necessary for a sustainable life. Between these two extremes, others feel squeezed as well. The economic boom of the late 1990s has helped upper- and lower-income Americans more so than it has those in the statistical middle—the working and lower-middle classes. Wages and salaries for middle-income people, many of them with college degrees, have not kept pace with the proportionate advances either for those at the top with their stock portfolios, or with those at the bottom with higher hourly wages.[32] Computer technology has diminished the need for clerks and secretaries at a time when corporate downsizing has made middle-income people feel less secure in their jobs and more reluctant to push for raises. With this loss of a middle ground has come increased anxiety and worries on the part of substantial numbers of Americans, and not surprisingly, revised views about their work opportunities. "It's not the way it was," a former secretary in a large business firm in Massachusetts told us, "I was laid off even though the company was making money. They said they didn't need as many of us working in the office." Her story goes against the grain of the financial boom many Americans are enjoying, yet it is not that uncommon. People in her situation look upon contemporary capitalism as out of control and perceive the growing gap between top executives and others who are earning huge salaries and often living in gated communities, and those who are either living on the margins like Luis Lopez or who have steady jobs and moderate pay but find themselves overextended in credit-card debt and in a tight, month-to-month financial squeeze. A sizable number of these people are first-generation college graduates trying to buy homes and to gain a footing into the middle class, and they want to send their children to college but, unlike Barney Stauffer, they do not readily have the means to do so and seriously doubt that their financial picture will improve anytime soon.

Unease and anxiety can translate into moral outrage and a declining confidence in hard work "paying off." Even back in 1988–89, Protestant Fundamentalists and Catholic traditionalists were less likely than all other constituencies to believe that the work ethic is rewarding. They were also more likely to think that it is society's fault—not the individual's—if a person is unsuccessful in life. When we spoke to them again in the mid-to-late 1990s, their views had hardened even more. People who voted Democratic in the past were now voting Republican, some claiming that Perot, or some other third-party candidate, was the only hope. "Top dogs will do whatever they have to do—rob, steal, stick it to other people—to hold on to their own money," a traditional-minded Catholic man in Ohio told us. A Fundamentalist in North Carolina put it as follows: "You try to get ahead but things are stacked against you." The feeling on the part of many conservative religious believers, especially from the middle-income category, was summed up in two moral axioms: one, opportunities for the individual to get ahead are not what they used to be, and, two, everybody's out to get what they can. Religiously, this translates into a defensiveness about one's own hard work and moral standards, and to a personal narrative of a burdened and struggling self in a secular wilderness. In its most strident expression, by white Euro-American males, there is some lashing out at women, minorities, and new immigrants, perceived to be the ones now getting all the breaks in the economic system.

The dilemma faced by the dogmatists is contrasted, interestingly, with that of the metaphysical believers and spiritual seekers, those the least likely to blame others, or society as a whole, when things go wrong for the individual. That these latter would challenge the cause of individual initiative is all the more striking considering that they are not generally bourgeois in orientation. Yet because they are so fiercely independent, and see themselves as having to assert control and direction over their inner lives, they assume a responsibility for what happens to them in the economic realm. The contrast between dogmatists and metaphysical believers and seekers is doubly interesting. We might have expected that the work ethic as linked to the moral asceticism about which Max Weber wrote so eloquently would apply to dogmatists, a group ideologically in rebellion against handouts and government-based welfare, yet they seem to have lost confidence in that ethic even as they affirm the moral duties of the individual to honor God, family, neighbor, and the faith community. And alternatively, metaphysical believers and seekers who have broken with so much of conventional morality and religious practice now emerge as the proponents of an individualism combining a vision of economic opportunities and work with an expressive moralism honoring, above all, the human spirit and the pursuit of goodness and higher truths. Here as elsewhere we observe a realigning of old religious and moral cultures.

To a considerable degree, the contrast between the two subcultures reflects the residues of an older, no longer highly coherent work ethic clashing with the need for a more deliberate, better-articulated strategy of action. An older work ethic is associated with a lingering, post-1960s discourse about "returning to stricter moral standards." Seventy percent of our respondents, in fact, so indicated that wish in the late 1980s, and there was no evidence of any massive change in outlook in our later survey and interviews. But that sentiment is counterbalanced by an equally strong trend within Boomer culture, even among conservative Protestants and traditional Catholics, honoring individual choice and the role of conscience in moral decision-making. Moral asceticism is deeply ingrained within the culture, yet when faced with a threat to individual autonomy the latter prevails. Commenting on this outcome, anthropologist Michael F. Brown is probably correct that a changing culture "signals a hope that religion will somehow foster a sense of personal ethics without restricting individual freedoms."[33] A highly privatized conception of religion encourages personal ethics in keeping with such freedoms, and ascetic moral discourse comes across as rather quaint, if not moralistic, to many Boomers. With regard to metaphysical believers and spiritual seekers, it is too soon to determine how successful they will be in establishing a work ethic encompassing morally expressive values. There is talk of a return to the land, of the importance of simplicity, of integrating leisure and work, of cooperation replacing competition, and of concern generally for the well-being of the whole world—but more talk really than practical implementation of a new ethic on any extended basis. Moreover, such worthy goals hardly characterize many affluent metaphysical believers and seekers who are unlikely to compromise their middle-class standing and who look for, more than anything else, spiritual well-being within the existing, or in an only slightly modified, economic system. Alternative ethical systems integrating work and life are still being formulated and actively promulgated by new spiritual entrepreneurs, but they are yet to be successfully institutionalized to any great degree. Here and there, are signs of a changing consciousness, but hardly of a magnitude to bring about a genuinely new course of moral action of any major consequence within the realm of work and economics.

The Environment

In contrast, perhaps the most success in shaping consciousness and courses of action relates to environmentalism. Since the first Earth Day proclaimed in 1970, concern about the ecological crisis has mounted to the point that today there are numerous, broadly based movements, some focusing on limited goals such as recycling and protection of wildlife reserves, others devoted to "deep ecology," or an all-encompassing shift in ways of seeing and valuing nature. With varied constituencies and ideologies, the movements attract Americans holding a range of religious and secular views. It should not be overlooked, however, that in the early days it was the spiritual seekers, many later known as New Agers, and secularists who played so crucial a part in galvanizing public opinion. The Vietnam War, long gas lines, and the Three Mile Island nuclear incident in the 1970s aroused considerable concern at the time. Among younger Boomers, the Vietnam War and long lines waiting at gasoline service stations were mentioned as the events that most influenced them when growing up; and 62 percent of metaphysical believers and seekers and 52 percent of secularists, far more than among any of the other religious constituencies, indicated that the potential nuclear disaster at Three Mile Island was what had most shaken them. Not unexpectedly, many of these people would become strong and vocal advocates for the environment. "I remember being at the Earth Day celebration when I was at Cal. State," Mary Coleman, a secularist in California, told us, "and then Three Mile Island happened, and I felt I just had to get involved. A bunch of us got together and held a rally down at Laguna Beach." A year or two later, she points out, "some of us who had gotten together at Laguna were demonstrating out in front of the nuclear power plant at Diablo Canyon."

The moral vision of healing a wounded environment and of restoring connection between humans, other life-forms, and the earth itself is powerful. For a generation in its early years that felt so alienated socially, the New Age language of transformation and of linking individuals in a common cause to save the planet filled a void. It still offers a vision, a "felt whole" experience of sorts, and inspires recycling and other behaviors in keeping with environmental consciousness. The language is born out of a metaphysical thread in American thinking since the nineteenth century, a "theory of correspondence" between the individual and the universe, and between the microcosm of society and the macrocosm of the universe.[34] Practically speaking, the language gives expression to an experience of interconnectedness and to the emergence of what has come to be called the "ecological self," which, as one commentator observes, "launches one on a process of self-realization, where the self-to-be-realized extends further and further beyond the separate ego and includes more and more of the phenomenal world."[35] A self-in-relationship is one deeply enmeshed within a larger narrative of creation and life-purpose, and thereby empowered to act on behalf of other life-forms, or of the larger whole of life itself. Human beings become, as eco-theologian Thomas Berry describes, "the self-reflexive function of the universe."[36] Or as Ruth McCarthy, a Catholic activist with a passion for the environment and influenced by Matthew Fox's creation spirituality, confessed, "When I think about how we are all related to one another, people, animals, plants, the stars, everything, I feel that power, that force—synergy, isn't that what they call it?"

Organized religion was slow at first to respond to the environmental crisis. In the aftermath of the 1960s, when so many social causes were before the churches, synagogues, and temples, ecological concerns were more peripheral than central in most institutional religious headquarters. But with the mounting voices of the secular environmentalists during the 1970s, and confronted with charges that religion was itself a major reason for the ecological crisis, the established Protestant, Catholic, and Jewish communities were pulled into the debate.[37] Over the next two decades virtually all religious communities became involved with discussion at local and national levels about environmental issues and how to respond to what was perceived as not just a national but a global crisis. By the 1990s, the topic was on the agenda for policy discussion and action by laypeople in many congregations. People like Sara Caughman, former religious dropouts who had now returned to more active involvement in these congregations, were in no small part responsible for raising consciousness about it. Because many of the returnees in their earlier, more rebellious years had concerns and causes similar to secular environmentalists, both deeply influenced by oil spills, nuclear disasters, and the pollution and destruction of corporate capitalism, they bring strong moral passions and sensitivities to these issues and thus have forced upon religious communities, particularly the more liberal, progressive ones, an ongoing theological and ethical discussion. In response, Jewish congregations reinterpret the Hebrew scriptures with holistic, creation-centered meanings of the words in mind, and Christians do the same with the teachings of Christ, medieval saints and prominent religious figures. But more than this, there is awareness of the need to change habits of thought and action, to adopt "green values" and to commit oneself to an ethic of environmental responsibility. Boomers, more so than other Americans, have insisted that environmental protection laws have not gone far enough, and that protecting the environment is so important that requirements and standards cannot be set too high. They are concerned about safety from pollution and nuclear disaster, born out of a fear of nuclear war and international conflict; safety and peace as concerns never really go away for a generation for whom the memories of Vietnam continue to be vivid.

Surveys show that Americans across all faith communities express considerable concern about the environment.[38] Among Boomers, we find no major difference in level of concern among Born-again Christians, mainstream believers, dogmatists, metaphysical believers and seekers, and secularists. Roughly 90 percent in every constituency favor more government spending on environmental issues. There are differences in theology and proposed courses of action. Secularists and metaphysical believers and seekers are much more likely to endorse values such as nonviolence, simplicity, and applied mindfulness, and to affirm the sacredness, interconnectedness, and life of nature as a general spiritual principle, if not more specifically by means of the Gaia hypothesis. Eastern spiritual teachings especially figure in the crafting of these views. Nothing short of a complete shift in ecological sensibilities, in thinking and action, will suffice for those radically committed to this vision. In contrast, majorities within all the major religious constituencies hold to a view that humans are a special creation who have stewardship responsibilities. Here there is considerable debate: what is meant by stewardship? Aroused as well are related disputes over imageries of God, creation, and community. Dogmatists among them emphasize a stern God who puts humans in dominion over nature and can cite chapter and verse in Genesis as proof. Many Born-again Christians share these views, although leading Evangelical periodicals, like *Christianity Today*, have moved toward redefining stewardship, stressing dominion less as human supremacy over the rest of nature, and more as duty and caring.[39]

Religious language in this instance is undergoing a process of re-spiritualization. There is considerable variation in the views of Protestant Evangelicals and Catholic Charismatics reflecting what amounts to a growing spectrum of theological positions voiced by religious leaders within these communities. Mainstream believers hold to an even wider range and mix of theological views: to all versions of the meaning of stewardship, to traditional notions of God as well as panentheistic conceptions of the earth as the body of God, to popular eco-theologies and spiritualities combining feminist themes, to views bordering on a mystical conception of a humanity united with nature as an ecological community replacing the traditional religious community. Unquestionably, the greatest ideological schism is over the matter of dominion between secularists and metaphysical believers and spiritual seekers, on the one side, who see this historic theology as legitimizing environmental destruction; and, dogmatists, on the other side, who believe strongly on biblical grounds that human beings are entrusted by God to be in charge of the world. While there are discernible differences in outlook and action between Born-again Christians and mainstream believers, the former more traditional-minded in their views of God and far less vocal on environmentalism, they appear to agree more than disagree. Commenting on recent Protestant trends, political scientist Robert Booth Fowler observes, "Much of the evangelical (but not fundamentalist) Protestant considerations on ecology these days are closer than one might predict to those of mainline and liberal Protestantism. . . . Many fewer within the evangelical world have as yet taken up cudgels for environmentalism, but those who have often sound the same themes as theological liberals."[40]

THE PUBLIC ROLE OF RELIGION

At a time when the religious boundaries are being redrawn, we would expect tensions and conflicts to easily surface. The "culture war" thesis is certainly correct in the sense that dogmatists, and especially Protestant Fundamentalists, continue to clamor for power and control over, as one leading conservative spokesman puts it, "available truth claims, explanatory systems, myths, stories, memories, loyalties, dreams and nightmares by which society lives."[41] Yet, as we have seen, the tensions are not polarized along a single continuum, nor are they necessarily of a level of intensity that would call for a war metaphor; rather, what we observe are differing patterns among the religious constituencies, depending on the moral issues involved, and varying levels of concern. People feel the same way about the public role of religion. Conventional wisdom would have it that the country is in deep conflict over religious ideology, with theological conservatives wanting churches to battle against abortion and homosexuality and opt for prayer in schools while theological liberals oppose such measures in defense of personal freedom and choice. Conservative ideology prescribes assistance to private individuals, such as soup lines for the hungry and prison ministry, whereas liberal, "Social Gospel" ideology is directed toward bringing about structural changes in society, such as welfare reform and greater social justice to the poor, to minorities, and to women. Private versus public dimensions of faith and commitment are to some extent still theologically structured in this way. But for many Boomers, this sharp ideological contrast more fitting to the earlier Fundamentalist-modernist conflicts of this century fails to ring true in their lives in the late twentieth century.

For one thing, the public-private distinction is arbitrary and calls forth differing responses depending on the issues involved. Already we have noted the strong feelings many Boomers have about preserving privacy. Yet religiously speaking, a holistic impulse leads in the direction of de-privatizing, of restoring some unity of the personal and public aspects of life. "Is abortion private or public, or both?" asks a liberal Methodist in Massachusetts. Issues like abortion and gay and lesbian rights, once thought of as private concerns, have become highly politicized, and thus redefined as public issues. "Faith doesn't make so clear-cut a decision between what I do privately and what I do as a citizen or member of society," comments a thoughtful Catholic, also in Massachusetts. Older boundaries between public and private, moral and religious, even religious and secular are being redrawn in an age of grassroots negotiation and discursive legitimation.[42] Luis Lopez's church is a good example of a religious community now engaged in political mobilizing in the local community. His is one of a growing number of churches, mosques, and temples in urban settings providing community-based social services in the post–welfare state. Community organizing involves establishing food banks, immigration and health services, information networks about employment, and active petitioning of the city for better police protection, job opportunities, youth programs, and the like. A powerful force behind such efforts is a theology based on praxis, or reflexive action. Liberationist theology is clearly making an impression on Lopez: "Jesus cared not just about people's souls," he says, "but about how they get along, if they have food and work and if babies can get help when they get sick." To the extent such religious movements can bring about social and economic change, there is some chance of generating a more hopeful vision among the urban poor for economic success, for greater family stability, and meaningful civic participation in the society. That hope hangs in the balance for great numbers of poor, unskilled Boomer Americans.

More broadly, there is a growing tendency for many religious communities to conjoin social/political *and* spiritual transformation. "Life politics," described in Chapter 3, is about human hopes and aspirations, about experiences of community, about moral and spiritual issues that reach deeply and broadly. Such politics involves the redrawing of boundaries between the public and the private, or better put, a blurring of those boundaries in an existential sense. "I can't box my feelings up, as if these belong to my life at work, and these I leave at home," an African American community organizer in Boston told us. "The old welfare program is no more," a social activist minister in a Los Angeles suburb emphasized. "We have to create new partnerships between religious groups, the city and the state, and with private foundations. Our bodies and souls are wrapped up in it." The most visible result for a wide range of religious communities is the emergence of a more holistic language, combining spiritual, political, economic, and self-development concerns, which is having a depolarizing effect ideologically. On both sides of the theological divine, we see developments pulling them closer together: an older theologically liberal language is being modified through recognition of the importance of personal faith and commitment, and theologically conservative language is incorporating a greater appreciation for addressing local community and civic concerns. On the basis of extensive fieldwork in Los Angeles, a team of researchers including this author conclude: "Left and right have converged toward the creation of political ministries that merge the search for practical political and economic solutions to urban tensions with the search for city-wide, racial, ethnic, and individual spiritual/moral transformation. . . . Spiritual renewal, community organizing, personal hygiene, and entrepreneurial skills are of a piece."[43]

This is not to minimize religious tensions and theological divisions that obviously exist across the United States and on occasion flare into serious confrontations. Dogmatists making absolutist religious claims are quick to draw lines, and some Born-again Christians are unyielding on certain moral views. Yet these latter often cannot agree on doctrines, and the "New Voluntarism"—described earlier as an individualistic stance toward religion increasingly embracing cultural-based notions of tolerance and pluralism—is making a far deeper imprint upon them than even they generally recognize. Inevitably, a tension is set up for Born-again Christians: how to reconcile faith in God and a religious order that should be all-encompassing and embrace the world, and yet accept tolerance and pluralism as desirable realities. It is largely a war "within," and particularly so for middle-class Boomers deeply wedded to achievement values—no matter what the religious subculture, whether Evangelicals, Charismatics, metaphysical believers, seekers, or mainstream believers.[44] And in this war "within" the individual's own conscience, increasingly voluntary and relativistic norms are winning out, except for theological conservatives and traditionalists who hold firm and wish we could turn the clock back to a simpler time. This inward war need not imply a weakening of religious conviction, only that such conviction is based more on personal conscience and an awareness, perhaps, that the moral and ethical issues of our time cannot be solved simply by religious maxims or ethical postulates. Theologies and spiritual teachings recognizing the severe challenges before us, resonating to the human struggles of addressing those challenges and of working life out in the face of its messiness, offer a decided advantage to serious-minded members of the spiritual vanguard of all the religious subcultures, except at the ideological extremes.

This drift toward a new centrism may yet blur other divisions, or conversely, lead to greater clarification of the boundaries that divide. So fundamental a contrast as that between traditional theism and the "new spirituality" shows signs of blurring. Considerable differences in beliefs exist between those who stress faith in a transcendent God, whether of a monarchical or nonmonarchical conception, and those who stress the inner self as sacred, either in a monotheistic or polytheistic sense. Obviously more than just opposing views, contrasting ontologies and epistemologies are at stake. And for sure, voices can be heated. Fundamentalist and Evangelical Protestant writers complain about "those other gods—the humanistic and occultic influences—that have made inroads into our homes, schools, businesses, and even our churches."[45] They readily acknowledge an "invasion" of alien spiritual themes, and particularly from the East. "No one is laughing at the new Eastern way of looking at things anymore,"[46] one Fundamentalist author writes, which in itself bespeaks a growing fear and recognition among religious conservatives that their members are being drawn into new and more holistic forms of thinking and believing. They emphasize how New Age and humanistic spiritualities have "seduced" ministers, teachers, doctors, television producers, and even taken up residence at the White House.

Based on the level of fear and worry expressed by these religious leaders, it seems for the people themselves, the new spiritualities have indeed invaded.

The reference above to the White House refers to the widely covered media event in June 1996, when it was reported that First Lady Hillary Rodham Clinton was consulting with self-described "sacred psychologist" Jean Houston and was engaged in imaginary conversations with Eleanor Roosevelt. Some commentators quickly accused her of engaging in cultlike behavior, others simply described her activity as tending toward the strange and bizarre. Talk about God and country was one thing, indeed, the expected thing for a first lady, but visualization techniques and guided meditations involving conversations with deceased people were something else. It was quite natural for presidents and their families to seek advice from clergy and religious leaders on matters public and private, but she had transgressed the limits—turning to alternative spiritualities.

Of interest were public reactions to the news reports. Conservative Christians took shots at New Agers, and the latter—whatever name they prefer—fired back. But except at the extremes, interestingly, reactions were fairly mild, more so than we might have expected, and apparently more so that media executives expected. News reporters expressed surprise that the story turned out not to be a story. Polls taken in the week following the news reports found actually very few Americans who thought her behavior was all that strange or who felt that it had lowered their opinion of the first lady.[47] Some people rushed to her defense arguing that what she was doing was "legitimate" human potential exploration. Far from being a cultlike or guru-activity, it was hailed as a type of creativity-enhancing exercise no different from that practiced in businesses and corporations.[48] Others hailed the first lady as a serious Christian, deeply committed to the values and teachings of her Methodist background, and claimed that the process and practice of "soulmaking" (Jean Houston's term) using contemporary techniques was not antithetical to belief in Jesus Christ and other Christian doctrines. Mixing of the two was no big issue. Moreover, it was pointed out that prayer as practiced by Christians historically was often approached as a form of conversation and that monastic orders like the Jesuits had long had their "Spiritual Exercises," a means of cultivating spiritual awareness by imagining one's own involvement in the Gospel story. Religion, it was argued, changes with the times; indeed, some change was essential if it was to be of continuing relevance in people's lives. While contemporary New Age teachings and practices can and on occasion do provoke sharp reactions, the paradox, as *New York Times* journalist Peter Steinfels points out, is that large numbers of Americans, including many conventionally religious people, "snap up its books, rely on its alternative medicines and pay coaches and consultants to teach its techniques for reducing stress and focusing attention."[49]

This episode, so illustrative of Boomer sensitivities, prompts two observations, both important for our understanding of the remaking of religion at present. One is how very quickly this media-created event became old news, not of much interest except to a few Neotraditionalists with loud and persisting voices. Perhaps because Americans are now accustomed to almost anything of a religious kind happening or because the media makes so much hype out of such happenings—or both—the public becomes quickly saturated. What on the surface would appear to be an event that would grab people turns into a non-event almost overnight. Media scholars speak of "communicative moments," and of the capacity of a story to "hold" such moments for extended discussion by means of narrative elaboration and through use of religious formulas and symbols.[50] From this standpoint, the communicative moment in the Hillary Rodham Clinton story did not happen. It is instructive to reflect upon why it did not happen. It might reasonably be argued that the media presumed the existence and power of an older religious narrative in the United States, one that would provide a basis for surprise and negative response to the first lady's actions. The fact that the story was received and interpreted very differently than expected suggests that the media misjudged the hold of that older narrative and failed to recognize the changing religious and spiritual mood of the country. A revealing episode in itself, this tells us a great deal about both media construction of religion and the extent to which "lived" religion can be at odds with presumed public religious norms.

A second observation, building on the first, is how amazingly tolerant and open-minded Americans of the Boomer generation can be regarding religious and spiritual practices. Fortunately we were interviewing some people soon after the news broke about Hillary Rodham Clinton, and the responses we received were almost all supportive of her. A man in Ohio with no religious affiliation said, "Religion's a personal matter—it's up to her what she does. Why should anybody care?" An Evangelical woman in North Carolina summed up the situation as "a bit weird I must admit, but if that's what she wants and it helps her, that's what counts." Still another North Carolinian, a mountain man, simply noted, "Well,

I've seen things more than that up here where I live." Norms of tolerance and open-mindedness are deeply rooted in American culture, and now more than ever are extended to religious matters. The sacred has come to be pretty much what people define it to be, or at least Boomer Americans are loath to question what others regard as sacred. A recent study of the American middle class speaks of a "capacious individualism"[51] with regard to religion—the notion that when people talk about faith or spiritual conviction, they have in mind not just their own, but that of others. If respect applies to one person's commitment, it must apply to all. Religious individualism as Americans understand it, according to this study, is a "compromise position between immoral selfishness and coercive conformity." As a normative framework, it describes not just the situation of the middle class, but of Boomers more generally. Rigidly minded and highly marginalized Fundamentalists and traditionalists do not take easily to compromise in such matters, yet even some of them, too, struggle with a culturally defined individualism that is in tension with moral and religious absolutism. Conservatives pick and choose when to invoke absolute principles. But clearly, the drift generally is toward a *moral* stance toward religion acknowledging that an individual's choice—to be religious or not, and if religious, in what ways—must be honored in a democratic society, where all options are to be kept open and people do not face undue pressures of coercion. It is an ethos that builds on a historic American freedom of religion, but in its popular style and practice represents a level of normative acceptance that is greater now than in the not-so-distant past.

PATCHWORK QUILT

It has been said that a patchwork quilt, more so than a mosaic, describes the American Evangelical subculture. The latter's beauty lies, as historian Randall Balmer points out, "in its variegated texture and even, sometimes, in the absence of an overall pattern."[52] That metaphor can appropriately be extended to the religio-moral cultures of middle-aged Baby Boomers. I would modify the metaphor to think of it as a quilt still in the making—more like the AIDS blankets members of this generation created with many hands over a long period of time. Culturally speaking, those hands are still very much at work as they seek to work out satisfactory solutions to the pressing concerns of gender and family life, of sexual orientation, of work and material values, of the environment.

Obviously there are other issues members of this generation are deeply concerned about, such as schools, guns, and safety on the streets, not reviewed here. The practicality evident in their ordinary religious lives extends to their moral positions, not in some unprincipled manner but in the sense that pragmatism, common sense, and creative response play a big part in meeting whatever challenges come their way. In their mid-life we glimpse a generation that is very much down to earth, dealing with everyday life and its promises and dilemmas, yet one that hardly lost its moral idealism and visionary fervor.

As the metaphor of a patchwork quilt suggests, Boomers respect individualism to the point that their moral visions and values do not conform to any simple or even very consistent pattern. What we most certainly do not find is a generation broadly caught up in a highly polarized cultural war as perpetrated by the media and ideologues. There are some wars—skirmishes really—over one or another issue, but the constituencies do not fall out always in predictable ways. Neither is there attitudinal consistency across issues nor as much polarization as some commentators seem to think. At both ends of the moral and political ideological spectrum, our two subcultures—the dogmatists and the secularists—hold views that are rather predictable. As we saw in Chapter 6, these two enclaves are to a considerable degree structurally separated in the contemporary United States; their contrasting social worlds are maintained by distinct organizational affiliations and friendship patterns. Continuing skirmishes between the two are certainly to be expected considering the depth of moral and religious differences that separate them, yet at present there is not the level of heated and vicious exchange in the public arena that existed in the early-to-mid 1990s. Whether the Clinton impeachment of 1998 will regalvanize the radical religious right politically, and if so to what extent and in what directions in the years ahead, is unknown at the time of this writing.

But in the long run, the centripetal forces of American society are likely to produce a moderating influence. The evidence is rather substantial that Born-again Evangelicals, Charismatics, and Pentecostals, as compared to Fundamentalists and traditionalists, are moving, gradually but discernibly, in a more centrist direction. On moral issues their positions are diverging from those of die-hard fundamentalists, traditionalists, and dogmatists of other stripes, whose politics are conservative to reactionary. This progressive schism within both the conservative Protestant and Catholic communities is not inconsequential: for Protestants, it means continuing institutional schism, but more than this, ever more

291

distinct and separate religious identities; for American Catholics, it means continuing and unresolved tension within its institutional structure. If, as our analysis suggests, mainstream believers are increasingly being joined by Born-again Christians in moral visions and values, that means a substantial religious middle may now be in the making. However splintered its institutional expression, at the level of popular faith and outlook this religious middle is potentially a powerful cultural force. But two further points ought to be underscored. One is that Born-again Christians, propelled as they are toward the center, still have theological (and in the case of Catholics, institutional) ties with their more conservative counterparts. This means that they are positioned somewhat flexibly, and depending on the moral issue involved, they are likely to posture themselves variously, joining with either conservative or more liberal-minded religious constituencies. In religion, as in politics, much depends on the unity and stability of this religious middle and how well it holds in the future. A second and related point is that this middle expands and contracts, which means that potentially mainstream believers, metaphysical believers, and seekers may be drawn closer together as well. Certainly on an issue like the environment, this coming together seems likely. As always, the nation's religious middle is a precarious cultural reality, always in a state of re-formation, and therefore constantly changing its colors—again, at any given time somewhat like a patchwork quilt, with some pieces stitched in bold colors separating them from others, and still other pieces woven in faded colors that blend together.

Not to be overlooked in this shaping of the moral climate is the spiritual factor itself. Moral and ethical challenges are now arousing deep spiritual concerns on the part of this generation. As we have seen, this dimension surfaces in the midst of the most mundane of human experiences—in work, in gender-based bondings, in love as mutuality and equal regard, in reassessing material values and aspirations, in coming to terms with the environment. Spiritual awareness is bound by no set script or prescription of where it should occur; it happens where and when it happens, in religious contexts but also outside those contexts, for some people but not for others—all of which makes for a more democratized, highly accessible conception of the sacred. Even among those who do not speak of the spiritual or the sacred, there is respect for those who do—itself a sign of a generation bonded around some sense of the ineffable. But a spiritual presence also forces questions about its depth and long-term significance. To pose the question again that was raised at the beginning of the chapter: Is the spirituality of this generation sufficiently grounded and robust enough to be transformative? Can it make a lasting impact on the course the country takes in the new century? If so, what and how? Having dealt with these questions only in passing, avoiding what inevitably we must deal with, we turn to a concluding assessment and interpretation of the terrain we have described.

"Whirl Is King, Having Driven Out Zeus"

A QUOTE FROM Aristophanes, cited by Walter Lippmann in his *Preface to Morals* in 1929,[1] captures the central motif running throughout this book. The United States at the turn of the century is a fragmented society in its normative underpinnings, as reflected in its meaning systems, values, goals, purposes, and moral orders. My objective throughout this book has been to advance a perspective on the post–World War II generation—the "lead generation" as we move into the twenty-first century—as being at the center of the cultural and religious changes now whirling around us. Generations are carriers of distinctive values and sensibilities; and Boomer Americans, by virtue of their numbers and location in midlife, are in a position to influence the moral and religious mood of the country for some time to come. That Lippmann used this metaphor seventy years ago referring to the "acids of modernity" reminds us that the changes of which we write are hardly new. Our more recent period is distinctive only in its magnitude and rapid pace of social change. Globalization, the changing dynamics of immigration, increased pluralism, the increased influence of the media, the social and institutional dislocations of the 1960s, the decline of older religious hegemonies, and an evolving psychological culture have all helped to accentuate conditions he and others have addressed. A more complex, heterogenous world makes for an environment in which human loyalties and commitments often pull at one another simultaneously, and where the psychological integrations of work, family, citizenship, beliefs, and values pose formidable challenges. Moral and religious coherence remains more an ideal than a practical reality. Americans often cannot articulate very well such descrepancies but they feel them.

For this reason, any mapping exercise to help us grasp the broad parameters of religious change poses a challenge. What I have sought to accomplish in identifying the five subcultures—dogmatists, Born-again believers, mainstream believers, metaphysical believers and seekers, and secularists—is to locate the enclaves that are themselves differentially shaped by the moral and religious fragmentation of our time and to chart their distinctive moral and spiritual responses. In this process, I have sought to offer an interpretation of this pivotal generation recognizing its own religious and spiritual styles, but without succumbing to easy, commonplace assumptions about its being "less religious" or "more secular" than earlier generations. Research on generational change in religion and culture is inhibited by stereotypes and often tainted by presumptions of increasing secularization and religious decline. The latter run like a master narrative throughout much of the academic study of religion and are widely shared by cultural elites. To be sure, I have no illusion of having broken through that paradigmatic dilemma, but attention to ordinary "lived religion" does help to shed old, fixed categories that oversimplify, and to refocus attention on the thick descriptions of religious realities. It is also to be hoped that such attention can orient us to a more dynamic, evolving religious world and its social environment or, as one scholar proposes, open our eyes to "the unfolding interplay of religious idiom and immediate circumstance that constantly reconfigures both."[2] Hence I have focused less on the institutional analysis usually done in the sociological study of religion, and more on the actual religious and spiritual narratives of individuals encountering modernity. The intent has been to let people speak as much as possible for themselves, and to look on their practices as strategies of religious action, strategies themselves open-ended and in search of greater fullness and drawing off a rich array of beliefs, symbols, imageries, techniques, and popular discourses. This perspective on religion in no way diminishes the significance of religious institutions or distracts attention from particular meaning systems they embody; indeed, to the contrary, this approach affirms the rootedness and deep sensitivity of all such institutions to their wider cultural contexts.

In this Conclusion I attempt to bring together themes that run through the previous chapters and to address some unresolved issues pertaining to the spiritual dimension of contemporary life. Unfortunately, spirituality remains more of a buzzword than a topic attracting serious analysis, among both students of religion and religious leaders; and the notion of a spiritual quest culture now permeating the United States attracts little attention as yet. Social scientists are more comfortable in restricting their analysis to traditional religious institutions as if they were intact entities, cut off from their environments. Religious leaders are inclined to dismiss talk about spiritual quest as New Age psychobabble, and typically do so without seriously coming to terms with all that it might imply. My own view is obviously very different, not because

I am deaf to much that I, too, recognize as babble, but because I judge that which lies behind it—the "anxious stuttering," to cite MacIntyre's phrase again—to signal something profoundly important about our times. Nor do I accept the view of many scholars that religion will simply move into the future attending to its business as usual, without having to address the changing cultural contexts we have tried to identify. Rather, the social and cultural dislocations underlying the anxious stuttering seem too far-reaching and much too serious to overlook. The twin notions of quest and reflexivity provide a framework for developing what is, I think, a useful and insightful perspective on current trends: quest, because it alerts us to a perennial human condition, but which can take many forms and may be more pronounced in some times than in others; and reflexivity, because it is so crucial a feature of the advanced modern world in which we now live. Combined, the two notions yield insights into the spiritual ferment of our time and into changing patterns of religion and culture which otherwise might easily go unnoticed.

CREATIVITY WITHIN RELIGION

One advantage of this perspective is that it sensitizes us to the resilience and creativity of the human spirit. The latter may be so obvious as to go without saying, yet something so basic often gets lost in religious interpretations privileging its conserving and legitimating functions within society. Too exclusive a focus on religion as institution, in fact, can lead to this oversight. Most certainly, religion conserves and legitimates, and these are indispensable social and psychological functions, but by its very nature more is involved than this singular abstraction would imply: religion is also process, movement, aspiration, quest. These liminal qualities point to its effusive and creative potential, its recurrent capacity to combine elements into new forms, its bumptiousness, or ability to reinvent itself on occasion. To overlook religion's transforming force, in both personal and social life, is to lose sight of a fundamental feature of human quest, the hope that lies in an indeterminate and unrealized future. Openness to that future is enshrined in all the great religious traditions as virtues and what ultimately sustains human life: to wait, to meditate, to pray, to expect, to dream, to seek. And in a time of chaotic social change and institutional dislocations—when "Whirl is King"—

such aspirations are likely to surface. Where and in what contexts they will surface, or what personal and institutional consequences they will have, we cannot always predict, but our lack of powers of discernment is not to be confused with the reality and potential impact of human yearnings in the face of chaos and uncertainty.

As elaborated in previous chapters, my argument rests on the role of narrative and its embodiment in ritual and practice. Religion in its most basic sense is a story involving symbol, metaphor, and language, all having the power to persuade and to fan the imagination. Symbol, metaphor, and language are in fact the means by which human beings come to self-awareness and articulate a sense of self in relation to others. That is, the very notion of the self implies reflexivity, or the capacity of a being to be an object to itself. By their very nature, too, symbol, metaphor, and language are creative resources undergirding not just cognition, but emotions and bodily experience. Whatever else it might suggest, the spiritual implies the transforming presence of the sacred, a presence made real, indeed created, through the persuasive power of narrative and symbol. And that which is created—the presence of the sacred—is something that enlivens and quickens, something felt within the body. Through repeated practice and ritual performance, religious emotions are "triggered," as William James would say; and when or wherever that happens, the body is the locus of the experience. That we are rediscovering "the body as the existential ground of the sacred" in our time may be an "artifact of history," as it has been argued,[3] but it is a rediscovery crucially important to religious analysis. At the turn of the century, and for the Boomer population especially, the body is a major venue to a dimension of experience that has come to be identified by many as deeply spiritual. That which is intimate, that which is spontaneous, that which empowers, that which is imagined, all potentially have a felt and, by inference, a sacred presence. And if not felt, the force of religion becomes greatly diminished.

By no means does this imply a purely personal, or simply a bodily-based, conception of the sacred. Creativity arises out of social practice and ritual performance; the liminal is hardly contained by an individual. For many Americans experience of the sacred happens through regular and committed involvement in religious organizations. In religious community, in the shared context of worship, ritual, and affirmation of faith, the spiritual is kept alive. It is sustained through familiar religious language and symbol. Yet for others, as we have seen, spiritual quest can lead to the evolution of new structures: to small groups, to extended networks, to informal gatherings and celebrations, to renewed activities within families and businesses, to direct marketing agencies that offer spiritual services in exchange for fees, to reliance on the media and emerging forms of electronic communication. Many religious leaders, commentators, and church-oriented researchers will of course be quick to argue that such forms are not on a par with the traditional congregation and that, all things considered, religious community is on the decline. And in a strict sense, they may be correct. Religious community as traditionally conceived is perhaps in some degree of jeopardy. Stable forms of face-to-face religious belonging and closely knit community may be declining with the Boomer generation. The survey evidence hints of this, although it is equally clear that people can, and still do, create community—including religious community—in various forms, old and new, and in ways often not immediately apparent; what we lack is a broadened conception of community appropriate to our times.

Yet clearly the local congregation, or religious assembly, remains the most common religious form in the United States. It is the vehicle through which most of what is identified as religious is nurtured and the means through which most voluntary religious activity and service is channeled. It is the key structure around which stable religious life is sustained and passed from one generation to the next. De facto congregationalism is alive and well, considering that as an institutional form it increasingly cuts across traditions, including non-Christian traditions; there is a convergence, as sociologist R. Stephen Warner argues, "more or less on the model of the reformed Protestant tradition of the congregation as a voluntary gathered community."[4] For the majority of Boomers, the congregation remains the dominant religious form whether for the large Euro-American constituency or for the growing Muslim, Latino, Asian, and Buddhist populations. Given continuing inmigration of new populations and given American propensities, the congregation will likely remain the dominant religious structure for the foreseeable future.

But we cannot overlook other kinds of spiritual networks and metaphysical enclaves, often hidden from social view, yet whose influence is not to be disputed. Most Americans live in "temples," it is said, but some people live in "tents"—the latter referring to more loosely knit associations less bound to a stable, geographic location and, to extend the metaphor, easier to repitch in the sense that they do not involve as much bureaucracy or theological orthodoxy constraining them. Because they are less permanently structured, and often less visible, we should not assume such gatherings and networks are inconsequential. Ours is an age of loose ties to organizations of many kinds, a trait hardly peculiar to religion. Also, we should not be blind to changing congregational forms themselves. The meaning of religious community has itself undergone major transitions over the course of American history—moving generally away from a singular, homogeneous community toward more diversity, becoming essentially a "group of groups," its members active often only in a select number of groups or activities.[5] That proliferation of groups in response to new niches and spaces for religious sociability and conversation continues to expand, encouraging institutional innovation and higher levels of reflexive monitoring within religious organizations. Media and communication technology, combined with skilled entrepreneurs ever ready to seize new opportunities, virtually assures this proliferation will continue. From the perspective of the traditional congregation, this entails risks and developments that may not be very attractive. Already among some Born-again Christians, there are signs of strain within Evangelical, Pentecostal, and Charismatic communities over how to maintain a normative conception of a unified congregation when it is splintered into so many subgroups. When as many as one-fifth of the Born-again population tell us they do not relate to any congregation and choose instead a small, informal sharing group with little or no ties to a congregation or, as is more likely the case, they simply hold to their own personal faith without regular involvement in any type of religious community, such numbers speak for themselves about the erosion of older patterns of community.

Several other considerations beg for attention as well. If, in fact, what we witness today is the rise of the "participatory congregation"—the demand of laypeople to participate within them on their own terms—it seems reasonable to assume that congregations will adapt to conditions even more striking than those we have witnessed thus far. The "seeker church" already signals the rise of a multilevel religious community, a coexistence of "seekers" and "believers" in which there is creative dialogue between the two. In one reading of this newly evolved structure, it simply accelerates the pace of religious accommodation to the larger culture by institutionalizing a serious encounter between the religious and the secular. It seems only reasonable to expect more such structures. The broader trend toward incorporating small groups within congregations suggests a restructuring that itself may evolve into forms as yet unimaginable. The multi-ethnic church with separate racial and ethnic communities celebrating their own cultures and periodically coming together to share some level of commonality already exists in large urban centers and may serve as a model for a more diversified church. In a multicultural and multireligious world, where as a society we struggle to find satisfactory solutions to civic life and global challenges, experimentation in modeling the life of the spirit and in forging new religious forms are virtually assured. At another level altogether, we might expect kin- and family-based religious activities to flourish. Metaphysical believers and spiritual seekers are committed to devising new rituals for families, and they are likely to continue to do so as their numbers increase. The continuing influx of Latino, Asian, and Middle Eastern immigrants into the United States will reinforce existing religious cultures with an emphasis on the family as a center of worship and celebration—and, to some extent, challenge the congregation as the dominant model of shared religious life in those traditions. Finally, we can expect new institutional alignments among work, family, and religion to unfold, opening up yet more spaces for sociability and no doubt giving rise to, as yet, unanticipated structures. In the broadest sense, these will be voluntary groups, or congregations, but they may not continue to share all the features of the gathered community model as inherited from an older Protestant culture, and still regarded as normative for congregational life.

The challenge currently facing religion in its evolution of forms is not unlike that of the so-called crisis in civic membership and participation. Robert Putnam, in his widely circulated article "Bowling Alone: America's Declining Social Capital,"[6] argues that civic participation has greatly declined since midcentury. Bowling alone has increased, while league bowling has declined, he observes, suggesting that democracy suffers as a result of declining associational life. He amasses an impressive amount of historical evidence on voting patterns and memberships in the PTA, the League of Women Voters, Lions, Shriners, and other voluntary organizations, all pointing to a decline in participation—and by inference, in conversation about civic matters. In contrast, those groups that are growing are largely 12-step support groups, the nonprofits, and specialized memberships like the Sierra Club and the American Association of Retired Persons. Putnam's argument is seductive, considering that it pits our contemporary malaise against a Norman Rockwell background of the United States at midcentury when people seemed to express their religious, parenting, and civic concerns in ways that were more uniformly structured. Putnam's nostalgia, not unlike John McRae's, is fixed on church and civic group in a setting where boundaries were clearer, and the options fewer and more agreed upon. But the fact is, that world was not all that nurturing and uplifting for many Americans—most notably, women and minorities—nor is the present situation as bleak as Putnam's scenario would have it. To cite two counterarguments: one, Americans, including many Boomers, are expressing their deep concerns about children and families, about social injustices, about the environment and other causes in organizations and networks that may look different but actually have goals not unlike those of an older type of voluntary organization; and two, despite the inward-focusing of the many small groups today, people in those groups often report gaining clarity on their self-absorption and of becoming renewed in their commitments to family and community and to causes and concerns that matter most to them. "Religious capital"—like "social capital"—is not exhausted by any single set of institutional forms, neither those of the past nor of the present. If there is one thing a quest culture holds out for, it is the possibility of new ways of expressing commitments.

CENTERS OF VALUE

H. Richard Niebuhr, Protestant theologian at Yale (1894–1962), was fond of calling attention in his classes to the inscription on the Yale Tower downtown in New Haven: "For God, for country, for Yale." In this way he emphasized how the theological enterprise was, broadly conceived, always engaged in prioritizing centers of value. All values are to be judged relationally, in what might be thought of as a very American way of thinking about theology and ethics; "worth is worth in relation to God," he argued.[7] But God, for him, was "the God behind the gods." Human beings commit themselves to an infinite number of possible value systems, often substituting loyalties to proximate values—to a way of life, to nation, even to ecclesiologies and religious systems—loyalties belonging only to the transcendent. To be sure, Niebuhr lived and wrote at a time when talk about a sovereign God and of all things in relation to God—that Center of Value—was more readily accepted in the cultural milieu than in ours today. The notion of a radical monotheism still evokes a powerful vision of ultimate loyalties and trusts, but in a time of greater cultural and religious fragmentation, theistic rhetoric in the

301

public arena often breaks down. Sometimes it results in confusion over interpretation, other times it is reduced to "weightlessness" or insignificance. Niebuhr's "God beyond the gods" gets lost in the midst of so many conceptions of the divine, in what is often seemingly a cacophony of contending and at times feisty religious voices and where no single image of God, or of God in relation to other social values, or even a version of religious truth enjoys much in the way of a privileged status.

Now frequently, the professional theologian faces an audience of people who view themselves as theologians, at least insofar as questions about God and values apply to them. The religious subcultures we have identified might be thought of in this way, as moral and religious clusters, differing in what the people themselves regard as centers of value. Dogmatists would certainly resist the notion that they elevate dogma, morality, or institution to the level of an absolute, but in practical ethics their actions often accomplish just that. The absolutizing of existing and/or idealized religious forms in the presence of so much flux and ontological uncertainty is a strong temptation. Confronted with moral and religious relativism, with tradition embattled with modernity on so many fronts, the return to old religious formulations easily takes on the aura of an urgent, if not sacred mission—resulting in what Anthony Giddens calls the "assertion of formulaic truth without regard to consequences."[8] In this instance "frozen tradition" easily lends itself to use as a weapon of power and persuasion in culture war and thus greatly limits possibilities of negotiation through dialogue. This use of moral absolutes and religious doctrines as weapons is most evident in current disputes over gay rights, where the strong views of dogmatists clash with those of secularists. The close-mindedness of one and the hedonistic and narcissistic inclinations of the other make for a volatile encounter and inhibit the likelihood of finding a common ground of moral values.

But these two subcultures represent only the extremes of a changing religious landscape. There are other centers of value, arguably stronger culturally and of a more positive vision, easily neglected in drawing attention to the ideological extremes. If there is a cultural shift in the direction of defining love as mutuality in marriage, family, and intimate relations as advanced in this book, certainly that qualifies as an emerging and significant center of value. But what exactly might it hold for the future? As discussed above, imageries of the divine are deeply rooted and reinforced in intimate relations. Psychologists remind us that three types of images are likely to become conflated in the inner world of experience: parental images, divine images as inherited from tradition, and images derived from intimate relationships, particularly from marriage and other sexual unions, but also parent-child relations. This triad of influences stemming from family history, religious heritage, and the subterranean emotions and imageries arising out of intersubjective love and experience, makes for a powerful, creative mix. At one level love as mutuality and equal regard is only a proximate good, yet at another it has a much deeper transforming potential. It is the locus for the birth of new God-images, more egalitarian and intimate, near to people's everyday life experiences, and deeply connected to all things. The force of that set of energies and divine imageries could alter significantly not only attitudinal systems and mind-sets, but orientations and feelings toward religion itself. If indeed there is a generational shift toward greater mutuality in human relationships, and many mainstream believers, Born-again Christians, and metaphysical believers and seekers are embracing this ideal, a broader cultural consensus may well be in the making. Much depends on the course of Born-again Christianity. If it is drawn toward a more moderate position in the religious economy and a greater recognition of the human possibilities of love as mutuality, a greater consensus seems quite likely, but were it to become postured in a more conservative moral alliance with Fundamentalist and traditionalist forces, that will most certainly curtail any such possibilities. Evangelical Protestantism as a majority voice within Born-again Christianity is pivotal to future developments.

Another significant center of value with a broad base of support is that crystallized around the environment. Metaphysical believers and spiritual seekers have led the way in shaping a new ecological ethic, defining it as spiritual at its core—with emphasis on the connectedness of all creation. Now others are arriving at views on nature and the environment that, if not always in full agreement, lend themselves to the forging of a broadly based ecological ethic. As older monarchical conceptions of God fade, anthropocentric views of nature and notions of "dominion" over it should likewise give way. Theologians in all the major religious traditions, in Judaism and Christianity particularly, are "remaking" beliefs in the light of the environmental crisis and exploring creative ways in which to formulate the relation between human beings and nature. Tensions remain far from resolved over exactly what should be the goal of human interaction with the earth. The ideal of "sustainability," considering the complex cycles of nature and interdependence of all forms of life is increasingly accepted, yet as an ideal it comes directly into conflict with "economic expansionism," the philosophy that economic development is the means of solving global poverty.[9] Linking ecology and economics will be a continuing challenge for the twenty-first century, itself a motivation no doubt for looking to deeper spiritual reasons in support of a viable ethic. In addressing the crisis of the environment, this emerging center of value touches on a wide range of issues, far from resolved but all having potential religious significance, such as cosmology and worldview, creation as an ongoing process, connectedness as a principle for understanding all forms of life, global eco-spiritual narrative, and ethics and human responsibility. As with the ideal of mutual love, given the fact that so many Americans across the religious subcultures share concern for the environment and define it as a deeply spiritual concern, reinforced in their views by a larger global cause, there is every reason to think that a change of consciousness of some magnitude is underway. What this expanded environmental consciousness might mean at its deepest levels and the actions it might inspire are less than clear, but its possibilities for unifying and reorienting large sectors of the population are becoming more apparent.

All this is not to give the impression that the future is one of mutual love and environmental sensitivity. These are but two evolving centers of value in a world of multiple values and competing loyalties. Contending forces born out of broad structural changes in society, dependent in no small part on the global economy and developments in corporate capitalism, will determine their success. Obviously other compelling values will emerge to galvanize religious and spiritual consciousness. Amid what will probably continue to be a fluid religious economy, an underlying axis of tension will probably be that between theists, on the one hand, who stress belief in an external, transcendent God, and the "new immanentalists," on the other, who think of the divine in the here and now, either present in the world or within themselves. Old discussions of transcendence and immanence in a theistic mode are giving way to new ways of conceptualizing sacred reality, but more so outside of organized religion than within it. To date this has not given rise to serious ideological dispute because of a history of thinking about God using theological categories of transcendence and immanence, but this may well increase in the years ahead. One possibility is that the traditional faiths will distance themselves from an expansionary subjectivism and draw theological boundaries in keeping with historic conceptions of a transcendent God; already in some mainline church circles there are voices expressing concern about trends toward "polytheistic sacredness," "syncretism," or "fantasies" of a self preoccupied with its own ego as the center of the moral and spiritual universe.[10] It is also possible that the emerging, far more pluralistic religious context will offer ripe opportunity for dialogue and engagement. Such opportunity could actually turn into a creative moment for traditional religious communities to affirm theocentric perspectives and to clarify their own spiritual resources, provided they are able to keep in check reactionary, dogmatic responses. But if this is to happen, progressive leaders within all the major religious communities will have to chart a middle course, making a case for transcendence while at the same carefully circumscribing their position vis-à-vis both die-hard traditionalists and a more self-focused spiritual culture. To a considerable extent, the future shape of the religious scene in the United States hangs in this balance.

Assessing "Spiritual Capital"

The nagging question throughout our analysis remains: What about spiritual depth and its power to transform individuals and society? My premise is that there is now greater spiritual maturity on the part of Boomer Americans which, if correct, implies that the potential for transformation is considerable. Certainly no one questions that the spiritual currents flowing today are incredibly diverse, even if baffling to assess: they are at once visible yet invisible, well-formed and articulated at times but vaguely understood and expressed at other times, obviously of some depth and importance to many but also shallow and seemingly insubstantial in ways. All this makes for uneasy generalizations with regard to depth and potential, though lived religion tends to be like that—that is, very much subject to interpretation, and even more so when we stand so close in time to it. Historian R. Laurence Moore points out that "selling God" runs the span of American history, meaning that whatever goes by the name of "religious" or "spiritual" will likely in its lived expression have its tacky, superficial, and commodified aspects, even as its power and hold over human lives continues to astound anyone who carefully examines it.[11] And probably anything described first and foremost as "spiritual" (more so than "religious") adds to the perplexity of any balanced assessment of it; the subjectivity and fluidity make for a limitless configuration of personal meanings, uses, and misuses, adding to the task of the commentator.

Today especially, it is difficult to arrive at a balanced analysis, if for no other reason than that so many of the boundaries once taken for granted in religious analysis are blurred. Increasingly we do not know the nature of the beast we are examining. Moore himself offers a vivid illustration:

> Fifty years ago we were fairly sure that we could distinguish a clinic organized by disciples of Carl Jung from a Christian Science church. The line is less certain now when we try to decide which of the following has qualified for religious tax exemption: the Esalen Institute, the Rolf Institute, the Erhard Seminars, the Institute of Esoteric Transcendentalism, the American School of Mentalvivology, the Life Study Fellowship Foundation, Inc., and the Institute for the Development of the Harmonious Human Being.

He goes on to say that Gordon Melton, who chronicles American religious groups of all kind, "lists only the last four in his *Encyclopedia of American Religions*, but slight repackaging could shift any of them in and out of the categories 'religious' and 'secular.' "[12] Interpreters of the contemporary scene cannot escape the slipperiness (and messiness) of existing conceptual categories.

But this problem aside, scholars will disagree over the depth of the spiritual meaning even as they agree they have implications of some kind. Consider the small-group movement, for example, which itself is open to widely differing interpretations.[13] Much of the debate on this movement centers on (1) whether small groups have any lasting impact on a person's life; (2) whether they can be institutionalized as lasting religious forms, and thereby be embedded in custom and practices; and (3) whether this movement reinforces existing patterns of religious faith and practice.

Considering the size and diversity of the small-group movement, each of these three deserves comment. On the first, the weight of the evidence from our research points to a positive assessment. Even if some people flit from one small group or spiritual experience to another, and levels of spiritual understanding are shallow and inconsequential—flaky, some would say—the majority are inclined to stick with a particular group or spiritual discipline over a period of time long enough to benefit from those experiences in ways that often do affect their outlooks and identities. Certainly, regarding the people we have studied over the past ten years, as they have aged they have become more serious in their spiritual pursuits and more inclined to give outward expression to those concerns, be it assuming family responsibility, commitment to social justice causes, volunteering to work within the community, or assuming responsibilities within a religious or spiritual group. There are signs of a deepening of commitment to religious and spiritual practices, and an incredible array of visible expressions—undermining any notion that they remain self-absorbed. Indeed, there is still much fluidity, but among the older cohort of Boomers in particular, meaning systems resemble that of a concentric circle—with a core of beliefs and loyalties defining these and becoming stronger over time, but spanning outward in a constellation where they are more permeable. The practical effect is that the core wields a dominant and stabilizing influence. Perhaps more than anything else, age and life-course are factors operating here; among older Boomers we can expect more mature, seasoned views of life.

The second consideration—institutionalization—is for much that passes as spirituality a serious problem: its beliefs and practices remain inchoate, their pattern as yet unclear. Often there is little agreement among followers as to what are the most basic teachings or practices; there is little of a sustained communal basis matching the rhetorics of spiritual quest. To a considerable extent, the survival of this type of spirituality depends on secondary institutions—radio and television stations, bookstores, publishing houses, resorts, retreat centers, the music, video- and audio-cassette industries, and bulletin boards at upscale laundry mats. Because much of popular spirituality is highly personalized and largely dependent on the individual's own private or small-group practice, it has the advantage of being highly adaptable in a mobile world where people's lives change often, yet suffers from a lack of long-term, shared face-to-face exchanges among its followers. Such exchanges are crucial for their reinforcement of individual commitments. Spiritual seeking suffers from another problem as well. Research evidence suggests that intense, instrumental approaches to spirituality—that is, wanting the benefits of believing but in the absence of strong conviction about such beliefs and practices—can be self-defeating.[14] Without some level of commitment, spiritual seekers are likely to remain tourists and never become pilgrims.

But not all seekers are so highly instrumental in their orientations. With greater maturity and spiritual well-being, a growing constituency are becoming more committed to the truth-claims of whatever philosophy or tradition they hold as their own. Yet the fact remains that many spiritually minded people who may be well disciplined in some respects are not all that anchored in communal enclaves. The "New Spirituality," as this less-grounded style of spirituality is sometimes called, is probably a forerunner of what to expect of a substantial segment of the population in the next decade that will rely less on sustained patterns of group interaction and more on informal networks, publications, and visual and media resources as a means of cultivating spiritual life. Finding structures for institutionalizing these spiritual resources that ensure a long and lasting impact is problematic, but the possibility of adaptable responses to these challenges are not to be ruled out. Clearly, without such responses much that passes as the "New Spirituality" will be short-lived.

With regard to the third consideration in assessing the small-group movement—reinforcement of established faith and practice—it seems fairly clear that spiritual ferment within the churches, synagogues, temples, and mosques is bringing about some constructive reforms. The basis for saying this rests not simply, or even primarily, on the major institutional innovations like "seeker churches," but in the numerous instances in our research where individuals and groups wanted to learn more about their own traditions. Large numbers of people, and many of them mainstream believers, are actively participating in Bible and Torah study groups, in women's groups and men's groups, in base communities, looking to cultivate a deeper, transforming inner life. To say self-transforming actually underestimates what is going on in many places. Had the stories we heard sounded like "finding myself," or the same old version of "self-fulfillment" of two decades ago, there would be no little basis for our argument. Rather, what we heard were stories about how small groups had often provided the leadership for restructuring congregations, for raising consciousness about social justice issues, and for reorienting mission statements of churches and synagogues. At the level of both faith and praxis, signs point to a more decentralized, multilevel religious structure for the future, one where grassroots input and styles of commitment are better accepted as options. Feminine sensitivities are finding an important place in those new structures and communities marking a major, if long overdue, accomplishment. Institutional innovations are occurring at many levels, sometimes very visibly, other times in small steps one at a time. One thing clear is that collective life, shared faith and spiritual experience, in one form or another are not about to be replaced by some new "irreducible church of solitary worship," as has been speculated.[15] Individualizing trends in the culture are strong, but so too still are the forces that lead people to come together in worship and celebration of a common faith.

Looking to the future, religious communities are likely to become understood and appreciated as depositories of symbols, practices, teachings, and moral codes for assembling and reassembling strategies of faith and action. That is to say, they will function less as a unified normative body prescribing a singular religious or spiritual style and will better institutionalize internal pluralism and the acceptance of diversity; individuals and small groups will turn to traditions as resources yet exercise freedom in making religious choices and in modes of spiritual cultivation. It will be taken more for granted that symbolic and spiritual resources within any tradition are diverse and to be drawn upon selectively, and that life forces upon people over and over again the need to reshuffle the deck, or to think through "what coheres with . . . changing experiences in the tortuous passage through life in a world where the old, allegedly comprehensive charts no longer command confidence."[16] Lived tradition will become even more highly textured, but even more importantly, more consciously embodied in response to personal and collective concerns. The more serious, reflexive-minded mainstream believers and, to some extent, even Born-again Christians should they continue on course toward a moderate position—each comprising a relatively small but highly committed vanguard—are a force to be reckoned with and constitute the leadership that will press religious institutions toward further innovation. As we move into a new century, we ought not underestimate the force of such pressures.

But as Peter Berger astutely observes,[17] the basis on which any religious group comes together in a world where old assumptions of religious certainty are no longer held is to a considerable degree "fragile." That is most certainly the case for the more liberal religious traditions, but in a broader ontological sense this situation now faces all religious organizations. Such is also the starting point for a reflexive spirituality, since rather than presume a foundation of taken-for-granted certainties it accepts uncertainty and forces on believers and seekers alike a posture of humility toward their religious claims. Given a fragile religious world, reflexive spirituality has two qualities to commend it. One of these raised to the level of a theological principle by Berger, is that this situation throws people back upon faith, or some fundamental assumption of trust in powers beyond themselves. Referred to in the past as the

"Protestant principle," it means that even institutions and absolutes cannot be held up in any final analysis as an object of loyalty. Boomers on the whole have an intuitive appreciation for such a principle, given their skepticism and distrust of institutions and high levels of personal freedom. Except for the dogmatists among them, they refuse easy answers of religious certainty whether that be based on the Bible, on the teachings of a particular guru, or on the authority of a religious institution. Often they appear to have turned to easy answers as promised in the latest spiritual fads, but their very active spiritual pursuits bear a deeper testimony to a generalized restlessness. In Niebuhr's terms, they may not always recognize the "God behind the gods," but they do recognize that the gods offered to them often are simply that, gods. So they bring with them a mind-set prepared to entertain questions at a most basic level about religious life and institutions, and do so in a way that encourages honesty and authenticity. The challenge for religious communities is to find ways to tap this creative potential and to be open to where its impulses may lead. Even more challenging for institutions, of course, is truly placing the message above the medium: easily preached, not so easily practiced.

A second quality is that reflexive spirituality reorients notions about religious and spiritual strength, away from custom, institution, or doctrinal formulation toward greater focus on the inner life and its cultivation. The spiritual emptiness that so many Boomers feel can actually present opportunities for deepening religious life. As mystics in all the great world religions have taught, in silence may be discerned a paradox: the sacredness of absence, or the absent presence. Ours is an age for the rediscovery of this fundamental insight. A reflexive stance also has the advantage of placing responsibility on the individual, forcing one to think through the options, and to commit to an option with critical self-awareness. In an age when the religious establishments cannot claim a monopoly on the culture, when religious tradition does not play as much of a role integrating society, integration—if it is to be achieved—must begin with the individual, or ideally with individuals in supportive, sharing communities cognizant of the massive transformations of religion in the modern context. Under such conditions, the primary task for religion is to break out of any social fictions it may propagate and to focus its energies explicitly around cultivating the interior life. The challenge is to become religious "from within," to start with a personal commitment in search of a religious center.[18] More than just humility, this involves a radical openness, acceptance, reaching out and, perhaps most important of all, recognition on the part of believer and seeker alike that at a most basic level, *both* are engaged in the rebuilding of a richer spiritual life. Admittedly, such a shared undertaking is daunting to imagine, much less to carry out. Yet for both believer and seeker the possibilities for spiritual formation are enormous. This need not imply an open-ended retrieval of religious resources, only that spiritual rebuilding—whether, most commonly, within a tradition, or through incorporation of elements from several traditions such as Christianity and Buddhism—be undertaken as a serious enterprise. Nor does this mean that spirituality is reduced to the personal dimension, that social consciousness is overlooked, but to stress simply that in a spiritual quest culture, it must begin in earnest at the personal level if it is to begin at all. Only in this way can there be any genuine spiritual deepening or discernment of directions to take in rebuilding personal lives and society—a "testing of the spirits," as it was called in an earlier time.

If the religious establishments are to meet these challenges, they will have to make some shifts in strategies. Aside from becoming serious about spiritual formation, they must find ways to institutionalize a greater level of deliberateness within their structures, a serious and on-going commitment to marshaling and monitoring their own resources. In an earlier age of greater religious certainty, so high a level of consciousness was not necessary; tradition as Berger is fond of saying, was "taken-for-granted." But not so in a fragmented, more secular world. Defining and perpetuating tradition becomes much more of a conscious undertaking and responsibility: "Every continuation of tradition is selective," writes the European sociologist Jürgen Habermas, "and precisely this selectivity must pass through the filter of critique, of a self-conscious appropriation of history."[19] What is called for is an interrogative stance toward that which is appropriated in the name of tradition, and a readiness to engage it in the face of cognitive pluralism and uncertainty, proclaiming its heritage of symbols, teachings, practices, and moral codes as spiritually edifying, and as a basis for making truth-claims. Triumphalist and exclusivistic theologies have no place in this circumstance, and adopting a more modest posture, humbling to be sure, might in the long run even have positive benefits for individuals and society. Modesty, even in making faith claims, has a certain virtue that commends itself; indeed serious believers in various traditions down through the ages have recognized that virtue.

311

Greater modesty in truth-claims might make posssible serious engagement of the quest culture. The resulting dialogue could in the long run have important consequences. The line between those seriously cultivating spiritual depth and those who are not may become more sharply defined, and religious communities be pressured to give greater attention to cultivation of the interior life. Should present trends continue, we would expect a further religious falling away of the casually involved, but also a nucleus of highly committed people trying to rebuild religious communities from within. Revitalizing activity of this sort will rely not just on the strengths of custom, tradition, or institution, but on people's own conviction and interiority—perhaps the most valuable form of "spiritual capital" of all. Should this common ground lead to more serious dialogue between religious and spiritual traditions, that may bear fruit of its own. It will most certainly add yet another layer to what is already a complex, multilayered religious reality in the United States and further confound attempts at understanding American religion relying on any simple set of categories or boundary definitions—theological, institutional, or otherwise.

There could be still greater confounding for religious analysis if, in fact, for perpetual seekers like Vicki Feinstein, the discontinuity is too great for any genuine connection with religion in its present institutional forms. Our character from Chapter 1 lacking a spiritual anchor, she does not easily connect with any inherited religious language. Metaphysical truth seems less her goal than the experience of spiritual searching itself. There is little in the way of a memory that might be described as religious; even her Jewish past is dim, and what she knows of it seems not to matter greatly to her. It is not inconceivable that she herself recognizes metaphysical homelessness as a state of mind, that religious truth in the forms it has been inherited since the Enlightenment does not suffice for her. That uncertainty coupled with her intent to focus on her own experience marks her as a seeker who regards as corrupted all theological and philosophical accommodations of religion to modernity as they have evolved over the past three hundred years. As the Jewish scholar Arthur Green might say of her, she is one for whom the long, drawn-out struggle of Western religious traditions in the face of secularization is over, for whom secularity, not religion, is now the starting point of any genuine spiritual quest.[20] That amounts to a whole new context for defining religion and one that we cannot yet fully envision.

But of course, the extent to which Vicki Feinstein will be an icon of the age remains to be seen. History may prove that her numbers are greater than here envisioned, but as judged by current religious demographics, she remains in the minority. For the great majority of her peers, she is hardly the example to which they aspire for themselves, or for their children. Older members of the generation do not relate to her frantic, seemingly endless trail of searching. It is not that the world has gone secular, lost all its scripts embedding the sacred; instead, the world has become a gigantic maze of alternative paths requiring of individuals a level of decision-making and accountability on a scale unlike anything previous Americans have known—and involving in a most fundamental way, things of the spirit. Most of them look on religion or spirituality, or both, and the master narratives, practices, and moral values that go with them as significant personal and family resources. Their own life stories are among the most diverse and conflicted of any generation's in American history, but that only adds to the sense of distinctiveness that they already greatly enjoy. Treasuring storytelling as they do, the narration of life experiences is itself elevated to something only slightly less than an art form; it might even be said that in some respects this is a generation held together by its stories.

What really stands out about those stories is their capacity to absorb so much experience and to pull it all into some coherence. Doubt and unbelief seem as much a part of those stories as affirmation and belief, and these elements hanging together seem workable somehow. Pragmatism as ideology and practice has a strong hold on them, as it has for Americans historically. Except for dogmatists, Boomers generally accept the view that certainty in any religious or ultimate sense is illusory, beyond human grasp, and therefore truly a leap; ambiguity and paradox seem to be built into life, not just in its organizational and institutional expression but in its deepest ontological sense. Perhaps the religious tensions felt are not so much those of belief versus nonbelief as of wanting to enjoy the material gains, power, and status associated with religious heritage without at the same time losing one's spiritual self.[21] By no means is this generation alone in feeling this tension, so deeply embedded is it in American culture, but it plays out differently in their case, with greater skepticism and curtailing whatever temptations they might have to flaunt a self-righteous piety. They are, after all, a generation whose multiple "centers of value" defy simple characterizations of singular loyalties and reduction to any single axis of ideological polarization; for whom tolerance toward diversity in most things is a matter of principle and a starting point for much public debate; and for whom the "politics of meaning" carries some resonance, urging on them an openness to truth-claims but not blindly so or without worries about the power plays that inevitably are involved. If metaphysical certainty is not possible, there are provisional approximations to hold on to even if they are no more than just that. As both creators of, and those created by the world in place at the turn of the century, hodgepodges and criss-crossings of once, taken-for-granted social boundaries come a bit more naturally to them, though not without a measure of anxiety. "Whirl is King," and they know it.

Methodology

THE DATA

THE ORIGINAL DATA for this project were collected in the fall of 1988 and spring of 1989 by Focused Group Interviews, Inc., a research firm in Chapel Hill, North Carolina. Supported by the Lilly Endowment, Inc., the firm randomly sampled 2,620 households in four states: California, Massachusetts, North Carolina, and Ohio. The states were selected to provide some degree of regional variation. We used a stratified sampling process to allow for approximately equal numbers of respondents in each of the four states. Only one person in each household was interviewed by telephone. The overall response rate was 60 percent. For the Boomer subsample, we chose people born in the years from 1946 to 1962, a procedure yielding 1,599 cases.

A second phase of follow-up telephone calls with 536 of the 1,599 boomers was conducted within three to nine months after the FGI completed its survey. Those interviewed were randomly selected using stratified sampling procedures, allowing for proportionate numbers of loyally religious participants, dropouts, returnees, and nonparticipants. These interviews gathered still more, in-depth information on religious biographies. Combining questions from both of the telephone interviews, people were asked to respond to approximately 120 items. In addition, 64 of the people were visited in 1989 and 1990 for face-to-face taped interviews. A supplemental grant from the Lilly Endowment, Inc., made it possible to carry out 75 additional in-depth interviews on religious biography during the years from 1992 to 1995.

The third phase of interviewing occurred in 1995 and 1996, when we sought to contact the 536 who had been interviewed in both previous phases. As a panel study we attempted not just to interview the same people but to repeat some of our most important questions. A total of 21 questions, about half of them repeats, were included in this third phase. A first round of contacts yielded 212 completed interviews and was then followed by a second round completing 197, or a total of 409 completed interviews (76 percent). Though interviewing began in summer 1995, most were conducted in the fall of that year and spring of 1996. Two of the interviewees had died, five would not talk with us, and the remainder we could either not locate at all or even reach because of uncooperative family members. As in the earlier interviews, the response rate was lower in Massachusetts than anywhere else. We simply do not know if, and to what extent, this lower response rate biases our results. In this latter phase of interviewing we spoke with more women than men (59 percent to 41 percent), slightly more so than in 1988-89, but otherwise we have no basis for assuming any serious biases. Following the completion of this round of telephone interviews in 1996, I personally spoke with approximately 40 of the interviewees during 1997 to obtain additional information, mostly opinions on public issues and to confirm responses. Face-to-face interviews were conducted with 14 of the people interviewed in the third phases, mostly in California but also in the other three states.

Independently of the panel survey, I had access to well over two hundred interviews with Boomers from other research projects focusing on ethnic and religious populations in Southern California. In a few instances, I have drawn from these interviews for qualitative materials in this book. The results in this instance were made available from projects funded by the Pew Charitable Trusts and Randolph and Dora Haynes Foundations between 1992 and 1996.

While the text summarizes results from a considerable amount of statistical analysis, it excludes quantitative tables, to enhance readability for an audience more oriented toward both the social sciences and humanities. For statistically trained specialists, further commentary on analysis and additional results in some instances are provided in the methodological notes that follow for the chapters. Unless otherwise indicated, cross-tabular analysis is used throughout with Chi-square as a measure of statistical significance and a probability of 0.05 on this and related measures of association for establishing statistical significance. The analysis was carried out using the Statistical Package for the Social Sciences.

ADDITIONAL COMMENTARY

Chapter 1: Varieties of Spiritual Quest

The terminology beginning in this chapter, and throughout the book, on "mainline" or "mainstream" Protestantism and "conservative" Protestantism conforms to the generally accepted usage in social science research. Rarely in the book does statistical analysis involve categorizing people into such clusters, but where it does we use the Protestant classification scheme of denominational families as found in Wade Clark Roof and William McKinney, *American Mainline Religion: Its Changing Shape and Future*,[1] Liberal Protestants (Episcopalians, United Church of Christ, Presbyterians); Moderate Protestants (Methodists, Lutherans, Disciples of Christ, Northern Baptists, Reformed); and conservative Baptists (Southern Baptists, Churches of Christ, Evangelicals, Fundamentalists, Nazarenes, Pentecostals/Holiness, Assemblies of God, Churches of God, Adventists). There are separate African-American denominations with which many blacks are affiliated, many in the same tradition as the white denominations; in most of the aggregate analyses here, blacks are not singled out from their white counterparts in the various institutions but treated as part of the total. Exceptions are made clear. The term *oldline* as applied to Protestant institutions refers mainly to our liberal Protestant category, composed of denominations that were all established early in the country's history prior to the rise of the large nineteenth-century Evangelical religious movements.

Chapter 2: The Making of a Quest Culture

The analysis of cohorts born in this century relies on the original 1988–89 survey of 2,620 individuals. Cohorts were arbitrarily divided for birth years as follows: Cohort 1, 1926–35; Cohort 2, 1936–45; Cohort 3, 1946–54; Cohort 4, 1955–62. Cohorts 3 and 4 constitute the early and later waves of the Boomer generation. Additional cohort analysis relies on General Social Survey data as documented in note 9 (of Chapter 2).

With regard to levels of confidence in the country, only 24 percent of the total Boomer sample in 1988–89 said they had "quite a lot" of confidence in the country, down from 49 percent as they recalled from their days growing up. Both measures were related to countercultural items such as smoking marijuana, attending rock concerts, participating in demonstrations, marches, or rallies (with gammas = .293 to .346). In 1995–96, we did not ask a question on confidence in the country, but we did ask, "Since we last talked, have you become more optimistic or less optimistic about where our country seems headed?" Twenty-five percent said they were more optimistic, 45 percent less optimistic, 30 percent no change. The question was asked prior to the crisis of the Clinton presidency in 1998.

Chapter 3: Spiritual Marketplace

Age controls on the spirituality items discussed in the first part of the chapter showed younger respondents to be somewhat more likely than older ones to encourage exploration of faiths, to stress personal benefits rather than duty to institutions, to prefer to be alone and meditate rather than worship with others, and to think of all religions as equally true and good. Except for the item on exploration of spiritual alternatives as opposed to sticking to a faith, age-based differences, however, were not statistically significant. In the 1995–96 survey, with a much smaller battery of items, we relied largely on two items as an index of spiritual interest. One self-identifying item was worded as follows: "In thinking about God, or whatever is sacred, do you think of yourself as a strong believer, as someone who tries to believe despite occasional doubts, or as a seeker, not always sure what to believe but who is exploring?" Responses were as follows: strong believer, 55 percent; believe but doubt, 25 percent; seeker, 18 percent; don't know, 2 percent.

The same agree-disagree item was included in both surveys: "People have God within them, so churches aren't really necessary." Opinions shifted very little, 31 percent agreeing in 1988–89, 34 percent in 1995–96. An increase on an item like this one for an aging population, however, is worthy of note. Age controls show younger Boomers to agree somewhat more than older Boomers, but differences are small, by 4 percent earlier, by 5 percent later, and neither statistically significant.

Chapter 4: On Being Fluid and Grounded

Loyalists, dropouts, and *returnees* are terms used in this chapter to refer to degree of institutional religious involvement. Operationally, these descriptions were measured by means of two questions in the first survey. We asked, "Has there ever been a period of two years or more when you did not attend church/synagogue, apart from weddings, funerals, and special holidays?" For those respondents who answered yes, we also asked, "Did you ever start attending church/synagogue again?" Those who said no to the first question were defined as loyalists, the assumption being that they were highly committed; if yes to the first and no to the second question, we defined them as dropouts; if yes to both questions, they were defined as returnees. It is a crude and somewhat conservative estimate of movement in and out of religious participation, considering

TABLE A-1
Weekly Attendance at Religious Services
(in percentages)

	Age			
	8–10	Early 20s	1988–89	1995–96
Roman Catholics	95	28	43	43
Liberal Protestants	82	18	27	31
Conservative Protestants	91	40	50	52

that it does not account for repeated periods of religious activity/inactivity. In some instances people told us about four or five times of movement in and out of religious and spiritual activities.

While the institutional loyalists are not discussed as much in the text as the returnees, it should not be assumed that they themselves remained loyal up until the time of our second survey. A core of loyalists have remained committed over the period of almost ten years that we followed them, but as a whole this constituency, too, is quite fluid in their commitments. Among those we identified in 1988–89 as the most institutionally committed, only 46 percent in 1995–96 remained active in any religious group; 25 percent said they hardly ever or never attend a religious service. Sixty percent say they are "strong believers," which means that 40 percent see themselves as "doubters" or "seekers." They were the faithful remnant of the Boomer population when we first interviewed them (one-third of the total), but now their numbers are much smaller. More than just switching from one religious group to another, as many of have done, significant numbers of them have abandoned religious institutions altogether.

Detailed analysis of self-reported religious attendance over time for the three large religious constituencies is shown in Table A-1. Respondents were asked in 1988–89 about the extent to which they attended religious services when they were "8 or 10 years old" and when older, "in their early 20s." Shown as well in the third and fourth columns are responses to questions about attendance at the time the surveys were administered. Reported are percentages describing weekly attendance.

Self-reported answers to the question about childhood religious tradition and more recent religious preferences are shown in Table A-2. Percentages are based on the total sample. For example, whereas 35 percent

Table A-2
Religious Background and Preferences
(in percentages)

	Childhood Tradition	Religious Preference 1988–89	Religious Preference 1995–96
Roman Catholic	35	30	32
Liberal Protestant	23	27	29
Conservative Protestant	29	21	18
Black Protestant	5	5	5
Jewish	4	4	3
Other	1	3	4
None	3	10	9

of our sample was brought up Catholic, fewer of them claimed a similar affiliation in 1988–89 and 1995–96. The same data are available for the other major clusters.

Chapter 5: A Quest for What?

To explore the relations between religious individualism and the self-reported "religious" and "spiritual" identities, we created an index of religious individualism using the following items: (1) "An individual should arrive at his or her own religious beliefs independent of any church or synagogue"; (2) "A person can be a good Christian or Jew if he or she doesn't attend church or synagogue"; and (3) "A good Christian or Jew should follow his or her conscience, even if it means going against what organized religion teaches." The three were positively correlated (average gamma = .292). Using a summated index with scores from 0 to 3 for increasing levels of agreement with the items on individualism, the percentage distributions were as follows: 93%, 88%, 78%, 64% on religious identity, and 37%, 45%, 54%, 71%, respectively, on spiritual identity. That is, with increasing individualism religious identity declines, and spiritual identity increases.

Using this same index of religious individualism, we found the following pattern for the four cohorts in the first survey: for the 1926–35 cohort, an average mean score of 2.56; for the 1936–45 cohort, 2.72; for the 1946–54 cohort, 2.90; for the 1955–62 cohort, 2.81. For the general population the pattern is one of increasing religious individualism by birth cohort, although second-wave Boomers (born 1955–62) scored slightly lower on the scale than did first-wave Boomers (born 1946–54).

The typology at the end of the chapter relies on two direct questions: "Do you consider yourself religious?" and "Do you consider yourself spiritual?" asked in that order but not consecutively in the interview schedules. Much social science research has shown that simple, direct questions often yield valid and reliable results equal to, if not greater than, multi-item indexes. Based on our argument, we would expect a moderate positive association between the two sets of responses, but not one that is exceptionally strong. And that is what we find (gamma = .291). Moreover, when we checked the association between "being religious" and "being spiritual" by subconstituencies, it emerged strongest for the majority population identifying themselves as "strong believers" (gamma =.439) and much less for self-proclaimed "seekers" (gamma = .196). This is exactly the pattern we would expect, since those who would identify themselves as "seekers" are far less likely to draw on religious language.

Other validity checks also confirm the index. Respondents were asked, "Which is best: to follow the teachings of a church, synagogue, or temple, or to think for oneself in matters of religion and trust more one's own experiences?" Sixty-five percent said think for yourself, 30 percent follow church, 5 percent said they try to do both. Cross-tabulated by our religious/spiritual typology, we find: those religious but not spiritual (dogmatists) are twice as likely to prefer following institutional teachings as those both religious and spiritual (mainstream believers and Born-again Christians); those spiritual but not religious (metaphysical believers and spiritual seekers) are twice as likely to say one should think for oneself and trust one's own experiences; those rejecting both a religious and a spiritual identity (secularists) likewise are predisposed toward trusting one's own experience. Important to note as well, many of the social and psychological correlates of the typology uncovered in this research are consistent with findings of two major empirical research efforts to disentangle the religiosity/spirituality complex.[2] Thus, on the basis of its face validity, predictive validity, and criterion validity, this measure of religious versus spiritual identities proves to be acceptable.

On the basis of this index, the percentage distribution for the five subcultures is as follows: dogmatists 15%; Born-again Christians 33%; mainstream believers 26%; metaphysical believers and seekers 14%; secularists 12%.

TABLE A-3
Subcultures and Beliefs
(in percentages)

Percent Believing in	Dogmatists	Born-again Christians	Mainstream Believers	Metaphysical Believers and Seekers	Secularists
Eternal Life	84	79	78	90	84
Reincarnation	22	27	26	28	32
Devil	78	62	72	61	52
Astrology	18	38	31	41	24
Ghosts	31	22	39	42	28
God as Father	82	57	55	31	30
God as Mother	6	21	17	17	4

Chapter 6: Redrawing the Boundaries

A summary of beliefs by subculture is shown in Table A-3. Only the differences on astrology and the God images are statistically significant. Additional interesting correlates include the following: one, secularists are more likely than others to practice meditation (20%); two, dogmatists are more likely to report reading the Bible weekly, although majorities within all the subcultures including the secularists say they do so; and three, roughly 40% across the subcultures report saying grace before meals regularly, but slightly fewer dogmatists claim to do so than the others. However, these differences do not reach statistical significance.

Chapter 7: Realigning Family and Religion

The influences of parental religiosity on a respondent's current religious or spiritual activity as reported in the text are statistically significant except in some instances of small-group participation. Mother's influences are almost always significant; father's influence is weaker on respondent's involvement in Bible study, prayer, and spiritual support groups and not statistically significant.

Chapter 8: Moral Vision and Values

All data pertaining to the issues described are reported in the text. As is pointed out, all statistics reported here were based on surveys prior to the crisis in the Clinton presidency. To gauge the political mood in

1995–96, we did ask two questions on politics, one on the 1992 presidential vote and a second on intentions for voting in 1996. On the first: metaphysical believers and seekers were more likely than any others to say they voted for Clinton (72%), secularists second (63%), and mainstream believers third (52%); 27% of Born-again Christians and 21% of dogmatists voted for him; 52% of Born-again Christians and 38% of dogmatists voted for George Bush; 16% of dogmatists, the most of any subculture, voted for the independent candidate Ross Perot; and 19% of dogmatists, by far the most who abstained among any of our groups, did not vote.

On the second: 48% of metaphysical believers and seekers said at the time that they planned to vote for Clinton, followed by secularists (36%), mainstream believers (34%), Born-again Christians (18%), and dogmatists (9%); 9% of dogmatists, far greater than for any other subculture, also said they planned not to vote.

✣ Notes ✣

INTRODUCTION
ON MAPS AND TERRAINS

1. H. Paul Chalfant, Robert E. Beckley, and C. Eddie Palmer, *Religion in Contemporary Society*, 3rd ed. (Itasca: F. E. Peacock Publishers, 1994), 5.

2. "Notebook," *The New Republic* 211 (12 Sept. 1994): 8. One is reminded, of course, that the same has been said of the devil—even further reason, I suppose, for caution in relying too much on any one map.

3. Thomas J. Ferraro, "Not-Just-Cultural Catholics," in *Catholic Lives, Contemporary America*, ed. Thomas J. Ferraro (Durham: Duke University Press, 1997), 14.

4. Martin E. Marty, *A Nation of Behavers* (Chicago: University of Chicago Press, 1976), 18.

5. Jonathan Z. Smith, *Map Is Not Territory: Studies in the History of Religion* (Leiden: Brill, 1978).

6. Marty, *A Nation of Behavers*, 1–16.

7. Eve Arnold-Magnum, "Spiritual America," *U.S. News and World Report* 116 (4 April 1994): 48–59.

8. Marty, "Where the Energies Go," *Annals of the American Academy of Political and Social Science* 527 (May 1993): 11–26.

9. Ibid., 15.

10. The eminent physicist John Wheeler of Princeton University uses such language. Stephen Hawking, the British cosmologist, ends his book, *A Brief History of Time* (London: Bantam Press, 1998), with the hope that, through science, we may one day "know the mind of God." See discussion of Wheeler and Hawking in Sharon Begley, "Science of the Sacred," *Newsweek* 124 (28 November 1994): 56.

11. It will be obvious to readers that many of the ideas expressed in this book resonate with the thinking of some "postmodern" intellectuals. Despite my indebtedness to these intellectuals, however, I do not use that term—it has become something of a buzzword, convoluted in its meanings, and ideologically loaded in ways that often obfuscate more than clarify. I think it is more appropriate to hold to assumptions of modernity, or late modernity, recognizing that the descriptive characteristics alleged to characterize "late modernity" and "postmodernity" often overlap.

12. R. Laurence Moore, *Selling God: American Religion in the Marketplace of Culture* (New York: Oxford University Press, 1994), 256.

13. My use of spiritual *searching* or *seeking* is not to be confused with the narrow conception of these terms as proposed by John Lofland and Rodney Stark in "Becoming a World-Saver," *American Sociological Review* 30 (1965): 862–75. Many sociologists have followed their view that seekers are prone to joining "cults" and "floundering among religious alternatives," unable to embrace any specific ideology. My view is closer to Ernst Troeltsch's formulation of spiritual and mystical religion, which he expected to flourish in the modern world. These issues are dealt with in greater detail in Chapters 4 and 5. See also Colin Campbell's

defense of this broader concept of seeking in his essay on "Cult," in *Encyclopedia of Religion and Society, ad. loc.*

14. Daniel Yankelovich, *New Rules: Searching for Self-Fulfillment in a World Turned Upside Down* (New York: Random House, 1981), xiv.

15. A review of publications on "General Spirituality" in the library at the Graduate Theological Union in Berkeley, California, in the summer of 1996 revealed that of the 204 entries only 4 address sociological (including topics such as "role," "power," and "social action") concerns. This reflects not on the GTU library but on the state of scholarship on spirituality.

16. San Francisco: HarperSanFrancisco, 1993.

17. Will Herberg, *Protestant-Catholic-Jew* (Garden City: Anchor, 1955).

18. Robert N. Bellah et al., *Habits of the Heart: Individualism and Commitment in American Life* (Berkeley: University of California Press, 1985).

19. Peter L. Berger, *The Precarious Vision* (Garden City: Doubleday and Company, 1961).

CHAPTER 1
VARIETIES OF SPIRITUAL QUEST

1. William James, *The Varieties of Religious Experience* (New York: Macmillan, 1961), 55. This classic first appeared in 1902.

2. All are actual people, but names and incidentals have of course been changed to protect their privacy. They are not to be identified with the characters described in my earlier books, *A Generation of Seekers*.

3. Robert Coles, *The Spiritual Life of Children* (Boston: Houghton Mifflin, 1990), 37. Coles attributes the comment to William Carlos Williams in the context of a doctor listening to hospital patients.

4. Twenty-two percent of Americans are involved in such groups according to the Princeton Religion Research Center, *The Unchurched American* (Princeton, New Jersey, 1988), 54. On Jewish *havurot*, see Riv-Ellen Prell, *Prayer and Community: The Havurah in American Judaism* (Detroit: Wayne State University Press, 1989), 12–24. On work-related religious groups, see the lengthy coverage in David W. Chen, "Fitting the Lord into Work's Tight Schedules," *The New York Times*, 29 November 1997, A1.

5. See Joan R. Gundersen, "Women and the Parallel Church: A View from Congregations," in *Episcopal Women: Gender, Spirituality, and Commitment to an American Denomination*, ed. Catherine M. Prelinger (New York: Oxford University Press, 1992), 111–32.

6. Miriam Therese Winter, Adair Lummis, and Alison Stokes, *Defecting in Place: Women Claiming Responsibility for Their Own Lives* (New York: Crossroad, 1994). Their research focuses primarily on women in mainline Protestant and Catholic churches. For a study of women within Fundamentalist Christian churches and the empowerment that comes from their participation within them, see Brenda A. Brasher, *Godly Women: Fundamentalism and Female Power* (New Brunswick: Rutgers University Press, 1997).

7. For a discussion of the "tourist," see Zygmunt Bauman, *Life in Fragments* (Oxford: Blackwell, 1995), 95–98. Bauman suggests that the tourist is caught

between "homesickness" and fear of "home-boundedness." The tourist is contrasted with the more familiar "pilgrim" who travels within a religious world.

8. Elsewhere I examine such issues as they relate to West Coast religious experience in the United States. See Wade Clark Roof, "Borders and Boundaries: Challenges for Future Study," *Journal for the Scientific Study of Religion*, 37 (March, 1998), 1–14. For a more general and systematic treatment of these issues, see Robert Orsi's informed discussion of the "hermeneutics of hybridity" in his "Everyday Miracles: The Study of Lived Religion," in *Lived Religion in America*, ed. David D. Hall (Princeton: Princeton University Press, 1997), 3–21.

9. Robert M. Torrance, *The Spiritual Quest* (Berkeley: University of California Press, 1994). After reviewing the literature extensively in the biological sciences, social sciences, philosophy, and literary theory, Torrance roots spiritual quests as a fundamental human activity across cultures. He writes: "By *spirit* I mean the dynamic potentiality latent but unrealized in the given (much as form, in Aristotle's terminology, is potential in matter), and by *quest* the deliberate effort to transcend, through self-transformation, the limits of the given and to realize some portion of this unbounded potentiality through pursuit of a future goal that can neither be fully foreknown not finally attained." p. xii.

10. Paul Tillich, *Systematic Theology*, vol. 3 (Chicago: University of Chicago Press, 1963), 24.

11. Steve Jacobsen, *Heart to God, Hands to Work: Connecting Spirituality and Work* (Bethesda: The Alban Institute, 1997), 11.

12. Thomas J. Csordas, *Language, Charisma, and Creativity: The Ritual Life of a Religious Movement* (Berkeley: University of California Press, 1997), 64.

13. Robert Wuthnow, *Christianity in the Twenty-First Century: Reflections on the Challenges Ahead* (New York: Oxford University Press, 1993), 108.

14. The term comes from Robert N. Bellah et al., *Habits of the Heart: Individualism and Commitment in American Life* (Berkeley: University of California Press, 1985).

15. Andrew M. Greeley spells out these characteristics. See *The Denominational Society: A Sociological Approach to Religion in America* (Glenview: Scott, Foresman, and Company, 1972), 3.

16. Nancy Tatum Ammerman's *Congregation and Community* (New Brunswick: Rutgers University Press, 1997), especially chapter 9, is helpful in offering a balanced perspective and challenging those sociological theories that would suggest unilinear secular decline as the dominant story about religion in modernity.

17. Meredith B. McGuire distinguishes between "official" and "nonofficial" forms of religion. See chapter 4 of her *Religion: The Social Context*, 4th ed. (Belmont: Wadsworth Publishing Company, 1997).

18. See Robert Wuthnow, *Sharing the Journey: Support Groups and America's New Quest for Community* (New York: Free Press, 1994), 47. Wuthnow finds 42 percent of the age category closest to the Boomer generation saying they are in a small group. Twenty-six percent of group participants describe their group as self-help. See chapters 2 and 3 of Wuthnow's book.

19. R. Marie Griffith, *God's Daughters; Evangelical Women and the Power of Submission* (Berkeley: University of California Press, 1997), 34.

20. Ibid.

21. Roy F. Baumeister advances this thesis. See his *Escaping the Self: Alcoholism, Spirituality, Masochism, and Other Flights from the Burden of Selfhood* (New York: Basic Books, 1991).

22. The term comes from *Lived Religion in America: Toward a History of Practice*, ed. David D. Hall (Princeton: Princeton University Press, 1997). "Lived religion" has the advantage over some other terms like "popular religion" as opposed to "official religion" in that it does not force a distinction between them and instead privileges the comprehensive religious expression of the actor.

23. See Alasdair MacIntyre, *After Virtue: A Study in Moral Theory*, 2nd ed. (Notre Dame: University of Notre Dame Press, 1984), 221–23. Sherry B. Ortner's essay is helpful as well, "Theory in Anthropology since the Sixties," *Comparative Studies in Society and History* 26 (1984): 126–66.

24. Susan Harding, *The Afterlife of Stories* (Berkeley: University of California Press, forthcoming).

25. Book publisher Thomas Cahill recently wrote in *The New York Times*: "There are all these people I know and meet, especially in communications: publishing, journalism, television, the theater and arts. They have feelings and promptings that they don't know what to do with; they have no vocabulary and terms in which to explain these things; and they have no suspicion that these experiences might have something to do with any religious tradition." See Peter Steinfels's column "Beliefs," *The New York Times*, 24 February 1996, A11.

26. The distinction receives empirical support in recent psychological research. See Vicky Genia, "The Spiritual Experience Index: Revision and Reformulation," *Review of Religious Research* 38 (June, 1997): 344–61.

27. Robert Orsi, "Everyday Miracles" (above, n. 8), 7.

28. Debra Orenstein, ed., *Lifecycles: Jewish Women on Life Passages and Personal Milestones*, vol. 1 (Woodstock: Jewish Lights Publishing, 1994), 370.

29. R. Laurence Moore, *Selling God: American Religion in the Marketplace of Culture* (New York: Oxford University Press, 1994), 8.

30. Thomas A. Tweed, *Rethinking U.S. Religious History* (Berkeley: University of California Press, 1997), 22.

31. See chapter 6 of C. Daniel Batson, Patricia Schoenrade, and W. Larry Ventis, *Religion and the Individual: A Social-Psychological Perspective* (Oxford: Oxford University Press, 1993).

32. See Robert Wuthnow's *Sharing the Journey* (above, n. 18) and Peter L. Berger's *A Far Glory: The Quest for Faith in an Age of Credulity* (New York: The Free Press, 1992).

CHAPTER 2
THE MAKING OF A QUEST CULTURE

1. Jack Miles, "Religion Makes a Comeback. (Belief to Follow.)," *The New York Times Magazine*, 7 December 1997, 58.

2. Peter L. Berger, "Protestantism and the Quest for Certainty," *The Christian Century*, 26 August 1998, 783.

3. Robert Wuthnow, *The Restructuring of American Religion: Society and Faith since World War II* (Princeton: Princeton University Press, 1988).

4. See François Ricard, *The Lyric Generation: The Life and Times of the Baby Boomers*, trans. Donald Winkler (Toronto: Stoddart Publishers, 1994). For other accounts of generational changes in Canada, see Doug Owram, *Born at the Right Time: A History of the Baby Boom Generation* (Toronto: University of Toronto Press, 1996) and Michael Adams, *Sex in the Snow: Canadian Social Values at the End of the Millennium* (Toronto: Viking Penguin, 1997).

5. Daniel Bell, *The Cultural Contradictions of Capitalism* (New York: Basic Books, 1976), 3–30.

6. See Wade Clark Roof, Jackson W. Carroll, and David A. Roozen, *The Post-War Generation and Establishment Religion: Cross-Cultural Perspectives* (Boulder: Westview Press, 1995).

7. See the essays in William R. Hutchison, *Between the Times: The Travail of the Protestant Establishment in America, 1900–1960* (Cambridge: Cambridge University Press, 1989). For a study of the Presbyterians, see Benton Johnson, "From Old to New Agendas: Presbyterians and Social Issues in the Twentieth Century," in *The Confessional Mosaic*, ed. Milton J. Coalter, John M. Mulder, and Louis B. Weeks (Louisville: Westminster/John Knox Press, 1990), 208–35.

8. Much has been written on the youthful defections from the mainline churches especially. See Dean R. Hoge and David A. Roozen, eds., *Understanding Church Growth and Decline, 1950–1978* (New York: Pilgrim Press, 1979); Wade Clark Roof and William McKinney, *American Mainline Religion: Its Changing Shape and Future* (New Brunswick: Rutgers University Press, 1987); and Dean R. Hoge, Benton Johnson, and Donald A. Luidens, *Vanishing Boundaries: The Religion of Mainline Protestant Baby Boomers* (Louisville: Westminster/John Knox Press, 1994).

9. *Composite Sample*, 1983–1994, General Social Surveys (University of Chicago: National Opinion Research Center).

10. This index is reported in *Religion in America—Approaching the Year 2000* (Princeton: Princeton Religion Research Center, 1990).

11. See David A. Roozen, "Denominations Grow as Individuals Join Congregations," in *Church and Denominational Growth*, ed. David A. Roozen and Kirk Hadaway (Nashville: Abingdon, 1993), 15–35.

12. Ibid., 31.

13. See Gustav Niebuhr, "Is Satan a Real Being? Most Americans Think Not," *The New York Times*, 10 May 1997, 26. His data show that 62 percent of Americans believe that Satan is "not a living being, but is a symbol of evil."

14. The General Social Surveys (Composite Sample) reveals that among pre-Boomers, 68.5 percent affirm the statement as compared to 57.4 percent of Boomers and 57 percent of Busters. See David W. Machacek, "Generation X and Religion: The General Social Survey Data" (unpublished paper, Department of Religious Studies, University of California at Santa Barbara, 1996).

15. There is as well the sheer fact of religious pluralism within higher education, among both students and faculty. According to Andrew M. Greeley, the University of Chicago at the time of Robert Hutchins was said to be "an institution where Baptist money was paid to agnostic professors to teach Roman Catholic philosophy to Jewish students." See Andrew Greeley, *The Denominational Society: A Sociological Approach to Religion in America* (Glenview: Scott Foresman, 1972),

232. For an analysis of the impact of higher education on Christian faith, written from a theologically conservative perspective, see George M. Marsden, *The Soul of the American University: From Protestant Establishment to Established Nonbelief* (New York: Oxford University Press, 1994).

16. Major critiques include Peter L. Berger, *The Noise of Solemn Assemblies: Christian Commitment and the Religious Establishment in America* (Garden City: Doubleday, 1961); Gibson Winter, *The Suburban Captivity of the Churches: An Analysis of Protestant Responsibility in the Expanding Metropolis* (Garden City: Doubleday, 1961); Will Herberg, *Protestant, Catholic, Jew* (Garden City: Anchor Books, 1955, 2nd ed., 1960). Those writing on the Death-of-God include Gabriel Vahanian, *The Death of God: The Culture of our Post-Christian Era* (New York: George Braziller, 1961); Thomas J. J. Altizer, *The Gospel of Christian Atheism* (Philadelphia: Westminster Press, 1966); and Paul M. Van Buren, *The Secular Meaning of the Gospel* (New York: Macmillan, 1963).

17. James Hudnut-Beumler, *Looking for God in the Suburbs: The Religion of the American Dream and Its Critics, 1945–1965* (New Brunswick: Rutgers University Press, 1994), 207.

18. Ronald Inglehart, *Culture Shift in Advanced Industrial Society* (Princeton: Princeton University Press, 1990), 211. See also Paul R. Abramson and Ronald Inglehart, *Value Change in Global Perspective* (Ann Arbor: University of Michigan Press, 1995). Inglehart's argument rests on Maslow's "hierarchy of needs" principle that youth reared in a time when physical and economic needs were largely met are now governed by more personal and expressive needs.

19. Gail Sheehy, *New Passages: Mapping Your Life across Time* (New York: Random House, 1995), 58.

20. I am indebted to Catherine L. Albanese for this definitional framework. She uses ideas drawn from Joachim Wach and Charles Long. See her *America: Religions and Religion* (Belmont, CA: Wadsworth, 1992), 6–9.

21. Peter L. Berger, *The Sacred Canopy* (Garden City: Doubleday, 1967), 111.

22. Jürgen Habermas, *The Theory of Communicative Action*, vol. 2 (Boston: Beacon Press, 1987), 345–47.

23. Sharon Parks, *The Critical Years* (San Francisco: Harper San Francisco, 1986), 12.

24. Georg Simmel, *Essays on Religion*, trans. and ed. Horst Jurgen Helle in collaboration with Ludwig Nieder (New Haven: Yale University Press, 1997), 10.

25. John Murray Cuddihy, *The Ordeal of Civility: Freud, Marx, Levi-Strauss, and the Jewish Struggle with Modernity* (New York: Basic Books, 1974), 10.

26. A good review of the 1950s is found in James Hudnut-Beumer, *Looking for God in the Suburbs* (New Brunswick: Rutgers University Press, 1994), 1–174.

27. William Atwood, "How America Feels," *Look*, 5 January 1960, 12.

28. Robert Wuthnow, *The Restructuring of American Religion* (Princeton: Princeton University Press), 55.

29. See N. J. Demerath III, "Cultural Victory and Organizational Defeat in the Paradoxical Decline of Liberal Protestantism," *Journal for the Scientific Study of Religion* 34 (December 1995): 458–69.

30. David F. Wells, *God in the Wasteland: The Reality of Truth in a World of Fading Dreams* (Grand Rapids: William B. Eerdmans, 1994), 88–117.

31. This is Loren Baritz's term from his book *The Good Life: The Meaning of Success for the American Middle Class* (New York: Alfred A. Knopf, 1988), 301.

32. Robert Wuthnow, *Meaning and Moral Order* (Berkeley: University of California Press, 1987), 201. I am indebted to Wuthnow for his insights about individuality as a modern theme.

33. Robert Jay Lifton, *The Protean Self* (New York: Basic Books, 1993).

34. See Charles Taylor, *Multiculturalism and "The Politics of Recognition"* (Princeton: Princeton University Press, 1992), 28. As Taylor points out, this conception of the self first emerges at the end of the eighteenth century, emphasizing that understanding of right and wrong is anchored in our feelings. Also see his *Sources of the Self* (Cambridge: Harvard University Press, 1989).

35. Landon Y. Jones, *Great Expectations: America and the Baby Boom Generation* (New York: Ballantine Books, 1980), 51–52.

36. Reported in Stewart M. Hoover, "Religion in the Media Age," *Perspectives*, June/July 1995, 17–18.

37. Much press attention was given to this event. As an example, see Diane Balay, "'Sophia' Worship Rocks United Methodists," *United Methodist Reporter*, 14 January 1995.

38. In an interview with actors appearing on the popular television series *Touched by an Angel*, Della Reese responds to a question about how God is represented on the show—as the God of Christians, Jews, Muslims—as follows: "We don't talk about that. We talk about a Supreme Being, who loves us all. Religion is a man-made thing. We deal in spirituality. That's a God thing." Roma Downy comments: "This is not a religious show; this is a spiritual show. Anybody who has ever been on any kind of spiritual journey knows there is a very distinct difference." See Daniel Howard Cerone, "Angels and Insights," *TV Guide*, 29 March–4 April 1997, 45.

39. The term is adapted from Richard A. Peterson's "cultural omnivores" discussed in his "Understanding Audience Segmentation: From Elite and Mass to Omnivore and Univore," *Poetics* 21: 243–58.

40. Catherine Albanese, "From New Thought to New Vision: The Shamanic Paradigm in Contemporary Spirituality," in *Communication and Change in American Religious History*, ed. L. Sweet (Grand Rapids, Eerdmans, 1993), 335–54.

41. Stewart M. Hoover's research is very helpful in understanding these processes. See his "Media and the Construction of the Religious Public Sphere," in *Rethinking Media, Religion, and Culture*, ed. Steward M. Hoover and Knut Lundby (Thousand Oaks: Sage Publications, 1997), 283–97.

42. See Gustav Niebuhr's piece on film and religion "A Question About God? Just Hand it to the Usher," *The New York Times*, 1 September 1996, 16. Also see Margaret R. Miles, *Seeing and Believing: Religion and Values in the Movies* (Boston: Beacon Press, 1996).

43. The affinity between the Internet and process theology emphasizing an evolving Deity and human species is advanced in *Time* magazine's cover story by Joshua Cooper Ramo Chama, "Finding God on the Web," 16 December 1996, 60–67.

44. See chapter 9 of Steward M. Hoover's, *Mass Media Religion: The Social Sources of the Electronic Church*, (Newbury Park: Sage Publications, 1988).

45. See Robert Cummings Neville, *The Truth of Broken Symbols* (Albany: State University of New York Press, 1996).

46. Roger Friedland and Deidre Boden, *NowHere: Space, Time and Modernity* (Berkeley: University of California Press, 1994), 3.

47. See chapter 1 of Anthony Giddins, *The Consequences of Modernity* (Stanford: Stanford University Press, 1990).

48. Ibid., 79–100.

49. William E. Paden, *Interpreting the Sacred: Ways of Viewing Religion* (Boston: Beacon Press, 1992), 3. The term "reflexive" is taken from Anthony Giddens, *The Consequences of Modernity*. See also Ulrich Beck, Anthony Giddens, and Scott Lash, *Reflexive Modernization: Politics, Tradition and Aesthetics in the Modern Social Order* (Stanford: Stanford University Press, 1994).

50. See Richard M. Zaner, *The Context of Self: A Phenomenological Inquiry Using Medicine as a Clue* (Athens: Ohio University Press, 1981). Also see William E. Paden, *Interpreting the Sacred*, 3–5. Here Paden briefly discusses the importance of interpretive "frames" in thinking about religion in the contemporary world.

CHAPTER 3

SPIRITUAL MARKETPLACE

1. Frances Fitzgerald, *Cities on a Hill* (New York: Simon and Schuster, 1981), 390. Her general thesis is put forth in the last chapter, which is entitled "Starting Over."

2. James Clifford, *The Predicament of Culture: Twentieth-Century Ethnography, Literature, and Art* (Cambridge; Harvard University Press, 1988), 14.

3. Robert Wuthnow, *Producing the Sacred: An Essay on Public Religion* (Urbana: University of Illinois Press, 1994), 3.

4. Pierre Bourdieu's concept of "social field" is found in many of his writings. See especially his *Distinction: A Social Critique of the Judgment of Taste* (Cambridge: Harvard University Press, 1984).

5. Wendy Griswold speaks of a "cultural diamond" involving these four components. See her *Cultures and Societies in a Changing World* (Thousand Oaks, CA: Pine Forge Press, 1994). For related discussion on "production of culture," see Robert Wuthnow, *Producing the Sacred: An Essay on Public Religion* (Urbana: University of Illinois Press, 1994). This approach overlaps but is conceptually different from economic market analyses of supply and demand, sometimes described as "supply-side thinking," as proposed by Roger Finke and Rodney Stark, *The Churching of America. 1776–1990* (New Brunswick: Rutgers University Press, 1992) and in Roger Finke and Laurence R. Iannaccone, "Supply-Side Explanations for Religious Change," *Annals of the American Academy of Political and Social Science*, 527 (May 1993): 27–39. In particular, more attention is given to symbolic construction in society including but not limited to that of religious organizations.

6. The distinction is not altogether obvious even in James's thought. James writes about religion as if it were purely personal, but when he describes religious experiences, he draws heavily on accounts of major figures who have been influenced by communal traditions.

7. Anthony Giddens, *The Transformation of Intimacy: Sexuality, Love, and Eroticism in Modern Societies* (Stanford: Stanford University Press, 1992), 30.

8. Harold Bloom, *The American Religion: The Emergence of the Post-Christian Nation* (New York: Simon and Schuster, 1992), 17. Interesting in this respect are the survey results of a Republican Party polling organization that routinely questions, "Has something happened in your life that has caused a recommitment to Christ?" Forty-three percent of this already highly Evangelical Christian population report a recommitment to Christ in its latest survey. See Christopher Caldwell, "The Southern Captivity of the GOP," *The Atlantic Monthly* (June 1998): 64.

9. Robert S. Ellwood, *The Fifties Spiritual Marketplace: American Religion in a Decade of Conflict* (New Brunswick: Rutgers University Press, 1997), 12.

10. See Martin E. Marty, "The Spirit's Holy Errand: The Search for a Spiritual Style in Secular America," *Daedalus* 96 (Winter 1967): 99–115. Here Marty offers his own trenchant analysis of the religious situation at the time, quoting Tillich as a commentator on religion and culture.

11. The notion of "religious capital" or "cultural capital" is Pierre Bourdieu's. See his *Distinction: A Social Critique of the Judgment of Taste*, trans. Richard Nice (Cambridge: Harvard University Press, 1984); for an excellent exposition of this term, see David Swartz, "Bridging the Study of Culture and Religion: Pierre Bourdieu's Political Economy of Symbolic Power," *Sociology of Religion* 57 (Spring 1996): 71–85.

12. See various writings of Pierre Bourdieu, but most especially his "Genesis and Structure of the Religious Field," originally published in *Revue française de sociologie* 12 (July-September): 294-334. He uses "social field" in the general sense in analyzing society, and "religious field" as one type of social field.

13. R. Marie Griffith, "The Promised Land of Weight Loss: Law and Gospel in Christian Dieting," *Christian Century* 114, 7 May 1997, 452.

14. Ibid., 453.

15. For a discussion about Alpha courses, increasingly popular in churches, see Tom Verde, "Crash Course in Christianity Is Winning Over Churches and the Wayward," in *The New York Times*, 27 December 1998, A20. It is said that "through a combination of humorous anecdotes, personal reflections and passages from many theological sources—from the Scriptures to C. S. Lewis to Charlie Brown," questions are raised about life and its meaning.

16. Web pages are filled with themes of this kind, such as the one I ran across surfing the Internet that uses a quote from General Colin Powell, "You can be anything you want to be," followed by the injunction "Explore Your Potential" that was posted by the Episcopal Church in the Houston area (Website: http://www.epicenter.org).

17. *Sojourners* is a magazine on the Evangelical left that had done a great deal to address contemporary social problems from a Christian perspective. See as well the book by the editor of *Sojourners*, Jim Wallis, *The Soul of Politics* (New York: Orbis Books, 1994).

18. The term belongs to Steven Seidman, *Contested Knowledge: Social Theory in the Postmodern Era* (Cambridge, Mass.: Blackwell, 1994). I am indebted to Michele Dillon for the use of the term and application to Catholics. See her "Rome and

American Catholics," *Annals for the Academy of Political and Social Science* 55 (July 1998): 122–34.

19. Dillon, 132. On the basis of the Catholic case, Dillon also observes that the religious economy model advanced by Rodney Stark, Roger Finke, and others may be more Protestant than Catholic, since "it does not allow for the autonomy of 'consumers' to reflexively produce doctrine themselves from within a doctrinally differentiated tradition in ways that fit with their own life contexts." This is an important observation pointing to a limitation of the religious economy model.

20. Women of Faith, an Evangelical Christian movement, for example, is a subsidiary of New Life Clinics, a private company that is the largest Christian counseling chain in the United States. Revenues in 1997, largely from fees and souvenir sales, totaled $6.1 million. See Nadya Labi, "The Female of the Species," *Time*, 13 July 1998, 62–63.

21. Charles Trueheart, "Welcome to the Next Church," *The Atlantic Monthly* (August 1996): 37–52.

22. The Willow Creek Association, originating with the huge Willow Creek Community Church outside of greater Chicago, and Zondervan Press have joined forces in producing resources such as music, drama scripts, novels, curriculum, videos, and the like "to reach seekers and to minister to believers" (reported on 15 April 1998 on the Willow Creek Association Website http://www.willownet.org).

23. Trueheart (above, n. 21): 37–52. Willow Creek Community Church, located in South Barrington, Illinois, is often cited as an example of a "seeker-sensitive" or "seeker-friendly" church with its more than fifteen thousand people showing up on a weekend. Some estimates of the growth in numbers of such churches is found in James L. Kidd, *Megachurch Methods: Church for the Unchurched* (Nashville: Abingdon Press, 1997).

24. Rodney Stark and William Sims Bainbridge distinguish among what they call "audience cults," "client cults," and "cult movements." Audience cults rely especially on the latest technology as a means of disseminating information. Groups workshops are an example of a client cult. See chapter 10 of their book, *The Future of Religion* (Berkeley: University of California Press, 1985). For a good case study of channeling as a client cult, see Michael F. Brown, *The Channeling Zone* (Cambridge; Harvard University Press, 1997).

25. Malise Ruthven, *The Divine Supermarket: Shopping for God in America* (New York: William Morrow and Company, 1989).

26. John Renesch, "Spirit and Work: Can Business and Consciousness Co-Exist," in *The New Bottom Line*, ed. John Renesch and Bill DeFoore (San Francisco: Sterling and Stone, 1996), 29. Other essays in this volume are of interest to this topic as well.

27. See Phyllis Tickle, *Rediscovering the Sacred: Spirituality in America* (New York: Crossroads, 1995), 16–19. She reports statistics from the Association of American Publishers showing the sale of books in the Bible/religion/spirituality category up by 59 percent nationally in the period from February 1992 to February 1994. Also, she refers to a Gallup study that projects that the largest sales increase in nonfiction books in the early years of the twenty-first century will be in religion/

spirituality (82 percent growth from 1987 to 2010), followed at 59 percent growth by second-place investment/economic/income tax books. Also see Sandra Dallas, "Onward Christian Publishers," *Business Week*, 31 July 1995, 44. She reports annual revenues of approximately $3 billion, up from about $1 billion in 1980.

28. Phyllis A. Tickle, *God-Talk in America* (New York: The Crossroad Publishing Company, 1997), 33.

29. Ibid., 36.

30. In December 1997 *Self* magazine brought out a Special Inspirational Issue entitled "Your Spiritual Life." It carried articles on meditation, fasting, Buddhism for beginners, the Ten Commandments, and even a spiritual inventory for people to administer to themselves.

31. See Nicholas Dawidoff, "No Sex. No Drugs. But Rock 'N' Roll (Kind of)," *The New York Times Magazine*, 5 February 1995, 40–44, 66–72. According to Dawidoff, Christian music is the fastest-growing form of popular music, grossing $750 million a year. For a history of the role of music in revivalistic Christianity, see Charles E. Fromm, "New Song: The Sound of Spiritual Awakening," paper presented at the Oxford Reading and Research Conference, Oxford, England, July 1983.

32. Tickle, *Rediscovering the Sacred*, 39. Tickle's categorization of books is based on sales over a three- to four-year period prior to the publication of her book.

33. Ibid., 48. Interestingly, the Evangelical book publishers now produce novels dealing with sex themes in two general categories, a mild version in "romance" novels and a heavier version in "temptations." As one critic observes, you can usually tell the difference between the two depending on which chapter contains the sex scenes, either chapter two or around chapter eight. See Hanna Rosin's commentary on Christian novels, "Books of Virtue," *The New Republic*, 24 November 1997, 12–13.

34. Jack Canfield and Mark Victor Hansen have sold over 14 million "Chicken Soup" books, beginning with *Chicken Soup for the Soul: 101 Stories to Open the Heart and Rekindle the Spirit* and followed by titles such as *Chicken Soup for the Surviving Soul, Chicken Soup for the Soul at Work, Chicken Soup for the Soul Cookbook, Chicken Soup for the Teenage Soul,* and four to seven more such books scheduled to come. Reported in Linton Weeks, "Ever-Hungry Readers Enjoy a Steady Diet of 'Chicken Soup,'" *Los Angeles Times*, 29 June 1997, E3.

35. Robert Wuthnow is somewhat negative, certainly ambivalent, in what he sees happening to the conception of the sacred within the small-group movement in the United States. See his volume *Sharing the Journey: Support Groups and America's New Quest for Community* (New York: Free Press, 1994). On panentheism see David Ray Griffith, *God and Religion in the Postmodern World* (Albany: State University of New York Press, 1989) and Marcus J. Borg, *The God We Never Knew: Beyond Dogmatic Religion to a More Authentic Contemporary Faith* (San Francisco: HarperSanFrancisco, 1997).

36. This is based on a content analysis of articles in *Christianity Today* and *The Christian Century* from 1970 to 1995. Earlier publications examined were *The Christian Century* (1920–50), *Methodist Review* (1920–31), and *Presbyterian Advance* (1920–34).

37. It is reported that approximately twelve thousand such messages come in daily. "Focus does not just answer mail," one writer says, "it maintains relationships." See *U.S. News and World Report,* 4 May 1998, 23.

38. In this discussion on Lazaris, I rely on the observations of Elijah Siegler, "Marketing Lazaris: A Rational-Choice Theory of Channeling" (M.A. thesis, University of California at Santa Barbara, 1998).

39. Judith Plaskow, "Jewish Memory from a Feminist Perspective," in *Weaving the Visions,* ed. Judith Plaskow and Carol Christ (San Francisco: Harper and Row, 1989), 46.

40. William H. Becker, "Spiritual Struggle in Contemporary America," *Theology Today* 51 (1994): 259.

41. Emile Durkheim, of course, located the constitutive experiences of the sacred within the social realm. For a more recent phenomenological analysis linking the self and the sacred by means of such bodily experiences, see Thomas J. Csordas, *The Sacred Self: A Cultural Phenomenology of Charismatic Healing* (Berkeley: University of California Press, 1994).

42. As Anthony Giddens puts it, "What an individual eats, even among the more materially deprived, becomes a reflexively infused question of dietary selection." See his discussion in *The Transformation of Intimacy: Sexuality, Love, and Eroticism in Modern Societies* (Stanford: Stanford University Press, 1992), 31–32.

43. With the "Weigh Down Diet" alone, it is reported that today there are 10,000 workshops with a quarter of a million participants who meet in the churches across the country. The very first workshop was held in a Memphis mall. Another program started in Houston, First Place, is now in ten thousand churches and estimated to be growing at 20 percent a year. The Hallelujah diet reports a circulation of sixty thousand. See Anna Mulrine, "A Godly Approach to Weight Loss," *U.S. News and World Report,* 5 May 1997.

44. Meredith McGuire (with the assistance of Debra Kantor), *Ritual Healing in Suburban America* (New Brunswick: Rutgers University Press, 1988), 244. I draw also here from Csordas's excellent study of charismatic healing, *The Sacred Self.*

45. Pierre Bourdieu, *Outline of a Theory of Practice,* trans. Richard Nice (Cambridge: Cambridge University Press, 1977), 124.

46. Frances Fitzgerald, *Cities on a Hill.* Also see my article "The Church in the Centrifuge," *The Christian Century,* 8 November 1989, 1013–14.

47. Anthony Giddens, *Modernity and Self-Identity* (Stanford: Stanford University Press, 1991), 210–31.

48. Wade Clark Roof and William McKinney, *Mainline American Religion: Its Changing Shape and Future* (New Brunswick: Rutgers University Press, 1987).

49. Marsha G. Witten, *All Is Forgiven* (Princeton: Princeton University Press, 1993), 30.

CHAPTER 4

ON BEING FLUID AND GROUNDED

1. *Time* magazine, 5 April 1993, cover story by Richard N. Ostling, "The Church Search," 45.

2. See Peter Collier and David Horowitz, *Destructive Generation: Second Thoughts about the Sixties* (New York: Summit Books, 1989). They see the rise of the post-

Vietnam New Left as inspired, in part, by liberal preachers like William Sloan Coffin who, they write, "infuse[d] Christianity with a 'liberation theology,' which postulated a Marxist God who had enjoined the faithful to establish a Communist heaven on earth through 'solidarity' with revolutionary movements." (151)

3. *Emerging Trends*, vol. 16, no. 2 (Princeton: Princeton Religious Research Center, February, 1994), 2.

4. Robert S. Ellwood, *The Sixties Spiritual Awakening* (New Brunswick: Rutgers University Press, 1994), 335.

5. Dan Wakefield, *Returning: A Spiritual Journey* (New York: Doubleday, 1988).

6. See David Roozen, William McKinney, and Wayne Thompson, "The 'Big Chill' Generation Warms to Worship: A Research Note," *Review of Religious Research* 31 (March 1990): 314–22. Also see the research described in David A. Roozen, Jackson W. Carroll, and Wade Clark Roof, "Fifty Years of Religious Change in the United States," in *The Post-War Generation and Establishment Religion,* ed. Wade Clark Roof (Boulder: Westview Press, 1995), 74–77.

7. Wade Clark Roof and Sr. Mary Johnson, "Baby Boomers and the Return to the Churches," in David A. Roozen and C. Kirk Hadaway, eds., *Church and Denominational Growth* (Nashville: Abingdon Press, 1993), 310.

8. George Barna's polls on Evangelical Christians show similar results. See John Dart's article on these data, "Survey Finds Drop in Evangelicals' Ranks for 2nd Year," *Los Angeles Times*, 13 August 1994, B4. He finds striking shifts within this conservative sector in this same direction.

9. Americans generally move in and out of religious organizations. But based on David A. Roozen's extensive analysis of the patterns of defection and re-entry, there appears to have been a significant increase in this movement beginning in the 1960s. See his "Church Dropouts: Changing Patterns of Disengagement and Re-Entry," *Review of Religious Research* 21 (Supplement 1980): 427–50.

10. C. Kirk Hadaway and Penny Long Marler advance this argument citing data from the Archdiocese of San Francisco. The archdiocese has kept records on Mass attendance since 1961 which show substantial declines, despite surveys in 1972 and 1996 reporting a stable proportion of Catholics saying they have attended Mass. See their article "Did You Really Go to Church This Week? Behind the Poll Data," *The Christian Century*, 6 May 1998, 472–75.

11. See John P. Hoffmann, "Confidence in Religious Institutions and Secularization: Trends and Implications," *Review of Religious Research* 39 (June 1998): 321–43. Analyzing General Social Survey data for the period 1974–94, he shows declining confidence in religious institutions particularly for younger cohorts and an increasing gap in confidence between the religiously active and the nonactive. Barna's data reported in note 8 above plus Gallup's finding of an overall decline in religious attendance in 1997 are consistent with my general conclusion.

12. Langdon Gilkey, "The Christian Congregation as a Religious Community," in *American Congregations*, ed. James P. Wind and James W. Lewis, *New Perspectives in the Study of Congregations*, vol. 2 (Chicago: University of Chicago Press), 128. For an extended discussion on the problems facing these churches, see Robert Wuthnow, *The Crisis in the Churches: Spiritual Malaise, Fiscal Woe* (Oxford: Oxford University Press, 1997).

13. See Michael Hout and Andrew M. Greeley, "The Center Doesn't Hold:

Church Attendance in the United States, 1940–1984," *American Sociological Review* 52 (1987): 325–45.

14. The term is Andrew M. Greeley's. See his article "American Catholics: Going Their Own Way," *The New York Times Magazine*, 10 October 1982, 28–29, 34–38, 68–76.

15. The groups mentioned most frequently by our respondents were very similar to those that Barry A. Kosman and Seymour P. Lachman report as "other religions" in their huge survey of 113,000 people in 1990. See their *One Nation under God: Religion in Contemporary American Society* (New York: Crown Trade Paperbacks, 1993), 15–17.

16. "Invented tradition" is Eric Hobsbawm's term. He observes that traditions that appear to be old sometimes are rather recent in origin. Christian Fundamentalism as we know it, for example, emerged in the early decades of the twentieth century. See his "Introduction: Inventing Traditions" in Hobsbawm and T. Ranger, *The Invention of Tradition* (Cambridge: Cambridge University Press, 1983).

17. C. Kirk Hadaway and Penny Long Marler, "All in the Family: Religious Mobility in America," *Review of Religious Research* 35 (December 1993): 104. The point is relevant considering that the "Nones" as a category of people tend to be unstable, a population often recruited to religious faiths.

18. Robert Wuthnow, *Sharing the Journey: Support Groups and America's New Quest for Community* (New York: Free Press, 1994), 45. Wuthnow finds in his national survey 40 percent of Americans involved in some type of small group.

19. Robert Wuthnow, *Poor Richard's Principle: Recovering the American Dream through the Moral Dimension of Work, Business, and Money* (Princeton: Princeton University Press, 1996), 312. Wuthnow cites data from an "Economic Values" survey finding that 75 percent of the workforce fails to see any connection between religious values and their work. Two-thirds of them, however, believe "God wants me to have the kind of job that will make me happy."

20. The rise of the "neo-Evangelical" movement is often dated with the founding of the National Association of Evangelicals in 1942. In Chapter 6 there is further discussion of this movement and its importance for shaping a more accommodating religious style.

21. Mark Shibley's research on Evangelicalism is insightful here. Based on analysis of data from the General Social Surveys, Shibley finds that "personal need" indicators better explain Evangelical affiliation than do the more customary socio-economic variables looked at in social research since the time of H. Richard Niebuhr. The latter's classic *Social Sources of Denominationalism* (New York: Meridian, 1965), first published in 1929, shaped sociological perspective on sectarian Protestant movements.

22. See James Davison Hunter, *Evangelicalism: The Coming Generation* (Chicago: University of Chicago Press, 1987), 50–75.

23. David F. Wells, *God in the Wasteland: The Realities of Truth in a World of Fading Dreams* (Grand Rapids: William B. Eerdmans, 1994), 90.

24. Philip Cushman, *Constructing the Self, Constructing America* (Reading: Addison-Wesley, 1995), 78.

25. Ibid., 79.

26. See "Religion in America, 50 Years: 1935–1985," *The Gallup Report*, No. 236 (May 1985), 1–57. The General Social Surveys show a modest decline in church-related activities in the period when these annual surveys began in 1972. The Barna Research Group Ltd. of Glendale, California, shows striking declines in religious involvement, year by year in the more recent period of the 1990s. See Larry B. Stammer, "Church Attendance Falls to 11-Year Low," *Los Angeles Times*, 2 March 1996, B4.

27. Robert Jay Lifton, *The Protean Self: Human Resilience in an Age of Fragmentation* (New York: Basic Books, 1993), 9.

28. For a recent theoretical statement, see Glen H. Elder Jr., "The Life Course as Developmental Theory," *Child Development* 69 (February 1998): 1–12. Elaborations of such turning points in people's lives are well documented in John Clausen, *American Lives: Looking Back at the Children of the Great Depression* (New York: Free Press, 1993).

29. On the tendency for Americans to create "adhesional" faiths combining identity-themes, see Mark Silk, *Spiritual Politics: Religion and America since World War II* (New York: Simon and Schuster, 1988).

30. Mary Catherine Bateson, *Composing a Life* (New York: Atlantic Monthly Press, 1989), 2–3.

31. Lifton, *The Protean Self* (above, n. 27), 94. On simultaneously affirming yet distancing oneself from faith as a feature of Generation X spirituality, see Tom Beaudoin, *Virtual Faith: The Irreverent Spiritual Quest of Generation X* (San Francisco: Jossepy-Bass, 1998), 129–42.

32. Penny Long Marler and David A. Roozen, "From Church Tradition to Consumer Choice: The Gallup Surveys of the Unchurched American," in David A. Roozen and C. Kirk Hadaway, eds., *Church and Denominational Growth* (Nashville: Abingdon Press, 1993), 266. For a more general discussion of cultural trends, see Joseph Veroff, Elizabeth Douvan, and Richard Kulka, *The Inner American: A Self-Portrait from 1957–1976* (New York: Basic Books, 1981). They argue that three types of changes have occurred in people's coping styles: 1) the diminishing of role standards as the basis for defining adjustment; 2) the increased focus on self-expressiveness and self-direction in social life; and, 3) a shift in concern from social organizational integration to interpersonal intimacy.

33. Robert N. Bellah et al., *Habits of the Heart: Individualism and Commitment in American Life* (Berkeley: University of California Press, 1985), 235.

34. Robert N. Bellah, *Beyond Belief: Essays on Religion in a Post-Traditional World* (New York: Harper and Row, 1970), 42.

35. Reginald W. Bibby, *Unknown Gods: The Ongoing Story of Religion in Canada* (Toronto: Stoddart, 1993), 152–68.

36. Psychologist Paul Pruyser uses the term *playful* to refer to the capacity to extend the imagination, to place one self within what he called the "illusionistic" world of the mythical and the metaphorical. This discussion is found in his book *A Dynamic Psychology of Religion* (New York: Harper and Row, 1976), 189–91.

37. Reginald W. Bibby, *Fragmented Gods: The Poverty and Potential of Religion in Canada* (Toronto: Irvin Publishing, 1987), 62–176.

38. Martin E. Marty, "An Exuberant Adventure: The Academic Study and Teaching of Religion," *Academe* 82 (1996): 17.

39. Richard Quebedeaux, *By What Authority: The Rise of Personality Cults in American Christianity* (San Francisco: Harper and Row, 1982), 80.

40. One good example is Richard Wolman's "PsychoMatrix Spirituality Inventory," consisting of 105 items. Of Wolman, a Harvard Medical School psychologist, it is written: "To avoid quibbling about definitions, he excluded questions about belief, such as 'Do you believe in God?' Instead, his inventory explores actual experience—of a God figure, a Higher Power, or a transcendent energy source; of religious activities, including study and prayer; of trauma and healing; of conscious-living choices such as meditation and yoga; and of contact with other dimensions, including out-of-body and near-death experiences," in Linda Weltner, "In the Spiritual Dimension," *Santa Barbara News-Press*, 16 May 1998, D1.

41. See Robin Marantz Henig, "Medicine's New Age," *Civilization* 4 (April-May, 1997): 42–49 and "Making a Place for Spirituality (Spirituality and Healing)," *Harvard Health Letter* 23 (February, 1998): 1–3.

42. A full-page advertisement of the Pentecostal churches in *USA Today*, 16 May 1997, D carries the following statement: "Computers, fax machines, copiers. They all need power to keep going. What about you? Where do you find the power to keep going? It's time to plug into an inexhaustible supply. Jesus said, 'Ye shall receive power, after that the Holy Ghost is come upon you.' Acts 6: 8. Experience the power of Pentecost. For more information, call 1-888-HOLY GHOST."

43. Thomas J. Csordas, *Language, Charisma, and Creativity: The Ritual Life of a Religious Movement* (Berkeley: University of California Press, 1997), 53.

44. Ernst Troeltsch, *The Social Teachings of the Christian Churches* (London: George Allen and Unwin, 1931), 730.

45. Garrett E. Paul writes about the breadth of Troeltsch's vision: "Troetlsch, at the beginning of the century, was keenly aware of many trends that became apparent to most observers only at its end: the collapse of Euro-centrism; the perceived relativity of all historical events and knowledge (including scientific knowledge); an awareness that Christianity is relative to its Western, largely European history and environment; the emergence of a profoundly global pluralism; the central role of practice in theology; the growing impact of the social sciences on our view of the world and of ourselves; and dramatic changes in the role of religious institutions and religious thought." See his article "Why Troeltsch? Why Today? Theology for the 21st Century," *The Christian Century*, 30 June 1993, 676.

46. Ralph W. Hood, Jr., "Mysticism," in *The Sacred in a Secular Age*, ed. Phillip E. Hammond (Berkeley: University of California Press, 1985), 287.

CHAPTER 5
A QUEST FOR WHAT?

1. *The Unchurched American* (Princeton: Princeton Religious Research Center, 1978), 9.

2. See "The New Rebel Cry: Jesus Is Coming," *Time*, 21 June 1971, 56–63. Ministers in mainline Protestant churches were particularly critical and conde-

scending. Evangelical sympathizers at the time, however, were much more charitable in their view of the movement. Also see Robert F. Berkey, "Jesus and the Jesus People," *The Christian Century*, 22 March 1972, 336–38.

3. Robert N. Bellah et al., *Habits of the Heart: Individualism and Commitment in American Life* (Berkeley: University of California Press, 1985), viii.

4. Other commentators would include Christopher Lasch, *The Culture of Narcissism: American Life in an Age of Diminishing Expectation* (New York: Norton, 1978); Richard Sennett, *The Fall of Public Man: On the Social Psychology of Capitalism* (New York: Vintage, 1976); and Jürgen Habermas, *Legitimation Crisis* (Boston: Beacon Press, 1976).

5. Bellah et. al., *Habits of the Heart*, 236.

6. Actually there was critique from feminist theologians and scholars. See Lauve H. Steenhuisen, "Deconstructing Bellah's 'Sheilaism,'" presented at the annual meeting of the Society for the Scientific Study of Religion in 1993. Also see Mary Field Belenky et al., *Women's Ways of Knowing: The Development of Self, Voice, and Mind* (New York: Basic Books, 1986) and Sherry Ruth Anderson and Patricia Hopkins, *The Feminine Face of God: The Unfolding of the Sacred in Women* (New York: Bantam Books, 1991).

7. Alexis de Tocqueville, *Democracy in America* (New York: Mentor Books, 1956), 155.

8. On the "second disestablishment" of the 1920s, see Robert T. Handy, *A Christian America*, 2nd ed. (New York: Oxford University Press, 1984). William McKinney and I proposed a "third disestablishment" thesis in *American Mainline Religion: Its Changing Shape and Future* (New Brunswick: Rutgers University Press, 1987), 33–39. Phillip E. Hammond addresses a similar thesis in his *Religion and Personal Autonomy: The Third Disestablishment* (Columbia: University of South Carolina Press, 1992).

9. Hammond, *Religion and Personal Autonomy*, 169.

10. Robert Wuthnow's contributions are voluminous. Major books bearing on these specific themes would be his *Acts of Compassion: Caring for Others and Helping Ourselves* (Princeton: Princeton University Press, 1991); *Christianity in the 21st Century: Reflections on the Challenges Ahead* (Oxford: Oxford University Press, 1993); *Sharing the Journey: Support Groups and America's New Quest for Community* (New York: Free Press, 1994); and *Poor Richard's Principle: Recovering the American Dream through the Moral Dimension of Work, Business, and Money* (Princeton: Princeton University Press, 1996).

11. The word *bumptious* is used by Jon Butler. See his *Awash in a Sea of Faith: Christianizing the American People* (Cambridge: Harvard University Press, 1990), 1.

12. Nathan O. Hatch, *The Democratization of American Christianity* (New Haven: Yale University Press), 1989.

13. Much research has been carried out on religious switching. Estimates vary from 20 percent to a third of Americans who switch denominations or faith communities. For a recent summary and interpretation, see Wade Clark Roof and J. Shawn Landres, "Defection, Disengagement and Dissent: The Dynamics of Religious Change in the United States," in *Religion and the Social Order*, ed. Mordichai Bar-Lev and William Shaffir (Greenwich: JAI Press Inc., 1997), 77–95.

14. Albert T. Rasmussen, "Contemporary Religious Appeals and Who Re-

sponds," in *Religion and the Face of America*, ed. Jane C. Zahn (Berkeley: University Extension, 1958), 4.

15. See Catherine L. Albanese, "Religion and the American Experience: A Century After," *Church History* 57 (September 1988): 337–51. Albanese also points out differences, particularly the expansiveness of New Age religion as contrasted with the more contractive quality of Evangelical-Fundamentalist faith.

16. Harold Bloom, *The American Religion: The Emergence of the Post-Christian Nation* (New York: Simon and Schuster, 1992).

17. Catherine L. Albanese, *America: Religion and Religions*, 2nd ed. (Belmont, California: Wadsworth Publishing Company, 1992), 422.

18. Barry A. Kosmin and Seymour P. Lachman, *One Nation under God: Religion in Contemporary American Society* (New York: Crown, 1993), 1.

19. Peter Clecak, *America's Quest for the Ideal Self* (New York: Oxford University Press, 1983), 10.

20. See Roland A. Delattre, "Supply-Side Spirituality: A Case Study in the Cultural Interpretation of Religious Ethics in America," in *Religion and the Life of the Nation*, ed. Rowland A. Sherrill (Urbana: University of Illinois Press, 1990), 84–108. Delattre charts the connections between spiritual supply and the material expectations of Americans as well.

21. See Penny Long Marler and David A. Roozen, "From Church Tradition to Consumer Choice: The Gallup Surveys of the Unchurched American," in *Church and Denominational Growth*, ed. David A. Roozen and C. Kirk Hadaway (Nashville: Abingdon Press, 1993), 253–77.

22. Ibid.

23. Stephen Warner, "Change and Continuity in the U.S. Religious System," Lecture at Princeton Theological Seminary, 6 February 1989.

24. Similar results from a survey hold, according to Robert Wuthnow, in the relation between individualism and altruism. He reports a slight positive correlation between self-oriented values and placing importance on charitable activities. See his *Acts of Compassion: Caring for Others and Helping Ourselves* (Princeton: Princeton University Press, 1991), 22.

25. Allison Stokes, "'Re-Imagining' and Women's Spiritual Support Groups: Their Challenge to the Church" (unpublished paper).

26. Robert Wuthnow, *Acts of Compassion*, 292.

27. See Michael J. Piore, *Beyond Individualism* (Cambridge: Harvard University Press, 1995), 9–28.

28. Daniel V. A. Olson, "Fellowship Ties and the Transmission of Religious Identity," in *Beyond Establishment: Protestant Identity in a Post-Protestant Age*, ed. Jackson Carroll and Wade Clark Roof (Louisville: Westminster/John Knox Press, 1993), 35. Olson speaks of a subcultural model of modernization as follows: "The very forces of modernization that disrupt the homogeneity of the preindustrial community simultaneously give moderns greater control over the construction of their personal networks, control that can be used to rebuild networks of shared identity. The difference between contemporary subcultures and the preindustrial community lies in the greater freedom of moderns to choose which elements of their identity they will emphasize in the construction of their personal networks and the degree of their involvement in sub-cultures based on

those identities. Moderns are freer to shape their personal networks and thus their own identity" (36).

29. Robert Wuthnow, *Sharing the Journey* (above, n. 10), 31–58.

30. I am indebted to Daniele Hervieu-Leger and insights from her paper "Modernity and Spirituality," presented at the Consultation on Spirituality at the University of California at Santa Barbara, March 6–8, 1998.

31. Alasdair MacIntyre, *After Virtue: A Study in Moral Theory*, 2nd ed. (Notre Dame: University of Notre Dame Press, 1984), 219.

32. Ibid., 221.

33. Robert Bellah et.al., *Habits of the Heart* (above, n. 3), 20–26.

34. The term *speech-act* is associated especially with Jürgen Habermas's theory of communication. For an insightful adaptation and extension of the work of Habermas with an emphasis on the transformative force of narrative constructions in women's lives, see Maria Pia Lara, *Moral Textures: Feminist Narratives in the Public Sphere* (Cambridge: Polity Press, 1998).

35. Peter L. Berger, *The Heretical Imperative* (New York: Doubleday, 1979).

36. Alasdair MacIntyre, *After Virtue: A Study in Moral Theory*, 223, 222.

37. Dorothy C. Bass, "Congregations and the Bearing of Traditions," in *American Congregations: New Perspectives in the Study of Congregations*, vol. 2, ed. James P. Wind and James W. Lewis (Chicago: University of Chicago Press, 1994), 185.

38. Robert M. Torrance, *The Spiritual Quest: Transcendence in Myth, Religion, and Science* (Berkeley: University of California Press, 1994), 4.

39. Andrew M. Greeley, *Religious Change in America* (Cambridge: Harvard University Press, 1989), 95.

40. See Marsha G. Witten, *All Is Forgiven: The Secular Message in American Protestantism* (Princeton: Princeton University Press, 1993), 29.

41. The notion of culture as a "toolbox" is advanced by many prominent social scientists. See especially Ann Swidler, "Culture in Action: Symbols and Strategies," *American Sociological Review* 51 (April 1986): 273–86.

42. Steward M. Hoover provides an interesting account of a guided tour through the Willow Creek Community Church near Chicago. His description is as follows: "As a group of visitors is ushered into the auditorium, one of the tour guides asks 'What don't you see here?' After someone responds that there is 'no cross,' he goes on to say: 'Right, there are no Christian symbols. We do have a cross. When we do baptism, we have a cross here. . . . The last time we had baptism, we had the people write their sins on pieces of paper. . . . And then they pinned them on the cross. All my life I have had a hard time understanding the redemptive power of the cross, but in that moment, I said "Yes, I get it . . ." I mean, to see that cross just covered with realms of paper . . .' And then, the most significant statement of all, from the perspective of contemporary symbolic sensitivities, the tour guide says: 'So, you see we don't have a fixed cross out here. We don't need it here every day or every week. We would say it looks like a "prop" to us.'" See Hoover's unpublished paper, "The Cross at Willow Creek."

43. Paul Heelas, "On Things Not Being Worse, and the Ethic of Humanity," in *Detraditionalization: Critical Reflection on Authority and Identity*, ed. Paul Heelas, Scott Lasch, and Paul Morris (Cambridge: Blackwell Publishers Inc., 1996), 200–222.

44. Ibid., 216.

45. Ibid., 207. Heelas points to "rights which have become inscribed in constitutions and international law," and the activities of bodies like the Red Cross, the International Labour Organization, and the United Nations.

46. Other research supports this conclusion. Brian Zinnbauer et al., in a content analysis of the definitions given for the words *spirituality* and *religiousness*, find statistically significant differences. They write: "Descriptively, definitions of spirituality most often included references to connection or relationship with a Higher Power of some kind, belief or faith in a Higher Power of some kind, or integrating one's values and beliefs with one's behavior in daily life. As with definitions of spirituality, definitions of religiousness included belief or faith in a Higher Power of some kind and integrating one's values and beliefs with one's behavior in daily life, but they also commonly included references to organized activities such as church attendance and performance of rituals, as well as commitment to organizational or institutional beliefs or dogma" (557). See Brian J. Zinnbauer et al., "Religion and Spirituality: Unfuzzing the Fuzzy," *Journal for the Scientific Study of Religion* 36 (December 1997): 549–64.

47. For the distinction between "cultural-linguistic" and "experiential-expressive" approaches to religion, see George Lindbeck, *The Nature of Doctrine* (Philadelphia: Westminster Press, 1984). Helpful also is chapter 5 of James Gustafson's *Ethics from a Theocentric Perspective*, Theology and Ethics, vol. 1 (Chicago: University of Chicago Press, 1981). For an empirical test, see David Yamane and Megan Polzer, "Ways of Seeing Ecstasy in Modern Society: Experiential-Expressive and Cultural-Linguistic Views," *Sociology of Religion* 55 (Spring 1994): 1–25. Using General Social Survey data, they marshal evidence in support of a cultural-linguistic model for explaining religious experience among Americans.

48. Dorothy Bass, "Congregations and the Bearing of Traditions," 172.

49. "Strategies of action" is Ann Swidler's phrase emphasizing culture as habits, skills, and styles rather than as values or ends toward which action is directed. See her "Culture in Action: Symbols and Strategies," 273–78. The term *habitus* belongs to Pierre Bourdieu, defined by him as "a system of lasting, transposable dispositions which, integrating past experiences, functions at every moment as a matrix of perceptions, and actions and makes possible the achievement of infinitely diversified tasks . . . and an objective event which exerts its action of conditional stimulation calling for or demanding a determinate response . . . on those who are disposed to constitute it as such because they are endowed with a determinate type of dispositions." See his *Outline of a Theory of Practice* (Cambridge: Cambridge University Press, 1977), 82–83.

50. Wilfred Cantwell Smith, *Faith and Belief* (Princeton: Princeton University Press, 1979), 12.

51. Herbert W. Richardson, *Toward an American Theology* (New York: Harper and Row, 1967), 58–70.

52. James A. Beckford has written about "holistic spirituality," and the search for a more unified, experiential perspective. See his "Religion, Modernity, and Post-Modernity," in *Religion: Contemporary Issues*, ed. Bryan Wilson (London: Bellew Publishing, 1992), 11–23. On the tourist, see Zygmunt Bauman, *Life in Fragments: Essays on Postmodern Modernity* (Oxford: Blackwell Publishers, 1995), 95–98.

53. Bernard C. Farr describes the close similarity between searching for a spirituality and becoming a marijuana user, in that both involve engaging in a practice to produce a desired effect and in each instance it is a matter of "becoming" that category of person rather than "being" that kind of person. Drawing off Howard Becker's research on marijuana users, he points to a threefold process: learning a technique to produce the desired effect, learning to perceive its effects, and learning to enjoy the effects. See his "Becoming Spiritual: Learning from Marijuana Users," in *Modern Spiritualities: An Inquiry*, ed. Laurence Brown, Bernard C. Farr, and R. Joseph Hoffman (Oxford: Prometheus Books, 1997), 179–94.

54. Daniele Hervieu-Leger, "Modernity, Secularization, and Religious Memory in Western Europe" (unpublished paper), 17.

55. Mihaly Csikszentmihalyi, *Flow: The Psychology of Optimal Experience* (New York: Harper and Row, 1990).

CHAPTER 6
REDRAWING THE BOUNDARIES

1. Martin E. Marty, *A Nation of Behavers* (Chicago: University of Chicago Press, 1976), 18–19. The discussion here draws heavily on his insights into the role of those doing the mapping.

2. The term comes from Dean R. Hoge, Benton Johnson, and Donald A. Luidens, *Vanishing Boundaries: The Religion of Mainline Protestant Baby Boomers* (Louisville: Westminster/John Knox Press, 1994), 120–21.

3. See Christian Smith et al., *American Evangelicalism: Embattled and Thriving* (Chicago: University of Chicago Press, 1998), 117–19.

4. The notion of a "socio-religious" group comes from Gerhard Lenski, *The Religious Factor* (Garden City, N.Y.: Doubleday, 1961), 18–24. A good example of what Lenski had in mind is Michael Novak's description of American Catholics: "To be a Catholic is not so much to belong to an organization as to belong to a people. It is, willy-nilly, even without having chosen it, to have a differentiated point of view and sensibility, to have participated in a certain historical way of life, to have become a different sort of human being." See his essay "The Communal Catholic," *Commonweal* (January 1975): 321.

5. Clifford Geertz, *The Interpretation of Cultures* (New York: Basic Books, 1973).

6. A vexing problem for sociologists of religion is defining and developing survey measures for "Evangelicals," "Fundamentalists," "Charismatics," and "Born-again Christians." Various attitudinal, doctrinal, experiential, and affiliational measures are used in research with widely varying empirical results. An experiential question like "Are you a Born-again Christian?" is useful because it is widely understood and inclusive across not only Protestant subtraditions but also across Protestant-Catholic lines. This latter is usually overlooked. See Lyman Kellstedt, "Simple Questions, Complex Answers," *Evangelical Studies Bulletin* 12 (Fall 1995): 1–4.

7. For an excellent discussion of the growth of Evangelicalism in the 1950s, 1960s, and 1970s and reposturing in relation to the liberal churches, see chapter 8 of Robert Wuthnow's *The Restructuring of American Religion* (Princeton:

Princeton University Press, 1988). On the rise of the megachurch, see Lyle Schaller, "Megachurch!" *Christianity Today*, 5 March 1990, 20–24.

8. See Thomas J. Csordas, *The Sacred Self* (Berkeley: University of California Press, 1994), 18–20. He interprets how Catholic Charismatics appropriate these themes in healing rituals. Other books on this same constituency include Meredith McGuire, *Pentecostal Catholics: Power, Charisma, and Order in a Religious Movement* (Philadelphia: Temple University Press, 1982) and Mary Jo Neitz, *Charisma and Community* (New Brunswick: Transaction Books, 1987). While such themes as spontaneity, control, and intimacy may be more apparent in Charismatic communities, they are discernible in other "Born-again" Christian constituencies.

9. Evangelist Paul Crouch, in his television ministry on July 10, 1997, spoke of religion as "cold, calculating, and routine" and of a spiritual need to "loosen[ing] yourself up," "explore[ing] riches," and "pursue[ing] life's meaning." Based on observations of Evangelical programming by my students in a 1997 project observing televangelists, the distinction appears to be far more common among Pentecostals and Charismatics than other Evangelicals.

10. There are many historical accounts of the rise of the neo-Evangelical movement. See Joel A. Carpenter, *Revive Us Again: The Reawakening of American Protestantism* (New York: Oxford University Press, 1997). Other valuable accounts include George Marsden, *Reforming Fundamentalism: Fuller Seminary and the New Evangelicalism* (Grand Rapids: Eerdmans, 1987); Donald Dayton and Robert Johnston, *The Variety of American Evangelicalism* (Knoxville: University of Tennessee Press, 1991); and, for an analysis focusing explicitly on the evolving boundaries of Evangelicalism in the larger culture, see Jon R. Stone, *On the Boundaries of American Evangelicalism: The Postwar Evangelical Coalition* (New York: St. Martin's Press, 1998).

11. Samuel S. Hill, Jr., "The Shape and Shapes of Popular Southern Piety," in *Varieties of Southern Evangelicalism*, ed. David E. Harrell (Macon: Mercer University Press, 1981), 89–114. While his essay focuses on the American South, these varieties of Evangelicalism are found across the country.

12. For a similar conclusion, see chapter 6 of James Davison Hunter's *Evangelicalism: The Coming Generation* (Chicago: University of Chicago Press, 1987). Also see John Schmalzbauer's "Evangelicals in the New Class: Class Versus Subcultural Predictors of Ideology," *Journal for the Scientific Study of Religion* 32 (December 1993): 330–42. Schmalzbauer finds that while Evangelical "knowledge class" workers resist the liberalizing effects of class in the realm of the sexual mores, they are more liberal on abortion, gender roles, and civil liberties.

13. James Davison Hunter, *Evangelicalism: The Coming Generation*, 210.

14. Susan Harding, *The Afterlife of Stories* (Berkeley: University of California Press, forthcoming).

15. Samuel S. Hill, Jr., "The Shape and Shapes of Popular Southern Piety," 102.

16. Harvey Cox, *Fire from Heaven: The Rise of Pentecostal Spirituality and the Reshaping of Religion in the Twenty-First Century* (Reading: Addison-Wesley Publishing Company, 1995), 305. Mark Shibley demonstrates with national survey

data that the "personal need" factor (along with need for community) is powerful in explaining affiliation with Evangelical churches currently in the United States. More so than "ideological strickness" or "intolerance for secular culture," meeting "personal need" seems to be the key to popular Evangelical growth, especially outside the South. See his *Resurgent Evangelicalism in the United States: Mapping Cultural Change since 1970* (Columbia: University of South Carolina Press, 1996), 113–32.

17. These are churches that presume that Christendom is largely dissolved and are generally disillusioned with denominational hierarchies and structures, preferring instead to look to the New Testament for organizational styles designed to reach secular, or pre-Christian, people. The term relates to a great variety of nontraditional churches today. George G. Hunter III uses the term to include such churches as follows: Frazer Memorial United Methodist Church, Montgomery, Alabama; New Hope Community Church, Portland, Oregon; Willow Creek Community Church, Barrington, Illinois; Community Church of Joy, Glendale, Arizona; Saddleback Valley Community Church, Orange County, California; The Church on Brady, East Lost Angeles, California; New Song Church, West Covina, California; The Ginghamsburg United Methodist Church, Tipp City, Ohio; and Vineyard Community Church, Cincinnati, Ohio. See his book *Church for the Unchurched* (Nashville: Abingdon Press, 1996).

18. In our 1995–96 survey, 28 percent of Born-again Christians said they preferred to explore religious teachings than to stick to a particular faith. Fourteen percent identified themselves as either believers with doubts or as seekers. Gregory A. Pritchard confirms our survey findings in his observations at Willow Creek Community Church in Barrington, Illinois. He writes: "Individuals I interviewed who had not made a commitment to Christianity frequently identified themselves to me by saying, 'I am a seeker.' Thus, not only is 'seeker' the church's designation for unchurched people—but also unchurched Harrys often accept this label for themselves." See his book *Willow Creek Seeker Services: Evaluating a New Way of Doing Church* (Grand Rapids: Baker Books, 1996), 77.

19. I draw off chapter 1 of Donald E. Miller's book, *Reinventing American Protestantism: Christianity in the New Millennium* (Berkeley: University of California Press, 1997). Miller's is a study of the post-1960s, California-based Evangelical movements: Calvary Chapel, Hope Chapel, and Vineyard Fellowship.

20. I am indebted to Chuck Fromm, the owner of Maranatha Music, for this observation in an E-mail message, February 20, 1998. Walter Ong's notions of secondary orality are particularly pertinent. See his *Orality and Literacy* (New York: Methuen, 1982).

21. Dieter Zander, once a member of the staff at New Song Church, West Covina, California, comments: "We need to move the line of fellowship. People used to be allowed to cross the line into fellowship only after their conversion. Today, increasingly, we must first invite people into the fellowship so they can process what being in the fellowship is all about. So, at New Song, we created a fellowship that knew how to include seekers inside the circle." Quoted in George G. Hunter III, *Church for the Unchurched* (Nashville: Abingdon Press, 1996), 166–67.

22. Cheryl Townsend Gilkes, "Plenty Good Room: Adaption in a Changing Black Church," *The Annals of the American Academy of Political and Social Science* 558 (July 1998): 101–21.

23. See the cover story by Jerry Adler, "A Matter of Faith," *Newsweek*, 15 December 1997, 49–54.

24. For an analysis of religious language in one tradition, see Catherine M. Prelinger, ed., *Episcopal Women: Gender, Spirituality and Commitment in an American Mainline Denomination* (New York: Oxford University Press, 1992), 209–11.

25. Nancy Tatum Ammerman, "Golden Rule Christianity: Lived Religion in the American Mainstream," in *Lived Religion in America: Toward a History of Practice*, ed. David. D. Hall (Princeton: Princeton University Press, 1997), 196–216.

26. Gary Dorsey, *Congregation* (New York: Viking, 1995), 382.

27. Alan Wolfe, in his *One Nation, After All* (New York: Viking, 1998), a study of middle-class Americans, titles a chapter on religion "Quiet Faith," a theme he pulls out of Robert Wuthnow's research.

28. Nancy Tatum Ammerman, "Golden Rule Christianity," 207.

29. See Martin E. Marty, *The Public Church: Mainline-Evangelical-Catholic* (New York: Crossroad, 1981).

30. Martin E. Marty and Edith L. Blumhofer, *Public Religion in America Today* (Chicago: The Public Religion Project, 1997), 9. Also see William McKinney, "Mainline Protestantism 2000," *The Annals of the American Academy of Political and Social Science* 558 (July 1998): 57–66.

31. James L. Kelley, *Skeptic in the House of God* (New Brunswick: Rutgers University Press, 1997), 164. The church is St. Mark's Episcopal Church.

32. Ibid., 168. One indication is the coalescing of groups—including seekers—leading to the founding of a recent para-church group, The Center for Progressive Christianity, in Cambridge, Massachusetts. To quote Kelley, "According to its statement of purpose, the Center's work will focus on 'reaching people who have given up on organized religion' and on providing 'support for congregations who embrace search, not certainty.'" For an account of a congregation's transition toward greater openness to questers, see Nora Gallagher, *Things Seen and Unseen: A Year Lived In Faith* (New York: Knopf, 1998). Also see Richard Todd, "The Stranger in the Back of the Church," *Civilization* (December 1998/ January 1999): 30–32, for a story on how Boston's old Trinity Church is "reaching out to the uninitiated."

33. E. Brooks Holifield, "Toward a History of American Congregations," in *American Congregations*, vol. 2, ed. James P. Wind and James W. Lewis (Chicago: University of Chicago Press, 1994), 23–53.

34. I am much indebted to Ann Taves for discussion on Roman Catholic and Mainline Protestant spirituality. Her unpublished paper on this topic was presented at a conference on spirituality at the University of California at Santa Barbara, March 6–7, 1998.

35. See Michele Dillon, "Rome and American Catholics," *The Annals of the American Academy of Political and Social Science* 558 (July 1998): 122–34. She describes how members of the Women's Ordination Conference validate their identity as Catholic while disagreeing with papal teaching. I am also indebted to Lara Medina for her paper "La Vida es la Lucha: The Spirituality of Las Her-

manas," presented at the Consultation on Spirituality at the University of California at Santa Barbara, March 6–8, 1998.

36. Tamar Frankiel, "Jewish Spirituality," unpublished paper presented at the conference on spirituality at the University of California at Santa Barbara, March 6–8, 1998.

37. Michael Strassfeld and Richard Siegel, *The First Jewish Catalog: A Do-It-Yourself Kit* (Jewish Publication Society, 1989). It is popular largely because it was modeled after the *Whole Earth Catalog*. Arthur Waskow's *Down-to-Earth Judaism: Food, Money, Sex and the Rest of Life* (New York: William Morrow, 1997) is another popular, more recent book.

38. On interaction ritual, see Michael H. Ducey, *Sunday Morning: Aspects of Urban Ritual* (New York: Free Press, 1977).

39. See Jackson W. Carroll and Wade Clark Roof, "United Methodist Congregations in North Carolina and California: Regional and Generational Trends," in *United Methodism and American Culture*, vol. 2 of *The People(s) Called Methodist: Forms and Reforms of Their Life*, ed. William B. Lawrence, Dennis M. Campbell, and Russell E. Richey (Nashville: Abingdon Press, 1998), 74.

40. A good example is Martha Manning's *Chasing Grace: Reflection of a Catholic Girl, Grown Up* (San Francisco: HarperSanFrancisco, 1996). She organizes her book around the Catholic sacraments and discusses her family history.

41. Kathleen Norris, *Cloister Walk* (New York: Riverhead Books, 1996), 275.

42. Ann Taves quotes in an unpublished paper (see n. 34) from James F. White: "The amazing thing about use of the lectionary is how far it has spread across American Protestantism. It is not just the mainline churches but Brethren, Nazarene, and Mennonites who have latched on to it. And once they have bought it they soon realized they have purchased a much more extensive liturgical year as well. Now clergy groups in many American towns do their exegesis together, whether Catholic or Protestant, since they preach on the same texts." See White, "Roman Catholic and Protestant Worship in Relationship," *Studia Liturgica* 26 (1996), 165.

43. Frankiel (above, n. 36).

44. For a rich account by a Protestant, see Diana L. Eck, *Encountering God: A Spiritual Journey from Bozeman to Banaras* (Boston: Beacon Press, 1993). Also see Rodger Kamenetz's *The Jew in the Lotus: A Poet's Rediscovery of Jewish Identity in Buddhist India* (San Francisco: HarperSanFrancisco, 1995).

45. Taves (above, n. 34).

46. Robert K. C. Forman, "'Spirituality' in Grassroots Spirituality," unpublished paper delivered at the Consultation on Spirituality at the University of California at Santa Barbara, March 6–8, 1998.

47. George Barna, *Index of Leading Spiritual Indicators*, 124–25. I am indebted to Robert K. C. Forman for these data.

48. *Religion in America* (Princeton: Princeton Religion Research Center), May 1985, 50.

49. William Sims Bainbridge, *The Sociology of Religious Movements* (New York: Routledge, 1997), 390. Barry A. Kosmin and Seymour P. Lachman, in their large survey of American religious self-identification, estimate that the New Age population is roughly 20,000. However, this clearly underestimates the figures since

many Americans, as they acknowledge, are influenced by New Age ideas and beliefs but do not identify themselves as such. See their book *One Nation Under God* (New York: Crown, 1993), 153–156.

50. Robert Wuthnow, *Sharing the Journey: Support Groups and America's New Quest for Community* (New York: Free Press, 1994), 188.

51. Catherine L. Albanese, "The Subtle Energies of Spirit: Explorations in Metaphysical and New Age Spirituality," an unpublished paper presented at the Consultation on Spirituality, University of California, Santa Barbara, March 6–8, 1998, 7. The literature on Gnosticism, Theosophy, New Thought, and New Age is voluminous. See chapter 11 of Albanese, *America: Religions and Religion* (Belmont, Ca., Wadsworth Publishing Company, 1992); James R. Lewis and J. Gordon Melton, eds., *Perspectives on the New Age* (Albany: State University of New York Press, 1992); and Paul Heelas, *The New Age Movement* (Oxford: Blackwell Publishers, 1996).

52. Lars Johansson, "New Age—A Synthesis of the Premodern, Modern, and Postmodern," in *Faith and Modernity*, ed. Philip Sampson, Vinay Samuel, and Chris Sugden (Oxford: Regnum Books, 1994), 208–50.

53. J. Gordon Melton, *Finding Enlightenment: Ramtha's School of Ancient Wisdom* (Hillsboro, Oregon: Beyond Words Publishing, 1998), 43. Melton traces the importance of Theosophy as the most pervasive form of Gnosticism occultism, of how the Theosophical Society has helped prepare the West for the importing of Eastern ideas and spiritual practices, and how theosophical teachings prepared the way for the rise of the New Age movement.

54. Lars Johansson (above, n. 52), 221.

55. Ibid., 223.

56. This is Michael F. Brown's argument. See his *The Channeling Zone: American Spirituality in an Anxious Age* (Cambridge: Harvard University Press, 1997), 179.

57. Wendy Griffin, "Crafting the Boundaries: Goddess Narrative as Incantation," Unpublished paper, 4.

58. Brown, *The Channeling Zone* (above, n. 56), 91.

59. See Elijah Siegler, "Marketing Lazaris: A Rational-Choice Theory of Channeling" (M.A. thesis, University of California at Santa Barbara, 1998). Siegler also points out that channeling as one type of New Age activity has evolved, much like the life-cycle of Baby Boomers, from emphasis on exploration in the 1970s and conspicuous consumption in the 1980s to settling down, or nesting, and "working" on oneself in the 1990s.

60. Brown, *The Channeling Zone* (above, n. 56), 92.

61. A good example is found in M. Scott Peck's description of God: "God, unlike some organized religions, does not discriminate. As long as you reach out to Her, She will go the better part of the way to meet you. There are an infinite number of roads to reach God. People can come to God through alcoholism, they can come to god through Zen Buddhism, as I did, and they can come to God through the multiple 'New Thought' Christian churches even though they are distinctly heretical. For all I know, they can come to God through Shirley Mac-Laine. People are at various stages of readiness, and when they're ready, virtually

anything can speak to them." See Peck's *Further Along the Road Less Traveled* (New York: Simon and Schuster, 1993), 155.

62. The term *Fundamentalist* as used in the United States arises out of Protestant history and thus is too limiting for our purposes. *Moralist* as a descriptive term is often used in conjunction with *Fundamentalist*. *Orthodoxy* is sometimes used to imply generally what I have in mind—see James Davison Hunter, *Culture Wars: The Struggle to Define America* (New York: Basic Books, 1991)—but is misleading considering the rich spiritual heritage of many religious traditions that also go by that name. The term *ritualist* is used in Robert Merton's "Social Structure and Anomie," in his *Social Theory and Social Structure* (New York: The Free Press, 1957), 131–94, and bears some relevance with its distinction between cultural goals and institutionalized means. But I chose *dogmatist* because as a psychological category with a focus on adherence to dogma it cuts across religious traditions and comes closest to being a generalizable term useful for this analysis.

63. Peter L. Berger, *A Far Glory: The Quest for Faith in an Age of Credulity* (New York: The Free Press, 1992), 59.

64. See chapter 3 of Marcus J. Borg, *The God We Never Knew* (San Francisco: HarperSanFrancisco, 1997).

CHAPTER 7

REALIGNING FAMILY AND RELIGION

1. Alasdair MacIntyre, *After Virtue: A Study in Moral Theory*, 2nd ed. (Notre Dame: University of Notre Dame Press, 1984), 216.

2. Penny Long Marler, "Lost in the Fifties: The Changing Family and the Nostalgic Church," in *Work, Family, and Religion in Contemporary Society*, ed. Nancy Tatum Ammerman and Wade Clark Roof (New York: Routledge, 1995), 23-60.

3. A major, well-documented work on the "restructuring" of religion in this period, Robert Wuthnow's *The Restructuring of American Religion: Society and Faith Since World War II* (Princeton: Princeton University Press, 1988) does not list *family* in the book's index. While special-purpose groups devoted to family causes are mentioned, the book does not look at the family-religion link in any systematic way. Two works in the 1980s that do focus more explicitly on this connection are William V. D'Antonio and Joan Aldous, eds., *Families and Religions: Conflict and Change in Modern Society* (Beverly Hills: Sage Publications, 1983) and Darwin L. Thomas, *The Religion and Family Connection: Social Science Perspectives* (Provo: Religious Studies Center, Brigham Young University, 1988). See also Ammerman and Roof, *Work, Family, and Religion in Contemporary Society* (above, n. 2).

4. Quoted in Ann Douglas, *The Feminization of American Culture* (New York: Avon Books, 1977), 160.

5. Judith Stacey, *Brave New Families: Stories of Domestic Upheaval in Late Twentieth Century America* (New York: Basic Books, 1990), 9.

6. In our general population survey, we compared four cohorts: those born between 1926 and 1935, between 1936 and 1945, between 1946 and 1954, and between 1955 and 1962. Differences in childhood religious involvement did not vary more than two points between Boomers and those born earlier.

351

7. Landon Y. Jones, *Great Expectations: America and the Baby Boom Generation* (New York: Coward, McCann and Geoghegan, 1980).

8. Robert S. Ellwood, *The Fifties Spiritual Marketplace* (New Brunswick: Rutgers University Press, 1997), 230.

9. See Lewis J. Sherrill, *Family and Church* (New York: Abingdon, 1937) and Roy Fairchild and John C. Wynn, *Families in the Church: A Protestant Survey* (New York: Association, 1961). The tone of the two books is remarkably similar.

10. Judith Stacey, *Brave New Families* (above, n. 5), 10. Elaine Tyler May draws the parallel between an "ethic of containment" in the Cold War and within the home. See her *Homeward Bound: American Families in the Cold War Era* (New York: Basic Books, 1988).

11. J. Conger, "Freedom and Commitment: Families, Youth, and Social Change, *American Psychologist* 36 (December 1981): 1477–78.

12. Sydney E. Ahlstrom, "Theology and the Present-Day Revival," *The Annals of the American Academy of Political and Social Science* 332 (November 1960): 30; and "The Radical Turn in Theology and Ethics: Why It Occurred in the 1960s," *The Annals of the American Academy of Political and Social Science* 387 (January 1970): 1–13.

13. Benton Johnson, "Liberal Protestantism: End of the Road?" *The Annals of the American Academy of Political and Social Science* 480 (July 1985): 39–52.

14. Bonnie J. Miller-McLemore speaks of this "double message" exposed at the time. See her "Protestantism and the European-American Family: Like Oil and Water," in *The Religion Factor: An Introduction to How Religion Matters*, ed. William Scott Green and Jacob Neusner (Louisville: Westminster/John Knox Press, 1996), 166–83.

15. A good, albeit somewhat dated, summary of research findings on family and religion is found in Darwin L. Thomas, *The Religion and Family Connection: Social Science Perspectives* (above, n. 3). The "twig" metaphor is taken from an essay in the collection by Gerald N. Scott, "Familial Influence on Religious Involvement," 258.

16. Darren E. Sherkat's insightful research shows the complexity of religious socialization, life-course factors, and countercultural influences. He finds support for all three types of influence but argues that early religious socialization was the strongest. See his "Counterculture or Continuity? Competing Influences on Baby Boomers' Religious Orientation and Participation," *Social Forces* 76 (March 1998): 1087–1115.

17. Lester Kurtz, *Gods in the Global Village: The World's Religions in Sociological Perspective* (Thousand Oaks: Pine Forge Press, 1995), 134.

18. See chapter 5 of Mary Jo Neitz, *Charisma and Community* (New Brunswick: Transaction Books, 1987). Hers is an excellent interpretation of family-based religious symbolism in the Catholic Renewal movement.

19. Kathleen Norris, *Amazing Grace: A Vocabulary of Faith* (New York: Riverhead Books, 1998), 22.

20. John Wilson provides a good summary of earlier research on this point. See his *Religion in American Society: The Effective Presence* (Englewood Cliffs: Prentice-Hall, 1978), 262–64.

21. Cover article by Kenneth L. Woodward, "A Time to Seek: With Babes in

Arms and Doubts in Mind, a Generation Looks to Religion," *Newsweek*, 17 December 1990, 50–56.

22. These data are taken from Barry A. Kosmin and Seymour P. Lachman, *One Nation under God: Religion in Contemporary American Society* (New York: Crown, 1993), 226. I rely on much of their discussion in chapter 6 of their book for themes developed here.

23. Ibid., 224.

24. Marler, "Lost in the Fifties" (above, n. 2), 38.

25. See David Halberstam, *The Fifties* (New York: Random House, 1993), 591.

26. Marler, "Lost in the Fifties" (above, n. 2), 40.

27. Ibid., 42: Marler writes, "Perceptions of church programming for traditional families are based on memories of what was good about their own families' church life."

28. Dean R. Hoge, Benton Johnson, and Donald A. Luiden found in their study of Presbyterian confirmands that only 13 percent were currently active members of a religious body outside of mainline Protestantism. See their *Vanishing Boundaries: The Religion of Mainline Protestant Baby Boomers* (Louisville: Westminister/John Knox Press, 1994), 121.

29. Donald E. Miller has an extended discussion on the centrality of the "relationship" with Christ as a basis for marriages in the churches he studied. See his *Reinventing American Protestantism: Christianity in the New Millennium* (Berkeley: University of California Press, 1997), 114–18.

30. Bradley Hertel, "Gender, Religious Identity, and Work Force Participation," *Journal for the Scientific Study of Religion* 27 (December 1988), 574–92. The 1996 data are from Andrew J. Cherlin, "By the Numbers," *New York Times Magazine*, 5 April 1998, 39. In this section I rely on discussion found in the Introduction written by Nancy Tatum Ammerman and myself to *Work, Family, and Religion in Contemporary Society* (New York: Routledge, 1995).

31. Judith Stacey (above, n. 5), 11.

32. I rely here on Elizabeth Souza's multiple-regression analysis of the first Boomer survey for these results. Her findings are found in an unpublished paper, "Changes on the Home Front? Workforce Participation of Baby Boomer Women and Public, Personal, and Familial Religiosity," Department of Sociology, University of Massachusetts at Amherst (1998). For example, when controlling statistically for age, education, marital status, age of children, and attendance at church/synagogue or Sunday School as a child, the impact of women's full-time employment on "public religiosity" is a −.0041. The same variables are included in the regression equations for "private religiosity" and "family religiosity."

33. Bradley Hertel (above, n. 30), 115–16.

34. For an excellent analysis of this "individualist" approach to volunteering in one tradition, see Joanna B. Gillespie, "Gender and Generations in Congregations," in *Episcopal Women: Gender, Spirituality, and Commitment in an American Mainline Denomination* (New York: Oxford University Press, 1992), 167–221.

35. A 1968 University of Chicago study of 1961 alumni found that for approximately 60 percent of Protestant marriages and 11 percent of Catholic marriages, one partner had switched. These data are cited in Kosmin and Lachman (above,

n. 22), 242. Historical data show a virtually uninterrupted rise in the proportion of people marrying outside their faith since at least the 1930s, true about equally for Catholics and Protestants. See Larry Bumpas, "The Trend of Interfaith Marriage in the United States," *Social Biology* 17 (December 1970): 253–59.

36. Kosmin and Lachman (above, n. 22), 242.

37. Jerry Adler, "A Matter of Faith," *Newsweek*, 15 December 1997, 52.

38. Quote taken from Nancy Cleeland and John Dart, "Interfaith Families Blend Easter, Passover Rituals," *Los Angeles Times*, 10 April 1998, A24.

39. For an early study, see Gerhard Lenski, *The Religious Factor: A Sociological Study of Religion's Impact on Politics, Economics, and Family Life* (Garden City: Doubleday, 1961). Later commentaries include William D'Antonio, "The Family and Religion: Exploring a Changing Relationship," *Journal for the Scientific Study of Religion* 19 (June 1980): 89–102; Barbara Hargrove, "The Church, the Family, and the Modernization Process," in *Families and Religions*, ed. William D'Antonio and Joan Aldous (Beverly Hills: Sage Publications, 1983), 21–49; and Don S. Browning, "Religion and Family Ethics: A New Strategy for the Church," in *Work, Family, and Religion in Contemporary Society*, ed. Nancy T. Ammerman and Wade Clark Roof (New York: Routledge, 1995), 157–76.

40. Daniel Yankelovich, *New Rules: Searching for Self-Fulfillment in a World Turned Upside Down* (New York: Random House, 1981), 90.

41. David W. Chen, "Fitting the Lord into Work's Tight Schedules," *The New York Times*, 29 November 1997, A1. Work, faith, and spirituality receive attention from a variety of perspectives. For a theological perspective by a pastor, see Steven Jacobsen, *Hearts to God, Hands to Work: Connecting Spirituality and Work* (Bethesda: Alban Institute, 1997). On the spirituality movement within business, see John Renesch and Bill Defore, *The New Bottom Line: Bringing Heart and Soul to Business* (San Francisco: New Leaders Press, 1996).

42. Arlie Russell Hochschild, *The Time Bind: When Work Becomes Home and Home Becomes Work* (New York: Metropolitan Books, 1997), 44.

CHAPTER 8
MORAL VISION AND VALUES

1. Louis Dupré, "Seeking Christian Interiority: An Interview with Louis Dupré," *The Christian Century*, 16 July 1997, 657.

2. Peter L. Berger, "American Religion: Conservative Upsurge, Liberal Prospects," in *Liberal Protestantism: Realities and Possibilities*, ed. Robert S. Michaelsen and Wade Clark Roof (New York: Pilgrim Press, 1986), 19–36.

3. William Lee Miller, "American Religion and American Political Attitudes," in *Religious Perspectives in American Culture*, ed. James Ward Smith and A. Leland Jamison (Princeton: Princeton University Press, 1961), 94.

4. Four widely known conservative foundations—Bradley, Olin, Smith Richardson, and Scaife—called as the "four sisters" because they tend to act in concert, made grants of $57 million in 1993 alone to fund ideological causes. See Leon Howell, "Funding the War of Ideas," *The Christian Century* 19 July 1995, 701–3.

5. Rhys H. Williams, ed., *Cultural Wars in American Politics* (New York: Aldine de Gruyter, 1997), 2.

6. For a more detailed analysis of developments in the 1990s, see chapter 1 of Don S. Browning et al., *From Culture Wars to Common Ground: Religion and the American Family Debate* (Louisville: Westminster John Knox, 1997).

7. Hillary Rodham Clinton, *It Takes a Village: And Other Lessons Children Teach Us* (New York: Simon and Schuster, 1996) and Dan Quayle and Diane Medved, *The American Family: Discovering the Values That Make Us Strong* (New York: Harper-Collins, 1996).

8. Reported on *CNN Headline News*, 20 August 1998, in the aftermath of President Clinton's admission of sexual involvement with Monica Lewinsky.

9. On the first through the fourth observations, I rely largely on Rhys Williams's summary in his *Cultural Wars in American Politics*, 283–93. Especially helpful are the essays on survey data by N. J. Demerath III and Yonghe Yang, Nancy J. Davis and Robert V. Robinson, and Paul DiMaggio, John Evans, and Bethany Bryson. On the fifth, this observation is inspired by Timothy T. Clydesdale's research. See his "Family Behaviors among U.S. Baby Boomers: Exploring the Effects of Religion and Income Change, 1965–1982," *Social Forces* 76 (December 1997): 605–35.

10. N. J. Demerath III and Yonghe Yang, "What American Culture War? A View from the Trenches as Opposed to the Command Posts and the Press Corps," in Rhys H. Williams's *Cultural Wars in American Politics* (above, n. 5), 36.

11. Alan Wolfe's widely read book on middle-class American life in the 1990s relies on selected small-scale community surveys. See his *One Nation, After All: What Middle-Class Americans Really Think about God, Country, Family, Racism, Welfare, Immigration, Homosexuality, Work, The Right, The Left, and Each Other* (New York: Viking, 1998) for an example of both of these possibilities. Wolfe's study shows the views of middle-class America are far more complex than surveys and polls suggest. However, because he does not systematically examine differences between groups using a large population base, it is quite likely that he overestimates the extent of cultural unity within the class.

12. During the time of this writing, three new books on abortion appeared with war in their titles. See Cynthia Gorney, *Articles of Faith: A Frontline History of the Abortion Wars* (New York: Simon and Schuster, 1998); James Risen and Judy Thomas, *Wrath of Angels: The American Abortion War* (New York: Basic Books, 1998); and Rickie Solinger, ed., *Abortion Wars: A Half-Century of Struggle, 1950–2000* (Berkeley: University of California Press, 1998). Religious imagery is apparent in two of the titles.

13. Christopher Caldwell identifies this response associated with what he calls the "Hillary Cluster," noting that Bill Clinton has been astute in recognizing how to posture individual concerns versus social responsibility. He writes: "The American people are not 'for' or 'against' gay rights. They overwhelmingly say they favor equal rights for gays—but then draw the line at gays in the military. They're for AIDS-research funding—but think gays are pushing their agenda too fast. They believe that global warming is going on—but waffle on whether major steps should be taken to block it. They have shown a tolerance for paying more taxes to protect the environment, but few list it as their No.1 concern when asked by pollsters." See his "Southern Captivity of the GOP," *Atlantic Monthly*, June 1998, 71.

14. Demerath and Yang (above, n. 10), 31.

15. In fairness to James Davison Hunter, it should be noted that in a more recent publication, he moves away from his earlier binary model of the "orthodox" and the "progressives" and speaks of the country as divided into five groups: neotraditionalists, conventionalists, pragmatists, communitarians, and permissivists. His neotraditionalists are similar in profile in many respects with our dogmatists. See his report, *The State of Disunion: 1996 Survey of American Political Culture*, vol. 1 (Ivy: In Medias Res Educational Foundation, 1996), 11.

16. Kristin Luker makes this point about love, emphasizing the possibility of moral judgments relying upon "a subjectively reasoned application of moral principles rather than upon an externally existing moral code." See her *Abortion and the Politics of Motherhood* (Berkeley: University of California Press), 185.

17. See Marcus J. Borg, *The God We Never Knew: Beyond Dogmatic Religion to a More Authentic Contemporary Faith* (San Francisco: HarperSanFrancisco, 1997), 68–71; and Karen McCarthy Brown, "Fundamentalism and the Control of Women," in *Fundamentalism and Gender*, ed. John S. Hawley (Oxford; Oxford University Press, 1994), 175–99.

18. Luker's work on pro-choice and pro-life activities, mentioned in n. 16, fits in here of course. So does that of W. Barnett Pearce, *Communication and the Human Condition* (Carbondale: Southern Illinois University, 1989), especially chapter 2.

19. See chapter 4 of James Davison Hunter, *Evangelicalism: The Coming Generation* (Chicago: University of Chicago Press, 1987).

20. See Charles Hall, "Entering the Labor Force: Ideals and Realities among Evangelical Women," in *Work, Family, and Religion in Contemporary Society*, ed. Nancy Tatum Ammerman and Wade Clark Roof (New York: Routledge, 1995), 137–54. Hall's data are from a *Christianity Today* questionnaire sent to 1250 subscribers in 1990.

21. Sally K. Gallagher and Christian Smith, "Symbolic Traditionalism and Pragmatic Egalitarianism: Contemporary Evangelicals, Families and Gender," *Gender and Society*, forthcoming. See also Judith Stacey, *Brave New Families: Stories of Domestic Upheaval in Late Twentieth Century* (New York: Basic Books, 1990), 41–176. For related accounts of the diffusion of feminist ideas in religious traditions, see Christel Manning, *God Gave Us the Right: Conservative Catholic, Evangelical Protestant, and Orthodox Jewish Women Grapple with Feminism* (New Brunswick: Rutgers University Press, 1999).

22. Nancy Tatum Ammerman, "Golden Rule Christianity: Lived Religion in the American Mainstream," in *Lived Religion in America*, ed. David D. Hall (Princeton: Princeton University Press, 1997).

23. See Ana Maria Rizzuto, *The Birth of the Living God* (Chicago: University of Chicago Press, 1979) and Don S. Browning et al., *From Culture Wars to Common Ground* (above, n. 6), 290.

24. Findings from the "Love and Marriage Survey" are reported in Don S. Browning et al., *From Culture Wars to Common Ground* (above, n. 6), 18–21 and 289–92.

25. Timothy T. Clydesdale (above, n. 9), 605–35.

26. At the time of this writing, Women of Faith is a rapidly growing movement particularly among white Christian women. What is its appeal? *Time* reporter

Nadya Labi responds to that question with a swift reply: "Good old-fashioned therapy, cloaked in the Ten Commandments." But she also points out how speakers at these rallies bring up issues like abortion and homosexuality but stop short of taking a political position, which in itself of course sends a powerful message. See "Female of the Species: Complement and Antidote to the Promise Keepers, Women of Faith Moves from Strength to Strength," *Time*, 13 July 1998, 62–63.

27. Attention to children and parenting has been brought to the public arena by books such as the one by Sylvia Ann Hewlett and Cornel West, *The War against Parents: What We Can Do for America's Beleaguered Moms and Dads* (New York: Houghton Mifflin, 1998).

28. In this instance the issue was really over biology versus social environment, but it raised questions about divorce, single parents, and whether the two-parent, heterosexual family is superior for raising children. See Sharon Begley, "The Parent Trap," *Newsweek*, 7 September 1998, 52–59.

29. Kathleen Gerson, "Coping with Commitment: Dilemmas and Conflicts of Family Life," in *America at Century's End*, ed. Alan Wolfe (Berkeley: University of California Press, 1991), 35–37. The rise of the tough-parenting movement is described by Susan Bolotin, "The Disciples of Discipline," *The New York Times Magazine*, 14 February 1999, 32-37.

30. Loren Baritz, *The Good Life: The Meaning of Success for the American Middle Class* (New York: Alfred A. Knopf, 1989), 80. He quotes a General Motors executive at a sales convention in 1929 as saying that an advertiser's goal is to have as many people as possible "healthily dissatisfied with what they now have in favor of something better. The old factors of wear and tear can no longer be depended upon to create a demand. They are too slow."

31. See Robert Wuthnow, *Poor Richard's Principle: Recovering the American Dream through the Moral Dimension of Work, Business, and Money* (Princeton: Princeton University Press, 1996), 138–40.

32. Based on data from the Economic Policy Institute of the Bureau of Labor Statistics, and reported by Louis Uchitelle, "The Middle Class: Winning in Politics, Losing in Life," *The New York Times*, 19 July 1998, sec. 4, p. 1.

33. Michael F. Brown, *The Channeling Zone: American Spirituality in an Anxious Age* (Cambridge: Harvard University Press, 1997), 68–69.

34. Catherine L. Albanese, *America: Religions and Religion*, 2nd ed. (Belmont: Wadsworth Publishing Company, 1992), 362–63.

35. Johanna Macy, "The Ecological Self: Postmodern Ground for Right Action," in *Sacred Interconnections*, ed. David Ray Griffin (Albany: State University of New York Press, 1990), 45.

36. This reference to Berry's theology is found in Charlene Spretnak, "Postmodern Directions," in *Spirituality and Society*, ed. David Ray Griffin (Albany: State University of New York Press, 1988), 37.

37. The first major charge came from Lynn White, who argued that Christianity had long fostered a dualism between humanity and the rest of nature, leading to an obsessive anthrocentrism and disregard for nature. See his essay, "The Historical Roots of Our Ecological Crisis," *Science*, 10 March 1967, 1203–7.

38. A decade ago George Gallup, Jr., and Jim Castelli asked people if they identified with social movements and found the following regarding an

"environmentalist" identification: white Evangelical Protestants, 39%; white non-Evangelical Protestants, 40%; Black Protestants, 31%; white Catholics, 41%; Hispanics, 33%; Jews, 50%; and no affiliation, 48%. See *The People's Religion: American Faith in the 90s* (New York: Macmillan, 1989), 215–16.

39. This is the conclusion of Robert Booth Fowler after examining environmental themes over two decades. See his volume *The Greening of Protestant Thought* (Chapel Hill: University of North Carolina Press, 1995), 81–86. Also see Mark A. Shibley and Jonathan L. Wiggins, "The Greening of Mainline American Religion: A Sociological Analysis of the Environmental Ethics of the National Religious Partnership for the Environment," *Social Compass* 44: 333–48.

40. Ibid., 39. The Evangelical publication *Sojourners* has taken strong stands on the environment. See particularly Wesley Granberg-Michaelson, "At the Dawn of the New Creation: A Theology of the Environment," *Sojourners* 10 (November 1981): 12–16. Also see his book *A Worldly Spirituality: The Call to Redeem Life on Earth* (San Francisco: Harper and Row, 1984).

41. The quote is attributed to Richard John Neuhaus, Catholic priest and editor of *First Things*, by Leon Howell in his article, "Funding the War of Ideas," *The Christian Century* 19, 19 July 1995, 703.

42. The most cogent argument on deprivatization of religion in the 1980s and 1990s is that of Jose Casanova, *Public Religions in the Modern World* (Chicago: University of Chicago Press, 1994). Casanova describes it as "the process whereby religion abandons its assigned place in the private sphere and enters the undifferentiated public sphere of civil society to take part in the ongoing process of contestation, discursive legitimation, and redrawing of the boundaries" (65–66).

43. John B. Orr et al., *Politics of the Spirit: Religion and Multiethnicity in Los Angeles* (Los Angeles: University of Southern California, 1994), 7–8.

44. This is a finding in Alan Wolfe's research on middle-class Americans as well. See his *One Nation, After All* (above, n. 11), 88–132.

45. David Jeremiah (with C. C. Carlson), *Invasion of Other Gods: The Seduction of New Age Spirituality* (Dallas: Word, 1995), 8.

46. Ibid., 26.

47. Kenneth L. Woodward, "White House Soul Searching," *Newsweek*, 8 July 1996, 33, reported in its poll that only 12 percent said that Hillary Clinton's meetings with Jean Houston lowered their opinion of the first lady.

48. Best-selling author James Redfield observed that the episode helped to raise a question on "the human potential exploration itself: what indeed is this search for quality and spiritual fulfillment that is occurring everywhere?" See his newsletter *The Celestine Journal*, September 1996, 1.

49. Peter Steinfels, "New Age Presents Allures, Conflicts," *Santa Barbara News-Press*, 27 July 1996, B8.

50. See Robert A. White, "Religion and Media in the Construction of Cultures," in *Rethinking Media, Religion, and Culture*, ed. Stewart M. Hoover and Knut Lundby (Thousand Oaks: Sage Publications, 1997), 47–49.

51. Alan Wolfe, *One Nation, After All* (above, n. 11), 86.

52. Randall Balmer, *Mine Eyes Have Seen the Glory: A Journey into the Evangelical Subculture in America* (Oxford: Oxford University Press, 1989), 280.

CONCLUSION
"WHIRL IS KING, HAVING DRIVEN OUT ZEUS"

1. Walter Lippmann, *A Preface to Morals* (New York: The MacMillan Company, 1929), 3–4. The Aristophanes quotation in the chapter title is from *Clouds* 928.

2. Robert Orsi, "Everyday Miracles: The Study of Lived Religion," in *Lived Religion in America: Toward a History of Practice*, ed. David D. Hall (Princeton: Princeton University Press, 1997), 10.

3. Thomas J. Csordas, *Language, Charisma, and Creativity: The Ritual Life of a Religious Movement* (Berkeley: University of California Press, 1997), 264. Csordas observes that Caroline Bynum argues that the spirituality of the Middle Ages, for women especially, was more bodily oriented than we generally assume. See her volume *Fragmentation and Redemption: Essays on Gender and the Human Body in Medieval Religion* (Cambridge: MIT Press, 1991).

4. R. Stephen Warner, 'The Place of the Congregation in the Contemporary American Religious Configuration," in *American Congregations*, vol. 2, ed. James P. Wind and James W. Lewis (Chicago: University of Chicago, 1994), 54–59.

5. E. Brooks Holifield, "Toward a History of American Congregations," in *American Congregations*, vol. 2, ed. James P. Wind and James W. Lewis (Chicago: University of Chicago, 1994), 23–53.

6. Robert D. Putnam, "Bowling Alone: America's Declining Social Capital," *Journal of Democracy* 6 (January 1995), 65–78.

7. H. Richard Niebuhr, *Christ and Culture* (New York: Harper and Row, 1951), 18. Niebuhr's influential essay, "The Center of Value" is found in his *Radical Monotheism and Western Culture* (New York: Harper and Brothers, 1960), 100–113.

8. Anthony Giddens, "Living in a Post-Traditional Society," in *Reflexive Modernization: Politics, Tradition and Aesthetics in the Modern Social Order*, ed. Ulrich Beck, Anthony Giddens, and Scott Lash (Stanford: Stanford University Press, 1994), 100.

9. See Larry L. Rasmussen, *Earth Community, Earth Ethics* (New York: Orbis, 1998).

10. These are all terms found in L. Gregory Jones's review of Thomas Moore's book *The Re-Enchantment of Everyday Life*. See his "Spirituality Lite: Thomas Moore's Misguided Care of the Soul," *The Christian Century*, 6 November 1996, 1072–74. Jones is Dean of the Duke Divinity School.

11. R. Laurence Moore, *Selling God: American Religion in the Marketplace of Culture* (New York: Oxford University Press, 1994). For a delightful read and provocative defense of "tacky theology" by a respected Evangelical leader, see Richard J. Mouw, *Consulting the Faithful* (Grand Rapids: William B. Eerdmans Publishing Company, 1994).

12. R. Laurence Moore, *Selling God: American Religion in the Marketplace of Culture* (above, n. 11), 258.

13. Robert Wuthnow takes a cautious, somewhat negative view of the depth of the spirituality in the small-group movement, questioning the extent to which involvement within them genuinely change people. See his *Sharing the Journey: Support Groups and America's New Quest for Community* (New York: Free Press,

1994), 341–66. Nancy Tatum Ammerman disagrees, arguing: "No commitment fails to change the person who makes it. It is one of the ironies of social life that individualism and communalism are utterly intertwined." See her *Congregation and Community* (New Brunswick: Rutgers University Press, 1997), 353.

14. See Louis Schneider and Sanford M. Dornbusch, "Inspirational Religious Literature: From Latent to Manifest Functions of Religion," *American Journal of Sociology* 62 (March 1957): 476–81, and Robert P. Althauser, "Paradox in Popular Religion: The Limits of Instrumental Faith," *Social Forces* 69 (December 1990): 585–602.

15. Loren Baritz's, *The Good Life: The Meaning of Success for the American Middle Class* (New York: Alfred A. Knopf, 1988), 301.

16. Harvey Cox, *Fire from Heaven: The Rise of Pentecostal Spirituality and the Reshaping of Religion in the Twenty-first Century* (Reading: Addison-Wesley Publishing Company, 1995), 305.

17. Peter L. Berger, "Protestantism and the Quest for Certainty," *The Christian Century*, 26 August 1998, 794.

18. This is Louis Dupré's argument. See his "Seeking Christian Interiority: An Interview with Louis Dupré," *The Christian Century*, 16 July 1997, 655.

19. Peter Dews, ed., *Autonomy and Solidarity: Interviews with Jürgen Habermas*, revised ed. (London: Verso, 1992), 243.

20. Arthur Green, *Judaism for the Post-Modern Era* (Cincinnati: Hebrew Union College Press, 1995), 6–7.

21. I am indebted to Peter J. Gomes for this insight tucked away in one of his pithy endnotes to *The Good Book* (New York: Avon, 1996), 360. He observes that this anxiety in American religion arising out of the appearance of godliness mixed with the substance of godlessness parallels what Richard Hofstadter once described as the "paranoid style" of American politics.

Appendix
Methodology

1. Wade Clark Roof and William McKinney, *American Mainline Religion: Its Changing Shape and Future* (New Brunswick: Rutgers University Press, 1987).

2. This research has already been identified: Vicky Genia, "The Spiritual Experience Index: Revision and Reformulation," *Review of Religious Research* 38 (June 1997): 344–61, and Brian J. Zinnbauer et al., "Religion and Spirituality: Unfuzzing the Fuzzy," *Journal for the Scientific Study of Religion* 36 (December 1997): 549–64.